THE SAME JESUS

THE SAME JESUS:

A Contemporary Christology

Daniel A. Helminiak

LOYOLA UNIVERSITY PRESS

Chicago

Nihil obstat   the Reverend J. Patrick O'Brien, S.T.D.
   Censor Deputatus
Imprimatur   the most Reverend Anthony J. Bevilacqua, J.D.C., J.D.
   Bishop of Pittsburgh

   granted January 3, 1986

Two quotations from *Vatican Council II: The Conciliar and Post Concil-iar Documents*, Austin Flannery, General Editor, are reprinted with permission of the Costello Publishing Company, Inc.

Loyola University Press
3441 North Ashland Avenue
Chicago, Illinois 60657

Library of Congress Cataloging in Publication Data
Helminiak, Daniel A.
The same Jesus : a contemporary Christology.
Bibliography: p. 317
Includes index.
1. Jesus Christ—Person and offices.   2. Jesus Christ
—History of doctrines.   I. Title.
BT202.H424   1986   232   85-23190
ISBN 0-8294-0521-6

Design by C. L. Tornatore

To my Mum and Dad, my sister and brother, aunts, uncles and cousins, friends and neighbors, sisters and priests and the whole parish of St. Josaphat, South Side Pittsburgh—from whom I first learned to believe.

Contents

We can never be born enough. We are human beings for whom birth is a supremely welcome mystery, the mystery of growing . . . the mystery which happens only and whenever we are faithful to ourselves.

— *e. e. cummings*

Introduction

"Jesus Christ is the same yesterday and today and for ever." So reads the Letter to the Hebrews (8:13). Yet Christian understanding about Jesus has changed, and it continues to change. This book is about Jesus and our changing understanding of him.

This topic is very delicate. Jesus is no abstract issue, something on the sidelines of people's lives. To talk about Jesus is to talk about something personal to many people. Deep feelings and strong commitments are invested in the discussion. Jesus has been the focus of meaning in the lives of thousands of people. Belief in Jesus has governed communities, churches, nations, and for a time even the whole of Western civilization, christendom. Today, when secularism is the dominant ethos, Christians committed to varying beliefs about Jesus continue to influence the course of history. Whether one is a believer or not, one can hardly afford to be indifferent to beliefs—or shifts in belief—about Jesus Christ. So, to talk about Jesus is to touch a sensitive nerve. To present new thoughts about Jesus is often to irritate that nerve and upset people's lives.

In general, we can never afford to be casual about a central focus in people's lives. But today, in particular, the topic of Jesus is especially important. For something has indeed happened to the traditional understanding about Jesus, and in one way or another we are all aware of it. Church-goers hear their pastors preaching an insistence on orthodox beliefs about Jesus, and that very insistence tips them off that somewhere someone is "questioning the faith." The phenomenal rise of fundamentalist "Christian" groups and of the "electronic churches" tells us that something is threatening people's security; they are banding together to protect their beliefs and to be safe from the questioning. Theologians or not, we read the newspaper, we watch TV, we glance at the Christmas and Easter issues of national news magazines. We have heard that scholars are proposing new interpretations of the Bible and that the Vatican has called in theologians and questioned their thinking. We cannot avoid the issue. There is new speculation abroad about Jesus Christ. The issue is too important to ignore.

So what is the position in this book? Absolutely that Jesus Christ is God. He is the Eternal Son of the Father—and equally absolutely, that he became human, one like us in all things but sin. He did this for our sakes. By his incarnation, life, death, and resurrection, Jesus Christ changed the meaning of human life. He opened to humanity a new possibility, to share in the very life of God. That is to say, he saved us.

What is professed here is traditional Christian belief, but the way it will be presented may seem unfamiliar. After all, something has happened to our understanding about Jesus, and the goal here is to incorporate the new understanding into our insistence on the old. Nonetheless, the assurance is here from the start. Though in the end he may not look exactly like the Jesus of yore, this book presents the Christ of the Church, the Christ of the traditional Christian faith, the same Jesus.

I write as a Christian believer, and I address myself primarily to other believers. Moreover, I am Roman Catholic. Necessarily I will speak out of my own Christian tradition, the one I know best. But my words are not restricted to Roman Catholics. On the contrary, this book presents authentic Christian belief about Jesus, valid across denominational lines. In this sense it is addressed to all Christians. Indeed, the hope is that by clarifying belief about Jesus this book might make some contribution to the reunion of the Christian churches. But this book is also addressed to non-Christians. Anyone interested in knowing what Christians believe about Jesus and on what grounds they believe it should find this book helpful. This is true particularly because the intent is not to *convince* anybody about anything. The intent is simply to show how traditional Christian belief about Jesus Christ can still be a coherent, reasonable position.

Why Another Book on Christology

When so many books about Jesus are appearing on the market, why another one? Simply because there is something more to be said. There is need for a text that can hold together the conclusions of contemporary biblical scholarship and the teaching of the early Christian ecumenical councils.

Studies about Jesus abound. Most of them treat one or another aspect of christology. For example, many deal with the New Testament teaching about Jesus or with some one aspect of that New Testament teaching.[1] Others deal with the ecumenical councils or with later christological development.[2] Still others treat a particular aspect of, or focus on, Christian belief about Jesus.[3] Those works that do present an integrative position tend to represent particular opinions, new approaches, or creative stands that may leave non-professionals wondering what is to be believed, or lose them in a haze of philosophical subtlety or lengthy and tedious discussions.[4] The present book offers a comphrehensive position that unites the various aspects of study about Jesus while remaining accessible to the ordinary educated reader.[5] In many ways this account is already familiar since it affirms traditional teaching about Jesus without question and builds on philosophical presuppositions inherent in Christianity from the start. Moreover, since so many contemporary specialized studies about Jesus have already been written, the present study can presume that material and borrow its conclusions without in every case having to rehearse all the technical discussion. Most of what is written here is not new. What is new is the way in which all the pieces hold together.

This is a work in systematic theology. The task of systematic theology is to present a comprehensive picture of multiple individual beliefs. It is to make the whole make sense by relating all the elements within one comprehensive system—hence the name "systematic." Accordingly, this book integrates the various elements in any understanding about Jesus—the biblical, the doctrinal, and the speculative.

The overriding concern is to spell out a system of thought within which all the elements fit together. So this book will explain its presuppositions in detail, for the beginning points of any discussion actually determine where the discussion goes and limit the conclusions that result. By way of contrast: this book does not present a detailed account of the New Testament development nor of the later conciliar and speculative developments themselves. On these issues there are ample resources in the endnotes. Rather, the present study takes the conclusions of those other scholarly specializations and integrates them into a comprehensive whole. This study presents only the biblical and doctrinal detail needed to make its point and to construct the intended synthesis. Often an issue is presented only by way of example. Historical complexities are simplified for the sake of clarity in overall argument. Of course, such narrow focus on an integrative framework might easily obscure an accurate account of historical detail. The systematic theologian does have a blind eye. Nonetheless, I risk this endeavor because an integrated presentation is so sorely needed. And at this point in time such a synthesis is possible.

Specific Contributions

This book is a contemporary summary of standard Christian belief about Jesus Christ. Yet it is more than that. Any real synthesis also represents some advance, for every synthesis entails some creativity. So the unfolding of this contemporary christology inevitably leads to some original conclusions. I must acknowledge them and take responsibility for them.

First, Bernard Lonergan presented a masterly study of development of doctrine in a work published in English as *The Way to Nicea*. That book traced christological development from the second century up to the Council of Nicea. His later article, "Christology Today: Methodological Reflections,"[6] addressed the contemporary problematic. Following Lonergan, this book correlates his notion of "common sense" with the New Testament mentality and accepts his philosophical analysis of the shift from common sense to theory.[7] There results a theoretically elaborated account of the development from Jesus himself and the New Testament through the ecumenical councils. Such an account of this critical shift is the linchpin needed to hold the Christian tradition together.

Moreover, accepting Lonergan's revitalized explanation of the traditional notions of 'nature' and 'person', this book discloses fuller implications in the commonly accepted conciliar teaching about the humanity of Jesus. Then, as contemporary christology is concerned to do, this book can insist fully on Jesus' humanity—but without prejudice to his divine status. Specifically, the present approach highlights Chalcedon's teaching—not the summary definition so often cited about one person and two natures but the other—that the humanity and divinity in Jesus are "without change, without confusion," that is, the two are not mixed together to form some hybrid. The key here is to realize that what the Eternal Word brought with himself into this world was not divinity and its powers—he emptied himself of these—but himself, an individual subject, an eternal identity, a divine person. The unity of humanity and divinity in Jesus is hypostatic. This same point can be made by suggesting—carefully!—that in himself Jesus did not primarily show us what God is like but rather what he himself, Eternal-Son-of-God, is like.

Third, contemporary christology is enamored of the approach from below, the move from Jesus' humanity to his divinity. This approach could never be used legitimately to suggest that anyone or anything *became* God, and thus to explain the Nicene decree. Yet the approach from below makes an important contribution. Bernard Lonergan's understanding of human consciousness and its potential and his understanding of the distinction between the 'natural' and the 'supernatural'[8] are relevant here. Relating these three issues—the approach from below, dynamic human consciousness, and the supernatural—this book proposes a notion of human 'divinization' as an account of what happened to Jesus in the resurrection. The suggestion is that insistence on this real change in Jesus is the valid intent of the contemporary christology from below. Thus, Jesus' resurrection/divinization is a complement to the incarnation; it is the fulfillment of a possibility inherent in the incarnation. This fulfillment in Jesus is the paradigm of human salvation.

Fourth, contemporary christology is also concerned to integrate an account of human salvation—soteriology—with the account of the mystery of Jesus Christ. In the course of Christian history these two considerations had become separated. The present account does unite christology and soteriology, and in a way found nowhere else. This aspect of this book is perhaps the most original and so the most subject to scrutiny. Yet it follows naturally as an integral part of the christological position developed here. And the fact that at this point this christology necessarily entails trinitarian considerations confirms that this understanding is on target, true to the Christian tradition. Three main ideas constitute this soteriological understanding: 1) Jesus redeemed the human race by his *fidelity* even unto death—and not by his death itself. 2) It is inaccurate to say without qualification that Jesus saves us, for our immediate saving contact with God is through the Holy Spirit. And 3) Jesus' achievement of divinization constituted in human history a new possibility for human becoming, a new epitome. In this way Jesus became central to the salvation of all humankind, whether people know and reverence him or not.

Finally, Jesus is the model of Christian living. So one's christology is intimately related to one's spirituality. Whether we are aware of it or not, our understanding of Jesus determines how we conceive the ideal of Christian life. Therefore, sections throughout this book treat the practical implications of the Christian doctrines and so clarify the Christian position in contrast to other possible conceptions of life. These practical sections also show that firm insistence on traditional dogma does not entail a stifling legalism in Christian living. Rather, on the one hand, an adequate christology disqualifies the excessive christo-centrism that legitimates oppressive ecclesiastical institutionalism. And on the other hand, it highlights the work of the Holy Spirit who invites God's sons and daughters to new freedom.

Why a Popular Presentation

In light of the above list of technical issues, one would expect that this book itself is very technical, written for a circle of specialized scholars. It is not—for a number of reasons. Above all, I was concerned to provide a text for my own students. An introductory text could not presuppose technical christological background but would have to explain terms and arguments step by step as it moved along. Of course, this does not mean that this book avoids all technical issues. One simply cannot resolve contemporary christological questions without some technical considerations! Still one can introduce technical considerations in such a way that the ordinary educated reader can understand them. So oftentimes this book presents the same issue in different ways. Then, hopefully, in one way or another the reader will "catch" what is meant. At critical junctures there are not only suggestive accounts of the issue but also a full technical account. Those who wish to go that far may; others can rest content with an "intuitive" grasp of the issue. Nonetheless, throughout the book discussion is limited to issues essential to the overall argument. For example, varying theological opinions are seldom discussed in the text itself. Such discussion is relegated to the endnotes. The notes are deliberately placed at the end of this book so that they do not distract from the main argument. Admittedly, there is a danger in this. The novice reader might think that there is little difference of opinion among scholars on these issues when precisely the opposite is true. Let the reader be advised on this score here. For the other approach, including variant opinions in the text, also has its danger. It is likely to leave the reader overly informed and thus merely confused. Let the reader first understand the main argument. Then he or she can go on to consider the varying opinions that surround that argument. Advocating this approach, the teacher in me hopes to have presented a text that is sufficiently technical to deal adequately with the issues but still easily enough readable to speak to non-theologians.

Indeed, to present a contemporary christology for the church at large is becoming increasingly important. Many people are confused about their belief in Jesus. They want to be up-to-date in their understanding, but they have difficulty integrating the new theology with their former beliefs. The pieces do not seem to fit together. At this point in time the needs of ordinary committed believers seem more pressing than those of the trained theologians. So I want to provide a book that speaks also to pastors and ministers and priests and catechists and lay ministers and missionaries and vowed religious men and women and all those leaders of the churches—intelligent, dedicated, educated in the faith—whose main concern is pastoral ministry, though they know they also need sound critical theology. I want to provide a book for them—and also for committed lay people who, though not involved in ministry, want to understand the Christian faith and its role in our world. Most of these could not benefit from a highly technical christology text.

On the other hand, theologians will also be able to read this book and assess its worth. Seeing through the metaphors and stories and examples and easily filling in the broader implications of this popularized statement, they will readily recognize the underlying technical issues and be able to pass judgment on the theological moves. So I hope to address both the scholarly community as well as a more popular audience with this book.

One other set of considerations led me to write as I did. The major issues dividing theological and christological schools of thought today are presuppositional. What exactly this means will become clearer as this book unfolds. As it is, to write for the scholarly community, one would have to dedicate a major portion of one's book to philosophical presuppositions. But philosophy is not at issue here; christology is. I have already confessed my philosophical loyalties. The thought of Bernard Lonergan undergirds this whole christological enterprise. A number of places, especially Chapter Two, present an exposition of Lonergan's thought. But the presentation is popular, very popular indeed. Even scholars not trained in Lonergan's thought might not recognize this material as Lonerganian if the fact were not documented here or in the notes. This point is important for two reasons. First, despite its popular form, I consider this study to be well-grounded in Lonergan's cognitional, epistemological, and metaphysical—and so methodological—analyses. Second, presupposing Lonergan's own works, I believe that the philosophical background presented in this book is sufficient for the task at hand. Those who wish a technical presentation can read Lonergan himself. There is no reason to believe that a more adequate statement of his position could be presented here. Those who have quibbles about his position must, nonetheless, accept it here as a presupposition. It will not be argued at length. Rather, it will be implemented. Then, perhaps, not be being convinced of the position from the start but by recognizing its effectiveness, some might be willing to reconsider their judgment about the position and return to the original sources to study it. These considerations also encouraged me to write with so serious an intent about so complex a topic in so popular a style. Presupposing a philosophical position—the stage being set—I want to get on with the show. The hope is that under these circumstances both professionals and amateurs can enjoy the presentation.

Use of this Book in a Course

This book can be used as a basic text for an introductory christology course. Most importantly, it provides an overall context into which other christological material—contemporary and traditional—can be easily integrated. It provides the framework. Obviously, however, this book is not comprehensive. It is not sufficient in itself for an in-depth study of contemporary christology. An essential supplement is a text on recent New Testament studies like James D. G. Dunn's *Christology in the Making* or sections from his *Unity and Diversity in the New Testament* or Joseph A. Fitzmyer's *A Christological Catechism*. Bruce Vawter's *This Man Jesus* and Raymond E. Brown's *Jesus God and Man* are also very useful introductory biblical texts, though unfortunately they are no longer in print. Also needed is a text on the conciliar development of christological doctrine—to give students some appreciation of the complexity of the politics and theological issues behind the conciliar decrees. P. Smulder's *The Fathers on Christology* is an excellent little summary, and the christological chapters from Jaroslav Pelikan's *The Christian Tradition*, vol. 1, *The Emergence of the Catholic Tradition (100–600)*, are also useful. Finally, a book like John F. O'Grady's *Models of Jesus* can give students some hint of the breadth of opinion in contemporary christology. However, in an introductory course one can hardly do more than mention various opinions and approaches. To do some of them justice would require an additional seminar course.

A Note on Language

I must also comment on my use of gender language in this book. Language structures our worldview, and a consistent preference for male pronouns distorts that worldview. Therefore, this text renders all generic human references in non-sexist form. Unfortunately, this same principle is not applied in cases of God-talk in this book. This text continues to refer to "The *Father*" and "The *Son*" and to use masculine pronouns for them and the "Holy Spirit" and for references to "God." This is not to suggest that God is actually male. Neither is it to suggest that those male symbols—Father, Son—are so sacrosanct that they need to be preserved intact.[9] Theologically correct alternatives are available and have been used.[10] However, such alternatives proved to be counterproductive for the present text. Preliminary readers found the christological issues here challenging enough without being asked also to restructure their images of God and Trinity. In deference to those readers and with a concern that this christological statement be effective, the standard usage has been restored throughout the text. It is to be hoped that widespread concern about this issue will intensify and that generally accepted alternative formulations will quickly emerge. Then one could be theologically as well as socially responsible and still expect to be understood. Unfortunately, that time is not yet here.

Outline of this Book

This book is divided into three sections. The first treats the background for contemporary christology, the second treats the Christian tradition on Jesus, and the third presents a summary understanding about Jesus, a contemporary christology. Each section contains a number of chapters.

Chapter One deals with the major cause of the contemporary shift in understanding about Jesus—the development of historical-critical method. This chapter explains the emergence of this method, relates the history of its application to the Bible, indicates some results of that application, and discusses the validity of the method for scripture studies. Chapter Two continues to explain the contemporary intellectual climate and the problems it poses for christology. This chapter treats an issue related to historical-critical method—relativism. In so doing, it highlights a prevalent position contrary to the overall presentation here. The basic insistence is that christology is reflection about Jesus and, as such, must follow the general criteria of sound thinking. Chapter Three introduces, discusses, and criticizes the two major approaches to Jesus in contemporary christology: "from below" and "from above." Chapter Four introduces a further presuppositional issue, the distinction between kerygmatic statement and systematic statement. In so doing, that chapter forges yet another of the tools that will allow a retrieval and integration of the whole tradition on Jesus.

The next three chapters apply the tools to the tradition. Chapter

Five presents a brief summary of contemporary knowledge about
Jesus himself and reviews the development of Christian thought
about Jesus as witnessed in the New Testament. The conclusion is
that New Testament Christians certainly looked on Jesus as God and
that late New Testament statements say as much. Chapter Six jumps
225 years to the Council of Nicaea. There the further question was,
"But *is* he God?" And the answer was, "Yes." That chapter is crucial. It
explains and defends as legitimate the milestone shift in Christian
theology from kerygmatic to systematic statement. It provides the link
between the New Testament and later conciliar teachings. Granted
the argument of Chapter Six, Chapter Seven follows easily. It summarizes and interprets the teaching of subsequent ecumenical councils about Jesus. With the conclusion of Chapter Seven, all the
spadework in the garden of Christian tradition is finished, and the
ground is prepared for a new, comprehensive account of Jesus.

The final three chapters present that new account. Chapter Eight
makes a summary statement of this contemporary christology. This
chapter is the core of this book. It elaborates a picture of Jesus that
integrates the traditional and the contemporary, the "from above"
approach and the "from below" approach, the incarnational and the
resurrectional, the concern for the mystery of Jesus Christ in himself
and the concern for human salvation through Christ. Chapters Nine
and Ten provide a more detailed account of some important questions
raised by contemporary concerns in general or by Chapter Eight in
particular. Chapter Nine treats the difficult but burning questions
about Jesus' consciousness and knowledge and his freedom and
sinlessness. With these questions the insistence that Jesus was the
Eternal Son of God and still human like us comes to the crunch.
Finally, Chapter Ten develops an account of human salvation in accordance with, and integral to, the christology of the previous chapters. Here, more than anywhere else, the practical implications of
christological doctrine come to the fore.

A Contemporary Christology

The picture of Jesus that emerges may be summarized as follows.
Because of love for us, the Eternal Word, Son of God, stripped himself
of divine glory and became human, being born of the Virgin Mary.
While on earth, he was empty of all divine knowledge and power. He

had surrendered his divine prerogatives. In all things he was human as we are. The critical difference is that that human life was the life of God the Eternal Son. His was a divine and eternal identity. Nonetheless, like all human beings, he had to live his life from day to day, relying on what human knowledge and sensitivity he had, deciding at each moment what he would make of himself. Would he be true to himself, or not? Would he repress the sense of himself that burned in his heart, or not? Would he live out his contribution to others as he saw it, or not? Unlike us who are sinners, he was absolutely true to himself. Faithful to his eternal identity, he was by that very fact also faithful to his heavenly Father, faithful even in the face of death. On earth as in heaven, in history as in eternity, he was perfectly Son-of-the-Father, Child-of-God.

Because of his fidelity, the Father raised him from the dead. In the resurrection the Father gave his human Son the glory that was his in eternity, the glory that could have been rightly his from the first moment of his human conception but was withheld according to divine wisdom. Through his human life and the power of God, in the resurrection Jesus became the first human being who in his humanity shared—insofar as is possible for a human being—in certain aspects of the divine nature. He did not become God; he always was God. Rather, his humanity was transformed. Now his human mind knew as God knows; his human heart loved as God loves. This human being was divinized.

Jesus' divinization introduced into human history a new possibility for human becoming. Before Jesus' resurrection, there was no divinized human being. Before then, who could say if human divinization was even possible? But divinization happened to Jesus. Then it is a human possibility. If it happened to one human being, it must be also possible—under certain circumstances—for other human beings. With Jesus' resurrection, a new possibility entered human history. This was Jesus' contribution to human salvation, and the Holy Spirit completes what is still needed. Through the Holy Spirit, a divine principle enters our own lives. In some way we become as Jesus was. In Christ we can now actualize the possibility of human divinization in our own lives. We, too, can live a life of fidelity to a divine lead within us and so attain a full share in divine life as the

xxii

man Jesus did before us. Such attainment would be our ultimate salvation.

This is the picture that emerges in the chapters that follow. This is a picture of the same Jesus whom Christians have always loved and worshiped: Eternal Son of God, completely and fully human, raised to divine glory, Redeemer of the world.

Acknowledgements

I am profoundly grateful to many people who helped in various ways to bring this book to completion: Father Bernard Lonergan, who taught me how to think logically and coherently—indeed, who taught me the meaning of thinking—and whose methodological and theological research provided the basis for this book; *requiescat in pace*. Fred Lawrence of Boston College, who was my prime mentor in Lonergan studies. Frederick J. Cwiekowski of St. Mary Seminary in Baltimore, from whom I first learned and continue to learn the complexities of New Testament christology and whose extensive professional criticism, along with that of Patrick O'Brien of the Office for Religious Education of the Diocese of Pittsburgh, was invaluable for improving and correcting this text. Friends, colleagues, and students in San Antonio and at Oblate School of Theology, Mary Hope Doudard, Thomas J. Dougherty, Nedra Jacks, Michael Kiefer, Roy Rihn, and Juana Villescas, whose criticism helped me revise this text. Lu Ann Hartnett, who faithfully, patiently, supportively, and expertly typed and retyped the manuscript of this text. And Sylvia Chávez-García and Frank LeClerc, who helped with proofreading and endnotes.

PART I

The Contemporary Situation

CHAPTER ONE

A New Way of Reading the New Testament

Practically everything we know about Jesus is found in the New Testament. There are no other significant sources.[1] The New Testament has been with us since the end of the first century, and the texts have not changed. Why, then, has our understanding of Jesus changed? Why, after so many centuries, are scholars claiming radically new insight into the life and meaning of Jesus Christ?

The present chapter addresses this question. Certainly the full answer is complex. Many strands of human concern weave together to form the fabric of any significant movement in history. Yet one strand in particular is of concern here. If the sources on Jesus have not changed, the way of reading them certainly has. There is the difference, and this chapter highlights that difference. These considerations are not strictly a part of the study of Jesus. They are a preliminary to it. But this preliminary is of utmost importance. No one can understand the recent revolution in thinking about Jesus without some understanding of the revolution in reading the Bible. For this reason this chapter will present a brief introduction to the historical-critical method of biblical interpretation used by contemporary scholars.

1

The Emergence of Historical-Mindedness

Something has happened to our understanding of Jesus. But more broadly than this, something has happened to our world as a whole. A new awareness has emerged, namely, historical-mindedness.

Since the nineteenth century, a new approach to historical studies has taken hold.[2] Critical scholarship arose. Formerly historians read their historical sources as clear testimony about what had happened. They took their documents at face value. But the critical method of historical scholarship took a different approach. Historians began asking questions of the sources, pitting them against one another, wondering why they said what they said. Historians began to question the sources rather than accepting reverently whatever they said. The conclusions were striking.

Two examples will clarify the point. Throughout the Middle Ages the pope claimed political sovereignty over huge territories in Italy and beyond. In fact, only in 1870 did the Vatican surrender control over the last of the Papal States. This political claim was based on an ancient document, the Donation of Constantine. According to this document, the Roman Emperor Constantine conferred on Pope Sylvester I (314–335 A.D.) and his successors primacy over Antioch, Constantinople, Alexandria, and Jerusalem—the four patriarchal sees in the East—as well as dominion over all of Italy and the provinces in the Western Empire. Though questioned at times, this document was generally considered to be authentic and the pope's reign over the Papal States legitimate. However, in 1440 Lorenzo Valla, an Italian humanist and priest, argued conclusively that the Donation of Constantine was a forgery. Valla mounted a whole series of arguments. He showed that the state of affairs described in the Donation did not square with what was otherwise known about the history of that time. And he did a linguistic analysis to confirm his argument: the barbarity of the document's Latin and the mistakes in its terminology show that it could not have been written in the fourth century.[3] Historians today have been able to date the so-called Donation of Constantine as an eighth or ninth century fabrication. Valla's critical study of that historical document shed new light on medieval history. Things were not what they had seemed to be. On the basis of the same historical

2

document but read differently, a different understanding of the facts emerged. Valla's work anticipated the now prevalent historical-critical method.

Or again, at the turn of the first century, Ignatius of Antioch was being taken to Rome to be martyred. On the way he wrote a number of letters—epistles—to various Christian communities. Among other things, the letters emphasize the important role of the bishop in the Christian community. Ignatius insists that in each community only one is bishop, that the bishop has authority over the community in all things pertaining to the faith, and that the bishop speaks for God. Christians owe obedience and respect to their bishop. Now, these letters used to be taken as clear evidence about the structure of a diocese from the earliest times: the hierarchy is three-tiered; a monarchical bishop, presbyters (priests), and deacons are set above the laity. For this is exactly what these very early Christian letters prescribe. But critical historians began to wonder why Ignatius was so insistent on the monarchical bishop and the reverence due him. They began to ask questions of the sources. Why was Ignatius' exhortation so forceful? Why were the Christian communities resisting this hierarchical system? Could it be that, in fact, the system Ignatius proposed was not everywhere accepted, that it was an innovation? Then Ignatius' insistence was intended not to confirm a system already long established but to bolster one being newly proposed. Whereas before councils of elders led the churches, now in each church one elder was to have authority over all. Renewed scrutiny of those letters and of other contemporary sources confirmed that this latter explanation fit the evidence better than the former. What was really going on was not what was previously supposed. Today historians agree that the three-tiered hierarchy was not established by the apostles but was a later development in the history of the Church. Ignatius himself played a critical role in that development. The accepted conclusion is now the reverse of what used to be held.[4]

Notice how a different reading of the same documents leads to different conclusions. This "different reading" is called historical-critical method. As a widely accepted and refined technique, it is barely a century and a half old. Its implications are far-reaching. The above examples make this obvious. Generally, we tend to read into the past what we know from the present. Then everything appears firm, stable, unchanging. We believe—indeed, we have been taught with religious conviction—that "it has always been this way." In fact, however, things have changed. Critical history shows that things were not always as they are. Despite the insistence of Qoheleth (Ecclesiastes 1:9), there are new things under the sun. The very emergence of contemporary historical-mindedness is one of them. The simultaneous and related emergence of a developmental world-view in Darwin's theory of evolution is another, and the emergence of a pervasive psychological awareness in Freud's psychoanalytic theory is a third. These nineteenth century novelties have shaken and broken our older, static understanding of the human world. We now readily understand things in terms of history, development, movement, change. Historical-mindedness has taken hold.[5]

The Further Impact of Historical-Mindedness

The same kind of critical scholarship that was applied across centuries in the study of history could also be applied across cultures in the study of anthropology. Cross-cultural studies were the result, and the very notion of culture changed. Formerly, the notion was normative. There was one culture, Western European. All else was—if not barbarian, as the Greeks would have held, then—primitive, undeveloped, uncultured.[6] Now the notion has become descriptive. "Culture" refers to any set of meanings and values that structure any society. There are many cultures. They are all valid in their own right, and they are all different! Not all peoples are alike.[7]

Again, the conclusion is the same. There are discontinuities within the human race, just as there are discontinuities within history. Humanity is not homogeneous, and history is not an unbroken line. To speak about eternal verities or even about universal human nature becomes problematic.[8]

A major philosophical issue surfaces. Lurking behind the conclusions of critical history and companion to its development is the specter of relativism.[9] Is there such a thing as truth? Can we really know reality? Are we all locked into our own culture and era, irreparably biased? Is one position as good as another? How could one ever assess the difference? Are all "truths" and "values" relative? Such fundamental questions had clearly emerged by the end of the last century. They have filtered down to a popular level in our own day.

They show themselves in familiar slogans: "You do your thing, I'll do mine." "If it feels good, do it." "Do your own thing." This issue will be treated in detail in Chapter Two, and it will resurface periodically throughout this book. It colors discussion about Jesus or anything else—especially when truth-claims are involved. Here I only want to draw attention to the issue. Note that such relativist thinking is a pervasive influence in the contemporary world, and recognize its connection with the emergence of historical-mindedness.

Historical-Critical Study of the New Testament

For the study of Jesus, the immediate impact of critical scholarship came when the new historical methods were applied to the New Testament. Even a cursory comparison of the gospels shows provocative differences among them. Most obviously, the style and structure of John differ from those of the other three gospels. Scholars refer to Matthew, Mark, and Luke as the synoptic gospels—from the Greek *syn* + *optikos:* common view or viewed together—because they parallel each other so closely. John focuses on only certain aspects of Jesus' activity and presents long, meditative discourses. John reads like poetry, and even John's Jesus speaks in elusive and deepening circles. In contrast, the Jesus of the synoptics speaks in brief, pithy sayings and in short parables. Obviously the gospel of John is in a different class compared to the other three gospels. John appears to be an extended reflection on Jesus, while the synoptics appear to be a more straightforward history of Jesus' career. Or so it seems on first sight.

However, comparison of the synoptic gospels with one another reveals other discrepancies. Mark is short and terse. Matthew and Luke are more elaborate. Yet even these two show provocative differences. In Matthew the word of Jesus' birth comes to Joseph; in Luke, to Mary. Matthew's account of the Lord's Prayer has seven petitions; Luke's only five. Matthew has eight beatitudes; Luke has four beatitudes and four woes. The account of Jesus' resurrection differs in all three synoptics. An interesting exercise is to compare those accounts while asking these questions: How many angels were there? Where were they located? In what position? To whom did they speak?

5

Formerly, people suggested ways to reconcile these differences in the gospel accounts. The presupposition was that the gospels give an eyewitness, newspaper-like report of Jesus' life. Any discrepancies in the reports were glossed over. Differences were explained away. They were not considered important. The various accounts were weaved together into one continuous story. But critical scholars began to take the discrepancies seriously. They asked why the differences are there. They asked questions of the texts: Why does Matthew say it this way and Luke that way? What difference in the overall message does it make? The resulting understanding of the gospels is remarkable.

Aspects of New Testament Criticism

It is almost impossible to exaggerate the importance of this new way of reading the New Testament. A review of the major aspects of critical biblical method will highlight the issue.[10]

The first task for biblical scholars was to determine the correct text of the Bible. History has bequeathed us many manuscript copies or fragments of copies of Bible books. Not all read alike. Copied by hand and derived from different parts of the ancient Christian world, the various manuscripts differ in part from one another. Scholars had to study and compare these various manuscripts and determine which were original and authentic, and which were alterations. Today all scholars, Catholic and Protestant alike, recognize the same authentic New Testament Greek text. Where minor "variant readings" still allow some differences in interpretation, the lines of difference do not fall along denominational lines.

Another task was to understand better the language used in the New Testament. The New Testament is written in Greek. However, it had long been recognized that the Greek of the New Testament is not the Greek of Homer and other classical Greek authors. It was supposed that the Greek of the Bible was "God's language." For that reason it differed from classical Greek! Recent archeological finds—like the Dead Sea Scrolls, first discovered in 1947—included copies of Old Testament writings as well as non-biblical texts prior to and contemporary with the New Testament period.[11] Here was a rich source for new insight into the New Testament era and its everyday language and culture. The language of the New Testament is now known to be nothing other than the common Greek language spoken

6

around the beginning of the Christian era. It is called *koine* Greek: common Greek.

Such recent archeological discoveries furnish a new context for reading the New Testament texts. When nothing except the New Testament texts themselves were available, they could easily be read as if they "dropped down from heaven." There was nothing with which to compare them. When other texts of the same era are available, the New Testament texts can be read in their own contemporary context. Obviously, the intended meaning of any spoken or written statement can be determined only within the statement's context. Take a statement out of context and it might be made to mean anything. Accurate interpretation becomes impossible. Then one tends to read the text as if it were written yesterday. One takes the words and phrases to mean what *we* would mean by them, forgetting that they were spoken in a different culture, in a different age, in a different language.

Consider this statement still familiar to many people: "You're out in left field." What would someone who does not know American culture make of such a statement? Yet it means the same thing as the seventies expression, "You're a real space cadet!" In the eighties someone might simply say, "You just don't compute." Even within our own experience, different generations make the same point by saying different things. Without a familiarity with the culture in which the statement arises, it is impossible to determine its meaning. No wonder, then, that for centuries interpretation of the Scriptures was open to easy error. No wonder, too, that recent archeological discoveries bring new certainty to contemporary interpretation of the New Testament.

Another step toward new understanding of the gospels was to determine the relationships among them. This task is called source criticism. Today it is generally agreed that Mark is the oldest of the synoptic gospels, written about 65 A.D. Matthew and Luke were both written about 80 A.D., and John was written sometime between 90 and 100 A.D. As suggested above, John is in a category of its own. On the other hand, Matthew and Luke tend to follow Mark in much of their account. Besides, Matthew and Luke also seem to rely on another common source, denoted by scholars as Q—from the German *Quelle,* which means "source." In addition, both seem also to have independent sources of their own—denoted as M and L. Thus, the interdependence of the synoptic gospels is generally agreed to be as follows:

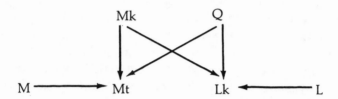

Determination of such relationships among the gospels represents a remarkable new understanding of the gospel texts. They have a history. They have a cultural context. They all have concerns of their own. They were not simply dictated by God to an entranced evangelist. In turn, this new understanding offers a new possibility for interpreting the gospels in themselves and for explaining the differences among them.

A further stage in the critical understanding of the gospels was to distinguish the different literary genres or literary forms incorporated into the same text. This task is called form criticism.

We are very familiar with various literary forms in our own culture. A novel is not a documentary. An editorial is not a news story. A spoof is not an analytical commentary. How one assesses any piece of writing depends on what kind of writing it is. In our everyday reading we take this for granted. Yet only with the discovery of literature which was contemporary with the Bible did scholars realize the diversity of literary forms included in the Bible. And by the early twentieth century, scholars were realizing that the gospels themselves are composites of many different types of writing.

There are *sayings*, rather short and straightforward teachings. Matthew's "Sermon on the Mount" is really a collection of various sayings of Jesus, strung together sometimes because of similarity of theme, sometimes because of mere repetition of words. Sometimes sayings are placed side by side seemingly at random, as in this case: "You hypocrite, first take the log out of your own eye, and then you will see clearly to take the speck out of your brother's eye. Do not give dogs what is holy; and do not throw your pearls before swine, lest they trample them under foot and turn to attack you. Ask, and it will be given you; seek, and you will find; knock, and it will be opened to you" (Mt. 7:5–7). *Parables* are another literary form in the gospels, clearly different from sayings. Parables are provocative teachings that make their point by unexpected and ironic twists in a story. Jesus' comparisons about the Reign of God—it's like a fishnet, a mustard seed, a hidden treasure—and his extended story of the Prodigal Son are familiar parables. *Pronouncements* are a still different literary form. They are the punchlines often attached to a story: "Render to Caesar the things that are Caesar's, and to God the things that are God's" (Mk. 12:17); "The Sabbath was made for people, not people for the Sabbath" (Mk. 2:27). Then, there is the *narrative* with which the evangelist ties other pieces together. For example, Matthew concludes the Sermon on the Mount with his own commentary: "And when Jesus finished these sayings, the crowds were astonished at his teaching, for he taught them as one who had authority, and not as their scribes" (7:28–29).

This determination of different literary forms gives further insight into the actual formation of the gospels. The evangelists did not write the gospels as completely original pieces. And the pre-existing elements that went into the gospels had histories of their own. Oral traditions played a major role in the formation of the gospels. Then, how the different evangelists use the inherited pieces reveals something about each evangelist's own intent. Furthermore, the analysis of literary forms has implications for understanding Jesus himself. For example, it is no longer tenable to think that in one sitting Jesus delivered extended discourses like the "Sermon on the Mount."

A final stage in the development of historical-critical interpretation of the New Testament was to determine the particular themes proper to each of the gospels. This task is called redaction criticism. Its concern is how the evangelists redacted—or edited—the final drafts of the gospels. Comparison of the gospels with one another and study of each in itself reveal the intended theme of each evangelist. For example, in Jesus' teaching on prayer, both Matthew and Luke are following Q. But whereas Matthew writes, "How much more will your Father who is in heaven give *good things* to those who ask him" (7:11), Luke writes, "How much more will the heavenly Father give *the Holy Spirit* to those who ask him" (11:13). Why this slight difference?

9

Does the gospel of Luke perhaps seek to emphasize the role of the Holy Spirit as a particular concern? Study of the remainder of Luke shows that this is, indeed, the case. Or again, Matthew has Jesus ascend to the Father from Galilee. In Luke Jesus ascends from Jerusalem in Judea. This discrepancy might appear serious for someone seeking historical accuracy as *we* define it. But further study of Luke and Acts of the Apostles—both written by the same author—reveals that Luke portrays Jerusalem as the center of salvation and all history. The gospel of Luke ends in Jerusalem, and Acts begins there. To Jerusalem Jesus' life ineluctably leads, and from it the message of Christ spreads to all the world. So it appears that the focus on Jerusalem is a literary device for Luke. These considerations lead us to conclude that the evangelists were more concerned to convey their theological messages than to document geographical or chronological details about Jesus' life. They wrote to share their Christian faith and not to present a biography of Jesus nor to write history as we understand it.

Thus, each of the gospels presents its message with a particular focus, and the picture of Jesus is different in each.[12] For Mark Jesus is the Son of Man who must suffer and die. Fidelity to God entails as much. Those who are faithful to Jesus will share the same fate. For Matthew Jesus is the authoritative, ethical teacher, founder of the New Israel, the Church. For Luke Jesus is the perfect gentleman, filled with the Holy Spirit and gifted in preaching. In addition, Luke emphasizes joy, compassion, prayer, and the role of women in Christian life. Finally, John presents a lofty, theological picture of Jesus come from glory, returning to glory, and filled with glory even during his life on earth.

The Quest of the Historical Jesus

This brief review of contemporary historical-critical method in New Testament interpretation raises an important question: Can we know what Jesus himself was like? It must now be obvious that the gospels do not give us a biography of Jesus as we would like. Rather, they present an interpretation about Jesus, and the interpetation is somewhat different in each of the gospels. Yet the gospels are our only source of information about Jesus. So we are left wondering what Jesus himself was really like.

10

The problem can be expressed in another way. Contemporary scholars speak about Jesus himself as *the historical Jesus.* This is the Jesus that any historian could know—a man born sometime around the beginning of the Christian era, an itinerant preacher, crucified in Palestine during the time of Pontius Pilate. But Christians affirm much more about this man. They believe that Jesus was the Son of God, that he was born of a virgin, that he rose from the dead, and that he was the Savior of the world. Scholars refer to this Jesus as *the Christ of faith.* Now, what the gospels present is the Christ of faith. But what we want to know is the historical Jesus. Limited as we are to the gospels for a source of information, can we know the historical Jesus?

This question first arose in the late eighteenth century. A review of the history of this question will focus this introduction to biblical criticism on the topic of this book, Jesus.[13] The source of this question was a book by Hermann Samuel Reimarus. Between 1774 and 1778 Gotthold Ephraim Lessing published excerpts from that book. Reimarus had suggested there was a difference between the aim of Jesus and the aim of the disciples. Jesus, he said, intended to be a political Messiah but was foiled and died on the cross. The disciples decided to use Jesus as the focus of a new religion and so fabricated the resurrection story. Of course, this suggestion was offensive and was violently rejected. Still, it had an important impact. It surfaced the harsh awareness that the gospels do not present a simple picture of the historical Jesus. Thus for the first time it raised the question that concerns us here. And it demonstrated the need for hard historical facts about Jesus of Nazareth.

Many people accepted the challenge that Reimarus raised and attempted to write a life of Jesus. These lives differed considerably as each successive scholar presumed to find a new angle on the historical Jesus. This era is known as the Old Quest of the Historical Jesus. The Old Quest rested on the naive presupposition that as historical sources Mk and Q were so primitive as to be free from theological interpretation. It was thought that on the basis of these sources one could actually write a biography of Jesus.

The Old Quest came to an end at the beginning of the twentieth century. For a number of reasons biblical scholars despaired of ever writing Jesus' life. In 1901 William Wrede's *The Messianic Secret in the Gospels* struck a first blow to nineteenth-century optimism. Wrede showed that even the gospel of Mark is a theological interpretation of Jesus' life and work. Wrede argued that the "messianic secret"— evidenced in Jesus' repeated injunction that the disciples not tell anyone that he was the Christ—was a literary device created by Mark and not traceable to Jesus himself. According to Wrede, Jesus had not claimed to be the Messiah. The disciples recognized him as the Christ only after the resurrection. Then Mark used the messianic secret to explain why, if Jesus was Christ, his disciples and the other Jews had not known him as such during his lifetime. In any case, Wrede showed that Mark's gospel, too, is a highly theologized interpretation of Jesus' life and work and not a pure source of information on the historical Jesus.

Albert Schweitzer, Nobel Peace Prize winner, renowned musician, and medical missionary in Africa, was also a theologian. When his book appeared in 1906, *Von Reimarus zu Wrede*—translated into English as *The Quest of the Historical Jesus*—struck the death blow to the Old Quest. As the German title suggests, *From Reimarus to Wrede,* this book recounts the attempts to write a life of Jesus, beginning with Reimarus' milestone piece and working through the nineteenth century up to Wrede's book. The implication of Schweitzer's long and tedious work was unavoidable: despite a century of effort, there was no consensus whatsoever on the historical Jesus. In fact, all the lives of Jesus to date were different. As Schweitzer suggested, the authors looked into the well of history and saw their own faces. That is, they projected their own lives and experiences into Jesus—much as believers still tend to do, making Jesus the ideal model for whatever happened to be the current social, political, or psychological trend. Besides, Schweitzer also uncovered a fundamental aspect of Jesus' teaching that all the previous lives of Jesus missed: Jesus' concern for the eschatological, that is, for the coming of God's reign at the end of time. According to Schweitzer's exaggerated opinion, Jesus was obsessed with the end of the world; and, discouraged with attempts to bring on God's Reign, in a last desperate move, Jesus went up to Jerusalem to get himself killed. In any case, the implication was obvious: if so central a part of Jesus' teaching had been overlooked, could anyone ever really know the historical Jesus on the basis of the gospels? The accepted answer was "No," and a new era began. The

12

Quest of the Historical Jesus was called off, and attempts to write Jesus' biography were abandoned.

Another factor worth noting had added to the abandonment of the Old Quest. It was during these same early years of the twentieth century that form criticism was being developed. As noted above, this approach to the gospels moved behind the inherited text and attempted to discern various pre-existing segments that the evangelists wove together to produce the final drafts of the gospels. As scholars began to realize how complex the process was that formed the gospels, they lost hope in the possibility of discovering the historical Jesus beneath the Christ of faith presented in the gospels.

For about half a century the Quest of the Historical Jesus was called off. A new figure in biblical scholarship, Rudolf Bultmann, dominated the field. Bultmann insisted that not only can we not know the historical Jesus but also that it is not important to know him. One major influence on Bultmann's thinking was his Lutheranism, which emphasized the importance of preaching the Word and insisted on justification by faith alone. A second influence was the existentialist philosophy of Martin Heidegger, which calls humans to appreciate their responsibility for themselves and their world and to decide for authentic being. So influenced, and faced with the seeming impossibility of knowing the historical Jesus, Bultmann argued that knowledge of the historical Jesus is not central to Christianity. Rather, the message about Jesus that is preached and heard—the kerygma—is central. The Christian message confronts us with an existential challenge to conversion. This is what matters. So, for example, whether or not Jesus rose from the dead is not worth debating. What is important is to choose to live in faith and hope because of the resurrection message. The kerygma is the heart of Christianity, not the historical facts about Jesus. To argue otherwise, Bultmann supposed, would be to make faith dependent on historical scholarship—as if having the historical facts would make faith unnecessary!

In view of the issues prevalent in his times, Bultmann's position is understandable. And for those times it became a major force in preserving the influence of Christianity. Moreover, it fostered an appreciation for the existential significance of the Christian message. But by the same token, that position downplayed the importance of

13

the historical ground of Christianity. Christianity claims to be a historical religion, not just a set of inspiring ideas, a philosophy of life. If what Christians believe about Jesus did not really happen, can they go on believing and preaching it? In Chapter Two I will answer with a definitive No! The notions that God became human and that a man overcame death may be reassuring; they may even inspire to heroism. But if they are not true, should one honestly base one's life on them? If Christian belief about the Christ of faith cannot be grounded in the historical Jesus, can Christians continue to hold their beliefs as true—unless they change the meaning of that word or are dishonest? These questions present an urgent challenge to contemporary Christianity. Although before 1774 these questions had not arisen, today they cannot be avoided. The questions are real and, once raised, they will not disappear.

By 1963 these considerations and further developments in biblical criticism brought another swing of the pendulum. Ernst Käsemann, a disciple of Bultmann, called for a New Quest of the Historical Jesus. Christianity could not simply ignore its historical basis. And refined techniques of historical research now made it possible to isolate some gospel material as Jesus' own. No one would ever again think it possible to write an actual biography of Jesus. Still, it might be possible to discover enough information about the historical Jesus to ground basic Christian beliefs about him. In any case, the effort to do so must be renewed.

The results of that effort appear later in this book. Scholars today are generally agreed that if we cannot know much about Jesus himself we can at least know something. Chapter Five will summarize current historical information about Jesus and argue that what we know about Jesus is sufficient to ground Christian beliefs about him. The Quest of the Historical Jesus has a happy ending, though what is found in the end is only a fraction of what scholars had hoped to find at the beginning. But through it all, this much has become clear. The picture the gospels present is not that of the historical Jesus. So what we can now legitimately say about Jesus is quite different from what we used to say.

Validity of the New Method

The results of historical-critical interpretation stand in stark contrast to what we used to read from the gospels. Accordingly, some might think that such an approach, new in the history of Christianity, is a betrayal of our tradition. This, of course, is the position which Fundamentalist groups hold. They insist on reading the Bible "literally," just as it sounds to the sincere ear of today's man or woman on the street. They reject a questioning, scientific reading of the divine texts as irreverent. But as a result, they advocate an unthinking religion, exposing people to the control of any preacher whose message is attractive. They risk exchanging the saving Word of God for the spontaneous opinion of some human being (cf. Mk. 7:1–13). For no one can read or preach the Scriptures—or anything else!—without employing some process of interpretation. The markings on a page are not words and so are not meaningful unless they pass through someone's mind. And that passing through entails interpretation. To appeal to a supposedly "literal" reading and so to refuse to consider how one ought to interpret the Scriptures is naive and ultimately irresponsible.[14]

If historical-critical interpretation of the gospels is new, it is not without reason. In fact, today we know more about the New Testament, its language, and its historical context than ever before. Our present dictionaries of New Testament Greek are the most complete and accurate in human history. We are farther from the New Testament period than, say, St. Jerome, who translated the Bible into the Vulgate Latin edition at the end of the fourth century. Nonetheless, our knowledge of Hebrew and Greek and the biblical world far surpasses that of Jerome or any others. If the implications of contemporary scholarship are revolutionary—and, indeed, they are—they are also well-grounded.

Christian scholars across denominational lines now accept historical-critical interpretation of the Scriptures as standard.[15] Protestant scholars initially developed the method. Recently, even the official Roman Catholic Church has approved it. This fact alone stands as persuasive testimony about the validity of this method. Typically, before allowing it, the Catholic Church waited until the method was significantly refined and its conclusions could be safely reconciled with traditional beliefs. In the meantime many Catholic pioneers in biblical criticism were censured for the conclusions they derived by using historical-critical method. Finally in 1943, Pope Pius XII published *Divino Afflante Spiritu*, an encyclical letter that supported critical study of the Scriptures. In 1964, the Pontifical Biblical Commission published its "Instruction on the Historical Truth of the Gospels." This document outlines three stages in the writing of the gospels: One, the actual words and deeds of Jesus himself; Two, the early disciples' preaching about Jesus, including their increased understanding and interpretation about Jesus; and Three, the evangelists' active work of writing the actual gospels. In its *Dogmatic Constitution on Divine Revelation*, article 19, in 1965 the Second Vatican Council summarized this understanding of the history of the gospel formation as follows:

> Holy Mother Church has firmly and with absolute constancy maintained and continues to maintain, that the four Gospels just named, whose historicity she unhesitatingly affirms, faithfully hand on what Jesus, the Son of God, while he lived among men, really did and taught for their eternal salvation, until the day when he was taken up (cf. Acts 1:1–2). For, after the ascension of the Lord, the apostles handed on to their hearers what he had said and done, but with fuller understanding which they, instructed by the glorious events of Christ and enlightened by the Spirit of truth, now enjoyed. The sacred authors, in writing the four Gospels, selected certain of the many elements which had been handed on, either orally or already in written form, others they synthesized or explained with an eye to the situation of the churches, the while sustaining the form of preaching, but always in such a fashion that they have told us the honest truth about Jesus. Whether they relied on their own memory and recollections or on the testimony of those who 'from the beginning were eyewitnesses and ministers of the Word,' their purpose in writing was that we might know the 'truth' concerning the things of which we have been informed (cf. Lk. 1:2–4).[16]

This official Roman Catholic statement stands as a summary account of the common prevailing Christian understanding of the formation of the gospels. This understanding is at the root of the historical-critical method of interpretation.

It is now clear that 'gospel' is a particular literary form in itself. The gospels are not historical accounts in the sense that we understand history. They are not biographies of Jesus. Rather, true to history in their own way, the gospels are documents of faith. They record what the early Church believed about Jesus, and they encourage others to believe the same. John 20:31 states this plainly: "these

16

things are written *that you may believe* that Jesus is the Christ, the Son of God, and *that* believing *you may have life* in his name."

The present understanding rules out any simplistic, literalistic, Fundamentalist reading of the Bible. It warns us not to confuse Stage Three with Stage One as if Stage Two never happened and Stage Three itself were not a creative process. The gospels do not give us picture-perfect, transcribed tape-recorded accounts of Jesus. Therefore, it will not be so easy as we had thought to learn from the gospels what Jesus himself was actually like. And when we do finally uncover the real Jesus, he may not appear as we have been led to imagine. The picture of Jesus that emerges from historical-critical study of the gospels is considerably different from the traditional pious accounts based on the literal reading of the gospels.

Summary

This, then, is what happened to our understanding of Jesus. Contemporary methods in scripture interpretation have revolutionized our knowledge about him. Now he appears much more human than we ever imagined. In fact, he appears so much like us that some people have begun to question traditional teaching about his divinity. Or, in any case, it has become much more difficult to hold together what the New Testament says with what later church teaching says.[17] The tension between the two is showing itself in the debates and rifts appearing in the whole of the Christian Church. The old questions are being seen from a new perspective, so new answers are emerging. And new questions are transposing or disqualifying old questions, and the result is much uncertainty. The crisis is real. Simple decree, regardless of its source, will not resolve it. The questions are real; they must be answered. No facile dogmatic solution will suffice. Something has happened to our understanding of Jesus. A primary cause of that happening was the application of the historical-critical method to the New Testament texts.

CHAPTER TWO

Christology: Thinking About Jesus

A new way of reading New Testament texts has changed our understanding of Jesus and provoked a real crisis in scholarship and faith. The focal problem is to reconcile an historical-critical reading of the New Testament with the dogmatic decrees of the early church councils. The New Testament, interpreted according to contemporary methods, and the traditional belief of the Christian churches seem to be in tension, if not at odds. A major task of this book is to address this tension and to suggest a resolution of it. This chapter begins that task by considering in some detail the human endeavor to understand the mystery of Jesus Christ. The topic here is christology itself. The guiding question will be, What is 'christology'? This question will quickly lead us to the heart of the matter.

Two Definitions of 'Christology'

There is an immediate and easy answer to the question, "What is christology?" Just as theology is the study of God and psychology is the study of the psyche or mind and cardiology is the study of the heart and epistemology is the study of knowledge, so christology is the study of Christ. In this sense, christology is a subject matter, and

19

it is the name of a course, one among many offered for study in a university or school of theology. In this same sense, this essay is a contribution to christology. It is a book on christology.

Yet there is a more profound answer to the question, and it is this answer which will concern us throughout this chapter. The suffix "-ology" comes from the Greek word *logos*. The word *logos* has many meanings, but basically it refers to the mind, its activity, and its product. So *logos* could be translated "intelligence" or "thought" or "word" or "statement." Accordingly, -ology can simply mean "study of." But it also means "word on" and "thought about" and "statement about" and "articulation of" and "verbalization of" and the like. So a christology is a particular understanding of Christ or someone's thought about Christ or a position on Christ or a particular attempt to articulate the mystery of Christ. In this sense we speak not only of 'christology' in the singular as the study of Christ in general, a particular subject matter, but we also speak of "christolo*gies*" in the plural as many possible understandings about Christ. There can be John's christology and Paul's christology, the christology of the Council of Nicea, Thomas Aquinas' christology, Karl Barth's or Karl Rahner's christology, and your or my christology. We can even speak of Jesus' own christology as we ask, "What did he think about himself?"

Notice that central to this second understanding of christology is the realization that all christology is thinking about Jesus. As different people think differently about Jesus and prefer different ways to express what they think, they have different christologies. But whatever christology one may hold, it is always an expression of thought or reflection. It is the product of a human mind. Here is the point. Christology is reflective: it is thought *about*, articulation *of*, position *on*. Christology is the product of one's *reflecting back on* Jesus.

Thinking About Thinking

To understand christology as reflection on Jesus is to make some far-reaching presuppositions. For one, it is to presuppose that there is a difference between Jesus and our reflection about him. This sounds ordinary enough. But when said in general terms, it appears much more significant. It is to presuppose, namely, that reality is one thing and our thought about reality is another thing. More about this below.

20

Then, it is also to presuppose that through the use of our minds we can know reality; our thoughts can express what really is. Moreover, it is to presuppose that some thoughts are correct and others are not; some agree with reality and others are mere delusion. Finally, it is to presuppose that some correct thoughts are more complete than others which, though correct, are less complete.

When these presuppositions are ennumerated, the discussion changes from thinking about Jesus to thinking about thinking. The topic switches from christology to epistemology. Now the questions are not about Jesus Christ but about what it means to know. What is knowledge? What is reality? What is truth? Can we really know reality? Or are we caught up in our own worlds and not able to break out of them? Is one opinion as good as another? Do these questions really matter?

It may be disturbing to face all these questions so early in the discussion. They are the "big" questions of life, and it is not easy to achieve agreement on the answers. Yet these are the very questions on which contemporary christology is foundering. Today's crisis in theology is more a crisis of epistemology than a crisis of any theological question—Jesus, Trinity, Bible, Church, Grace, Eucharist. Epistemology underlies every attempt to do any theology. When uncertainty about the possibility of certainty prevails, the "motor" for all the disciplines is in the repair shop. Nothing moves forward.

Human Reality: A Social Construct

Epistemological concerns will resurface periodically throughout this essay. They are the heart of the matter. So it is important to point them out at the beginning. It is also important that from the beginning I be clear about my own presuppositions on this matter.

Some may wonder, "Why even make an issue of this? It's just common sense!" In some ways, it seems so. It is one thing for it to be raining outside and another thing for me only to think it is raining. If it is not really raining, all my thinking does not change that fact. And if I am so determined that I insist on carrying my opened umbrella, everyone will simply think I am some kind of kook. There is not much doubt here.

Yet I remember that once as a child I was at the cinema watching a movie that ended with a rain storm. The sense of dark clouds, splashing water, and a chill up my spine was so real that I fully prepared myself for such weather as I stepped out of the theater. Lo and behold, the sun was shining brightly. It was a beautiful summer day. I was shocked.

It was easy enough for me to realize that the movie had so affected me that for a moment I had been out of touch with the "real world." I adjusted quickly and realized that I had only been thinking it was raining. Actually it was not. I chuckled at the little joke I had played on myself. I marveled at that exciting experience. I was young and quite impressionable at the time.

Things seem easy enough when we are talking about rain or other such aspects of the physical world. But when it comes to the more important questions about life, knowing what is real becomes much more difficult. For example, Am I in love? Or is this just some crazy thing going on in my head? We hear so much about love through TV, movies, popular songs, and novels. Could it be that this is all just propaganda? Do we want to believe in love so much that we convince each other that love is real? If we lived before the early Middle Ages, the whole question of romantic love would never come up. The same is still true in many cultures outside of Western civilization. So, is love real? Or is it just an instance of mass delusion? Are we all caught up in some dream? Are we overly affected by some bigger-than-life movie?[1] Could it be that we do not know what the "real world" is? Such questions are not so far fetched. On the contrary, they are too real.

If you can, recall the days before television. When I was about seven years old, my Aunt Helen, who lived across the yard, was the only person in the neighborhood who had a television set. We kids used to invite ourselves into her kitchen shortly before seven every weekday evening so we could watch "Captain Video." Those fifteen minutes of space adventure were a real treat. When we walked down the street of the shopping district—there were no malls then—crowds would be gathered in front of the furniture stores, watching TV through the display windows. To get a glimpse of a TV was something special. And today? No one marvels at a TV set. Almost every household has at least one. Evening TV entertainment is taken for granted. Live news coverage around the world is taken for granted. This is all

22

part of life. Anyone not old enough to relate to my childhood memories might find my marvel at television quite peculiar. Those who were born into a TV society never knew things otherwise. For them "it has always been this way"! This is what is real.

The same can be said about airplane travel, long distance telephone service, interstate highway systems, and so much else. What impact will computer technology and today's movements—like black, brown, women's, and gay liberation or holistic health—have on our society? In the past fifty years our world has changed considerably. Life is not what it used to be. What we now understand life to be is not what we used to understand it to be. The reality has changed, and it has changed because we have structured it differently. In many ways we create our own reality.

Roman Catholics may remember the church of pre-Vatican II days. Mass was in Latin. The priest faced the altar. The altar boys held up the priest's chasuble during the Elevation. People went to confession at least once a month so they could receive Holy Communion on Holy Name Sunday or Sodality Sunday or CYO Sunday. Nuns wore long habits and were hardly ever seen in public, certainly never alone. When anyone visited them in their convent, they would bring out a snack of tea and cookies, but they themselves would never eat in front of others. Priests wore their cassocks and birettas as they walked the streets of the parish. Catholics avoided getting very friendly with their Protestant neighbors and would never think of going to church with them. And generally, the Protestants felt the same way about the Catholics. All of that seemed so right. Few ever thought of doing otherwise. That is the way things were. That is how it was *supposed* to be. That is what was "real." Yet today few Catholics would think of Mass in Latin, and Christians of most denominations consider it proper to work and pray together with Christians of other denominations or with non-Christians.

Our world—human reality!—is certainly different from what it used to be. No one ever thought, before the changes came, that things should have been different. Now it is difficult even to imagine how things used to be. How quaint the past appears! In view of this experience, we can easily wonder, "What is real?" Are we, all of us together as a group, deluding ourselves? Will we look back someday on today's "reality" and wonder how we could have been so narrow-minded, so naive, so "out of touch with reality"? These questions are not silly.

The world we live in is more than the physical world. It is a human world. This world consists of people and relationships and shared understandings about things and customs and procedures and rules and punishments.[2] Its reality is consensus reality. It is what we have agreed on as real.[3]

Realizing that what I say is true, many have given up the acknowledgement and pursuit of truth. "Truth," they say, "is what is meaningful for me. And your truth is what is meaningful for you." If a conflict develops, "You do your thing, and I'll do mine." "We really can never know what is right, what is true." This position emerged clearly among philosophers and historians by the late nineteenth century and has come to inform popular culture in our own day. In Chapter One I noted how such relativism is related to historical-mindedness.

The Possibility of Sure Knowledge

The relativist position calls for a strong response. It is not easy, of course, to arrive at sound knowledge. And it is even harder to say what knowledge and truth are. Yet, despite the difficulty, the pursuit of truth must not be abandoned.

In the first place, we do know certain facts that are indisputable. As I write this in sunny San Antonio, it is not raining outside. In the past fifty years there have been major changes in our society. The human world we live in is in great part the product of social consensus. We do know these things to be true.

In the second place, we can and do change our minds. We learn. We reject former understandings and adopt new ones. We are not boxed into the consensus world in which we were raised. Though we are considerably conditioned by the world in which we live, we are also able to transcend it. Anyone who has ever made a mistake and has been lucky enough to recognize it and honest enough to admit and correct it knows this to be true. Wherever people remain open to reality and honest about facing it, the possibility of approaching the truth remains. We are not doomed to relativism.

That same position can be expressed more technically. What we

24

experience is not pure data. The real world, the human world, is a construct; and we ourselves are part of that world. We, too, are constructs. As we grow, we are formed and we form ourselves. Necessarily, then, we approach reality through the "filter" of our own conceptions and values. So the object of our experience already contains interpretation.

Nonetheless, there is a difference between the data we interpret and the interpretations we make. Data are not interpretation. We are able to distinguish the two. We go on to insist on the verification of any interpretation we discern. Our interpretation might be wrong. We want evidence for what we accept as true. Only when we have sufficient evidence do we allow that we really know something. Then we have fact. Then we have moved toward the truth.

Fact is *interpretation* that is *verified* in *data*. This formula sums up the complex process of human knowing.[4] It articulates the working of the human mind in every case, however complex or however simple. Its terms apply on a sliding scale to whatever is being considered in any particular case. The data in question may be a sensible experience in the physical world or an internal experience in the world of the psyche. The data may be that about which an infant has a first thought or that which a team of physicists have understood about molecular structure. The knowing process, enunciated in this capsule formula, is the same in all cases.

The process is open-ended. Whatever comes into awareness becomes data for the process. The knowing process itself can become data for the process. Then the knowing process can be understood and articulated, even as I am articulating it here. Once articulated, the norms inherent in the process can become the deliberately chosen norms of all thought and so enhance the possibility of accurate knowing.[5] Moreover, any product of that process can become further data for the process. Our knowledge can itself become the data for further reflection, so the process is self-correcting.[6] It breaks through past misconceptions. The dynamism of this process, built into the human person, moves relentlessly to know more and more. It directs itself toward everything there is to be known. Its object is reality. Reality is that which there is to be known. Through the unbiased functioning of this process, we do know reality. Reality and knowledge are correlates.[7]

Christology, An Instance of Thinking

The above paragraphs summarize my understanding of the human process of knowing. Now let us apply that understanding to the issue at hand, christology; for christology is but a particular instance of human knowing. Christology, in the verbal sense, is one's actual thinking about Jesus, one's reflecting on Jesus. In this sense, to christologize is to do something. It is to think about and understand Jesus. Christology, in the nominal sense of the word, is the product of such thinking and understanding. Any particular christology is someone's articulation of his or her understanding of Jesus. Clearly, then, at the core of christology is the human process of knowing: acknowledging data, questioning their meaning and arriving at an interpretation, and verifying the suggested interpretation against the data. Christology is but a particular application of the human knowing process. This has implications.

It follows that it is completely legitimate to distinguish between Jesus himself and any understanding of who/what Jesus is. Data are one thing, interpretation another. Granted, we do not know Jesus apart from our understanding of him, so it may not always be easy to sort out the two. Still, the two are not the same thing. Jesus himself and our understanding of Jesus are distinct. So, given the self-correcting process of knowing, there is an opening to and a possibility of eventual correct and complete understanding of Jesus.

It follows further that Christian understanding and expression about Jesus Christ may change as time goes on. The process of knowing is on-going and cumulative. So christology develops.[8] Christians grapple to find some way to understand and to express what they experience in Jesus. Through the years, building on past efforts, they may come to understand more accurately and to express more precisely the Jesus they know. The development of christological thought and doctrine is the result.

According to this understanding, we would not expect earlier statements to be as detailed or precise as later statements. Going back to Jesus himself and granting he was limited to understanding with a human mind while on earth, we would not even necessarily expect Jesus to be able clearly to articulate who/what he was. Yet in every instance, the lack of a fully adequate statement about Jesus does not cancel out the reality of Jesus. Even if Jesus himself cannot completely say who/what he is, this does not stop him from being himself. Jesus is Jesus, regardless of how well or how poorly he is understood and regardless of who is doing the understanding. Reality and our reflection on it are not the same thing. Jesus Christ and Christian reflection about Jesus are not the same thing. The reality does not stand or fall on the reflection, and the reflection is not necessarily adequate to the reality. The reflection can change while the reality remains the same.

Although we will treat this issue in more detail later, perhaps a brief digression about Jesus' possible ignorance about himself is needed here. Most Christians believe that Jesus knew everything about everything, so he certainly knew everything about himself. Whether or not this was the case is not the issue here. Later it will be. Here I would just like to pose a question that takes us more surely to the real issue: How human are we willing to allow Jesus to be? We claim to believe that God, the Eternal Son, became human, like us in all things but sin. We claim that in this we see how much God loves us. But how much are we willing to let God love us? How far are we willing to let God go? If Jesus was really human, while he was among us he knew only with a human mind; but human minds do not know everything about everything. They know piecemeal, bit by bit, little by little. If Jesus was really human, why do we presume that Jesus' mind was different from our own? And as for his knowledge about himself—what human being can give a complete and adequate statement about him- or herself? Does any of us really know who we are? Is it not rather this way: only after we have lived our lives, people come to appreciate who and what we were and are able to say it? If Jesus was really human, why should it be different with him? God can do anything that is not self-contradictory. Evidently God can even become human. But how much humanity are we willing to allow God? How far do we let God bend down to us? Does it shake our faith to think that as human the Eternal Son might not have been able to say clearly with a finite human mind who and what he was? If so, what faith is being shaken? Our faith in how *we* think God ought to behave or our faith in the incomprehensible love of God for us? If we are overwhelmed by what this reasoning might mean, perhaps we have caught a glimpse of the mystery of the incarnation. Jesus Christ was much more human than we generally allow. To grapple with this is the real issue.

Christological Development

The distinction between reality and human reflection on reality suggests that christologies may change throughout the centuries while Jesus Christ remains one and the same. What this "change" means needs to be clarified. If reflection on Jesus is really about Jesus, each christology will say something accurate about Jesus. And the succession of christologies will expand and complement one another. The change will not be random. Rather, it will be an orderly and cumulative process of growing understanding. It will be development.

Development entails two aspects: change and continuity. If there is only change but no continuity, the result is not development but only a series of random, disconnected ideas. In this situation, anything goes and nothing is worth very much. Further reflection does not lead to increased understanding but only adds another theory, more idle speculation. On the other hand, neither is there development if there is strict continuity down the centuries but nothing new ever emerges. In this situation, there is only constant repetition of what others thought and said before; and, again, there is no increase in understanding. Development entails both change and continuity.

Change results when new situations provoke new questions and new questions demand new answers.[9] Then reflection makes a step forward. On the other hand, continuity results from two factors. First, throughout the centuries one and the same Jesus Christ is the object of all reflection. So all christologies find grounding and coherence in the common object of their concern, Jesus Christ. Second, throughout the centuries one and the same process of human knowing is at work. The movement of mind—from data to interpretation to verification of interpretation in the data—remains the same and insures the same formal structure to all christology. In summary, all christology is reflection, and all christology is reflection on Jesus; in this there is continuity. But continued questioning and reflection brings new insight; in this there is change. Change amidst continuity is development.

Development of christology finds control in the process of human knowing. The process imposes its own criteria.[10] The process demands that every new interpretation be verified against the data.

28

So, as an instance of human knowing, every christology must be true to the reality, Jesus Christ. If a new interpretation arises that cannot be reconciled with Jesus himself, that interpretation must be rejected as idle speculation. But this criterion cuts both ways. If an old and accepted interpretation proves irreconcilable with Jesus himself, it too must be rejected as mistaken. As new research uncovers more about Jesus himself, Christians must review and rethink all that has been said about Jesus, and they must propose more adequate accounts of Jesus. Throughout, the criterion of adequacy of interpretation to data prevails.

The Reasonableness of Christianity

To call for adequacy of interpretation to data is to call for reasonableness. To be reasonable is to follow the intrinsic norms of the human process of knowing. It is to provide evidence for one's claims. It is to ground one's interpretation adequately in the available data. Here, assuming that christology is an instance of human knowing, I am insisting that any acceptable account of Jesus must be reasonable. By the same token, I am suggesting that Christian belief about Jesus itself must also be reasonable. Thus, another presupposition underlying this whole presentation comes to light: faith must be reasonable.

Let me explain. If faith is reasonable, it is not silly. It is not without some basis. It may not be completely explainable, but it is not without grounds. Obviously, then, reasonable faith is not "blind faith," faith without reason, unthinking faith. Faith is not the same as whim. Faith is not a matter of caprice. Faith is not blind decision. To take something so completely "on faith" that one has no reasons for accepting it is to act irresponsibly. To believe without reason is to betray the very workings of one's own mind. It is also, then, to slight the God who made us as we are. Religion is no excuse for irresponsibility. Religious faith does not excuse us from reasonableness. Faith must be reasonable.

Reasonableness still leaves room for faith and mystery. For example, though we can use it, no one really understands what electricity is or how it works. Even physicists cannot explain it. Nonetheless, it is reasonable to believe that electricity lights our homes and cities. To accept that is to believe it, for no one can explain it. Yet it is a reasonable belief. Moreover, the reasonableness of this belief does not

take away the mystery—the marvel—from the operation of electricity.[11] Or again, love is a mystery. Who could explain it? Yet even
when one's love is reasonable, one still makes an act of faith when one
loves; one takes a risk. And the mystery remains, despite the reasonableness of the love. In some similar way, Jesus Christ is a mystery of
faith. To say that our belief in Jesus must be reasonable is not to deny
the mystery nor the need for faith. On the contrary, the reasonableness of our faith is precisely what allows us to believe a mystery,
and to believe responsibly.

To believe without reason is to play the fool. Such irresponsibility
is not what Christianity advocates. Neither Paul's comment about
being a fool for Christ's sake (1 Cor. 4:10), nor Jesus' rebuke of Thomas
for refusing to believe without first seeing (Jn. 20:26–28), nor Paul's
teaching that we are saved by faith (Gal., Rom.), nor any other New
Testament teaching encourages belief without some reasonable basis.
The point of these texts is something else. In view of the recent
mushrooming of Fundamentalist "Christian" groups, this issue must
be emphasized. No Christian is called to surrender intelligence and
good judgment in the name of religion. On the contrary, the Judeo-
Christian tradition affirms the goodness of creation. Christian belief in
the incarnation implies that God places his ultimate seal of approval
on humanity. So authentic Christianity does not entail the suppression of the human mind or the disqualification of human life. Rather,
authentic Christianity entails the fulfillment and perfection of these.
Faith and reason are allies, not foes. If faith transcends reason, it does
not contradict it. Truth is one, just as the source of truth is one. There
can be no real conflict between accurate human knowledge and the
revealed mysteries of the faith.[12] No one who is unquestioning and
unthinking—and thus irresponsible—should think that he or she is
for that reason justified before God. Such a suggestion is a travesty of
Christianity and an insult to God and humanity.

Reasonableness is not Proof

On the other hand, reasonable is not the same as provable.[13]
Though they should be reasonable, one should not expect the beliefs
of faith to be proved. A position is reasonable if it is internally
coherent and has sufficient evidence to warrant its acceptance. Said

negatively, it is not self-contradictory and not without basis in reality. In contrast, a position is provable if it can be demonstrated so cogently that doubt is not possible.

Obviously, proof is hard to come by. No matter how brilliant an argument is, if someone does not want to believe it, that person will not be convinced. Depending on which presuppositions one has chosen to hold, one can explain—or explain away—any evidence one wishes.

The October 19, 1981 issue of *Newsweek* carried an article entitled, "Footnote to the Holocaust." According to the article, the California-based Institute for Historical Review maintains that "the Holocaust is a myth perpetuated to generate sympathy for Jews and Israel." The Institute concedes "the European Jews were forced into camps, but . . . only 500,000 to 800,000 died—mostly from overwork, typhus and other diseases. The gas chambers, they say, were mortuaries—the gas itself used only to delouse clothing . . . the admissions of Nazi war criminals at the Nuremburg war trials were coerced." The Institute claimed the evidence of an eyewitness "falls short of proof. 'He doesn't say he saw his family killed. . . . He saw his family led off into what he later determined to be a gas chamber.'" In a court suit against the Institute, a Los Angeles Superior Court Judge ruled that the Holocaust was a fact "not reasonably subject to dispute" and that "This court does take judicial notice of the fact that Jews were gassed to death at Auschwitz." In response, a representative of the Institute suggested that the judge "had been hoodwinked by history books." Evidently, there is more to proof than reasonable argument.

Not even science develops by the imagined flow from one logical deduction to another. Recent research into the history of science shows that major advances occur when prevailing presuppositions are revised and new guiding paradigms emerge.[14] A paradigm is a complex of presuppositions that explains known data and determines further research. The slow acceptance of the heliocentric over the geocentric theory or of Einsteinian physics over the older Newtonian physics is an example here. A new paradigm is accepted not because of the cool insistence of logic but because of the hardwon victory of one school of thought over another. Oftentimes a new approach is accepted only after the advocates of the old approach die off. This is not to say that the new approach need only be new. It should also be better. It should provide a better approach to the old questions and also open up new questions. It should point to a more comprehensive and coherent understanding of things. A new scientific paradigm generally represents an advance over the old. But this only makes its acceptance more appealing. It does not insure its acceptance. In the final analysis, after weighing all the factors, scientists must *choose* to accept a new paradigm. That the position is reasonable does not mean it is proved; that is, its demonstrable reasonableness does not mean that everyone will accept it. Not even science works this way.

Proof is rigorous only within an agreed-upon set of presuppositions.[15] Granted common presuppositions, people can easily enough prove things to one another, and the logical deduction of new conclusions follows compellingly and routinely. Yet the more important step is to alter one's paradigm. Real movement occurs when people decide to abandon, change, or broaden their presuppositions. Then openness to whole new perspectives or significant broadening of a former perspective occurs. Horizons shift. Everything is placed in a new context. Everything is seen in a new light. Without a change in presuppositions—which can rightly be termed "conversion"—thinking and thinkers remain static.[16]

Christology: Reasonable Account, not Proof

Accepting Christianity is like making a paradigm-shift. Christian conversion sets one in a whole new position vis-à-vis the meaning of life. Of course, belief about Jesus is the heart of Christianity.[17] To accept Christian belief about Jesus—and to live out its implications!— is to be Christian. So christology is important to Christian conversion and to continued Christian faith.

Because of that, some might expect a christology to be a proof of Christian belief about Jesus. This is not the case. Christology does not prove the faith for non-believers; it confirms it for believers. Christology does not offer a proof of Christian belief about Jesus; it provides a reasonable account of that belief, already presupposed. An adequate christology will ground its statements about Jesus in the data we know about Jesus himself. It will show that Christian belief is a reasonable interpretation of those data. It will show that the evolution of Christian belief about Jesus follows a line of legitimate development. And it will make sense of that belief in light of other

Christian beliefs and of ordinary human experience. That is, an adequate christology presents an understanding of Jesus that is coherent in itself, consonant with our data on Jesus, consistent with Christianity, and true to life.[18] But all this does not constitute proof.

For non-believers such a christology will not prove Christian belief. There can be no presentation such that whoever understands it could not but become a believer. The case is not so watertight, and the stakes are high. Other interpretations, myriad ways to explain the evidence, are always possible. People do not arrive at faith by deduction, nor can they be coerced by logic into believing. In the last analysis, people believe because they choose to believe. The present christology might offer some people reason to believe, if they are looking for such reason, but it does not pretend to prove anything to anybody. On the other hand, such a christology will provide Christians the reasonable reassurance that they are not fools for believing. It will let them see that the Christian position does hold together, coherent in itself and responsible to the data. Christianity need not avoid questions nor neglect evidence in order to stand. Indeed, it will be clear to Christians that their belief answers the questions and does justice to the evidence better than any other interpretation. For Christians Christianity makes sense eminently! If non-believers protest that this is sheer arrogance, Christians can only respond, "Try it and see." For the present christology does not claim to prove Christian belief. Rather, this christology assumes Christian belief as one of its presuppositions. Then it shows the reasonableness of the Christian belief. In this way it just might open the way for non-believers to embrace Christianity, but conversion is not expected. More certainly, however, it will allow Christians to be secure in the belief that they already hold.

The Subjective Context of Christology

As must be obvious now, I do not pretend that this christology is objective in the sense that it can stand apart from a Christian believer. Indeed, one does not expect to find Christianity except in a Christian—even as one does not expect to find human understanding except in a human subject. The human subject is essential to the matter. Only the human subject attains human understanding, and accurate human understanding means precisely that which the open, intelligent, and reasonable human subject attains. Desire for human objectivity that requires elimination of the human subject—the supposed "God's eye view" on things—is sheer fantasy. There is no human objectivity apart from an authentic human subject. "Genuine objectivity is the fruit of authentic subjectivity."[19] And since christology is a form of human understanding, neither can christology avoid the issue of the believing human subject.

Then how does one insure objectivity? The answer is simple but not always welcome: No one can *insure* objectivity! Only openness and honesty give some reassurance that we are on the path toward the truth. Where openness and honesty are lacking, the truth will never be known. Nothing can substitute for authenticity in the human subject. And nothing can guarantee that it is there. Each one, present to himself or herself in the secret precinct of conscience, must provide whatever guarantee there can be. Yet the conclusion is not that objectivity is unattainable, that relativism again rules the field. Let those who are open experience to the full. Let those who are intelligent rejoice in deeper insight. Let those who are honest answer only in truth. Let those who are responsible desire to know accurately and fully. Then the process will take care of itself. Then together we will increasingly achieve objectivity and truth.

That is so when the issue is any human enterprise whatever. But when the issue, like christology, is one of faith, another factor enters in: the Holy Spirit. Some would think that this new factor completely changes the situation, that the influence of the Holy Spirit takes the issue out of the arena of human discussion, that through the Holy Spirit Christians know accurately apart from the workings of the human mind, that where there is faith and the Holy Spirit thought is superfluous. Some would opt for a dogmatic or fundamentalist position. Obviously, I disagree with that position, and for good reasons. On the one hand, I have already implicitly acknowledged the Holy Spirit. The christologist is a Christian believer. And the Christian believer is one who is graced by the Spirit with the gift of Christian faith. So, if the present christology presupposes Christian belief, it also presupposes the work of the Holy Spirit. Now my implicit acknowledgement of the Holy Spirit is explicit. This statement here is sufficient to account for the Holy Spirit and the gift of faith insofar as these are relevant to doing christology. The present position does incorporate the Holy Spirit. On the other hand, I continue to insist

34

that the belief one accepts, even under the inspiration of the Holy Spirit, must be reasonable. Even the gift of the Holy Spirit does not excuse us from being responsible in what we believe and do. If anything, the Holy Spirit transforms our minds so that we are more perceptive, more insightful, more reasonable, and more responsible. The Holy Spirit does not destroy but rather perfects our God-given human mind. Granted, then, that the Christian position is wholly reasonable, one may appeal to the Holy Spirit to explain why some accept Christianity and others do not. God's gifts are inscrutable. What we cannot understand we may still legitimately attribute in an undifferentiated way to the mystery of Divine Providence. Nonetheless, those who do believe must do so responsibly. Appeal to faith and to the Holy Spirit does not free them to accept what is unreasonable.

The immediate practical implication is obvious, and I do not hesitate to state it. If people sincerely find that their Christian belief is unreasonable, then they should abandon it! I say this fearlessly, for the central beliefs of Christianity are wholly reasonable. Still, the challenge must be given. The seriousness of my argument must be affirmed. The risk of appeal to honesty must be accepted. Those who cannot honestly believe should at least honestly admit their unbelief! Such action would be truer to Christianity than any feigned faith. For Jesus himself called for strict honesty when he taught, "Let what you say be simply 'Yes' or 'No.'" (Mt. 5:37) Such action would at least denounce the relativism of our day that says one belief is as good as another. Such action would at least reject the growing agnosticism of our day that says we can know nothing certainly so we should at least believe something—anything!—mightily. Honest admission of unbelief is a noble path.

There is another path, however, less noble and far too easy to follow. Because the questions are complex, because the relevant data are overwhelming, because the epistemological issues are subtle, because the mood of the day is permissive, and because the distinctive claim of Christianity seems preposterous—God became human!—many prefer to reinterpret the message rather than admit unbelief in it. So the same words are spoken, but the meaning is changed. The message is watered down, and the tradition secretly dribbles away. No doubt, contemporary Christians sincerely attempt to remain true to the Christian tradition while making some acceptable sense of it.

Yet people understand knowledge and its possibility differently, so they read the tradition differently and have different criteria for reasonableness. How I make sense of the tradition dictates in practice what the tradition is for me. But when a whole culture obscures the difference between what something is for me and what something is in itself, I can go on thinking that what the tradition is for me is what the tradition actually is. Then you have "your truth" and I have "my truth." "My truth" is what is meaningful for me, and "your truth" is what is meaningful for you. And each of us has a group of "fellow believers" to support us in our construction of "reality." The further question, "But is it so?" no longer makes sense. And who is to say whether we are still truly Christian or not?[20]

Summary

These considerations bring us full circle, back to our starting point. Epistemological concerns surface again. At the beginning, epistemology overshadows christology—and rightly so. If christology is thinking about Jesus, then what one thinks about thinking will significantly determine what one thinks about Jesus.

This chapter has developed a position on epistemology. There is a reality in itself, Jesus Christ, distinct from any thinking about the reality. There is the possibility of knowing that reality and all reality. There is development in thinking about Jesus—without prejudice to the reality of Jesus, who is thought about. Moreover, what is thought must be reasonable; it must square with the available data; though no one pretends that a reasonable account constitutes proof. The believing Christian is central to the christological process, even as the human subject is central to any process of human knowing. Nonetheless, there remains the possibility of objectivity in knowing, and where openness and honesty prevail, one can expect that people will come to know the truth.

All this has been said in the abstract; it is the theory that guides my christology. If we would now answer some of the specific questions about Jesus himself, we must turn to that concrete data on Jesus and see the theory at work. There, too, will come the test of the usefulness of this approach as contemporary concerns and traditional beliefs encounter one another.

CHAPTER THREE

Christologies "From Above" and "From Below"

Christology is reflection on Jesus. Different christologists have different approaches and so there are different christologies. Despite the diversity of christologies which are possible, contemporary theology distinguishes two basic approaches: "from above" and "from below." Simply stated, a christology from above has a storyline that moves from heaven above to earth down below: God "comes down" and becomes human, living among us. A christology from below moves in the opposite direction, from earth to heaven: the man, Jesus of Nazareth, is seen to be or becomes for us Lord and God. Much more needs to be said about these two general approaches, but the basic storyline is what characterizes each of them.[1]

Christology From Above

The christology from above is the one most familiar to Christians today. It represents the traditional way of speaking about Jesus Christ. It is the Christmas story: God's Son took flesh of the Virgin Mary and was born among us. In this approach the emphasis is on the incarnation, that earth-shaking event wherein divinity and humanity came together as the Word became flesh in Mary. According to this understanding, the most important thing about Jesus Christ is that he is divine: he is the divine one who became human. When asked who Jesus Christ is, most people will answer without thinking, "He is God." The christology from above so emphasizes Jesus' divinity that his humanity is overshadowed. That he is God is the most important thing. That *God* became human is the most important occurrence. That he was human tends to get lost in the telling of the story. He was God!

A christology from above highlights Jesus' divinity and downplays his humanity. As a result, the life, death, and resurrection of Jesus play a minor role in such a christology. After all, the important thing is than humanity and divinity were united in Jesus Christ; and this happened at the incarnation. Is there anything more to look for? What else could one expect? Nothing, of course. When humanity is united perfectly with divinity, redemption is achieved. All that remains is for that salvation to be applied to others.

So Jesus' life is understood mainly as an example to us. We should live lovingly as Jesus did if we are to gain the salvation he brought. His miracles are understood mainly as signs—even proofs—that he really is God, come to live among us. The resurrection is the greatest miracle of all; it proves that Jesus is who we say he is and that we ought to follow his teaching. His death is understood as the cost of our wickedness, the price of our sins. The fact that the crucified Jesus was God highlights all the more how atrocious our sins are and how much God loves us despite our sinfulness. In Jesus, God died for us. Jesus' death then becomes the supreme appeal for us to repent. It also invites us to endure suffering willingly because the Lord himself suffered even death on a cross—and for us.

In the traditional christology from above the life, death, and resurrection of Jesus appear secondary in importance and even, at times, superfluous. The incarnation is the central mystery; the rest is almost an automatic consequence of the incarnation. On this basis, the central question in academic christology was, How could divinity and humanity come together in Jesus Christ? The other issue, Jesus' death and resurrection, became a separate consideration. It was treated in another doctrinal tract called soteriology, the study of salvation. Though related, according to the older understanding, soteriology was not strictly considered a part of christology.

The pervasive emphasis on christology from above resulted in a tacit oblivion to Jesus' humanity. Oh, when asked, Christians would clearly affirm that Jesus was indeed human. But they also thought of him as having knowledge and power hardly possible for a human being. After all, Jesus was God. Popular faith represented a crypto-docetism. Docetism—from the Greek *docein* which means to seem—is the heresy that Jesus Christ was not really human but only seemed to be so. He looked and acted like a regular human being, but in fact he was beyond all that. He was God clothed over in human form.

Emphasis on the divinity of Jesus is understandable, and it appears early in the Christian tradition. Once Christians began to realize who their Jesus was, they began to highlight that realization. After all, his divinity is *the* critical factor about Jesus Christ, and they would not want it overlooked. Early accounts also seem to indicate a certain embarrassment over the very human characteristics of Jesus. These got toned down as reverence for the Lord grew. This process is already obvious when Mark, generally considered the earliest of the gospels, is compared with Matthew and Luke. In Mark's account of the cure of the man with the withered hand (3:1–5), the Pharisees were silent when Jesus asked whether it is lawful on the Sabbath to save life or to kill. "And he looked around at them with anger, grieved at their hardness of heart, and said to the man, 'Stretch out your hand.' " In recounting the same incident, Matthew (12:9–13) and Luke (6:6–10) completely omit all reference to Jesus' being angry and grieved. Or again, in the account of the stilling of the storm, Mark (4:35–41) quotes the disciples saying, as they woke Jesus, "Teacher, do you not care if we perish?" Matthew (8:25) rephrases this embarrassing question as "Save, Lord, we are perishing"; Luke (8:24) renders it, "Master, Master, we are perishing!" Or again, when the woman with hemorrhage touched Jesus' garment and was cured and when Jesus asked, "Who touched my garments?" Mark (5:31) has the disciples taunt Jesus with "You see the crowd pressing around you, and yet you say, 'Who touched me?' " Matthew (9:20–22) omits all reference to this interchange and Luke (8:45) has Peter not questioning Jesus but gently reminding him "Master, the multitudes surround you and press upon you!" And finally, where Mark (8:22–26) recalls Jesus' cure of the blind man from Bethsaida—this cure took two attempts—Matthew and Luke, who are following Mark's account at this point, omit all reference to this cure. The gospels already deemphasize the all too human characteristics of Jesus. Once the Council of Nicea (325 C.E.) defined that Jesus is "consubstantial with the Father," insistence on this Christian doctrine became all the more dominant. And so the tradition developed. We, then, inherited an understanding of Jesus that highlights his divinity and underplays his humanity—a one-sided christology from above. Such a christology is preoccupied with explaining the unity of humanity and divinity in Jesus Christ and sets aside for separate treatment the account of how Jesus redeemed us.

Contemporary Concern for the Human

In the past two decades, interest in Jesus has shifted. We want to know Jesus as one of us. The human Jesus has become the center of focus.[2] This shift did not come overnight. It reflects a major preoccupation of the contemporary world: the human being.

In the late seventeenth century, Isaac Newton made a major breakthrough. Building on the contributions of Copernicus, Galileo, Kepler, and others, Newton formulated a coherent mathematical explanation of the movement of the solar system. Modern science had come of age. Newton's achievement stunned his contemporaries. Since then, the power and precision of scientific understanding has fascinated and dominated the modern world. Philosophers also marveled at such "objective" knowledge and attempted to achieve similar results in their own field. In the process, human knowledge itself became the major concern of philosophy. Reflection on the human being—*die Wende zum Subjekt:* the turn toward the subject—characterizes modern philosophy. This is so among the British empiricists, the German idealists, the French existentialists, and contemporary phenomenologists and language analysts. The human and the human situation has become a preoccupation.

Modern psychology emerged from, and contributed to, this same movement. Mid-nineteenth century musings about the human psyche reached a well-known high point in Sigmund Freud. By 1933 Edna Heidbreder could write a book about *Seven Psychologies.*[3] Today almost every literate American has read some "pop" psychology—self-help books—or at least listened to psychologists' discussions on radio or television talk shows. Moreover, awareness of psychological development has become commonplace. Gail Sheehy's best-seller, *Passages,* was a popular landmark in this area.[4] We no longer think adulthood reaches its apex at age twenty-one. Concern for human development has all of us thinking about our further growth. We wonder what stage of development we are in. We find hope in theories of unlimited human potential. In brief, we have become our own most fascinating object of study.

No wonder, then, that Christians want to know more about the human Jesus. If today, as always, he is to be our model and inspiration, we must know him in his everyday humanity. As noted in Chapter One, contemporary biblical scholarship obliges us. Itself the expression of the intellectual and cultural history which we all share, it strips away the layers of early Christian reflection in the New Testament accounts and gives us some information about the man Jesus. It lets us glimpse the Master, in all his ordinariness, as he walked this earth before us. And he appears more human than we had ever imagined.

Christology From Below

Reflecting the times and challenged by contemporary biblical scholarship, contemporary christology prefers the "from below" approach. Emphasis is now on the humanity of Jesus, so it is not possible to obscure his humanness and to think of him as an incognito God. In the christology from below, resurrection—not incarnation—becomes the central event. This is an Easter christology. In the resurrection, humanity and divinity achieve perfect union in Jesus Christ. The story comes to its completion: the human Jesus is the divine Christ. Furthermore, the resurrection event is saving for us. Through it, Jesus' humanity, shared with all of us, comes to divinity. The highpoint of human history is achieved. This affects us all.

The christology from below overcomes the limitations of the christology from above. In the approach from below, Jesus' humanity is highlighted, not overshadowed. Jesus' earthly life is the path to his ultimate fulfillment, not merely a good example that he gives to us. Jesus' resurrection is central to the mystery of divine-human union in Jesus Christ and is not just a final proof of his divinity. The mystery of Jesus' life, death, and resurrection is intimately entwined with our own salvation and is not just an indication of what will also be ours. The contemporary emphasis on christology from below effectively redresses the one-sided emphasis of the christology from above.

Reservations About the Approach From Below

Hans Küng's *To Be a Christian* capitalizes brilliantly on the approach from below. Küng emphasizes the teaching of the historical Jesus and translates it into a form that speaks to us today. Thus Jesus becomes again for us—what Christianity always saw in him—God's advocate challenging us to a faith and love that revolutionize our understanding of God. But then, is Jesus nothing more than a great prophet? Did not Christianity see more than this in Jesus? Ah, there's the rub! While the christology from above leaves no doubt about the absolute divine status of Jesus Christ, the christology from below leaves one wondering.

A main concern of contemporary christology is to root Christian claims about Jesus in the historical Jesus, in the human Jesus. Mere dogmatic assertion is not enough, whether that assertion comes from ecumenical councils or from the New Testament itself. These assertions must be grounded in the historical Jesus. Hence, contemporary christology prefers the approach from below. But how can one move from the human being, Jesus, to absolute insistence on Jesus' supposed divine status? Justifying this move is the biggest challenge to a christology from below. A moderate form of the christology from below points to outstanding human qualities in Jesus and, on the basis of them, argues that Jesus was God. But what human quality, however sublime, justifies such a conclusion? A radical form of the christology from below suggests that in some sense the human Jesus actually *became* God. But how can a human being become God? Both forms of the christology from below have a problem. I will consider each in turn.

The moderate form of the christology from below focuses on outstanding qualities of Jesus and from them argues to Jesus' divinity.[5] For example, Jesus was compassionate, kind, and forgiving. He did not repay evil for evil. His behavior evidences an internal harmony and a personal integrity of the highest degree. The center of this integrity was his relationship with God, "Abba." Thus Jesus appears as the fulfillment of the human image and likeness of God, noted in the creation account (Gen. 1:26–27). So Jesus is the human face of God.[6] He is God's presence among us. And—if one would push this line of argument to its limit—he is God.

42

But this argument moves too fast. It does not show that Jesus is actually God.[7] At best, it provides a reasonable basis for the Christian *belief* that Jesus is God. But this belief is the presupposition of the argument, not the conclusion. This supposed christology from below is presupposing the christology from above! Indeed, would theologians even be involved in christology if they were not Christian and thus committed from the beginning to their "conclusion," that Jesus Christ is God?[8] As it is, belief in Jesus' divinity comes from one's acceptance of the teaching of the Christian community, mediated by a long historical tradition and grounded in the New Testament. In turn, the belief of the New Testament is grounded in the early disciples' experience of Jesus' life, death, and resurrection. As the Nicene Creed professes, Christian faith is "apostolic"; it depends on the witness of the apostles and early disciples.[9] One does not arrive at Christian insistence on the divinity of Jesus solely from a consideration of qualities in the human Jesus. This brings us to the point. The moderate form of the christology from below is not an adequate account of Christian faith. No argument from human qualities, however noble, can conclude to divinity. Humanity even to the nth degree is not divinity and does not necessarily indicate divinity in humanity. If a christology from below appears to arrive at Jesus' divinity, that is not because of the christology from below but primarily because of a prior Christian faith. The judgment must be that this form of the christology from below, strictly taken, entails an irresolvable problem. This approach does not successfully negotiate the move from knowing Jesus as human to professing him as divine.

The radical form of the christology from below makes a bolder move. While the moderate form deals with how one knows that the human Jesus is God, the radical form is concerned with Jesus' actually being God.[10] The radical form suggests that in Jesus Christ a human being actually *became* God.[11]

How can a human being become God? Some answer to this question may be suggested. We have tended to see God and humans in unbridgeable distance from one another. God is "totally other" in comparison to humans. Yet another understanding is possible. Consider that we are beings of amazing potential. Our minds and hearts are open to know and love all there is to be known and loved. We are open to everything. We are open to God. Our inner selves evidence

43

an infinite expansiveness. The contemporary worldview confirms such an understanding. Our appreciation for scientific evolutionary theory and our acceptance of psychological developmental theory make it easy for us to imagine a perfected human state. We conceive that perfected state as the fulfillment of all human potential, and we identify that fulfillment with a fullness that is divinity itself. In this way, we can conceive of a human becoming divine. And this, it is suggested, is exactly what occurred in Jesus. He was a perfect human being—so perfect, in fact, that he attained to absolute fullness, divinity itself. He was the first to do this. In doing it, he opened a way for us to follow. Jesus Christ, the divine-human one, thus allows us also to become divine.

Here is an answer to the question, How can a human become God? This answer is very appealing to contemporary people. It fits our worldview well and addresses our major preoccupations. But is it an acceptable answer? Does it represent sound thinking? No. This answer is more the product of fantasy and imagination than of intelligent and reasonable thought.[12]

Certainly humans do have amazing potential. They are open to all there is to know and love. Beginning with an image of this potential—say, a bright light—we can imagine the potential growing. The light gets brighter and brighter. We also imagine God to be an infinitely bright light. Our own light increases. We imagine it so bright that it, too, is infinitely bright. It is like God. It is God. Two lights, infinitely bright, must really be not two but only one. The light that is our own is but a spark of the divine light itself.[13] So we reason. We conclude that our potential is open to and can become fully God. Such, we suppose, is our very nature. And it takes no great effort to *imagine* this.

But the inquisitive mind will raise some further questions. We are indeed open to know and love all there is, potentially even God. But are not these two different: to know and love something, and to become that thing? Some clear thinking about thinking and thinking about being are needed here.

Moreover, we might even grant that *in some sense* we do become what we love. Yet, at this point in the discussion, we cannot afford to leave the precise sense undefined. Further reflection is needed.

Let us grant that God is creator. That means that God is self-explanatory. God needs nothing else to account for his existence. It follows that as creator God is without beginning. If God had a beginning, something else would have to account for God; it would explain God. Then that something else would be creator. However, thinking that something else could explain God and so God could have a beginning is just pushing the problem back one step, where the same problem recurs again. This thinking avoids the call for reasonable judgment and in imagination runs in an infinite series of back steps, never facing the issue squarely: To be creator means to be self-explanatory, period!

If God is creator, everything else is creature. There is no middle ground between the two.[14] When one conceives the issue intelligently and formulates it logically—that is, when one is not relying on mere fantasy or imagination—one is faced with an either-or. A reality is either created or uncreated. It is either a creature or God.

Conceived in this way, the difference between creator and creature is not something that can be fudged. What is created cannot become uncreated. What needs something else to account for its existence cannot someday become self-explanatory. What has had a beginning cannot someday become without beginning. Imagination may picture the growth from human being to God, but sound thinking does not allow a change from created to uncreated. What is created can never become uncreated. A human can never become God.

In summary, a radical christology from below does not—and cannot—account for Christian belief that Jesus Christ is God. It is simply unacceptable to suggest that in Jesus Christ a human being came to share so much in God's life that he actually became God. Likewise, as we have seen, even the moderate form of the christology from below does not satisfactorily account for the Christian belief. In both cases a major problem faces the christology from below. It cannot adequately account for the divinity of Jesus as traditionally affirmed by Christianity.

Final Assessments and Conclusion

This is not to suggest that the approach from below has nothing to offer. Its concern for Jesus' humanity, its insistence on his human development, and its focus on the resurrection as a saving event are recent and important emphases. The christology from below calls for an understanding of Jesus' human development even to the point of absolute perfection in the resurrection, and it suggests that through the resurrection Jesus' humanity came to participate in a new way in divinity. It implies, namely, a notion of human divinization—a human participation in God's way of being—first exemplified in Jesus Christ and so made possible for all of us. So conceived, the christology from below elaborates the mysteries of Jesus' life, death, and resurrection and inextricably binds them to the mystery of human salvation. If these mysteries can be seen as the unfolding of the incarnation in Jesus' life, then the christology from below appears as a complement to the traditional christology from above. The contemporary christology from below suggests the content of a new stage of development in the on-going Christian task of understanding Jesus more and more completely.

However, the christology from below does not replace the christology from above. The newer is not a substitute for the older. Nor can the older now do without the newer. The strengths of the one are the weaknesses of the other. Whereas the one emphasizes Jesus' divinity, the other emphasizes Jesus' humanity. Whereas the one dwells on the mystery of the union of humanity and divinity in the incarnation, the other dwells on the mystery of glorified humanity in the resurrection. Whereas the one focuses on the moment of the Eternal Son's human conception, the other treats Jesus' life, death, and resurrection. The two are complementary. An adequate christology requires both. The challenge facing christologists today is to unite the two in a way that is coherent, reasonable, relevant, and faithful to the Christian tradition.

I will propose such a synthesis in Chapter Eight. But first, some further considerations are needed. So Chapter Four will again turn to thinking about thinking as that applies to christologies from above and from below. These final preliminary considerations will allow us, then, to turn to Jesus Christ as presented in the New Testament and later conciliar teaching. Then, finally, we will come to the new synthesis.

CHAPTER FOUR

Kerygmatic and Systematic Statement

Back to our starting point. Christology is reflection on Jesus. Reflection results in statements—or articulations or formulations. In Chapter Three we saw that statements about Jesus can be said to follow two general approaches; there can be christologies from above or from below. However, there is another issue. We can consider statements—about Jesus or about anything else—from still another point of view: What purpose do the statements serve? Statements can serve different purposes. Depending on our purpose, we formulate our thoughts differently. In this chapter we will consider two different kinds of statements, kerygmatic statements and systematic statements. Then we will apply this understanding to christologies from above and from below. The conclusion will be that these christologies are kerygmatic in form, and not systematic.

The general purpose of all statements is to communicate our ideas to others. However, sometimes our concern is not simply to inform others. More than that and most of all, we sometimes want to move them. We want to interest others in what we think. We want to inspire them to accept what we are saying. We want them to appreciate the importance of our message. I call statements with such purposes 'kerygmatic.' On the other hand, sometimes our concern is simply to communicate accurate information. We assume that others are already interested in what we are saying. They would not be listening to us if they were not. We assume they already have some basic notion of our message. We are concerned about expressing our ideas clearly. Our main purpose is to explain more carefully what we are thinking. I call statements whose purpose is precise expression of meaning 'systematic.'

Kerygmatic Statement: Story, Image, Metaphor

Kerygmatic statement is concerned with announcing a message, proclaiming a word. Its purpose is to inspire and motivate. It looks for acceptance of the message. 'Kerygmatic' comes from the Greek word *kerygma,* which means proclamation or announcement. This word is used in the New Testament to speak of the message that is preached. Luke 11:32 says that the people of Nineveh repented at the *kerygma* (preaching) of Jonah. In Romans 16:25 Paul makes reference to "my gospel and the *kerygma* (preaching) of Jesus Christ." Elsewhere in the New Testament *kerygma* means simply the preaching or message of the apostles.[1] A kerygmatic statement is intended to motivate, inspire, and engage people with what is being said. Preaching, oratory, and most public speaking is kerygmatic in form. "Rhetorical" may be another name for what I am calling kerygmatic statement.[2]

Kerygmatic statement intends to inspire and motivate. This does not mean that kerygmatic statements have no content or that the speaker is not concerned about the accuracy of what he or she is saying. There is a message to be conveyed, and the speaker does want to convey it. But the main purpose is to get the message across. Accordingly, the kerygmatic statement does not get bogged down in the intricacies of logic and detailed argument or in technical terminology and subtle reasoning. It is not precision of thought but the main impact of the message that is the prime concern. Kerygma is popular presentation. It addresses the whole person—emotions, imagination, mind, choice. It does not appeal solely to the mind or understanding.

Kerygmatic statement makes use of different literary devices to engage the audience and to achieve its purpose. For example, every good public speaker knows that people of all ages like stories. Stories are very effective for making a point. In telling the story the speaker often exaggerates a bit, embellishes the storyline, fills in the details. The speaker does not think this is dishonest, nor does the audience. Everybody realizes that the speaker is just trying to make a point. He or she is not insisting on every detail in the story.

When President John F. Kennedy was in Berlin, he inspired the German people with his message. At one point in his talk, he insisted on his firm identification with the people of Berlin, who had suffered the forced division of their city but were still dedicated to freedom. He said he understood what they felt. He assured them he felt that himself. In German he declared, *"Ich bin ein Berliner!"* "I am a Berliner!" Following that speech there was some criticism of Kennedy. Someone claimed that he had betrayed his American citizenship by making that statement, for he was not a German but an American, and indeed the American president. How absolutely foolish! This complaint completely misses the point of Kennedy's statement. It confuses Kennedy's rhetorical statement—his kerygmatic formulation—with literal statement. The point Kennedy made was clear and poignant in that form. No one who really understood him thought he wanted to surrender his American citizenship.

You see how the story I just told easily conveys what I mean to say, better perhaps than a long, technical discourse. My use of this story makes two points. First, stories are an effective way of getting a point across. Second, not everything that a speaker says is to be taken absolutely literally; the point—and not always the exact words—is what is intended.[3]

The Bible is full of stories—Adam and Eve, Noah and the Ark, the call of Abraham, the Exodus from Egypt, Jonah and the Whale. Are these stories true? If we take them as stories, they certainly are true. The points they make are eternally true. But is every detail to be taken literally? That is another question which must be answered in each case by specialized research. Jesus, too, made powerful use of stories. His creative genius is clear in the parables he told.

Contemporary theology is rediscovering the power of stories.[4] In a more technical way, theology speaks of 'myth' rather than simply of 'story.' Here 'myth' does not mean a false account, a misbelief, a fairy tale, an illusion: "It's a myth that you can get along without money." "Much of what we're told about George Washington is myth." Rather, myth is a narrative statement, a story, which conveys a truth.[5] The

truth of myth is known not by critical analysis and literal interpretation but by personal entry into the story and experience of the reality
created by the story. Story and myth are important features of religion, for religion is kerygmatic: it wants to inspire, to motivate, to
advocate a new vision of reality.

Kerygmatic statement also makes use of other literary devices:
images and metaphors. "A picture is worth a thousand words," they
say. Whoever can present an image that captures the imagination has
a powerful tool for informing and motivating people. The gospels
make powerful use of images and metaphors. When Jesus stepped
from the boat and saw the people, "he had compassion on them
because they were like sheep without a shepherd" (Mk. 6:34). The
image of a flock of sheep spoke to the people of that day. John uses the
same image to convey an understanding of Jesus' intimacy with his
disciples. "I am the good shepherd; I know my own and my own
know me. . . . there shall be one flock and one shepherd" (Jn. 10:14–
16). This image of the sheep and the flock is attractive. With it we
imagine a peaceful gathering of all peoples, heeding the message of
the shepherd, Jesus. Images and metaphors convey messages easily
and powerfully.

In summary, kerygmatic statement uses stories, images, and
metaphors to make its point. Appealing to the whole person, it is a
powerful form of address. It not only informs people but also motivates them and inspires them to act on what they hear.

The Danger of Being Misunderstood

However, stories, images, and metaphors are inherently ambiguous in their meaning. They can be easily misunderstood. I have
already noted how John Kennedy's statement was mistaken to be an
act of treason. So his statement needed to be explained. It indicated
support for the Berliners, not denial of his American citizenship.
Images and metaphors are open to misinterpretation.

We are familiar with the metaphor, the Church is the flock of
Christ. But sometimes we need to be cautioned. This does not mean
we are dumb sheep! It does not mean that the laity must follow
unthinkingly whatever the bishops, or priests—the "shepherds of the
flock"—tell them. That was not the intent of the image. Nonetheless,
a common characteristic of sheep is to be rather stupid. Any shepherd

50

will tell you that. Or again, that Christians are the flock of Christ does not mean that members of the Church grow wool![6] Critical thought must be applied so that the real meaning of the images can be determined. For an image could suggest a variety of meanings. Some are pertinent. Some are absurd. Only some are really intended. Sheep are dumb. Sheep grow wool. Sheep readily follow their shepherd. What could the image mean? What does it mean?[7]

Stories, metaphors, and images are oftentimes not enough. The above examples make this clear. Kerygmatic statement is very useful for inspiring the heart, for stirring the imagination, for motivating action. But it is not always very useful when clarity of meaning is required. Precise expression requires another kind of statement, systematic statement.

Systematic Statement: Technical Terminology

Systematic statement moves away from poetic, imageful, suggestive expression and moves toward technical expression.[8] Words are defined. They mean this and only this. Contexts of discussion are set up. This issue is germane; that is not. Systematic statement tends to become esoteric. Only those who know the system can understand what is meant. Systematic statement is dry and tedious. Technical prose is precise in what it says, but it is not very inspiring.

When it comes to its perfect form, systematic statement is scientific statement, and the easiest example is the mathematical formula.[9] An example will help.

What is a circle? Kerygmatic statement would answer this question in a number of ways. The moon is a circle when it is full. Wheels are in the shape of a circle. Faces are something like circles, but they are not perfectly round. A circle is something that is round on all sides. It is equally round all around. Does this mean that a ball is a circle? No, but if you look only at the edge of a ball, that's a circle. For kerygmatic statement, examples, description, metaphors, and simile suggest what a circle is.[10] With enough suggestive clues and a little intelligence, one might "catch on" and know in some way what a circle is.

However, systematic statement can say exactly what a circle is. A circle is the co-planer locus of points equidistant from a given point. This is the standard definition of a circle from Euclidean geometry. It is precise. It is clear. It needs no interpretation. But it is also far from everyday experience and thinking. To understand it, one needs to have understood what a plane is, a point, a line as a locus of points, distance, and equality. This definition presupposes and uses a whole system of ideas. To understand it, one needs to know Euclidean geometry. Within that system, the definition is precise; it is clear. The definition is systematic. It leaves no room for various interpretations.[11] Circle is defined this way; this and only this is a circle.

Systematic statement about a circle can go even further. Once it becomes clear that distance from a given point is essential to a circle, one can inquire about the relationship between that point and that distance and the circle itself. Call the distance from that point to any point on the circle the radius (r). Call the distance around the circle the circumference (C). Discern the relationship between these two. Once grasped, it is expressed by the formula, $C = 2\pi r$. This formula expresses exactly what a circle is. It expresses the intrinsic intelligibility of a circle. The terms in this formula are no longer understood or defined by relationship to some particular radius and some particular circumference of some particular circle. *The terms are defined by relationship to one another.*[12] C is precisely and nothing other than $2\pi r$. r is precisely and nothing other than $C/2\pi$. π expresses the constant relationship between the radius and circumference of any circle whatsoever; π is precisely and nothing other than $C/2r$. The formula $C = 2\pi r$ expresses the essence of circle. It is true of any circle, anywhere and always. It does not depend on one's preferences, one's mood, one's inclination, nor even on one's good will. Apart from how anyone feels about it, $C = 2\pi r$.

To attain such precision of expression is the strength of systematic statement. Systematic statement isolates the intended meaning and prescinds from all other considerations. Focusing on only one dimension of human experience, the cognitive, it treats that dimension with clarity and precision. It says exactly what is meant. Of course, judged from other points of view, systematic statement has shortcomings. It is dull and boring. It is not very inspiring. It does not tend to motivate. It is not easy to grasp. It requires some training for proper understanding—not everybody is a mathematician, not everybody is a physicist, not everybody is a systematic theologian. Correct understanding of systematic statement takes some formal preparation. To the uninitiated, systematic statement is sheer jargon.

All this contrasts with kerygmatic statement. Kerygmatic statement is poetic and metaphorical. It is inspirational. It is vividly suggestive. It appeals to everybody. It conveys not only intended meaning but in addition it addresses the whole gamut of human sensitivities. This is its strength. This is also its weakness, for kerygmatic statement is ambiguous and sometimes vague. When questions arise—as they inevitably do—it needs to be explained. Then the initial impact of marvel and enthusiasm begins to wear off. Questions nudge us from kerygmatic to systematic statement.

The Danger of Being Misunderstood

Obviously, then, kerygmatic statement and systematic statement are complementary.[13] The one is needed to inspire and motivate; the other, to clarify what is meant. Both are valuable in their own right. Neither alone would be sufficient for human life. Yet it is important to recognize the two as distinct, and it is important not to confuse and misuse them. So, when it comes to religion, pulpit preaching or catechesis is not the same thing as systematic theology. One would expect to hear kerygmatic statement in a homily and systematic statement in a theology class. If all one heard in a theology course was preaching, one might want one's money back. If all one heard from the pulpit was technical, systematic theology, one might be bored or frustrated and feel the need to go to church again—or to stop going altogether! Certainly, technical theology enriches preaching, just as the achievements of research scientists eventually enrich daily living. And good preaching inspires theologians to new lines of thought, just as problems in daily life suggest research projects for scientists. Nonetheless, each form of thought has its proper place.

When systematic formulations are commonly used as public proclamations, the difference between kerygmatic and systematic statement is forgotten, and the meaning of the systematic statements is obscured and eventually lost. Then everybody, specialist and lay, uses the same terminology, and nobody is sure any more what the terms mean. Is this term being used popularly or technically? Are people aware that there is a difference? In any case, how could anyone succeed in retrieving the technical terms from the grasp of popular usage? Confusion and decline result on all fronts.[14]

Confucius is credited with the following commentary:

> If language is not used rightly,
>   then what is said is not what is meant.
> If what is said is not what is meant,
>   then that which ought to be done is left undone.
> If it remains undone,
>   morals and art will be corrupted.
> If morals and art are corrupted,
>   justice will go awry.
> And if justice goes awry,
>   the people will stand about in helpless confusion.

The demise of a theoretical theological system is an important part of Christianity's recent history. Terms forged in the highly rarified philosophical-theological atmosphere of medieval scholastic thought—like 'sanctifying grace' and 'actual grace', 'persons' in the Trinity, 'natures' in Christ, 'natural' and 'supernatural', sacramental 'causality' *ex opere operato*—these terms became the coinage of everyday preaching, teaching, and counseling. So belief formulas appeared foreign in comparison with everyday language. The words were strange. The common religious thought pattern became stilted and rigid. One had to learn by rote and take "on faith" the basics of one's religion. Few knew what was really meant. Imagination and impoverished piety filled in the meanings. Religion moved ever more visibly far from both common experience and accurate belief. The message became irrelevant, and the brave even said so. Eventually it was thrown off. Fresh air was needed. Only a return to the sources would restore life to religion.

In the Roman Catholic tradition, the Second Vatican Council called for and marked that return to the sources. Pope John XXIII's order to open the windows and let in fresh air became the theme of the day. The misused and so misunderstood and ineffective formulas of scholastic theology were generally put aside. The more popular and more provocative kerygmatic statements of the Scriptures became the vogue. Vatican II was a *pastoral* council. Roman Catholicism finally began to face some of the issues that Protestantism had been dealing with from the beginning. In Catholicism, as earlier in Protestantism, a return to the Bible became a necessary and appealing alternative.

In the meantime the meaning and value of systematic statement had been obscured and all but forgotten. Systematic statement is a delicate flower. It grows only under rarely achieved conditions. It easily withers and dies. Systematic thought first arose in the West among the Greeks, under the influence of Aristotle. It revived again in the Alexandrian School during the third and fourth centuries. Origin and Clement were its prime representatives. Significantly for our concerns, this flowering provided the background for the doctrinal resolutions of the early councils of the Church, which will be the topic of our Chapters Six and Seven. Systematic thought emerged again and reached a high point in the medieval synthesis achieved consummately by Thomas Aquinas. This was its last flowering in theological circles. There followed a slow decline, the decadence described in the paragraphs above. Finally, systematic thought arose in the secular sciences in the sixteenth century, consummately with Isaac Newton, as described in Chapter Three. It is only in the form of natural science that most of us today have any sense whatever of systematic statement. So it is most easily identified by calling it "scientific."

Christology—Kerygmatic or Systematic?

Naturally, the revival in christology followed the same path. The systematic formula inherited from the Council of Chalcedon and elaborated by subsequent medieval speculation—one person in two natures—no longer spoke to people's concerns. After all, the term 'nature' is not clearly understood, for it has taken on a variety of meanings. And the term 'person' has taken on a meaning very different from what it had at Chalcedon in 451 C.E. and during the high Middle Ages. The traditional formula itself became problematic. So in the move away from scholastic theology and toward biblical thought, the two basic approaches—"from above" and "from below"—came instead to characterize contemporary christology. But clear awareness of the difference between kerygmatic and systematic statement was not available. Indeed, the difference can be worked out only in a systematic context built on an understanding of understanding it-

55

self.[15] (The presuppositional issues treated in Chapter Two surface again!) In christology a serious confusion has resulted.

It is not clear if the contemporary christologies are meant to be taken as literal statements or, on the other hand, as merely suggestive statements of Christian belief. Are they systematic or kerygmatic? This issue is critical. The traditional statements were intended to be taken literally—I will argue this at length in Chapters Six and Seven. In fact, those statements were generally taken literally. That the unfortunate practical consequence, docetism, usually resulted is no argument against the intrinsic validity of the doctrinal definitions. That practical consequence merely highlights the peril of isolating systematic statement from its conceptual context. In any case, traditional christological statements were taken literally. So the natural assumption is that subsequent christological statements that claim to reinterpret the traditional ones should also be taken literally. Indeed, one gets the impression they are intended to be taken literally. They represent serious works in what is generally called "systematic theology."[16] Nonetheless, christologies "from above" or "from below" are not systematic statements. Rather, they are kerygmatic in form. As such, they are not patient of literal interpretation, and so they are not adequate for resolving the critical christological questions that disturb us today. Further clarifications about these christological approaches will explicate what I mean.

Some suggest that the "from below" approach is the natural approach.[17] It is the way the original disciples moved. First they experienced Jesus as one of them, a human being. Only later did they come to know him as Lord. This supposed experience of the original disciples is to set the model for all subsequent disciples. Christology from below is supposed to be normative.

Note that the christology in question here is the moderate form of the christology from below. It moves from Jesus' human qualities to his status as divine Lord—in the experience of the disciples! That is, it expresses how *the disciples* came *to know* Jesus as Lord. What is at issue is a process of knowing. But this fact is not clear in the presentation of the christology. The presentation confuses reality and thought about reality. It confuses what is experienced and one's understanding about the experienced. It confuses Jesus himself and the disciples' faith about Jesus.

56

Jesus Christ, whom the disciples experienced, is himself, Jesus Christ. Whatever he is, that is what the disciples experienced. They experienced no other than Jesus when they initially met him, when they had known him for a while, when he was crucified, and when they knew him resurrected. The one in question did not change. This is not to suggest that Jesus experienced no human growth during his time on earth. He did. Yet one and the same Jesus experienced that growth, and the disciples experienced one and the same Jesus throughout the whole of their experience of him. If, as Christian tradition holds, Jesus is the Eternal Son, then from the first moment they knew him, the disciples were experiencing the Eternal Son in human form. The fact that they did not know this from the beginning does not change the reality they were experiencing. Granted, their experience would have been richer had they not only experienced Jesus Christ but also known from the beginning the fullness of what they were experiencing. Still, all along they were experiencing Jesus Christ. And in experiencing Jesus Christ, from the beginning they were experiencing the Eternal Son, for that is who he is. Later they were also able to acknowledge him as Son of Man, Christ, Lord, God. This acknowledgement represented a change *in them*. Then they knew what before they had not known, though they had experienced it. That acknowledgement did not represent a change in Jesus Christ.

If it is true, as Acts of the Apostles states, that "God *has made* him both Lord and Christ" (2:36), the truth is that Jesus became that *for the disciples*. Whereas before he was not Lord or Christ *for them*, now they recognized him as such. Only in this sense had he literally *become* Lord and Christ. But here "become" speaks about the understanding of the disciples, not about the reality of Jesus Christ himself. Jesus remained one and the same. So, in fact, the disciples did not then hesitate to use the titles "Lord" and "Christ" when speaking about Jesus during his earthly ministry. They wrote back into their account of Jesus' life the understanding they achieved only after his resurrection. He had become Lord and Christ for them only later. Yet, once they knew him as such, they did not hesitate to acknowledge him as such from the beginning. Were they not aware that the Lord and Christ—and even God!—they came to acknowledge only after the resurrection was the very same one whom they had experienced all along? They do not hesitate to suggest as much.[18]

Of course, this is not to deny that something did happen to Jesus during his lifetime. As a result of his life, death, and resurrection, he was different from what he was before. There was a real change in him. According to God's good plan, it was necessary for Jesus to pass faithfully through human life in order to reconcile humanity with God. So in one sense he did become something that he was not before: the Redeemer of the world. Chapters Eight and Ten deal with this issue. Then, if "Lord and Christ" is taken in the sense of Redeemer, it is true that Jesus did *become* Lord and Christ—and not just for the disciples but also in himself. But the point being made here is different. The point is that whatever Jesus became during his earthly life, he remained ever the one and the same one who became that. And the one whom the disciples experienced, both before and after he had completed his redemptive work, was the one and the same one, Jesus the Eternal Son.

Therefore, it is incorrect to assume that the natural christology is christology from below. The natural process is not to move from knowing the human Jesus to knowing the divine one, Jesus Christ. Rather, the natural process is to move from experiencing Jesus—human and divine—to understanding and articulating ever more fully what one had experienced, and finally to verifying one's understanding against the experience. As noted in Chapter Two, this is the natural process of knowing—and so the natural process of christology. In this process one comes to recognize that Jesus is and was both human and divine; one realizes that that is what one had been experiencing all along.

If this christology from below is to be taken literally, it can only be speaking about the disciples. It relates how the disciples grew in their understanding about Jesus. It cannot be taken to speak about Jesus. It cannot be taken to suggest that Jesus himself, at first only human, subsequently became divine. Taken literally, then, it is not strictly a christology. It is not reflection *about Jesus*. Rather, it is reflection about the growing faith of the disciples. The conclusion follows: the moderate christology from below is not a literal statement about Jesus.

Now turn to the radical form of the christology from below. It suggests that Jesus actually became God. In this case it is clear that an assertion is being made about Jesus himself and not simply about how one comes to know Jesus. Evidently, this statement about Jesus *is* to be taken literally. However, then the irresolvable problem arises: explain how a human being became God, how the created became uncreated. There is no satisfactory answer. So one must conclude in this case, too, that the christology from below cannot be taken literally.

Two Stories, One Point

The conclusion is clear—because of the allowance for literal, systematic statement. However, most contemporary christologists are not as insistent on literality. More likely, they question the possibility of any literal statement or any literal interpretation whatsoever.[19] The result is real confusion. Either one looks for literal statement. Then it appears Jesus was really—and only—a human. There can be no account of how he is literally God. Or one rejects the possibility of literal statement. Then the councils which defined Christian belief about Jesus are treated as merely suggestive. Again, traditional belief is lost.

Of course, there is a third alternative. "Truth" means what is "true" for me, what holds meaning for me, what makes sense for me. On this account, the councils did speak the "truth" and are to be taken "literally." They stated, namely, what the council fathers held as "true." They enunciated the worldview that structures and motivates believing Christians' lives. They proclaimed what is "true for Christians." But it remains unthinkable that the councils intended to state what is true in itself, whether or not anyone holds it as true. Obviously, this alternative is unacceptable. It effectively dissolves the meaning of "true" or "literal" while still holding on to the terms. It is directly opposed to the presuppositions we enunciated in Chapter Two. Again, the issue is epistemological presuppositions.

There is also a fourth alternative, an acceptable one. Make a distinction between kerygmatic statement and systematic statement. Allow that both are valid in their own right. Be careful not to confuse the two. Demand of each only what it can offer.

On this basis, christology from above and christology from below are both kerygmatic statement. They follow the story approach to make their point. Their basic structure is that of a story. Each has a storyline. The storyline is opposite in each case, yet both storylines touch all the important elements of the story. And both hold all the elements together by the power of narration. They make their point by the effect of story. In the story from below, the man Jesus is finally known to be the divine one who came to bring us new life. Known in this way, Jesus is acknowledged as Lord, God, and Savior by all who appreciate the story. The purpose of the story is achieved in people's lives. In the story from above, the Eternal Son came to be one of us. This Jesus, then, a man living among us, is recognized as God himself. The marvel of the story conveys power and impact to his deeds and teaching, for we know who he is. Known in this way, Jesus is appreciated as Lord, God, and Savior by all who appreciate the story. The purpose of this story, too, is achieved in people's lives.

Both christology from above and christology from below are effective as kerygmatic statement. Both include the human and the divine dimensions of the Christ mystery. Both spark the imagination to get the point across. Christmas and Easter both have appealing, moving messages. Both affect people's lives and convey a word about salvation. As kerygmatic statement and understood as such, both are adequate.

The point in these christologies is made by the overall story. Whoever is caught up by the story appreciates the message. The story, as such, is not to be analyzed. Its parts are not to be taken literally. Specifically, the notion "became" is not presented for critical analysis in the story as such: God became human; the man Jesus became God. In a dream the bulldog becomes your uncle, your home becomes a cathedral. In a fairytale, the frog becomes a handsome prince, the witch becomes a pile of ashes. Symbol can combine meanings in ways that boggle the logical mind. So, too, in christology. Here "to become" indicates the combination of seemingly incompatible elements. The point is precisely that somehow Jesus is both God and human. The story makes the point amazingly well—but it does not claim to explain the thing.

Critically Valid Insight from Both Stories

Of course, for thinking beings like us, critical analysis of the story is inevitable. To the critical mind it appears that the storyline of the christology from above, "God became human," could be taken literally. There is no inherent contradiction in that assertion, and God can do whatever is not inherently contradictory. Certainly, exactly what such a becoming would mean and to what extent it could be true must be clarified. Such clarification is precisely a main concern of christology. These further questions aside for the moment, "God became human" could be taken literally. On the other hand, "Jesus became God" could not be taken literally. The statement involves inherent contradiction, as noted above.

Stories prompt us to think. They spark our imagination and engage our minds. Some of the ideas they inspire turn out to be nonsense. Some prove to be valuable insights. When such inspiration occurs, one has to look into the matter and come to reasonable judgment about it. As we saw, stories, images, and metaphors are basically ambiguous in meaning. One must discern carefully what they mean and what they do not mean. But this process of critical reflection already moves us out of the realm of story. It moves us from kerygmatic statement and toward systematic statement. One can accept that God became human, but one must reject that a human became God. This acceptance or rejection is a judgment of the reasonable mind. It is an expression of critical thought. That the critical mind can affirm the storyline of christology from above but must deny the storyline of christology from below says nothing about the validity of either of those stories as stories. Both are valuable approaches if one takes them only for what they are. The from above approach has an obvious added value. It suggests an understanding that is readily acceptable also to the critical mind. But this says more about the content of the story—God and humans, creator and creatures, and their relationship—than about the power of that particular story as such. As story both approaches are valuable.

In addition, the approach from below also has a specific contribution of its own. The critical mind cannot accept its storyline—Jesus became God—literally. Still, the critical mind can wonder if there is not some sense in which a human can become divine. One can wonder if the approach from below says something important about Jesus' resurrection. As noted, critical thinking would have to clarify the insight gained from christology from above. It would have to explain in exactly what sense God became human. Likewise, critical thinking would also have to explain in what exact sense a human can

61

become divine. This project, too, is now precisely one of the main concerns of christology. A creature cannot become the Creator; no human can literally become God. This much is clear. But to what extent can we say that a human comes to share in divinity? What could it mean that a creature, while remaining such, is transformed to participate to some extent in God's way of being? Here, again, a story has sparked the imagination and engaged the critical mind. New speculation arises. It deals with an aspect of the mystery of Christ that had not been treated extensively before. Here is a contribution of contemporary christology to the on-going understanding of the Christ mystery.

Summary and Preview

Both christology from above and christology from below are valuable as kerygmatic statements about Christ. As story, they can be equally powerful. Beyond that, each strikes the inquisitive mind in a particular way. Each has a particular contribution to suggest for the possible construction of a systematic statement about Christ. A comprehensive systematic christology will have to combine the storylines from both approaches. It will combine two movements: the movement of God to the human and the resultant possible movement of that human to share more perfectly in divinity. But the presentation will no longer be made by appeal to storyline. Systematic christology is not concerned with stories as such but with the possibly valid literal implications of the stories. In systematic statement the point is not made by a narration, a succession of one episode following another. The point is made by representing the simultaneous interrelationship of the essential elements. The point is made through one act of understanding that grasps the intelligibility of the whole, all at once. When I understand $C = 2\pi r$, I understand circle. In this one act of understanding, I combine many preliminary understandings. I understand a whole geometrical system, and within that system I understand circle. The same applies in systematic christology. I must first understand a conglomerate of christological concepts before I can possibly understand the interrelationship of them all. I must first be introduced into a system of thought, and within that system I can have some systematic understanding of Christ. These preliminary chapters have been introducing the notion of such a system. The next three chapters will continue developing this system of thought. They will introduce further elements which, when combined in Chapter Eight, will allow a comprehensive understanding of Jesus Christ.

A brief summary of this book thus far is in order. The emergence of historical-critical interpretation of the Bible has raised a serious challenge for traditional belief about Jesus. Jesus now appears to have been much more human than was previously realized. The question arises, How can contemporary biblical scholarship be reconciled with the teachings of the early christological councils? An answer requires a clear understanding about what christology is. Christology is reflection on Jesus. This conception presupposes a distinction between Jesus, the reality that is experienced, and christology, one's reflection on, and subsequent articulation about, that reality. This conception also presupposes that one can really know reality and that one's understanding of reality develops.

Statements about any reality—including christological statements about Jesus—can be of two kinds: kerygmatic and systematic. Kerygmatic statement makes its point through the suggestive use of literary devices like story, image, metaphor, example, and description. Kerygmatic statement attempts to inspire as well as to inform. On the other hand, systematic statement makes its point through the use of technical terms defined within a system by relationship to one another. Systematic statement intends only to clarify, to explain.

Contemporary christology speaks about christologies from above and from below. The approach from above relates closely with the traditional conciliar statements, which approach a systematic form. The approach from below appears at first sight to reproduce the lived experience of the early disciples, who knew Jesus first as human and only later as divine. An attractive oversimplification would suggest that the approach from below is the natural form of christology—a "biblical" christology—since it supposedly follows the experience of the disciples, whereas the approach from above results in an abstract and speculative christology—a more "systematic" christology—that is distant from life and the Scriptures. In fact, however, both the christology from above and the christology from below are forms of kerygmatic statement. They make their point about Jesus by following a storyline. As such, they may be equally valid and powerful ways to convey the Christian message about Jesus. But neither, as such, is a systematic statement. They are not intended to be interpreted literally. These distinctions must not be overlooked, and the different possible forms of christology must not be confused. Confusion of these issues is at the root of much of the confusion in christology today. Resolution of the confusion calls for a systematic christology.

Christology and its Multiple Forms

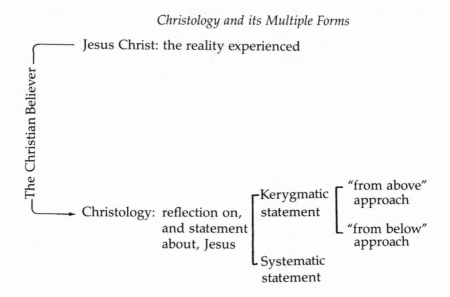

PART II

Retrieving the Tradition

CHAPTER FIVE

Jesus in the New Testament

Christology is reflection on Jesus. All human reflection is imperfect. It is capable of improvement. It develops. Development of christological thought is already evident in the New Testament. Over and above what modern scripture scholars can uncover about Jesus himself, they discern a number of different christologies in the New Testament.[1] Our task in this chapter is to summarize these conclusions of contemporary scholarship. Then we will have before us the basic known information about Jesus himself, the hard data on which Christian belief rests. We will have a summary of early Christianity's thought about Jesus, for this is what the New Testament records. We will have a good example of kerygmatic statements about Jesus, for the whole New Testament is kerygmatic in form.[2] And we will have an initial example of development of doctrine, for the New Testament statements about Jesus represent an advance over what Jesus said about himself.

Knowing the Historical Jesus

What was Jesus himself like? An unthinking response might suggest one need only read the gospels to answer this question. This response forgets that the gospels were not written as history in the sense that we think of history today. The gospels are proclamations of early Christian faith. They tell us what Christians believed about Jesus. They inform us about what the believing heart discerned to be "really going on" in the Jesus experience. In brief, the gospels do not present a picture as a video recorder would have made nor a message as a tape recorder would have picked up. Knowing what Jesus himself was like requires more than simply reading the gospels as they stand.

Contemporary biblical scholars now agree that we can get behind the overlying faith layers in the New Testament and uncover something of the historical Jesus himself. Such research work is extremely complex and delicate. Chapter One has already presented an overview of the method scholars use. Here we move more deeply into the problem of uncovering the historical Jesus.

If the gospels do not present an immediate picture of Jesus himself, how can we know him? How can we decide if the teachings and actions attributed to Jesus in the gospels are really those of the historical Jesus and not the added reflections of the early Church or the evangelist? Scholars have agreed on some simple criteria to address this issue. Only that which cannot be explained as an addition of the Christian Church or as part of the earlier Jewish tradition will be accepted as Jesus' own. Only that which has no other explanation will be attributed to Jesus.

These criteria are minimalist. They accept only that which is beyond doubt. They focus on what was unique about Jesus. As a result, they disqualify some otherwise legitimate data on the historical Jesus, all that would show him to be a typical product of his own times. This minimalist approach does not provide a very rich picture of Jesus. But it does provide a sure picture. Barring major new archeological finds, its conclusion is never again likely to be questioned. If this approach strips our valid knowledge of the historical Jesus down to a bare skeleton, this skeleton is firm and secure. As we will see, it is fully able to bear the weight of the whole developed tradition.

Jesus' Statements About Himself

Our question was, What was Jesus himself like? The answer will come in two parts. First, What did Jesus think about himself? Note that this is tantamount to asking, What was Jesus' own christology?

This question must be translated into a more workable form: What did Jesus say about himself? We know what he thought only through what he said. We presume that he said what he knew; and we do not presume he thought what, according to the record, he did not say. Granted, John (16:12) has Jesus say, "I have yet many things to say to you, but you cannot bear them now." But this statement represents more the christology of John than the words of Jesus. On the other hand, on occasion Jesus is portrayed as denying knowledge of certain things: he did not know who touched him in the crowd (Mk. 5:30–33); he did not know when the last day would come (Mk. 13:32). So we can rightly presume there were some things Jesus did not know. You may object that Jesus could have known much that he chose not to say or that he said things of which we have no record. There can be no refutation to this objection. Arguing that way, people can believe anything they want about Jesus. Imagination alone sets the limit. Yet I think it very strange that Jesus, able to do otherwise, would remain smugly silent about issues of critical importance to Christianity. In any case, I choose not to speculate about what he might have been thinking and rely on what evidence we actually have.

The discussion will be limited to what Jesus said about himself. On this score, there is very little evidence. Certainly, he never spoke of himself as God. The only clear New Testament statements to this effect are John's christology, not Jesus' own words: "Before Abraham was, I Am" (8:58); "I and the Father are one" (10:30). Jesus never said he was God.

Is that surprising? It should not be. How could he ever have expressed that he was God? For Jesus, God is the Father. Jesus certainly did not want to say, "I am the Father." Could he have said, "I am the Son of God"? Yes, indeed. But all would have calmly responded, "We know you are God's Son, Jesus. God is certainly with you." In Jesus' day, Son of God meant nothing more than someone particularly blessed by God. Then, could Jesus have used the terminology of the Council of Nicea: "I am *homoousios to Patri*—I am one in being with the Father"? Well, we have no evidence that Jesus spoke Greek. Then, had he used the Nicene formula, people would not have comprehended it; they would have thought him mad, mumbling unintelligible words and insisting on their importance. Finally, it is unreasonable to expect one human mind—even if it is Jesus'—to arrive at a formula produced only after some two hundred years of Christian reflection. Such expectation forgets that Jesus was working with a human mind, bound to the limitations of his own culture, language, thought forms, and concepts. In Jesus' day, there was simply no way to express who/what he was. Why should there be? It had never happened before.

Jesus never said he was God. Neither did he refer to himself as "Son" or "Son of God." His parables and statements that mention "Son"[3] might seem to be spoken about himself. Yet contemporary scholarship concludes there is no reason to think Jesus was referring to himself in those statements. The same must be said about the title "Christ" (= Messiah).[4] If in Mark's account of the trial Jesus clearly answers "I am" (15:2) when asked if he were the Christ, his answer is elusive in Matthew's (26:64) and Luke's (22:67) accounts of the same matter. Evidently the issue was not so clear as Mark would suggest. Then Mark's clarity must represent more a christological theme in Mark than an actual account of Jesus' own statements. Analysis of the rest of Mark's gospel and especially of the scene at Caesarea Philippi (8:27–33) confirms this supposition.[5] So it appears that Jesus did not think of himself, nor did he want to be thought of, as the Christ. On the other hand, there is evidence that Jesus used the title "Son of Man." However, it is not clear if he was referring to himself or to someone else. Scholars are divided on this issue. Some of Jesus' statements can be read both ways: "For whoever is ashamed of me and of my words, of him will the Son of Man be ashamed when he comes in his glory and the glory of the Father and of the holy angels" (Lk. 9:26).[6] Whether or not Jesus was referring to himself, he was at least claiming the authority of the Son of Man as his own. This is an important point. It provides a link with the Son of Man christology in the Palestinian church, treated below.

On the positive side, with absolute certainty only one thing can be said about Jesus' explicit self-understanding. He thought of himself as prophet. Referring to himself, he said, "A prophet is not without honor, except in his own country, and among his own kin, and in his own house" (Mk. 6:4), and "It cannot be that a prophet should perish away from Jerusalem" (Lk. 13:33). Jesus may even have thought of himself as the Last Prophet. He spoke with ultimate authority; judgment depended on acceptance or rejection of himself (cf. Mk. 8:38). As a prophet, he was *sent* to the outcasts and sinners;[7]

70

this suggests that the final expectation of Israel had arrived in him. After him the end was to come (Mt. 23:31, 36, 38). But nowhere did Jesus say outright that he was that Last Prophet. The most we can say about Jesus' explicit self-understanding is that he referred to himself as a prophet.

In Jesus' explicit statements about himself we find little to support later beliefs about him. This is not surprising. Why should we expect Jesus, in his human mind, to know everything about himself? We do not expect—nor do we find—the same in any other human being.

Jesus' Self-expression in Deeds and Teachings

As expected, Jesus' statements about himself do not give us much indication about who/what he is. But actions speak louder than words. So we have a second approach to our question, What was Jesus himself like? If we want to know about someone, we should look more to how they act than to what they say about themselves. I myself, in my own being, am the best expression of myself. With some halting words, I might be able to express something of what I think about myself. With more words, other people might be able to express—at times even better than I—who/what I am. Yet I myself in my very being am my own best possible self-expression. In the things I say and do, better than in any other way, I express myself.

The same is true of Jesus. So christologists have turned to Jesus' teachings and actions in order to find a basis for later statements about Jesus. More than this, it is even presumed that Jesus' words and deeds somehow express his own inner awareness of who he is. All of us have some inner sense of ourselves. We are not able to express this in words nor even to conceptualize it clearly in thoughts. Yet the awareness is there, and it expresses itself in how we behave and speak. So, unable to find an explicit christology in Jesus, scholars begin to talk about an "implicit christology." Jesus' implicit christology is what he *must have* "sensed" about himself as *implied* by what he taught and how he acted.

Note that the term "implicit christology" is an anomaly. On the one hand, actions do speak louder than words. So Jesus' deeds and teachings are a surer indication of who/what he was than even his own words about himself. One's real self comes across in one's be-

71

havior. Furthermore, it is legitimate to suppose that Jesus, as all of us, had a deep inner sense of himself and that this inner sense expressed itself in his actions. Call it an "intuition" or a "vague inner awareness" of himself, if you wish. Yet, on the other hand, christology is reflection on, and articulation about, Jesus. This vague inner awareness does not qualify as reflection; even less, then, is it articulation. Rather, the general inner awareness of self, which we all have, is that *upon which* we reflect and that which we try to articulate when we wish to state explicitly who/what we are. That inner awareness is the self-conscious experience that gives rise to reflection about ourselves. It is that way in the case of the man Jesus, too. Therefore, Jesus' inner awareness of himself—unreflected, unconceptualized, unthought, and so unarticulated—is not a christology. To refer to it as "implicit christology" is to set up a contradiction in terms. Christology, by definition, is explicit; it is reflective and articulate. The sense of self that Jesus had and that certainly overflowed into his actions and teachings was neither reflective nor articulate. It is not rightly called "christology." Technically, the term "implicit christology" is a misnomer. Its usage both distorts the meaning of "christology" and hinders correct understanding of the non-conceptualized self-awareness that every person has.

Nonetheless, the unhappy term "implicit christology" points to an important reality—the inarticulate presence of Jesus to himself that expressed itself in Jesus' teachings and deeds. The term helps us realize that Jesus' teachings and actions are themselves some expression of who/what he is. The term turns our attention to a valuable source of data on Jesus—his actions and his teachings.

The core of Jesus' preaching was the Reign of God or the Kingdom of God. People often think that love was the core of Jesus' preaching. In fact, love was secondary. One should love because that is proper to God's Reign. Mark summarized the whole of Jesus' ministry this way: "Jesus came into Galilee, preaching the gospel of God, and saying, 'The time is fulfilled, and *the kingdom of God is at hand;* repent, and believe in the gospel.' " (1:14–15) Jesus' numerous parables speak of the Reign of God. Jesus' dominant concern was God's Reign.

That Jesus preached about the Reign of God is not unique. Israel was long awaiting the coming of God's Kingdom, and the prophets of

Israel commonly spoke about it. But there is something unique about how Jesus preached the Reign of God. Jesus spoke and acted as if the Reign of God *had come—in him!* In response to the Pharisees' criticism, Jesus explained: "If it is by the Sprirt of God that I cast out demons, then the kingdom of God has come upon you" (Mt. 12:28). He congratulated those of his company, for they had experienced the expectation of Israel: "But blessed are your eyes, for they see, and your ears, for they hear. Truly, I say to you, many prophets and righteous men longed to see what you see, and did not see it, and to hear what you hear, and did not hear it" (Mt. 13:16–17). The final fulfillment of Israel's hope, the expectation of the ages, the arrival of the Reign which God alone could bring—this, Jesus claimed, was here in him. This is one piece of undisputed evidence on the historical Jesus.

There is more. Jesus' use of the term "Amen" was also new. In Jewish life, the response, Amen, indicated agreement with what someone else had spoken. It meant something like "Yes, indeed!" "Right on!" "So it is!" This usage is still prevalent in pentecostal groups where the congregation encourages the preacher with "Amen, Sister!" "Amen, Brother!" Amen was always used to affirm what another had said. But Jesus used Amen to affirm *his own* statements! This was unheard of. In so doing, he claimed to need no one else to validate his statements. He was claiming to be his own validation. On his authority alone his statements stood. Whereas the prophets of old had said, "Thus says the Lord," Jesus said, "Amen, amen, I say to you"! Moreover, what he said challenged the Law of Moses and the religious practices of the day. On his own authority he presumed to change what was believed to have come from God himself through Moses. On his own authority Jesus overruled the most sacred traditions of Judaism.

Other teachings and practices of Jesus have the same implications. Jesus disregarded the Sabbath law. The main point here is not simply that he dared to change the Law of Moses. More than this, he presented himself as the expected Sabbath of the Lord. For the Jews the Sabbath represented God's promise of a final rest from hard labor, the curse of Adam and Eve's sin (Is. 14:3). To expect the Sabbath of the Lord was to expect the Reign of God. When Jesus declared the Son of Man master of the Sabbath (Mk. 2:28) and on the Sabbath cured the man with a withered hand (Mk. 3:1–6) and the man born blind (Jn. 9), he suggested that the Sabbath of the Lord had come, and it was there in him. Likewise when Jesus performed exorcisms and healings, he himself became the living presence of God's Reign. Matthew 11:4-6 summarizes Israel's expectations in Jesus' answer to John in prison: "Go and tell John what you hear and see: the blind receive their sight and the lame walk, lepers are cleansed and the deaf hear, and the dead are raised up, and the poor have good news preached to them. And blessed is he who takes no offense at me." Finally, Jesus associated with the publicans and sinners. He declared their sins forgiven. He ate with them. Here he suggested that the salvation was not for Israel alone. He extended salvation to the outcasts. In his own actions he lived out what his parables taught about God (cf. Lk. 15). On his own authority he acted out fulfillment of the broadest hopes of the Old Testament. In himself he made real a Reign of compassion, honesty, justice, love, and forgiveness that surpassed the imagination of the deeply religious Jewish people.

Jesus always addressed and spoke about God as "Father." The exact term is *"Abba."* It is an Aramaic word. It is recorded in the New Testament in three places.[8] Evidently this Aramaic term was so well known among the early Christians that they could include it in a Greek text and use it in Greek-speaking communities. The term itself is diminutive in form, best translated in English by something like "Daddy." In Jesus' day children and even adults used *Abba* to address their father with loving reverence. The word implied deep intimacy. Now the Old Testament had spoken of God as Father. God was the Father of orphans[9] and the Father of the nation.[10] However, Jesus' usage was remarkable on two counts. It uses 1) the diminutive form 2) in personal direct address to God. The sense of intimacy with God expressed in the term *Abba* exceeded the generally accepted limits in Judaism. We have record of only one other instance of such usage.[11] Honi the Circle-Drawer, a first century B.C.E. Hasidic rabbi, addressed God as *Abba*. There is some evidence that a tradition of charismatic Judaism stemming from Honi flourished in Galilee, where Jesus grew up. This may be the source of Jesus' use of the term *Abba*. In any case, the usage was certainly uncommon among Jews in Jesus' day. The early Christians, themselves good Jews, would hardly have dared to initiate such usage. Jesus himself must be its source. To legitimate this usage, Jesus must have had somewhere within himself a tremendous

74

sense of closeness to God. That sense must have been strong enough to allow him freely to transcend the standard restrictions of Jewish religion. If we know of no instances when Jesus referred to himself as the Son, we are absolutely sure he spoke of God as "Daddy." This usage is remarkable in Jesus' culture and religion and bears witness to Jesus' profound sense of intimacy with God.

Jesus' preaching about the Reign of God, his use of the terms "Abba" and "Amen," his teaching about the Sabbath, his acceptance of outcasts, his healings and exorcisms—these are indubitable historical facts about Jesus. Understood against the background of the deeply religious, monotheistic Judaism of Jesus' day, these facts have far-reaching implications. They would easily lead one to look at Jesus and ask, "Who did he think he was?!" Indeed! Jesus never claimed to be God or the Son of God. He never even claimed to be the Messiah. Yet he acted with a self-validating authority that reinterpreted God's revealed word to Moses. He taught and acted as if the final, awaited, saving presence of God had come—in him. He set up acceptance of himself as the ultimate criterion of righteousness. If people were baffled and offended by this remarkable man, is that surprising? If the early Christians, especially when astounded anew by his resurrection from the dead, attributed to him the highest praises and titles, is that scandalous? If Christians began to relate to him, God's ultimate intervention in history, as to God himself, is that unreasonable? If, finally, Christians began to reverence him explicitly as God himself come to earth, is that dishonest? These provocative questions take us far from our study of the historical Jesus. They point out a line of development that exceeds anything explicit in Jesus himself or, indeed, in the New Testament. Still, they indicate a path back from Christianity's boldest claim to the man of Nazareth himself. They point to a solid foundation, indubitable data on the man Jesus. Of course, these data are open to various interpretations. They do not *necessitate* any one conclusion. Nonetheless, they offer a reasonable basis for the interpretation Christians have made. It remains to sketch the development of that interpretation.

New Testament Christologies

Contemporary biblical scholarship is able to uncover the historical Jesus beneath the overlay of faith interpretations in the New

Testament. The above section summarizes the conclusions of such research. Contemporary biblical scholarship is also able to sort out various strands—different christologies—that make up that overlay of faith interpretations. Now we turn to a consideration of this aspect of the New Testament.

The New Testament, when read critically, does not contain only one interpretation of the Jesus experience. There are several distinguishable christologies in the New Testament. These are weaved together, sometimes coherently, sometimes not, to suggest a summary Christian belief about Jesus.

Contemporary scholars want to account for the differences in the New Testament texts. They are able to sort out these different New Testament christologies. They do this through skilled and astute detective work. They comb the New Testament for belief statements about Jesus. They isolate these statements and line them up, comparing one with another. These experts use whatever clues they have to understand the historical text, the New Testament, before them. So they also attempt to relate the different christologies of the New Testament to the different cultural influences that were dominant at the time of Christianity's beginnings in the eastern part of the Roman Empire.

The influences of three cultures are important. There is the Jewish culture, which used the Hebrew Bible and spoke Aramaic. This group is also referred to as the Palestinian church, since the Aramaic-speaking Jews became the earliest Christian community in Palestine. Jesus and most of his followers were members of this cultural group. There is also the Hellenistic Jewish cultural group. "Hellenist" is another word for Greek. These were the Jews who, while remaining Jews, lived among the gentiles. They were the Jews of the *diaspora*. Accordingly, they spoke Greek—and not Aramaic—for Greek was the common language of the Roman Empire at that time. They read their Bible from a Greek translation called the Septuagint. Paul was a Hellenistic Jew. Finally, there was the non-Jewish world, the Greek or Hellenistic culture. The Hellenistic world, the gentiles, became the object of Christian missionary activity shortly after the beginning of Christianity in Palestine. Paul understood himself to be the apostle of the gentiles, so he visited and sent letters to Galatia, Corinth, and Rome.

76

As best they can, scholars make use of these cultural contexts to help sort out the strands of New Testament statement about Jesus. They are careful to note the three different languages involved: Hebrew, Aramaic, and Greek. And they are careful to discern expressions of the different thought patterns associated with the Palestinian, the Hellenistic-Jewish, and the Hellenistic worldviews. Until recently, it was thought that the clever examination of all these clues would point to some clear line of development in New Testament christology.[12] The assumption was that the line would lead from the Palestinian church through the Hellenistic-Jewish church and finally to the Hellenistic mission. The further assumption was that New Testament christology would evidence an increasing complexity as it moved through these subsequent communities. Today it is clear that the reality is even more complex than this![13] In fact, the Jewish and Greek worlds interpenetrated one another in the Palestine of Jesus' day. So it is virtually impossible to sort out the Hellenistic and Jewish affiliations of New Testament statements. These categories are now known to be artificial; they do not fit the historical reality.

Practically, this means that it is not possible to spell out chronological stages of development for New Testament christology. We must be content with something else. Below I will present three different New Testament christologies. Consideration of these will give us some appreciation of how the early Christians interpreted their experience of Jesus. By the same token, this consideration will provide the occasion for further insight into the process of christologizing. Finally, this study of New Testament christologies will highlight the development that occurred between the early Christians' experience of the Jesus of history and their statements about him as the Christ of faith. Though no easy move from stage to stage will take us through the development in New Testament christologies, the shift from the historical Jesus to New Testament Christian belief about Jesus will be clear.

What is presented below is a solution to a detective case. The solution is a hypothesis. It is a proposed interpretation. It responds to a question with a reasonable answer in accord with the available evidence. In every pursuit of sure knowledge one moves from available data, to an interpretation of the data, and to verification of the interpretation in the data. In this case the data are multiple, diverse,

77

and intertwined statements about Jesus found in the New Testament as we know it today. The question is, How can we make sense of these New Testament documents? How can we explain the diversity? How can we account for the final form? The proposed explanation is that the documents evidence a consolidation of various understandings about Jesus. To some extent these understandings can be associated with different cultural contexts, but no strict correlation between cultures and christologies and no sure developmental dependence among the christologies can be maintained. This explanation, incomplete as it is, does account for the evidence. It sheds light on the thought of early Christianity. General consensus among scholars lends credence to this explanation. It is the best available opinion of the day.

Of course, not everybody accepts this theory with equal enthusiasm. Some reject the whole outright because they do not allow the historical-critical method. Recall the discussion in Chapter Two about the impossibility of "proving" anything to anyone. Even among scholars who accept a critical approach to the Bible, there are differences of opinion. Not all the issues are easily resolved. The data are complex and challenging. Recall the ambiguity over whether or not Jesus spoke of himself as the Son of Man. Our knowledge of the historical period is limited. Questions remain about many fine points of this hypothesis. Yet the general consensus is there. We can responsibly accept this account of New Testament understanding about Jesus.

Jesus, the One Who Is To Come

One New Testament christology understands Jesus as the One Who Is To Come. Christians still rely on this christology when they profess that Jesus "will come again in glory to judge the living and the dead and his kingdom will have no end."[14] This christology relates most closely to Palestinian Jews who were predominantly Aramaic-speaking and who had associated with Jesus during his life on earth. This future-oriented christology appears in the New Testament in a number of guises.

Whether or not Jesus saw himself as the Son of Man, these first Christians made sense of their experience of Jesus by seeing *him* as the Son of Man. When the Son of Man would come, he would be no one other than Jesus himself. It was to Jesus that the words of Daniel 7:13–

14 applied. He was now at the right hand of the throne of the Ancient of Days. To him would be given dominion and glory and kingdom. All peoples, nations, and languages would serve him. His dominion would be an everlasting dominion that would not pass away, and his kingdom one that would not be destroyed. So during his martyrdom, Stephen expressed his experience of Jesus by saying, "Behold, I see the heavens opened, and the Son of Man standing at the right hand of God" (Acts 7:56). Remarkably, this passage is the only one in the New Testament in which someone other than Jesus refers to Jesus as the Son of Man. In the gospels, the title Son of Man is everywhere on the lips of Jesus. But only in the case of Stephen does it appear on the lips of a Christian speaking about Jesus. We must conclude that the early Christians did use the title Son of Man to refer to Jesus as the One Who Would Come. But since this usage occurs in only one place and in a situation that is historically early, we also conclude that this title must not have been very effective for conveying the Christians' understanding about Jesus. Evidently, it was not widely used. We do know that even among the Palestinian Jews Son of Man was an obscure and ambiguous title. There was no clear understanding of what it meant. It had little impact, so it had little appeal. It seems, then, that this title was quickly dropped.

There is an instructive irony in the account of Stephen's martyrdom. On the one hand, as far as can be determined, Stephen was a Hellenistic Jew, one of the many living in Jerusalem.[15] On the other hand, the title Son of Man relates most closely with the Aramaic-speaking church. Yet it is precisely on the lips of Stephen that we have the sole New Testament record of a Christian referring to Jesus as the Son of Man! Evidently, distinct New Testament cultural contexts cannot be easily separated.

All indications are that the title Son of Man was quickly replaced by another title—Christ. The same future-oriented christology appeared in another guise. The title changed, yet the meaning was still the same. Here "Christ" had a future reference. Jesus *would be* the Christ when he appeared. When the Christ came, it would be no one other than Jesus. Acts 3:19–21 records this future-oriented christology using the title Christ: "Repent therefore, and turn again, that your sins may be blotted out, that times of refreshing may come from the presence of the Lord, and that *he may send the Christ appointed for you,*

Jesus, whom heaven must receive until the time for establishing all that God spoke by the mouth of his holy prophets from of old." The sense was that Jesus had been designated as the Christ, and when the Christ at last appeared, he would be no other than Jesus.

Finally, this same future-oriented christology can be seen in the early usage of the title Lord. Jesus was the exalted Master, the Lord, who would come. So a theme of early Christian prayer was, "Come, Lord." It is important that in the New Testament this prayer is retained in two places in its Aramaic form: *Maranatha*.[16] The Aramaic language links this christology with the Palestinian church. And the retention of this Aramaic prayer in the Greek texts of the New Testament suggests that this christology was quite prevalent.

One way that the early Christians made sense of their experience of Jesus was to see him as the One Who Would Come, the expected one of Israel, and the reference was still to the future. However, later Christian belief more simply and directly says that Jesus is God. So from our point of view, this early Palestinian christology may not appear very impressive. It does not seem to make much of Jesus. Yet, from the point of view of those earliest Christians, it is an exalted christology, indeed. What more could they have said of Jesus? He was at God's right hand. That is, he shared in the very power of God. He would come as God's anointed one. God would act through Jesus. Jesus himself would be the one to execute God's own judgment. Jesus would reign over God's own kingdom. His rule would be without end. He is the one appointed by God to fulfill God's promises to Israel. Understood within the worldview of those early Christians, this christology makes Jesus supreme. He is the focus of Israel's hopes.

The development made through this christology is significant. The Palestinian Christians had put into words what Jesus had previously expressed only implicitly in his way of acting and teaching. They had put a first, tentative name on what they had experienced in Jesus. They granted to him the reverence his deeds and teachings called for. They made him the ultimate in their lives. He would be the one who would judge for God. He would be the ultimate criterion of their lives.

To summarize: this early christology was future-oriented. It made sense of Jesus by making him the agent of the fulfillment of God's promises to Israel. Jesus was the one who would be the Christ sent by God at the end of the ages. Though foreign to our way of thinking, this understanding of the early Christians exalted Jesus to the immediate, practical ultimate in their lives.

The Title "Christ"

Very early the Christians began calling Jesus the Christ. As noted, at first this title had a future significance. As we will see, this title also bears a present and a past significance as the Christians in another cultural context understood Jesus to have been the Christ all along. This central title Christ provides a good example for considering what goes on in the process of christologizing.

In fact, the Jews offered considerable opposition to the Christians' claim that Jesus was the Christ. This opposition is abundantly documented in the Acts of the Apostles. A prime concern of the early Christians was "proving that Jesus was the Christ" (9:22).[17] Why this difficulty? In no way was the Christ expected to suffer and die! But Jesus had suffered and died. How could he possibly be the Christ? The Christians had to alter the notion of Christ in a significant way if they were to use it to speak about Jesus. They had to combine that title with others in the Old Testament—like Suffering Servant in Isaiah.[18] In this way they could argue that the promised, saving one of the Lord did have to suffer and die. And his kingdom was not of this world. But note well, the Christians changed the specific meaning of the title Christ in order to make their point.

Struck by the impact of that last sentence, one of my students once protested, "Well, then, did Jesus really fulfill the prophecies of the Old Testament? Or did the Christians just use the Old Testament to try to justify their belief however they could? Or what?" The correct answer is, "Or what?" Let me explain.

When we speak of Jesus' fulfilling the prophecies, we usually have a notion of some one-to-one correspondence between detailed predictions and Jesus' actions. Actually, the "prophecies" of the Old Testament represent a *general* promise that God would indeed save his people. The "prophecies" are an expression of a fundamental trust in the invisible and mysterious "Yahweh" in the face of any occurrence whatever. This general sense of promise and trust was reinforced when the Jews perceived Yahweh's gracious pleasure working in every specific instance of Israel's life. The prophecies about an Anointed One—Messiah or Christ—were part of this general promise and hope. It was not that the title Christ included a well worked-out list of qualities, nor that the Christ was defined as a specific historical personage, nor that to be the Christ one had to match all the prerequisites as if filling the role expectations of a job description. The prophecies were not so cut and dried, not so specific and fixed. To ask whether or not Jesus *"really* fulfilled the Old Testament *prophecies"* betrays a misunderstanding of what the so-called prophecies of the Old Testament really were.

Well, then, were the Christians just trying to justify their beliefs? No. The Christians were actually quite conscientious about how they used the Scriptures and about what they claimed about Jesus. Of course, they and all in their day felt much freer about applying a Scripture than we might today. They did not interpret the Scriptures with a literalistic, logical-deductive mind-set that we tend to bring to things, especially when we get argumentative. When they quoted the Old Testament according to their way of thinking, generally accepted by all, they had good reason for applying particular texts to Jesus. Certain aspects of their experience of Jesus did recall certain statements in the Old Testament texts. And the Christians did understand Jesus to be the unexpected yet legitimate fulfillment of Jewish religious hopes. The Christians were not trying to prove their own point at any cost.

Finally, then, what was really going on? Very simply, the Christians were doing christology. They were attempting to find some way to express what they had experienced in Jesus. Remember, Jesus Christ was a first. There were no ready-made ways to speak about him. Not even the revealed Old Testament had precise statements that applied point for point, in perfect fit, to Jesus. The Christians struggled to find a way to express their experience. They reached into their religious tradition and pulled out anything that might be useful to make their point. They found the notion of Christ quite useful. So they used it. But, of course, even it did not say exactly what they had known in Jesus. So they adapted it. They altered it. They combined it with other Old Testament notions. Using whatever they could and firm in their personal integrity, they forged and reforged notions that would express their experience of Jesus. That the early Christians so

82

readily dropped the title Son of Man and latched onto the title Christ should be instructive for us. Their concern was not to have a finished formula to pass on, untouched, from generation to generation. Their concern was to convey a message about Jesus. Their intent was to speak to their contemporaries. They used whatever means would work. When Son of Man evidently proved ineffective, they took up the title Christ. In other cultural contexts they took up still other titles and conceptions. Of course, in taking up the title Christ, they were forced to rethink the whole issue. To what extent does this new title fit? How is it inadequate? How must it be altered and qualified to convey accurately what Jesus was? In every different cultural setting and for every possible different formula, the Christians had to work out their proclamation. Different situations and different formulas invited the Christians to expand and clarify their message. What they would not have suspected in one context came to mind in another context. What was not suggested by one formula was suggested by another. In each case an assessment had to be made. In each case the proclamation had to be forged. It must be both relevant to the hearers and true to their own experience of Jesus. It must make the point they intended to make. What was going on was christology.

Jesus, Lord and Christ through the Resurrection

Another New Testament christology conceives Jesus not as the future Christ but as already the Christ through the resurrection. Acts 2:36 gives evidence of this christology: "Let all the house of Israel then know assuredly that God *has made him both Lord and Christ,* this Jesus whom you crucified." Jesus is already Christ and Lord. This same basic understanding about Jesus is present in our text of the Letter to the Romans 1:3–4. This passage combines the titles Christ, Lord, and Son of God, and relates them all to the resurrection: "the gospel concerning his Son, who was descended from David according to the flesh and *designated Son of God* in power according to the Spirit of holiness *by his resurrection* from the dead, Jesus *Christ* our *Lord.*" Or again, Paul's speech at Antioch expresses this same christology, this time mentioning only the title Son: "And we bring you the good news that what God promised to the fathers, *this he has fulfilled* to us their children *by raising Jesus;* as also it is written in the second psalm, 'Thou are my *Son,* today I have begotten thee' " (Acts 13:32–33). In each case the same understanding is there. Jesus was constituted in power through the resurrection.

What was the cultural context of this second christology? Scholars link this christology with the Hellenistic Jewish community, the Greek-speaking Jews. Among the Hellenistic Jews, concern for the Christ's final coming was not intense. Expectation of a final fulfillment of Jewish hopes was a Jewish preoccupation, not a Greek one. So the impact of this Jewish notion had waned among the Hellenized Jews, and the title Christ did not have the strong eschatological overtones that it had in the Palestinian community. To understand Jesus as the one who would be the Christ was not very relevant; but to understand Jesus as already the Christ still did have meaning. Add to this another consideration. The Christians' early expectations of Jesus' speedy return were disappointed. Time was passing, and Jesus was not returning. It seemed more and more irrelevant to understand Jesus simply as the one who would come. This harsh reality militated against the acceptance of a future-oriented christology, especially in a cultural context where the future-orientation was not important. An understanding of Jesus as already the Christ squared well with the mind-set of the Hellenistic Jews.

Moreover, the Christians were already experiencing what they took to be the power of the risen Christ working among them. They performed miracles in his name. They understood their miraculous power, of course, to be the expression of Christ's power, and they related their miracles to Jesus' own miracles while he was on earth. So the very sermon in Acts of the Apostles that ended by saying "God has made him both Lord and Christ" began by describing Jesus as "a man attested to you by God with mighty works and wonders and signs" (2:22). This notion of a "wonder worker"—also known as the "divine man"—was prevalent and popular in the Greek world. To speak of Jesus as the Christ in power who had himself worked wonders while on earth and who now continues to work wonders through his power in his disciples—this was a very appealing way of expressing the Christian experience of Jesus among the Hellenistic Jews. All of these considerations played a part in the formation of the christology in question.

Finally, there is one other consideration that seems to link this christology with the Hellenistic-Jewish Christians. In this christology the title Lord is closely associated with the title Christ: "God has made him both *Lord and Christ*." Psalm 110:1, quoted immediately prior to this verse in Acts 2:35, is associated with Jesus' resurrection: "The *Lord* said to my *Lord*, Sit at my right hand, till I make thy enemies a stool for thy feet." The title Lord is the focus of interest here. Now, recall that for the Hellenistic Jews Greek was the common language. These Jews read the Scriptures in their Greek translation, the Septuagint. Their use of the Greek Bible had an important consequence. Whereas in the Hebrew Scriptures, used by the Palestinian Aramaic-speaking Jews, Psalm 110:1 would use two different words for Lord: *Yahweh* said to *Adonai;* in Greek, one word *kurios* translated all the Hebrew words for Lord. Moreover, *kurios,* Lord was the word the Hellenistic Jewish Christians also used to speak of Jesus in the sense of Master-Lord-Sir. So, speaking Greek, these Christians used the exact same word to speak of Jesus and to speak of God, Yahweh. To know Jesus as *kurios* and to refer to God, Yahweh, as *kurios* was automatically to associate with Jesus what was said of God. By sheer dint of language an important connection between Jesus and Yahweh was established. The phrase, "The Lord said to my Lord," now suggested a close association between the Lord and the Lord, that is, between God and Jesus. This association would not have been suggested in the Palestinians' Hebrew Scriptures or in the Palestinians' Aramaic speech. But to the ears and minds of the Hellenistic Jews, the Greek Scriptures suggested that through the resurrection Jesus came to share in God's own lordship over the Christians. In the resurrection Jesus became Lord, and the sense was that Jesus was Lord just as Yahweh was Lord.

Calling Jesus *kurios* had an important implication, that somehow Jesus was Lord for them just as Yahweh was Lord for them. Remarkably, the early Christians did not balk at this implication but actually affirmed it. They took Old Testament phrases that originally referred to Yahweh and referred them to Jesus: "the day of the Lord" (1 Thes. 5:2), "to call on the name of the Lord" (Rom. 10:13). A most striking example of this phenomenon is in the christological hymn recorded in Philippians 2:6–11. The hymn concludes with the declaration, "Jesus Christ is Lord." The sense of Lordship intended here is specified by the preceding verse: "at the same of Jesus *every knee should bow . . . and every tongue confess*." These words are quoted verbatim from Isaiah 45:23 in the Septuagint. There they speak of Yahweh, who is God, besides whom there is no other. In Philippians those same words are applied to Jesus! The application is deliberate. The implication is unavoidable. Clearly, the Christians relate to Jesus as Lord even as they do to Yahweh. For Christians Jesus is as God.

We are considering a second New Testament christology that sees Jesus as already Lord and Christ, constituted as such through his resurrection. Numerous considerations suggest that this particular christology was closely associated with the Hellenistic Jewish Christians. Like the Palestinian Christian christology, this one, too, interprets Jesus in terms that are relevant to its own particular cultural situation. But in contrast to that first christology, this second appears to be more explicit in attributing some divine status to Jesus. However, if both are understood in their respective cultural contexts, this difference is really not so pronounced. In fact, both are expressions of one and the same lived reality: radical commitment to Jesus as the ultimate authority in the Christians' lives. The Palestinian Christians express this commitment in terms of their vivid expectation of the fulfillment of Yahweh's promise to Israel; the Hellenistic Jewish Christians express it in terms of acknowledging one who is already filled with Yahweh's power and as such is acting in their lives. Both are acknowledgments of Jesus as ultimate in the Christians' lives.[19]

Nonetheless, it is worth highlighting this acknowledgment in the Hellenistic Jewish case, for here the acknowledgment comes to what is for us a more obvious expression. It seems that the Hellenistic Jewish Christians express more fully the implications of accepting Jesus as the ultimate in their lives. If he is the one who will judge them, if he is already God's ultimate instrument in this world, if he is effecting God's work among them, then he is to be revered even as God is revered. If he is God's power at work for them, then for all practical purposes he is as God for them. So when these Christians call Jesus "Lord," they freely associate with that title of Jesus what was said of the Lord Yahweh in the Old Testament. They do not hesitate to spell out in words the implications of what they had been living in fact all along. To them Jesus is like God. He is their Lord, established as such by Yahweh through his resurrection from the dead. In this way the Hellenistic Jewish Christians understood and expressed their experience of Jesus. Here is a second New Testament christology.

86

Functional and Ontological Mentality[20]

Notice how use of the title Lord has a very personal overtone. To say "Jesus is Lord" is to say, more accurately, "Jesus is *my* Lord." Even in current English usage, the title Lord has this overtone. For this reason, a consideration of this title may foster further understanding and appreciation of the New Testament mentality. It is precisely with this personal overtone that the title Lord is used in the New Testament. To acclaim Jesus as Lord is to acknowledge a personal commitment to Jesus.

It is important to appreciate this "personal overtone" in the New Testament statements about Jesus. For the whole of the New Testament speaks out of a mentality that presupposes personal commitment and that appeals for personal commitment. The personal commitment is the prime concern. In contrast, the mentality of the New Testament is *not* concerned about abstract definitions or doctrinal statements. To be sure, embedded in the New Testament are understandings that could be developed into formal definitions; there are firm beliefs that could be processed into precise dogmatic formulas. But the New Testament thinkers are not concerned about definition and dogma. That is not their mentality. Their way of thinking turns on personal commitment, on practical implications. So one could interpret the Palestinian Christian christology above as follows: if Jesus exercises the authority of the Son of Man, for all practical purposes—that is, insofar as it has any relevance to me—he *is* the Son of Man. This "is" does not represent formal definition or scientific analysis. It does not mean "is in himself." It means merely "is for me." The same applies in the case of the Hellenistic Jewish christology. If Jesus conveys the saving power of the Lord Yahweh to me, for all practical purposes—that is, insofar as I relate to him—he *is* Lord. The Lord (Jesus) is Lord (Yahweh), indeed. Again, this "is" does not mean "is in himself," "literally is." The Christians did not mean to say that Jesus is Yahweh any more than Jesus himself would have wanted to say he was God, the Father. Jesus is not the Father. The Lord Jesus is not—in any literal, speculative sense—the Lord Yahweh. Rather, this "is" means simply "is for me." It means, "*I* relate to him as Lord. He is *my* Lord."

87

Now someone might object: "There was some pretty shoddy thinking going on there. In a question as serious as this one, the early Christians should have been more precise. It is one thing to say, 'Jesus is Lord,' and mean I reverence him as I do God himself. And it is another thing to say, 'Jesus is Lord,' and mean that Jesus is in himself, literally, God. The two are significantly different. *One may relate to him as God, but one may be mistaken. Is he God or not?* This is a serious question. It should have been answered."

To appreciate the seriousness of this question is to begin to appreciate how different the New Testament mentality is from our own. We may say the early Christians *should have* addressed more precisely the question we pose about the precise status of Jesus as God. The fact of the matter is that they did not. The fact that they did not, that it never occurred to them to do so, that they felt no need to do so, indicates precisely the mentality they lived with. If we are ever to understand the development of christology in the New Testament and beyond, it is precisely this mentality that we must come to appreciate.

Scholars call this New Testament mentality "functional" thinking, and different ones define it in slightly different ways.[21] I understand functional thinking in terms of what Bernard Lonergan calls "common sense."[22] *Functional thinking* understands things from the point of view of how they relate to me. In contrast, there is *ontological thinking*. It understands things as they relate to one another. It correlates with what Lonergan calls "theory."[23] Ontological thinking is determined by a concern for what things are in themselves, apart from how I feel about them or am affected by them. Functional thinking is determined by a concern for what things are for me.

An example will help. When I say, "It's hot in here," what I really mean is, "I feel hot." I am operating out of a functional mentality, our everyday way of approaching the world. I consider things insofar as they relate to me. But perhaps I have a fever. Then my saying, "It's hot in here," really has little to do with the temperature of this room. On the other hand, if I note, "It's 85 degrees in here," I am clearly saying something about this room. And what I say is determined quite apart from myself. The indication, 85 degrees, depends not on how I feel but on a thermometer reading. The thermometer measures heat by relating on a calibrated scale the volume of a small amount of mercury

88

to the heat energy available wherever the thermometer is placed. Here heat is indicated by the relationship of various factors to one another—the heat in the room, the mercury in the tube, the numbers on the thermometer—quite apart from how I might relate to the heat. A thermometer gives a much more accurate reading on the heat in a room, better than anyone's feelings might. This is not to say that the functional mentality lives in its own, small, isolated world and understands nothing about objective reality in itself. When I feel hot, it may very well be—and usually is—that the room is hot. Unless I am lost in psychotic fantasy, my understanding of things as they relate to me does, indeed, say something about those things as well as about me. Functional thinking and ontological thinking are both concerned about reality. Not their *object* of concern but *how* they approach that object is what makes the difference between functional and ontological thinking. Both provide ways of relating to reality, but the ways are different. Functional mentality understands things according to what practical meaning they have for me. Ontological mentality understands things as they are in themselves.

These two mentalities—functional and ontological—relate to the two kinds of statements discussed in Chapter Four: functional thinking expresses itself in kerygmatic statement; ontological thinking expresses itself in systematic statement. Both kinds of statement say something about reality, but they say it differently because their intent is different. The precise intent of these different statements depends on the mentality from which they proceed. The functional mentality turns on personal commitment; it expresses itself in kerygmatic statement. It appeals to personal commitment, and it makes its point by using story, myth, metaphor, imagery, and other engaging techniques. Its purpose is practical. On the other hand, the ontological mentality turns on precise understanding of things in themselves; it expresses itself in systematic statement. It appeals to the pure desire to understand, and it makes its point by using terms defined technically by relationship to one another within a comprehensive system of thought. Its purpose is theoretical.

In the New Testament the functional mentality rules. New Testament statements proceed from a functional mentality, and they are kerygmatic in form. They express how the Christians relate to Jesus— exactly as they do toward God, Yahweh. Jesus will be the agent of

God's judgment. Jesus has been constituted as God's supreme regent. Jesus exercises the authority and power of God. Insofar as the early Christians understand the issue, *for all practical purposes* Jesus is God. So they relate to him as they do to God. This is what the New Testament statements about Jesus express. They are kerygmatic statements. They express the Christian's commitment to Jesus, and appeal for others' commitment to Jesus. The New Testament statements are the product of functional mentality.

The New Testament Christians never went on to ask the further question, "But is he really God?" For them, their point is made perfectly well by proclaiming that he is Lord—their Lord—and by appealing to others to accept Jesus as Lord, too. As will be seen below, even when they apply to Jesus the title of God, the meaning is the same. Of course, they understand this Lordship in the context of Old Testament statements about Yahweh, Lord, God. Their understanding of Jesus is exalted, indeed. To them, Jesus is as God. But the New Testament statements are not systematic. They are not to be read literally. The New Testament Christians were not operating out of an ontological mentality.

To grasp the difference between functional and ontological mentality is to be able to rightly assess the New Testament message about Jesus and to accurately appreciate the later conciliar decrees as a legitimate development of the New Testament message.

Jesus, Pre-existent Word and God

A third New Testament christology finds its most obvious example in the Johannine literature—the gospel and epistles of John. Here emerges the explicit theme of Jesus' preexistence. The Prologue to John begins, "In the beginning was the Word, and the Word was with God, and the Word was God. He was in the beginning with God; all things were made through him" (1:1–3). Elsewhere John has Jesus say, "Truly, truly, I say to you, before Abraham was, I AM" (8:58).

To our logical minds, the assertion of Jesus Christ's pre-earthly existence seems obvious. Christ is God. God exists forever, without beginning or end. Therefore, Christ exists forever, without beginning or end. So he preexisted his earthly life.

But that mentality is not the mentality of the New Testament, even in its most developed statements.[24] The New Testament does

90

not call Jesus God with the systematic statement of an ontological mentality. The New Testament acknowledgment of Jesus as God represents a personal commitment, not an abstract declaration. This is exquisitely exemplified by Thomas' statement in John 20:28: "Thomas answered him, '*My* Lord and *my* God!' " Obviously, this is a statement of personal commitment. It is not a dogmatic proposition.

Raymond E. Brown analyzed the development of christological belief in the Johannine community.[25] Brown points out that this final New Testament stage of belief about Jesus emerged because of a cultural situation. Evidently the Johannine community had very early made converts among the Samaritans. The Samaritan expectation of a Messiah differed from that of the Jews. Whereas the Jewish expectation emphasized descent from David, the Samaritans emphasized a Mosaic connection. As Moses had gone up and seen the face of God and so was able to come down and reveal God's word, so the Samaritan Messiah would come from God to reveal all things. So said the Samaritan woman at the well: "I know there is a Messiah coming; whenever he comes he will announce all things to us" (Jn. 4:25). This Samaritan conception sparked the mind of the Johannine Christians. Could this notion of one coming down from God to reveal all things help express their understanding of Jesus? Indeed it could. But unlike Moses, Jesus did not first go up to God before he could reveal eternal life. Rather, he was with God in the beginning: "In the beginning was the Word, and the Word was with God" (1:1). From God he came to earth: "The Word became flesh" (1:14).

This notion of one coming from God to reveal all things and later returning to God was attractively similar to a notion prevalent in Hellenistic culture. Many Greek myths included a theme of divine wisdom's descent to earth. Wisdom was to free humans from their darkened state, enslaved in the body. But wisdom was not well received, so wisdom returned to God.

This same general theme occurred in speculation about human intelligence. Intelligence is a spark of the divine mind, fallen to earth and embroiled in matter. The goal of human life is to free this divine spark to return to its natural abode.

It is worth noting that today this same theme is again becoming common in Western civilization. Many Eastern philosophies, so popular today, convey this theme in one form or another. The human spirit or mind is an emanation of the one, divine mind. Our goal is to return to unity with that one and be absorbed in it again. The path to that goal may be a long one; it may carry us through many lifetimes. If in this life we do not achieve perfect purity, we will return in another form to continue our struggle toward perfect enlightenment. The basic pattern—descent, stay on earth, and reassent—is the same. The suggestion that that which descended is divine is also the same. This theme was prominent in Greek speculation about wisdom. It developed in a highly elaborate form called Gnosticism sometime during and after the New Testament period we are considering. The resurgence of this theme today makes this period of christological development extremely relevant.

Of course, the Jews had already met and responded to Greek speculation about wisdom. The "wisdom literature" of the Old Testament—Job, Psalms, Proverbs, Ecclesiastes, Song of Solomon, Wisdom of Solomon, Ecclesiasticus—resulted in part from this meeting of the Jewish and Greek minds. The Jewish response was true to Old Testament insistence: there is but one God, and that God, Yahweh, is beyond all creation. The gap between the Creator and the created world is inviolable. The wisdom—intelligence—evident in all creation is the expression of Yahweh's work. It is not itself divine. Wisdom is no divine being alongside Yahweh. Nor is it some part or extension or emanation of Yahweh. There is nothing divine but Yahweh. Yahweh is absolutely God, and there are no degrees of divinity. Apart from Yahweh, all is but the result of Yahweh's marvelous handiwork, all else is created. The issue admits only a simple either-or.

The Christians were familiar with this Jewish tradition about wisdom. This tradition offered a rich touchpoint with the Hellenistic world at a time when the Christians were increasingly turning their missionary efforts toward the Greeks. The Johannine community's contact with the Samaritan messianic tradition provided the needed catalyst, and in yet another situation the Christian mind was on the move, forging yet another way to express who/what Jesus is. Jesus was "the Word." The Greek term is *Logos*. In Greek speculation *logos* was the term used to refer both to the intelligence immanent in the world and to the human mind itself. We already saw this word in Chapter Two, where christo*logy* was discussed. *Logos* was also commonly used as an alternative for the term *sophia*—wisdom! Thus all the pieces come together. The link between John's christology and the cultural situation emerges. The final result is the high christology of John.

No logical deduction from abstract principles but the confluence of cultural factors—Jewish, Samaritan, Hellenistic—in the life experience of faithful Christians gave rise to the preexistence theme. To understand Jesus in terms of the Old Testament wisdom tradition and the Samaritan messianic tradition was automatically to introduce the preexistence theme. Preexistence is part and parcel of the wisdom speculation. To accept one was to accept the other. The Johannine Christians did not hesitate to accept both. Evidently they found wisdom speculation a relevant and valuable vehicle for expressing their belief about Jesus. In accepting that vehicle, they were invited to expand Christian understanding about Jesus. They realized that Jesus, the revealer whom Christians reverenced as God, had come from God. He was in the beginning with God.

There were no ready-made formulas for expressing Christian understanding about Jesus. In each case the Christians took what the culture offered and altered it to suit their own purposes. The Logos christology is no exception. Developed from Jewish wisdom speculation and very appealing to the Hellenistic mind, it nonetheless differed from both the Jewish and Hellenistic notions of wisdom. For the Jews, wisdom was no divine being. Only Yahweh is God, Yahweh alone. But for the Christians, "the Logos was God" (Jn. 1:1)! Here is a serious departure from Jewish faith. It made the definite difference between Jewish faith and Christian. On the other hand, for the Greeks wisdom never became completely involved in the material world. Wisdom came from above, visited and was rejected, and returned again to above. Even the intelligence resident in earthly humankind was destined to be freed from the body to return above. The material world is an unworthy place for the glorious wisdom/mind. But for the Christians, "the Word became flesh" (Jn. 1:14)! Here is a serious affront to the Hellenistic viewpoint. Thus, the Christian view cuts down the middle between the Jewish and the Hellenistic. The result is something new under the sun. Neither is it found in its predecessors, nor can they account for it. From where, then, did the novelty arise? From the Christian community. And as the source of its inspiration that community points back to Jesus of Nazareth.

John's gospel includes the most advanced notions of New Testament christology: preexistence: "In the beginning was the Word" (1:1);[26] generation from the Father: "we have beheld his glory, glory as of the only begotten (Son) of the Father" (1:14);[27] and role in creation: "all things were made through him" (1:3).[28] These became the main points of discussion among post-New Testament Christians, and the discussion focused on the titles Logos and Son of God.

Only at the Council of Nicea in 325 c.e. was a precise understanding of these titles clarified. It is tempting to project back into the New Testament understandings that emerged only in a later era. After all, the words lend themselves so easily to such a reading: "the Word was God." Nonetheless, the mentality of the New Testament, even in its final stage of development, was functional. This is clear when one considers the literary genre of the three New Testament statements that undoubtedly call Jesus God.[29] The Prologue of John is commonly recognized to be a hymn; it is not a speculative formulation. Thomas' statement, "My Lord and my God," is a personal confession; it is not a doctrinal formula. And Hebrews 1:8—"But of the Son he says, 'Thy throne, O God, is for ever and ever' "—is quoting a psalm; it is not an abstractly conceived assertion. The statements about Jesus at the end of the New Testament era are more expansive than the earlier ones. They add considerations not found earlier. They even use the very title God in reference to Jesus. Nonetheless, the intent is no different from that implied by the title Lord, which we have already considered. Indeed, Thomas' confession combines the two: "My Lord and my God!" Contrary to what we are inclined to think, these latest New Testament statements are making no literal determination about the divine nature of Jesus Christ or about his eternal procession from the Father as Son. New Testament Christians simply did not think in these terms. They did not conceive the issue this way. How can one be certain about this? Because the speculative issue of Jesus' divinity was not resolved until the Council of Nicea. If this issue had already been clear in the New Testament, why did it take 225 years of Christian reflection and heated debate to produce the Nicene formula?

The New Testament mentality is functional through and through. The Logos christology of John, like those before it, is a kerygmatic attempt to convey in still another cultural context what Christians believed about Jesus. All who were familiar with the *logos-*

sophia speculation of the day would have attended to that proclamation and found it meaningful. They would have easily accepted all that came with it, for those implications—preexistence, generation from God, role in creation—were part of the *logos-sophia* speculation. And at the same time, in a form congenial to them, they would have heard the firm testimony of the Christians: we look on Jesus Christ, the Logos-Son of God, the wisdom through whom all was created, as God. He is the agent of God's salvation. To know him is life.

As the other New Testament christologies, the logos speculation was in its own right an effective vehicle to convey the Christian understanding about Jesus. If it brought with it provocative implications, the Christians found those implications acceptable, once adjusted to fit the new case, Jesus Christ. When further questions arose—as they soon did—Christian reflection would have to determine exactly how those implications were to be taken.

Summary

In summary, there are some sure conclusions that emerge from contemporary New Testament research. The historical Jesus never said he was God nor even the Son of God. At best, he said he was a prophet. Possibly he thought of himself also as Son of Man. In any case, he taught and acted as if God's ultimate intervention in history, long awaited by Israel, had come in him. He assumed such an intimacy with his Father, Abba, and such an authority even over God's revelation to Moses that anyone could wonder, "Who did he think he was?"

Inspired by his life and bolstered by his resurrection from the dead, his followers struggled to understand their experience of Jesus. Again and again they found ways to express what they experienced in Jesus. They were doing christology. Their functional mentality did not lead them to make abstractly conceived statements; rather, they used the tools available in their respective cultural situations to express kerygmatically their increasing understanding of Jesus. They proclaimed what Jesus was for them, and they called their listeners to respond with personal commitment to Jesus. From the beginning they acknowledged Jesus as the ultimate in their lives. God's own judgment was determined through him. By the end of the New Testament era, Christians did not hesitate to apply the title God and the qualities of Yahweh to Jesus. There is no doubt whatsoever that the New Testament Christians *related to Jesus as to God*. In their living, loving, and working, for all practical purposes, *for them* Jesus was God. Nonetheless, the New Testament statements may not legitimately be taken to say more than that. Nowhere does the New Testament contain an abstractly conceived declaration that Jesus Christ is literally God.

An important question still remains. The New Testament Christians certainly related to Jesus as God. But is he really God in himself? This precise question did not emerge until later. The Christian answer to it came only at the Council of Nicea. To this further issue, the stumbling block for much contemporary christological thinking, we turn in the next chapter.

CHAPTER SIX

The Council of Nicea: A Double Development

First-century Christians looked on Jesus as God. This is the clear testimony of the New Testament, especially in its later writings. The same attitude and the same functional mentality also dominated Christian thought beyond the New Testament era. In his study of the development of Christian doctrine, Jaroslav Pelikan exemplifies the prevailing state of affairs by quoting 2 Clement, an early second-century sermon attributed (mistakenly) to Clement, the third bishop of Rome: "Brethren, we ought so to think of Jesus Christ as of God, as of the judge of living and dead."[1] Discussion about the precise sense of this "thinking of Jesus Christ as of God" ensued for two and a quarter centuries. Finally, at the Council of Nicea in 325 c.e., the Church hammered out a declaration that clarified the divine status of Jesus. The Nicene creed was the culmination of those centuries of Christian thought. The contrast between it and the New Testament statements is stark. Nicea clearly represents another milestone in the development of christology.

The advance at Nicea was double, so it is of peculiar importance. Not only did Nicea further clarify Christian understanding about Jesus, even as each New Testament christology had done. Nicea also conceived and expressed its understanding of Jesus in a new way; it operated out of an ontological mentality and moved toward systematic statement. As well as an advance in christological clarity, Nicea evidenced a differentiation of consciousness among certain Christians. Thus, the Council of Nicea merits detailed consideration. It is the topic of this chapter.

A Jump of 225 Years

Undoubtedly, some people will criticize this seemingly blithesome leap over two and a quarter centuries of doctrinal debate. They will object to this supposed too easy acceptance of Nicea's decree and mentality. After all, they will argue, the ontological mentality canonized at Nicea was a foreign element for Christianity.[2] Its dogmatic attitude produced doctrinal formulae that irreconcilably split the Christian Church. Besides, the Nicene decree itself so startled the Church that a half century of conflict resulted. The Nicene position prevailed in the end only by the hair of its teeth. The Nicene position was but one of a number of possible trajectories that Christian doctrinal development could have followed. Stark and vivid contrast between orthodoxy and heresy is but the fable of Christian propagandists and pre-nineteenth-century uncritical historians. The historical reality is not so simple as one would like to think. In the end, some would suggest, orthodoxy was but the fortuitous product of political vote; heresy, the winner's name for the position that lost.[3]

No one would deny the complexity of doctrinal history nor discount the cultural-political forces that often move it along. Still, there is more to doctrine than the outcome of vote. Different doctrinal positions have different intrinsic rationales. Not all are equally adequate to previous tradition. Not all have the same practical implications for lived religion. Not all are equally valid as an understanding of life. In brief, there is truth, and there is falsehood. There is accurate understanding, and there is misunderstanding. Any position, so long as a person really holds firmly to it, is not as good as any other. This discussion brings us back to our starting point in Chapter Two. Epistemology is still the heart of the matter.

I continue to follow critical-realist presuppositions. On this basis, the decree of Nicea can be shown to be a legitimate development in the Christian tradition. That decree is in full continuity with what went before, yet it takes the tradition a giant step forward. If it introduces new complexity to doctrinal statement, at the same time it adds a precision and richness not had before. The Council of Nicea is a main focus of this novelty in Christianity. From this point of view, consideration can profitably and legitimately be limited to it. Such consideration will clarify beyond doubt Christian belief about the divinity of Jesus Christ; it will also significantly highlight the epistemological issues so central to contemporary christology.

The Teaching of Nicea

Behind the Council of Nicea stand Arius, a priest of Alexandria and the proponent of the condemned position, and Athanasius, deacon and later bishop of Alexandria and chief spokesperson for the Council.[4] Arius' concern was to defend the transcendence of God. Arius insisted that God is without beginning, without source. God is unbegotten and is the subject of no change or alteration. Therefore, the Word, born of the Father, is not God. The Word is a creature. "God's perfect creature, he is unlike any other creature; begotten, yes, but unique in the manner of his begetting."[5] Arius explained, "They persecute us because we say that the Son has a source and a beginning, but God has not. This is why they abuse us, and also because we use the phrase 'out of nothing' (*ex non exstantibus*); but we used this phrase because the Son is not a part of the Father, nor, on the other hand, was he made out of any preexisting matter."[6]

Arius' argument is crystal clear. In fact, the issue had never been phrased so clearly before. This was Arius' contribution. He phrased the question about the Word in terms that could not be sidestepped. No longer would he tolerate images open to ambiguous meaning. Arius wrote, "If some people understand the phrases *from him, from the womb* and *I came forth from the Father* and *I come* as implying that he is a consubstantial part of the Father, or a sort of emission, they make the Father composite, divisible and changeable; indeed God would be a body. . . ."[7] Arius is aware that images can be misleading. He begins to analyze them, and he rejects certain possible interpretations. He pushes the question toward systematic formulation. He poses the question in clearcut terms: Is the Word a creature or not? There can be no halfway house here. The question about creaturehood is an either-or question. Given that Arius defines God as the unsourced and given that the Word is born of God, the Word cannot be God; the Word is a creature.

With this understanding, Arius was still able to affirm the Scriptures and accept traditional statements about Jesus Christ. He wrote the following: "This one God, before all time, begot his only-begotten Son, through whom he made the ages and the universe. He begot him not just in appearance, but in fact; by his own will he made his son to subsist and he made him unchangeable and unalterable."[8] A key biblical text supposedly supports Arius' position: "The Lord *begot* me at the beginning" (Prov. 8:22). This text goes on to speak of Wisdom and its role in creation; it is part of the wisdom tradition that lies behind John's Logos christology. But the word "begot" is ambiguous in the Hebrew. It could also be legitimately translated "created." In the Syriac version, used in Antioch where Arius studied, it is translated, "The Lord *created* me at the beginning."

Arius was fully convinced that his teaching was in accord with the Scriptures. However, his teaching actually introduced a consideration that went beyond what the Scriptures had clearly dealt with. The question, Was the Word a creature or not? had never been posed before. So the Scriptures had not answered it. But once posed, the question had to be answered.

The Council of Nicea responded to Arius' position point for point. The response is a profession of faith, formulated at Nicea, revised at the First Council of Constantinople, and still proclaimed in the Christian Churches under the name "Nicene Creed." The creed reads: "We believe in one Lord, Jesus Christ, the only Son of God, eternally begotten of the Father, God from God, Light from Light, true God from true God." Thus far, Arius could agree. "Eternally begotten" would mean that the Son was born of the Father outside of time. But Arius insisted that the Son did not exist before he was begotten. The Father was when the Son was not. Of course, in this sense, the Son is not eternal, that is, not co-eternal with the Father. Still, Arius could provide an interpretation for the phrase, "Eternally begotten." Furthermore, Arius would not object to calling Jesus Christ God, Light, and true God. Nor would he object to saying that as such he came from God, Light, and true God. These things had been said about Jesus Christ for generations. Arius could accept the Nicene formula thus far.

However, the Council went on to say, "begotten not made, consubstantial (one in Being) with the Father." Here Arius could not agree. These phrases directly address and reject his teaching. According to the Council, Jesus Christ is indeed begotten; he is "sourced" from the Father. Still, he is not "made." The Greek word is the same one used earlier in the creed to say that the Father is "maker" of heaven and earth. It can also be translated "created." This is to say, though the Son is from the Father, the Son is not a creature. The issue could not be phrased any more clearly. Evidently, then, Arius' key assumption that the essence of God is to be without source is deemed erroneous. The Word is "sourced," but the Word is not a creature.

Note that here, as in the case of John's Logos christology, Christian faith again cuts down the middle between two seemingly sole alternatives. The Word is neither a creature, nor is he without source. Here is a completely new understanding of God. Again, its inspiration is the Christian experience of Jesus Christ. Again, Christians are forging new ways to express that experience of Jesus Christ. They are doing christology.

The next term, *homoousios* (consubstantial), is the key to Nicea's definition. In contemporary English the term is best rendered as "of the same stuff." The Son is of the same stuff as the Father. Whatever the Father is—and the Council does not presume to explain what God is!—that, the Son is also. With this notion the Council countered Arius' assertion that the Son is "out of nothing." God made all things out of nothing. The technical Latin term is *ex nihilo*. Before God created all things, apart from God there was nothing. God could not have made things out of something else that was existing, for nothing existed. Only God was. Had God "made" things out of himself, they would be eternal, divine, as God is. There is no third alternative. A reality is either God, of the divine substance, or a reality is a creature, made to exist by God out of nothing. In declaring that the Son is *homoousios to Patri*, of the same stuff as the Father, the Council clarified the divine status of Jesus Christ: He is God even as the Father is God. Whatever the Father is as God, the Son is that also.

The teaching of Nicea is clear. Arius asked whether Jesus Christ, the Son of God, is a creature or not. The Council responded that the Son is not a creature but is God even as the Father is God. Here

101

Christian belief in the divinity of Jesus Christ comes to unambiguous assertion.

Implications for Fundamentalism

The Council of Nicea was bold in using the term *homoousios.* Some participants in the Council complained: the word is not scriptural. The faith should be expressed only in terms found in the Bible. Worse than that, the term itself had been condemned in a previous local Synod at Antioch in 268 C.E. Paul of Samosata had used the term unacceptably to suggest that both the Father and the Son were expressions of the Divinity, prior to them both.

Despite these objections, the Council did incorporate the term *homoousios* in its creedal definition. In the first place, it was argued, the term was now safe. It was clear to all that *homoousios* was not being used in the condemned sense. Moreover, only use of some such term, it was argued, could adequately respond to Arius' position. As we saw, Arius could explain all the biblical statements in terms of his own understanding. No mere scriptural statement would be effective to answer him.

In adopting the term *homoousios,* the Council of Nicea made an important affirmation. To adequately express Christian belief, it is necessary to go beyond the mentality, phraseology, and vocabulary of the Bible. Clarifying for the first time the absolute divinity of Jesus Christ, this Council simultaneously excluded from Christianity any strictly fundamentalist adherence to the Scriptures.

There is an irony here. Fundamentalists who insist that the Bible alone determines Christian belief are hard pressed to safeguard a key fundamental belief in the divinity of Jesus Christ. In fact, clear and definitive assertion of Jesus' divinity emerged only at the Council of Nicea. Nicea is the historical path by which that assertion entered Christianity. Yet the very same council insisted that the Bible alone is not adequate to express Christian belief. On the basis of the Bible alone, Arianism is a defensible position! In light of the Council of Nicea, Fundamentalism should find itself facing disturbing alternatives: either insist on the Bible alone and so jeopardize belief in the divinity of Jesus Christ, or insist on unquestioned belief in the divinity of Jesus Christ and admit its basis in the Council of Nicea and so surrender supposed strict adherence to the Bible alone. In practice, of course, Fundamentalism would reject these present historical considerations just as it rejects historical-critical interpretation of the Bible. At the heart of Fundamentalism is the refusal to take *history* seriously. By implication, such refusal also entails the refusal to take seriously Yahweh, the Old Testament Lord of *history*, and the refusal to take seriously the incarnation of God's son in *history*, as well. These implications may appear subtle—though they are really at the core of Christianity—so they, too, are likely to be lost on the Fundamentalist movement. This is so because at the heart of Fundamentalism is also the refusal to think critically about religion. In any case, by continued insistence on the Bible alone, the Fundamentalist movement actually chooses the first alternative set out above. It chooses to be oblivious to history and so to a critical formative factor in the Christian tradition, the Council of Nicea. Under the circumstances, can Fundamentalism legitimately continue to call itself "Christian"?

Systematic Statement

Notice how technical the discussion of Nicea's decree becomes. To understand the decree of Nicea, one has to understand precisely what 'creature' and 'creator' mean. One has to understand the notion "creation out of nothing." These notions are not images or metaphors. They cannot be imagined. The very terms 'creature' and 'creator,' 'created' and 'uncreated,' are understood only in relationship to one another. They are part of an overall system of thought within which alone the intended meaning is grasped. We have moved into systematic statement and are confronted by ontological mentality. This change in the way of understanding things, evidenced so clearly in the Nicene debate, did not occur overnight. It is the achievement of generations of Christian thinkers. It is the heritage of the Alexandrian School, boasting such third-century theological giants as Origen and Clement of Alexandria. In moving from the New Testament to the Council of Nicea, we have jumped into a new world.

The budding ontological mentality that lay behind the Nicene discussion provoked and answered the question latent in Christian faith from the beginning: Christians reverence Jesus as God, but is he God? Is he God or creature? To respond, "We look on him as God. He is our Lord and our God," was no longer enough. A new question had been raised in an entirely new cultural situation. A new answer was needed.

The mentality behind that question was not concerned about how Christians relate to Jesus, whether they reverence him as God or not. The new concern was whether or not he is God in himself, literally so. The Council answered this question not by saying again how Christians relate to Jesus Christ, but by saying how Jesus Christ relates to other things: he is not a creature; he is of the same stuff as the Father. This declaration could almost be presented mathematically:

$$\text{Jesus Christ} \neq \text{creature}$$
$$\text{Jesus Christ} \cong \text{Father (God)}.$$

The kind of thinking that produced the formula $C = 2\pi r$ also lies behind the declaration of the Council of Nicea. The terms are defined by relationship to one another.

Nicea's statement leaves no room for doubt about Christian belief about Jesus Christ, the Son of God. He is God. The intent is not that you should reverence Jesus as God and so let him be God for you. The intent is not to clarify that Christians do reverence Jesus as God. This fact was clear for centuries. Rather, the intent is to insist on this: Christians affirm that Jesus *is* God—whether or not someone reverences him as such. If Christians do reverence Jesus as God, that is because he *is* God.

Understanding and Legitimating the Development

I have argued that the development of New Testament christologies was legitimate in itself and consistent with what preceded it, the historical Jesus. I make the same assertion regarding Nicea. This development, too, was legitimate in itself and consistent with the New Testament christologies. To validate this assertion, I present below an analysis of the intrinsic ideal structure of the Nicene development. I call this structure "ideal" because it is not an account of the complex and concrete history of the event. Rather, it is an account of the essential intellectual process that lay behind the concrete history. The process includes four factors, as follows:

The Council of Nicea: A Double Development

The transposition of functionally conceived New Testament belief into on-tologically conceived Nicene belief:

(1) Jesus is God for me. (The New Testament heritage)

(2) I am a person of integrity. (The subjective dimension: the authentic, graced Christian)

(3) But is Jesus God in himself? (The cultural catalyst: a new question arises)

(4) Yes, Jesus is God in himself, He is not a creature. He is consubstantial with the Father. Otherwise I would not reverence him as God. (The Christian's answer to the new question, the only possible consistent response)

First, notice that (4) and (1) are of the exact same value as knowl-edge statements in faith. This is so because the source of both is the same. Both rest on the same objective and subjective bases. The objective basis is the historical Jesus, known immediately in the flesh by the earliest Christians or mediately through inherited tradition by later Christians. The subjective basis is the authentic Christian subject consistent throughout history: (2). More on this below. The historical data on Jesus and the appropriation of the data by an authentic subject are constant throughout the tradition. The various statements of Christian belief proceed from this same—though double—constant source. So they are of the same cognitive value; that is, they are equally valid articulations of reality. Though conceived functionally in terms of how I relate to Jesus, (1) does contain some undifferentiated yet valid indication about the reality itself, Jesus, to whom I relate. (4) isolates that valid indication about the reality itself and articulates it in a differentiated form, with focus and precision. The valid cognitive indication about Jesus of both (1) and (4) is the same. Both are of the same cognitive value.

Second, the difference between (1) and (4) is not in the cognitive value of the statements but in how the statements are conceived. (1) proceeds from my functional mentality whereby I understand reality insofar as it relates to me. Yet, in this, I do understand reality. (4) proceeds from my ontological mentality whereby I understand things insofar as they relate to one another. In this, too, I understand reality; yet now my understanding has achieved a clarity and preci-sion absent in (1). In a sense, (4) is not saying anything that was not

105

already presupposed in (1) (given (2), of course). Yet what (4) says was not, in fact, said in (1); so (4) represents an advance over (1). Not the cognitive value but the form of the statements is the difference between (1) and (4).

Third, notice that (2) provides the context for, and influences, the whole developmental process. (The vertical arrow connected with (2) indicates this.) Therefore, the process is not one of mere logical deduction. The above outline is not a syllogism. Rather, the process proceeds by intelligent insight and reasonable judgment in a responsible subject. The above outline represents not a logical deduction, but an advance in understanding. The subject in question is, specifically, the authentic Christian.[9] Faith is also a dimension of this subject. However, recall that appeal to the Holy Spirit, grace, and faith is the Christian way to further qualify and explicate the meaning of the authentic subject. The Holy Spirit, grace, and faith do not alter or invalidate the meaning of "intelligent, reasonable, and responsible subject"; they merely add a further dimension and confirm what is already there. That further dimension is presupposed throughout this book, as noted in Chapter Two. Specific treatment of it need not be made here. The point to be made here is simply that the authentic subject determines the whole of this developmental process.

It follows that (4) is a statement of a human subject. Though its form is systematic—'scientific'—it is not an 'objective' statement in the sense that it represents a "God's-eye point of view." It is human statement. It is human affirmation. It is the statement of a human subject. In this sense it is subjective, as is all human knowledge. It is subjective not in the sense that it is biased, unobjective, or inaccurate. It is subjective in the sense that it is the statement of a human subject. To say in this sense that (4) is subjective is not to say that (4) is functionally conceived. It is *not* accurate to suppose that (4) is also functional because it is someone's 'subjective' statement. (4) *is* a subjective statement; it is the statement of a Christian believer. But it is conceived ontologically and formulated systematically. (1) is also a subjective statement; it, too, is a statement of a Christian believer. But it is conceived functionally and formulated kerygmatically. The subjective factor in (4) is the same as the subjective factor in (1). The whole developmental process is determined by the human subject: (2). It is mistaken to suppose that (1) is a 'subjective' statement while (4) is an 'objective' statement. Both are subjective. And, if Jesus really is what Christians say he is and if he is worthy of the reverence they give him, both are objective; that is, both responses arise from, and articulate, an accurate understanding of reality. This point needs to be emphasized. Misunderstanding here too easily allows the dismissal of the systematic nature of Nicea's statement because the proclamation of Nicea is a creed, a statement of faith. Indeed, the decree of Nicea is a creed. But the mentality that produced that creed was ontological; and the form of that creed's christological affirmation is systematic.

Finally, notice that when (3) emerges, it calls for an answer of either "Yes" or "No." There can be no third alternative. Even Arius knew this. He tried to place the Son somewhere between God and creation, outside of time yet not co-eternal with the Father. Nonetheless, he was forced to profess that the Son was, therefore, a creature and not God.

Granted that faith entails a stance vis-à-vis reality[10] and given (1) and (2), the only consistent response to (3) is "Yes." (4) must follow. If "No" is the response, then either (1) or (2) must also be negated. The Christian leaders at Nicea qualified on (1) and (2). When (3) arose within its new cultural context, they did not hesitate to reformulate their belief in Jesus in a new way. Consistent with the tradition and with themselves, they responded, "Yes. Jesus is God; he is not a creature."

Granted the consistency between (1) and (4), those who balk at (4)'s stark clarity should have earlier balked also at (1). It is symptomatic of today's epistemological confusion that many are enthusiastic over the return to the Bible, with its popular functional mentality and "relevant" kerygmatic statements, and readily accept New Testament statements as adequate expressions of Christian belief yet hedge when it comes to Nicea.[11] At the heart of the matter is epistemology: Do my statements and beliefs and structures of meaning relate me to reality in itself or do they, on the other hand, create only a personal reality, considered "true" because it is meaningful for me? Accept the latter alternative, and it is sufficient to hold, "Jesus is God for me." And the further question about reality in itself never comes up or is disallowed. But where the question does come up and is allowed and pursued, an answer must be given. The Christians at Nicea allowed the further question, and they answered it. They did not shun the critical mind or its demand for clearer statements of faith. They did not hesitate to introduce technical terminology to make their point. The answer they gave was consistent with the previous tradition. In hindsight, this consistency can be shown. The Nicene decree is a further clarification of the New Testament faith, which is itself a legitimate interpretation of the data on the historical Jesus. The Christian position, even at Nicea, continues to be reasonable.

Nicea's Challenge to Us

On the personal level, Nicea's statement presents a challenge. Nicea did not explain away the mystery of Jesus Christ; it merely clarified what that mystery is. Nicea clarified Christian belief about Jesus. We are left to decide if we will accept it or not. We are left to decide if we will be Christian or not. Acceptance of the Council of Nicea, acknowledged as a valid explication of New Testament faith, has been and remains the litmus test of true Christianity. Unqualified belief in Jesus Christ as Eternal-Son-Incarnate is the hallmark and determinant of the Christian tradition.

Perhaps the Council clarified the issue more than we want. One of my students burst into tears at this point in my christology course. Despite her desire to be a Christian and her self-identity as such, this intelligent and thoroughly honest woman realized she did not believe as Nicea defined. The issue had become too clear. She could live much more comfortably with the ambiguities of a New Testament faith that could see Jesus as a Christian parallel to Moses or Buddha or Mohammed: God's messenger, God's supreme messenger, and so even God *for us*—if not for others. She could live much more comfortably with what she then knew to be only a pre-Nicene faith. Yet once the ontological question was raised and clarified, the inherent implications of the New Testament faith were also unavoidable. . . . Perhaps one should not study theology!

I cried, too, one Christmas season. After four years of doctoral studies, including two years of work on my dissertation, I realized that my theological project had no resolution as long as Jesus was only another great prophet. I could not explain human divinization—salvation—if Jesus were not God. Along with this theological realization, I had the personal realization of my own unbelief. I prayed for faith and insight. That winter, huddled for a vigil service in the dark and cold chapel at Andover Newton Theological School, I heard the Christmas gospel with the ears of a child, though my understanding was that of a trained theologian.[12] And the message was the same! The marvel of Christmas overflowed in me. I was awed at the realization of God's great love for us. I was overwhelmed at the goodness and beauty of life. I could believe again.

For that moment I was a Christian. From time to time I again catch a glimpse of the mystery of God becoming human. For a moment, from time to time, I am again a Christian. But the notion of the incarnation is mind-boggling. The implications are astounding. Its claim sounds preposterous. If it were true, what all would that mean. . . ? It is very difficult to maintain such faith with constant intensity. Such faith is a gift. Rather, we must constantly pray, "I believe, help my unbelief!" (Mk. 9:24).

Yet the challenge which Nicea offers was not unique to Nicea. Every era offers the same challenge in its own way. Each person who hears is challenged to take a stand vis-à-vis Jesus. For Christians, he is the ultimate, the Lord, the Son through whom all was made, God from God, Light from Light, one in being with the Father. The Christian assertion about Jesus is clear, and it is challenging. The decision to accept or reject that assertion remains with each of us. Each is challenged to continue growing in faith.

A Differentiation of Consciousness

The advance at Nicea represented not only a clarification of Christian doctrine but also a differentiation of consciousness. Ontological thinking was emerging.

Functional thinking is concerned with practicality: what do things mean for me? It is concerned with acting and doing as well as with understanding. It appeals to feeling and deciding as well as to understanding. In functional mentality all the human conscious operations are bundled up in one package.

Ontological thinking, on the other hand, sorts out that package and focuses on only one element within it. Its concern is pure understanding. It seeks precision of thought. It gains this precision by turning its focus away from the subject and to the relationship of things among themselves. It prescinds from feelings and decision and action and concentrates on meaning.[13] Here 'meaning' takes on a particular meaning. Here 'meaning' does not mean what is significant for me, what moves me, what appeals to me: "That experience was very *meaningful* to me." Rather, here 'meaning' means the intelligibility within a thing or situation, the sense that something makes, the rationale proper to the matter: "What does the term 'christology' *mean?*" 'Meaning' takes on a completely cognitive significance.

It is clear that the Council of Nicea was concerned to determine the precise meaning of Christian belief about Jesus. The images traditionally used to express the relationship of the Son to the Father were no longer adequate. Their meaning was ambiguous. Even Arius could not continue to use them. The Council clarified the acceptable Christian meaning by introducing the term *homoousios,* consubstantial. Athanasius argues that what the term *homoousios* means is exactly what the popular images intended to convey.

> How can you aptly describe how the brightness is related to the light, or the stream to the source, or the Son to the Father, except by using the word, consubstantial?
> . . . thus, to be offspring, and to be consubstantial, mean one and the same thing; and whoever thinks of the Son as the offspring (*gennema*) of the Father, rightly holds that he is consubstantial with the Father.
> But then the bishops, seeing through the deceits of the Arians, went to the scriptures and there collected these words: brightness, source, stream and the figure of his substance. They also adduced the phrases, "In your light we shall see the light" and "I and the Father are one". Then, concisely and more clearly, they wrote that the Son is consubstantial with the Father; for that is what the other phrases all mean.[14]

Evidently, Athanasius is aware that meaning can be expressed in different ways and that the formulation of Nicea clarifies the meaning intended by the traditional images. The concern for precision in cognitive meaning is clear in these accounts of the discussion at Nicea. This concern evidences a differentiation of consciousness.[15] A new way of thinking was emerging.

This differentiation of consciousness shows itself again in a more precise understanding of the term 'truth.' For the biblical mentality truth is something to be done. 'Truth' refers globally to all that is to be thought and embraced and lived. Truth includes both the true and the good. One lives the truth. Thus, John writes, "He who *does what is true*

110

comes to the light" (3:21). The biblical notion of truth bears witness to an undifferentiated consciousness. In contrast, for the ontological mentality truth is what is correctly affirmed. The ontological mentality sorts out living and acting and affirming and focuses only on affirmation. Here a differentiated notion of truth emerges. Clement of Alexandria bears witness to this emerging new mentality when he speaks of truth in terms of the process of question and answer. Christian philosophy, he writes,

> has no place for any sort of strife. What it says is "Seek, and you shall find; knock, and it shall be opened to you; ask, and you shall receive" (Mt. 7,7; Lk. 11,9). Investigation by question and answer is, I think, knocking on the door of truth, asking that it be opened. When the door, which had been barring the way, is opened by investigation, scientific contemplation of the truth begins.[16]

The differentiation of consciousness under consideration shows itself in still another way, in the shift from use of images to use of propositions. Christians insist that their statements speak reality, so words are important. This Christian awareness has deep roots in the Judeo-Christian tradition. The prophets of old confirmed their statements with, "Thus says the Lord." Jesus urged, "Let your Yes be Yes." The church proclaims, "If anyone says . . . , let them be anathema." Inherent in these statements is a dogmatic realism: the insistence that on the basis of faith one knows what is real. Propositions can state Christian belief; they indicate reality. Belief statements relate one not to a personal or a collective fantasy world, but to reality. This mentality undergirds the statements of Nicea.[17]

How different is the mentality that rules our contemporary society. Political rhetoric offers a prime example. Politicians often say whatever they need to say in order to influence people's vote. People have come to take this for granted. Few are surprised, and even fewer incensed, when political promises are forgotten after election day. "That's just the way it goes." Everybody knows that. Few really expect accurate statements any more. In our society, one's political word and statements are cheap. Situations are construed in the way most favorable to the candidate or the officeholder. Statistics are manipulated. Embarrassing facts are overlooked. When pointed out by the opposition or the press, they are obscured with sophistries. They are reinterpreted. The lie no longer exists; rather, statements merely become "inoperative." Dishonesty is merely an "error in judgment." Few have any hope of restoring virtue to the scene. Honest living makes things hard for everyone. Propositions—statements—are merely part of a word game. The situation is sad, indeed.

In contrast, Athanasius certainly had an appreciation for the propositional expression of truth. His rule, which governs the relationship between the Father and the Son, presumes as much: "Therefore, because they are one, and because the divinity itself is also one, what is said of the Father is also said of the Son, except the name, Father."[18] This rule insists that reality about God can be expressed through sheer logical proposition. "What is said" indicates what is so. Since God is one, there is no duplicity about what is said of God. The same is said of the Father and the Son, for both are the same divinity. Yet, since the Father is not the Son, they are named differently. What is intended in this rule is not something that can be imagined; it cannot be accurately portrayed by metaphors. The standard metaphors—the sun and its ray, the root and its shoot, the river and its streamlet, the three-leafed clover—do not convey the same precision of meaning as the proposition, "what is said of the Father is also said of the Son." The proposition moves beyond image and metaphor; it indicates what is beyond imagination. It states precisely what is meant.

Athanasius' rule presupposes that meaning is our bridge with reality. We know reality when we affirm correct meaning. Now, images and metaphors can express meaning, and propositions can also express meaning. But only propositions can express meaning with precision and clarity. Since Christianity is concerned about reality and since Christian beliefs are accepted as indications of what is real, it is important that what is believed be expressed clearly and precisely. A Christian would not want to affirm what is not so. Thus the move from metaphorical expression of meaning to propositional expression of meaning comes naturally to Christianity. The move is an attempt to clarify and preserve the authentic tradition. It is an advance within the tradition. In form, Christian propositional statement of truth is a strict parallel with the Greek achievement of systematic statement. But this is not to say that Nicea represents the Hellenization of Christianity.[19] The motivating concern behind Nicea was strictly Christian. The doctrinal propositions that resulted from Nicea are strictly Christian. No Greek philosopher ever had to confront the conceptual issues raised at Nicea. Granted, the Nicene Christians shared ontological mentality and systematic statement with the ancient Greeks and with any others who attain a theoretical differentiation of consciousness. But in sharing this mode of conception and expression with others, Christians do not abandon Christianity. Rather, they understand their faith in a new way and express it more precisely. The Christian acceptance of doctrinal propositional statement comes directly from Christian concern for precise expression of meaning. And Christian concern for precision of expression comes directly from Christian concern for what is real. For "what is said" is a most precious human tool for attaining to what is real. So Christians, concerned for what is real, are very careful about what they say. Athanasius' rule and the whole development at Nicea bear witness to this fundamental realization.

The Pastoral Concern at Nicea

I have noted indicators of an emergent differentiation of consciousness within Christianity at Nicea: focus on the cognitive function of meaning, a differentiated understanding of the notion "truth," and an appreciation for the propositional expression of meaning. My attention to these subtle epistemological issues should not obscure the fact that Nicea's basic concern was human salvation. From this other point of view, the bishops of Nicea were very practical men. They were intensely concerned about Jesus Christ, who he is, and what impact he has on our lives. The fact that Nicene discussion pushed Christian teaching to such refinement indicates the intensity of their pastoral concern. Hindsight alone can highlight the subtleties of the development that they achieved. They themselves were not attending explicitly to those epistemological issues. Their prime concern was Jesus Christ and the salvation he wrought and the correct understanding of these two. Nicene insistence on the unqualified divinity of Jesus Christ did not result from logical deduction nor even from deliberately following the "ideal structure" presented above. A guiding force of the Nicene development was this insistence: "If he was not divine, we have not been saved." Certain that only God can save us and committed to Jesus Christ as Savior, the Nicene fathers

113

forcefully insisted that Jesus Christ was not a creature but was God eternal become human. The ruling issue was hardly abstract and speculative. It was very existential. It concerned the ultimate meaning of life and the worth of Christian faith. In its own way and in its new cultural context, Nicea was affirming what Christians had always proclaimed: because of Jesus Christ the ultimate significance of human life was changed. Now there is hope, hope that exceeds the wildest human imagination. God loves us so much as to intervene in our history and become one of us. In so doing, from inside he transformed the meaning of our lives.

Some pastoral implications of this position, clarified at Nicea, deserve comment. The Nicene decree implies that God embraces our very life, literally. God loves us that much. God is so involved with us. According to Arius, God would remain distant. Arius' God is so transcendent that he cannot become involved in human history. To save us that "God" must send a representative, a supreme creature who mediates between God and creation. For Arius, it would be beneath God for God himself to get involved with us. The Christian position is different: God's love for us is extreme. Our contact with God is immediate. The Nicene decree professes an unimaginably loving God.

On the other hand, the Nicene decree implies something about human life, and our world, too. In becoming human, the Eternal Word gives ultimate validation to human life. Humanity is worthy of God! Humanity itself, transformed in Christ, is itself a source of human salvation. The created world, worthy of God, is worthy, too, of our care. Here is the ultimate source of any concern for the earth and the ultimate validation of any incarnational spirituality. Now the words of Deuteronomy take on new meaning:

> For this commandment which I command you this day is not too hard for you, neither is it far off. It is not in heaven, that you should say, "Who will go up for us to heaven, and bring it to us, that we may hear it and do it?" Neither is it beyond the sea, that you should say, "Who will go over the sea for us, and bring it to us, that we may hear it and do it?" But the word is very near you; it is in your mouth and in your heart, so that you can do it. (30:11–14)

We need not—indeed, we must not—flee this world if we would live in God. We are free—indeed, we are obliged—to dedicate ourselves to

114

this world and its inhabitants. All human pursuits, all science, all art and creativity, all industry and government, all human services, all concern for our world—all are worthy of God, and in them we have saving contact with God.

The teaching of Nicea is lofty. The claim of Christianity may even seem pretentious. But it is profoundly paradoxical. "The foolishness of God is wiser than humans" (1 Cor. 1:25). Nicea unequivocally attributes to Jesus Christ the transcendence of absolute divinity. Some may find this preposterous. Yet precisely because of this and in the same stroke, Nicea gives ultimate validation to the created world. If the Eternal Word, God, is also one of us, then all of us, by sheer dint of our humanity, are caught up in the wake of his passage through our history. Nicea's intent and effect are of supreme pastoral importance. Detailed consideration of the epistemological subtleties of the Council must not obscure this fact. Only because of its pastoral implications does Nicea merit such meticulous study. By the same token, such study is necessary. If a deliberate, literal definition of Jesus Christ's absolute divinity cannot be validated in the discussion at Nicea, the linchpin of the entire Christian tradition falls out, the pieces pull apart, and Christianity crumbles. Not just a system of ideas, not a philosophical position, not a body of theological speculation, not simply a complex of doctrinal formulae, but a life-enhancing, vibrant, religious tradition is at stake here. The ultimate significance of the human race and its possibility for fulfillment are at stake here. A religion, unique on this earth, which affirms both the absolute love of God and the ultimate validity of creation might be lost to human history. The practical implications of Nicea and of the present argument are neglected only at mortal peril. For all the subtle intricacies inherent in its debate, in its own way Nicea was an eminently pastoral council.

Christianity's Precarious Status Today

I write with urgency as I consider these things. I began by presenting epistemological presuppositions that allow a reasonable account of the development of christological doctrine from the New Testament, through the Council of Nicea and beyond, to the present day. A differentiation of consciousness emerged within official Christianity at Nicea. Implicitly, yet none the less certainly and really, there was a move from a functional to an ontological mentality. To understand what such a shift means and so to recognize it in the discussion at Nicea is crucial to my overall argument. Only the understanding and appreciation of systematic statement as a valid expression even of religious meaning allows critical acceptance of the decree of Nicea. Such understanding and appreciation is the presupposition *sine qua non;* it is indispensable. Yet because of an epistemological confusion that rules our age, precisely this presupposition is lacking. So even believers of good will are unable to understand the intended meaning of Nicea's decree, and they are unable to discern the continuity of development beyond the New Testament. Nicea's decree is likely to be taken as just another kerygmatic statement, one further insistence that Christians look on Jesus as God. The possibility of saying what is so in itself—Jesus Christ *is* God—is dismissed by many. Christianity becomes one more system of ideas, locked in its own system's boundaries, alongside other such systems, themselves bound by their own limits. The ultimate validity of Christianity is deemed equal to that of any other religion that serves its purpose: to inspire and motivate, to make sense out of life, to give some reason for living—any reason, as long as it works. That religious statements speak about reality in itself is a rare opinion, for such reality is scarcely acknowledged; reality is generally taken to mean only "my reality" or "our reality." That religious statements express valid cognitive meaning is a rare opinion, for objective cognitive meaning is scarcely acknowledged; meaning is generally taken to mean only existential meaning, what something means in practical terms for me and mine. In the aftermath of Nicea, when almost the whole of Christianity had unknowingly accepted the Arian position, Ambrose of Milan—if my memory serves me well—commented on this startling turn of events: "The whole world awoke, surprised to find that it was Arian." The same statement, historically adjusted, could be said of increasingly broad pockets of Christianity today: "They awoke, surprised to find that they were Nietzschean."

A Case in Point

James P. Mackey's *Jesus the Man and the Myth* offers a clear example of the epistemologically confused state of contemporary christology. Reviewers suggest, "for the general reader there is no better book on Jesus."[20] And "*Jesus, The Man and the Myth* is the single

116

most important work on christology to come out of the English-speaking world for the last few decades. It is an outstanding book that will be with us for many years to come. It is destined to become one of the standard texts on Jesus for a long time in the future."[21] This book does stand as a telling specimen of contemporary christology. In this it may, indeed, be a classic. By the same token it stands as a classic example of the widespread position opposed throughout this book.[22] Because of its epistemological presuppositions, Mackey's presentation of Jesus cannot square with the Christian tradition. An extended criticism of *Jesus the Man and the Myth* will clarify my position by contrast with Mackey's.

Mackey's presentation presumes the conciliar christological tradition as summarized in the Council of Chalcedon (451 C.E.). To this extent, his presentation goes beyond the historical account presented thus far. Nonetheless, the watershed is at Nicea. The decree of Nicea already raises and responds to the epistemological issues. What followed merely drew out the logical implications of that decree, as will be shown in the following chapter. Thus, within the present context Mackey's presentation can already be legitimately criticized. Such criticism here will highlight the significance of epistemological presuppositions. The central issue is the understanding of myth and systematic statement as expressions of meaning and then, more particularly, the validity of the differentiation of consciousness that results in ontological mentality and systematic statement.

Mackey's final position on Jesus Christ is summarized as follows: in Jesus we encounter the one, true God. This is so because through Jesus we arrive at the same faith in God as Jesus himself had. Inspiring us to such faith, Jesus allows us to encounter God.[23]

Mackey insists repeatedly that to say "Jesus is God" is short for saying, "In Jesus we meet the one, true God." According to Mackey, this is all the Council of Nicea intended.[24]

Much of what Mackey says is correct. Jesus does inspire us to faith. In that faith we do know the God he called Father. We do have that faith because of Jesus. So we can rightly say that in Jesus we encounter the one, true God. Actually, Mackey presents a profound and complex analysis of the existential effect of Jesus on our lives. This is an important and typically contemporary contribution. Its concern is existential. It focuses on lived faith. But is that all Nicea intended to say about Jesus? Not at all. Nicea and later tradition went further. Mackey's position is not an adequate interpretation of the Council of Nicea. Consider his position.

Is the fact that through Jesus we know God in faith sufficient reason for saying, "Jesus *is* God"? No, not unless we mean merely "Jesus *is* God *for me*" and take this to mean "In Jesus—that is, through Jesus or because of Jesus—I meet the one, true God." But the further question—the one Nicea faced—remains unanswered. Pre-Nicene ambiguity perdures. For I also encounter the one, true God in many other people besides Jesus.

Oh, you object, it is only because of Jesus that I know I am encountering God in other people. It was through Jesus that we learned God is among us.

I grant that. But, then, what is the difference between my encounter with God in Jesus and in others? Is it simply more intense in Jesus, more astounding? Is it for that reason alone that we were tipped off by Jesus to God's presence in humanity? If so, then Jesus is still *only* one of us, and no more. Jesus is merely human, but at the same time he is more fully human, more perfectly human than we; and for that reason he allows us to encounter God in him. Is that it? We call him God for that reason, because he is more perfectly human and so points us to God, allows us to encounter God in him.

Oh, you object, this does not yet do justice to the tradition.

Granted, again; so let us push the issue further and suggest that to be fully and perfectly human is to be God. Then we can allow that Jesus *is* God because he is perfectly human. We, since we are not perfect in our humanity, are not God—not yet, at least. . . .

No, I object this time. This approach does not work either, for it obliterates the distinction between God and humans. God appears to be merely humanity perfected. Let us go back and ask the question again: What is the difference between my encounter with God in Jesus and in others?

Well, you suggest, Jesus is a special representative of God. He was sent particularly to allow us to encounter the one, true God in himself.

Granted, again. But the question still remains: is he God or is he just a mediator sent by God?

Well, he was certainly more than we who are merely human.

118

Granted, again. But I fear the discussion has not yet moved beyond the Arian position: Jesus was sent specially to mediate God to us. He is above all others. So exalted is he that we can even rightly call him Son of God and recognize the divine prerogatives which he exercises. We could even say he is "God from God, Light from Light, true God from true God." But, of course, he really is just a creature— the first creature, the highest creature, mind you, but a creature nonetheless.

Oh, you object to this as well? Does it too clearly contradict Nicea? Well, what other alternative is there? To confess that Jesus is God? Yes, but by this time it should be clear that "Jesus is God" means more than simply "In Jesus we encounter the one, true God."

Yes, Mackey is correct: *in Jesus we do encounter the one, true God;* but this is so because *Jesus is God.* This is what the tradition maintains. And the switch from the one statement to the other entails a shift in mentality, from kerygmatic to ontological mentality. Mackey's account will not allow for this shift. Therefore, it does not allow for the Council of Nicea, either.[25]

Mackey makes it perfectly clear that he rejects the post-New Testament move toward systematic statement.[26] He understands the notion of 'truth' only in its existential sense, the undifferentiated sense that includes feeling, motivation, desire, and action, as well as correct affirmation.[27] ". . . the truth in question here is not truth that can be satisfied with purely mental existence, and with the quiet contemplation which this suggests; it is rather, in the terminology of the Fourth Gospel, a truth which must be done."[28]

Again, as far as it goes, what Mackey says is correct. What Christianity or any religion is about is life and its living. Abstract propositions are not the essence of religion. ". . . the truth that heals is no theoretical system to be accepted in some single act of intellectual assent; it is the lived experience of all life and existence as God's good gift. . . ."[29] Systematic statements—doctrinal propositions—taken out of their context, can be and were misunderstood and misused. However, this misuse does not discredit their intrinsic validity. If precise expression of cognitive meaning is not the essential function of religion, still, no religion concerned about reality can neglect the issue of control of cognitive meaning. A differentiation of consciousness that allows an understanding of truth as correct cognitive meaning is not foreign to Christianity. What occurred at Nicea was no exercise in philosophical speculation. Important pastoral issues were at stake in that council. They could be resolved only by meeting them on the field where they arose. With Arius, Christianity could not refuse to move into ontological mentality. By the same token, Christianity today cannot refuse to deal with fundamental, subtle, and technical epistemological issues. To point to abuses and so reject a whole era of Christian history is irresponsible. To flee into obscurantism, to ignore further questions, to retreat to myth in the twentieth century, is unacceptable. Cliches come to mind: "To bury one's head in the sand," "To throw out the baby with the bath water." One can go too far.[30]

Mackey's reaction to abuses is to reject a major development within the Christian tradition. He does this deliberately. He admits his reason. Unbelievable as it seems, it is as follows: to distinguish functional and ontological mentalities—Mackey speaks in terms of function and nature—implies burdensome presuppositions. Briefly, the issue is too difficult to deal with! In his own words:

> One is sometimes at a loss to know precisely what is being suggested by such distinctions and discriminations . . .

> It seems to the present writer to be quite futile, in any case, to try to plot one's way through the intricacies of the early tradition about Jesus while one is burdened by any of the above presuppositions . . .

> So let us simply pursue our quest for the history and logic of the development of the myth of Jesus through its most formative years, *bearing in mind no further distinctions of Jew or Greek, Bible or philosophy, function or nature, bearing only in mind what has already been said in an earlier section on myth. . . .*[31]

Mackey's practical response, again unbelievable as it seems, is this: treat all statements as functional, regardless of their origin. For example,

> Nature, in short, is a functional term. To say that there are two natures, divine and human, in Jesus or more accurately that one and the same Christ is manifest in two natures, is simply tantamount to saying . . . that *Jesus functions as man and as God,* since in Jesus they [Jesus' followers] encounter one like themselves in all things, except that he was no sinner, and they also encounter the one, true God.[32]

120

Mackey's position is in obvious opposition with the generally accepted reading of the Christian tradition. And Mackey is well aware of this. He formulates his position quite deliberately. That is why his book is so good an example of a major school of contemporary thought. He knows that others understand the Councils clearly to teach that the Eternal Son, the Word of God, is the ultimate identity of Jesus Christ. Mackey responds that that is just one way of reading the evidence.[33]

Again we are faced with the issue of proving "beyond any doubt."[34] Again we are faced with the issue of different possible "trajectories" for the development of the Christian tradition.[35] I have already commented on these issues. I will not do so again. Instead, I will make two summary observations.

First, as a cautious historian, Mackey may well be correct. It may well be "scarcely possible to prove beyond any doubt that the Chalcedonian formula requires that we" conclude Jesus Christ is the Word of God.[36] Still, for a comprehensive christological position, this historical detail pales in significance in light of later conciliar teaching. The Second Council of Constantinople (553 c.e.) clarified the record beyond doubt. Constantinople II teaches that the Divine Word who became incarnate as Jesus Christ is one of the Holy Trinity.[37] This is to say, there is further evidence on the question, evidence which Mackey's position does not take into account.

Second, the root difference between Mackey's position and the one presented here is presuppositional. Because of his overriding concern for myth, his appreciation of the New Testament as mythic expression, his awareness of absurd excesses to which misunderstood systematic statements about religious issues might be taken, his reluctance to grant a cognitive as well as an existential import to religious statements, and his decision not to deal with the epistemological issues raised by post-New Testament christological discussion—because of all this, Mackey's position retains a New Testament mentality even when dealing with post-New Testament developments. His position canonizes the functional mentality and anathematizes the ontological mentality. His position views all statements as kerygmatic—or, in his terms, mythic—and disallows systematic statement. So his position cannot deal with the conciliar christological development, which then somehow must be discredited. Another set of

121

presuppositions, such as I have presented, can deal with New Testament christology as well as with later conciliar development. On these presuppositions, the whole account is coherent, consistent, developmental, and reasonable, adequate to the evidence. This is what has been shown here. Then where one stands on the issue depends on one's choice. For Christianity can represent a fully reasonable choice. Does one want to claim for one's own Christianity as it has been traditionally understood, or not? Does one choose to stand within the Christian tradition, or outside of it? This choice, too, is one of the critical presuppositions which determines the course of the christological enterprise. The difference between Mackey's position and my own is presuppositional. The presuppositional is constitutive of the contemporary problematic.

Summary

Certain epistemological presuppositions, common in contemporary culture and explicitly embraced by James Mackey, preclude the outright acceptance of traditional Christian belief about Jesus Christ, defined at the Council of Nicea. In contrast, other presuppositions allow that there was a legitimate development at the Council of Nicea. The development was double. Nicea clarified the status of Jesus Christ as absolutely divine. Nicea also ushered Christianity into an era of ontological thinking. These two achievements are intertwined. Acknowledgment of the one entails acknowledgment of the other. They mutually condition one another.

By acknowledging the epistemological issue, one is also able to acknowledge and affirm the christological issue and to present a reasonable account of the development through Nicea. According to the cumulative evidence of the New Testament, Christians relate to Jesus as to God. Arius raised the further question: but is he God? Arius urged this question not by asking how Christians look on Jesus but by asking whether or not Jesus Christ, the Word and Son of God, is a creature. The Council of Nicea responded in the terms in which the question was posed. The Council answered out of an ontological mentality and in systematically formulated statements: the one Lord, Jesus Christ, eternally begotten of the Father, is not a creature; he is of the same stuff as the Father.

As is to be expected, Nicea's christological clarification raised

122

other questions. As is also to be expected, these questions were answered within the same ontological mentality that prevailed at Nicea. Accepting the validity of this mentality, the following chapter will summarize post-Nicene conciliar teaching about Jesus Christ. Using the tools of contemporary historical scholarship and epistemological awareness, it will retrieve the tradition from the past and bring it up to the present. By the end of that chapter, this book will have dealt with the contemporary problematic and with the retrieval of the tradition within that problematic. Finally, then, Chapter Eight will present a comprehensive account of Jesus Christ—the same Jesus whom the Christian tradition always affirmed—as he appears in light of contemporary scholarship.

CHAPTER SEVEN

Christological Development after Nicea

Nicea clarified the absolute divine status of Jesus Christ. Thus, that council went beyond New Testament teaching. Not only do Christians look on Jesus as God. Jesus is God, literally so.

This new clarification of Christian belief turned christological thought in a new direction. The prime question was no longer, Who/What is Jesus Christ? Now the prime question was, How can Jesus Christ be both God and a human? In one way or another, subsequent ecumenical councils responded to this new question. Step by step, Christian understanding of Jesus Christ was further clarified. The present chapter summarizes this further clarification.[1]

The main concern of this book is not to present a detailed history of christology. Rather, it is to present a reasonable account of the christological development inherent in that history. The ultimate goal is to present a contemporary understanding of Jesus Christ which is still in accord with traditional teaching about Jesus. Accordingly, this chapter, too, will focus on doctrinal issues. It will consider the post-Nicene christological councils: Constantinople I, Ephesus, Chalcedon, and Constantinople III.[2] But it will use these councils more as occasions to discuss doctrinal issues than as specific topics of historical interest. It will not be so concerned to limit discussion to what can

125

be said on the basis of only the particular council in question. Rather, it will introduce into the discussion considerations that, in fact, emerged only at later times. That is, it will interpret these conciliar teachings in light of both medieval theology and, especially, the presuppositions noted at the beginning of this study. This chapter completes the contemporary retrieval of traditional Christian belief about Jesus. It completes the doctrinal foundation for the contemporary christology which is to follow.

Jesus' Complete Humanity: Constantinople I and III

After the Council of Nicea, various attempts were made to explain how Jesus could be God and still be a human being. Apollinarius, one-time bishop of Laodicea, made one such famous attempt. His teaching was condemned at the First Council of Constantinople in 381 C.E. Little is known for certain about Apollinarius' teaching. Most of his writings have been lost. This much is known: Apollinarius' teaching implied that Jesus was not a complete human being.

Apollinarius' concerns were quite legitimate. He wanted to insist on the unity of the Word of God and Jesus Christ: they are one and the same. It is not as if the Eternal Word came to dwell in the man Jesus at his baptism or some other time after his birth, as Paul of Samosata and others had suggested. This unacceptable position is called adoptionism: the Word "adopted" the human individual, Jesus, and dwelt in him as a companion. No, Jesus and the Word are one. Furthermore, Apollinarius wanted to insist that Jesus was holy—not just accidentally nor even just voluntarily but necessarily holy by his very constitution. To meet these concerns Apollinarius suggested that the union of the human and divine in Jesus is like that of the body and soul in the human being. For Apollinarius, the divine Word—the Logos—takes the place of the human soul in Christ. Thus, humanity and divinity are united, the Word and Jesus Christ are one, and Jesus' holiness flows inextricably from the Eternal Word in him.

According to another account, Apollinarius' position is more subtle. The human is constituted of body, soul, and also spirit. "Spirit" is here considered the highest dimension of humanity, sometimes equated with what we call reason, and named with the Greek term *nous*. According to this account, the Divine Logos takes the place

126

not of the soul but of the *nous* in Christ. Thus, at the apex of the human in Jesus is the Divine Word. Again, Apollinarius' concerns are met.

If Apollinarius' position as summarized here seems simplistic, it is. For one thing, we have no complete statement from Apollinarius himself. We can only generally summarize his position. For another thing, it is no easy matter to determine the essential factors that constitute the human. Even today there is no agreement whatever on this question. We are still left to choose our favorite formula: the human is body and soul; the human is body, psyche, and spirit; the human is body, mind, and spirit; the human is body, soul, mind, and spirit. In addition, Greek, Hebrew, Buddhist, Hindu, and other accounts could provide still more options. For Apollinarius the Logos replaced the human soul or human spirit in Jesus. That we might wonder exactly what this means is understandable. Yet, regardless of what it might mean, the point to be made is clear: Jesus Christ is not a complete human being if he lacks something that other humans have. Apollinarius' Christ is not really human.

On precisely this point Constantinople I condemned Apollinarius' teaching. The arguments were simple. Jesus Christ was truly human, so he had a human mind or rationality. Moreover, the Word became flesh to save us, so he must have taken on everything that humans are. If he did not have a human mind, the human mind was not saved and we are not fully saved. Here the slogan was, "What was not taken on was not saved." The insistence was that we are completely saved, so Jesus must have been completely human in every way that we are. He had a human mind or rationality. In 362 C.E., Athanasius, still alive and still involved in christological debate, phrased the issue this way:

> The Redeemer did not have a body that was inanimate or non-emotional or non-rational. For because the Lord became man for our sake, it was impossible that his body be non-rational, and in the Word took place the salvation not only of the body but also of the soul.[3]

The Council of Constantinople ratified this teaching. It insisted that Jesus did have a human mind (or soul or rationality).

Church teaching about Jesus' full humanity was further elaborated in the Third Council of Constantinople in 680–81 C.E. The question at Constantinople III centered not around Jesus' mind but around his will.

We commonly use the term 'will' in two different senses. When we say "to do God's will," we mean to follow a particular plan, a particular choice. Here 'will' has an existential meaning and refers to what we choose. But 'will' also refers to the principle of freedom that allows us to choose: "I have free will." Discussion at Constantinople III was concerned with Jesus' will in this second sense, the ontological sense. The question was, Did Jesus have a human will and a divine will, or did he have only one will, the divine one?

It is easy to understand how this question arose. The tradition insists that Jesus always followed the will of the Father. There was never any deviation from the divine will in him. Still, if Jesus had a human will as well as a divine will, there might be the possibility that his human will would not be in harmony with the divine will. Banish the thought! Concern for the absolute and necessary holiness of Jesus could not tolerate the suggestion of possible deviation between Jesus' will and the divine will. The two were always in perfect harmony. Phrase the issue another way and the point becomes even clearer: Jesus' will and the Father's will were one! The harmony was so absolute, it was suggested, that one should not speak of two wills but only of one. The insistence was that there is only one will in Christ, or said differently, only one principle of activity, one "energy," one "operation." This position is called monothelitism—from the Greek: *mono* means one, and *thelein* means to will. Monothelitism holds there is only one will in Jesus Christ, the divine will. According to monothelitism, Jesus always did the will of the Father because the divine will was the sole source of free activity in Jesus. Accordingly, Jesus was perfectly and necessarily holy. And in his perfect holiness, he, a human being, was our salvation.

The Third Council of Constantinople condemned monothelitism for the same reason the First Council of Constantinople condemned Apollinarius' position: trying to affirm the perfect unity of the human and divine in Christ, both compromised the full humanity of Jesus Christ. Constantinople III taught that Jesus Christ, like every other human being, has a human will. Jesus lived his life exercising human freedom just as every human does.

The composite teaching of Constantinople I and III is that Jesus

Christ is a complete human being. He has a human mind and a human free will. Said in more general and contemporary terms, Jesus has a human consciousness. He has a complete human psychology. Whatever is true of us mentally, psychologically, psychically, spiritually—or in whatever other terms you prefer to indicate that by which humans differ from brute beasts—that same is true of Jesus Christ. And because Jesus has human consciousness, he also has human knowledge, human understanding, human responsibility, human feelings, human experience, human intuition, human intelligence, human creativity, and all the rest. Jesus is totally and completely human. In technical terms, Jesus has a human nature; he has that which makes one human.

Unlike us, however, Jesus is also God. That means he also has a divine consciousness. And with that divine consciousness he has divine understanding, divine knowledge, divine freedom. So Jesus Christ has two minds, two freedoms—two consciousnesses, one divine and one human.

Already the specter of a schizophrenic being arises. This very specter leads many contemporary christologists to be very cautious, even hesitant, to speak about Jesus' divinity. Insisting that Jesus has two consciousnesses, we might begin to think of Jesus as some "split personality," switching from one mind to another as circumstances dictate. More will be said about this. Christian history did not ignore so obvious and crucial an issue. Here it is sufficient to note that Jesus was completely and fully human. The christology from above, which we generally learned, so emphasized Jesus' divinity as to obscure his real humanity. Nonetheless, the same conciliar tradition which in practice fostered emphasis on divinity also gives solid support to emphasis on Jesus' humanity. Contemporary concern to see Jesus more human has all the doctrinal basis needed in the early christological councils of the Church.

One Identity in Jesus: Ephesus

One result of Constantinople I was to highlight the duality in Jesus Christ: he is divine and he is human, absolutely so in each case. The next important christological debate focused on the unity in Christ. The central figure in this debate was Nestorius, a monk of Antioch and later (428 C.E.) bishop of Constantinople. Nestorius' leading opponent was Cyril, bishop of Alexandria. Political rivalry between these two important sees and the schools of thought associated with each played no small part in this debate.[4]

Nestorius was worried about devotion to Mary as Mother of God. Leading theologians had long called Mary *Theotokos*, Mother of God— from the Greek: *theos* means God, and *tokos* means bearer. Now popular piety was more and more commonly using this title. Nestorius thought the title inaccurate and its continued usage dangerously misleading. He argued, Mary was not the mother of God but the mother of Christ. He began to teach and insist on this in Constantinople.

Cyril of Alexandria and others, including Pope Celestine, objected to Nestorius' teaching. To say Mary was mother of Christ but not mother of God was to suggest that there were two in Christ, one who was born of God and another who was born of Mary. Nestorius' teaching suggested there were two individuals in Christ, one divine individual and one human individual. This smacked of adoptionism. For Jesus Christ and the Eternal Word are one and the same. They are one individual, one identity.

The Council of Ephesus in 431 C.E. resolved this debate by condemning Nestorius' position. The argument of the Council was straightforward and logical. Once the ontological mentality was in sway, further clarifications could be made almost by mere deduction. Since correct propositions indicate what is real, further analysis of those propositions and intelligent insight into their meaning can further clarify reality. Thus, following the creed from Nicea, the bishops noted that there was only one grammatical subject for all that was said about the Son of God:

> We believe in one Lord, *Jesus Christ,*
>> *who* was born of the Father as only begotten . . .
>> who came down from heaven, was made flesh, became human. . . .

The argument was a sheer logical exercise, an analysis of propositions. "What was said" at Nicea became the indicator for what should be said at Ephesus.[5] According to the creed, the *one who* was born eternally of God is the same *one who* was born in time of Mary. The subject does not change. Only one subject is in question. Only one identity is in question, only one individual. There is only *one*

130

who did a number of different things: this one was born of God and the same one was also born of Mary. Whatever is said about this one is predicated always of the one and the same one: born of the Father, God from God, agent in creation, born in the flesh, suffered, died, rose for our salvation. So the Council declared that Mary is rightly called Mother of God, *Theotokos*. For the *one who* was born of her is, indeed, the Son of God.

The teaching of Ephesus is subtle and profound; its implications are far-reaching. Further considerations will clarify the issue.

Nestorius was correct in insisting that divinity is not born in time. God is eternal. God, *as God*, has no beginning in time. It is absurd to suggest that Mary is the source of divinity. If this is all Nestorius meant to teach, he was perfectly correct.

However, the way Nestorius spoke suggested there were two *who* were in Christ—two "who's," if you will. The man born of Mary was one, and the Eternal Son of God was the other. For if Mary was not the mother of God, the Eternal Son, she must have given birth to someone else, to another individual called "Christ." Then Christ and the Eternal Son were not one and the same individual. Thus, Nestorius' argument implied that there were two subjects in Christ, *two who* were in Christ. As we saw, this position differs both from a grammatical analysis of the Nicene Creed and from traditional affirmations about Jesus Christ: there is only one who is begotten eternally of the Father and was born in time of Mary.

Here is another way of approaching the same issue. Consider this. What is it that is born of a woman? Is it a body that comes forth? No, not unless the birth is stillborn. Is it a body and a mind that comes forth? That is, is it a human nature that comes forth? Does a woman give birth to a "humanity"? No. What is born is *someone*. A particular individual is born. Someone, this one and not that one, a particular identity, is born. Now, Nestorius' position suggests that what was born of Mary was Jesus' humanity, his human nature: Mary was the mother of the human in Christ. But mothers do not give birth to human natures. They give birth to people, to "someones." Then who was the someone born of Mary? What was the ultimate identity of Mary's child? Ephesus insisted that the someone born of Mary is the one and the same someone who is born eternally of God the Father. So the one born of Mary is

131

Son of God; that is *who* Mary's child is. Then it is completely correct to say that God was indeed born of Mary at a particular point in time—born, of course, as human.

Note a practical implication of this teaching. There is an important difference between God in Jesus Christ and God in us. In me there is a distinction between God-in-me and myself. I am not God, though God is in me. I was not eternally. Rather, I had a beginning in time, namely, when I was born of my mother. In no way do I suppose that I am eternal. Jesus' case is different. In him there is no distinction between God in him and himself. Jesus *is* the Eternal Son, he is God. So there is strict identity between God-in-Jesus and Jesus himself. He is himself. He is God the Eternal Son. The one who was born as a human baby, Jesus, was no other than the Eternal Son of the Father. In this Jesus differs from us, who also have God in us, but in another way. Though in some sense we are all divine, Jesus' way of being divine is different from ours.[6] Moreover, he was eternally. His existence did not begin only when he was born of Mary. Indeed, his human existence began then, but the one born of Mary had already existed in God eternally.

Eastern philosophies, and much contemporary spirituality inspired by them, attribute to us what Christianity attributes only to Jesus Christ. They suggest that we existed before this earthly life we now live. Then talk of "prior lives" arises. These philosophies find it difficult to conceive that we simply were not before we were conceived and born of our parents. These philosophies suggest we have some kind of an eternal existence. The further implication is that we are some part of the Eternal, that at the depth of the mystery of our being is really the divine. In other words, we are really God—or sparks of the divine, or weak emanations of the divine. In one way or another, we are supposedly chips off the Old Block! Here is an important difference between Christianity and those other philosophies. Christianity makes an inviolable distinction between God and us, between creator and created. It insists that we were created, we had a beginning in time. It insists that Jesus Christ as human also had a beginning in time; he was born of Mary. But his existence is eternal. The one born of Mary is eternally as God. He exists before he was born into our world. On this score, there is a chasm of difference between Jesus Christ and us. These issues, so relevant in spiritual circles today, were at stake in the Council of Ephesus. Appreciation of them offers another way of understanding what Ephesus meant.

Persons and Natures

With the above considerations, I hope to have suggested the meaning of the terms 'person' and 'nature' as developed at Ephesus. We are all well aware that traditional christology is phrased in terms of "one person and two natures." This summary phrase was canonized only by the later Council of Chalcedon, but the notions 'person' and 'nature' are at the heart of the discussion at Ephesus and need to be treated here. The meaning of these terms is not always clear. The difficulty is multiple. Not only are the technical terms subtle in what they mean. They are also now used in a sense completely different from what they meant at Ephesus.

We use the term "person" frequently. We say, "Treat me like a person." "I have feelings as well as you; I'm a person, too." "Every person is entitled to certain rights. Each has a dignity that should be respected." "What a magnificent person she is! So sensitive, so compassionate, so intelligent, so fair!" We also use the term in adjectival forms and in compounds. "Well, if you really want to get personal, let me tell you how I feel." "He is so personable. I always feel so at ease with him." "Interpersonal relationships are the most important part of life."

There is a general meaning behind all these usages. In today's language, "person" comes to be another way of saying *"human being"*—with emphasis on the "human." The word "person" emphasizes those characteristics that are peculiarly human. "I'm a person" means I have feelings, rights, thoughts, responsibility. The terms "personable" and "interpersonal" emphasize the fact that humans are relational beings. One of our most precious capacities is to share deeply with others and to develop bonds of intimacy. We use the term "person" to highlight that about us which gives us special dignity and worth, which demands some reverence, which makes us different from things or brute animals. That is to say, today the term "person" indicates *what kind* of a being is in question. In most instances, person is another word for human. According to common understanding, only humans are persons, and to be a person is to be human. To name someone a person is to emphasize the humanity of that one. All the characteristics that define persons are qualities of humanity: intelligence, sensitivity, responsibility for one's own life, creativity, capacity for intimacy and love.

This usage is in sharp contrast with the classical meaning of the term 'person,' as developed in the christological councils and medieval philosophy. What we today commonly mean by "person" is what classical usage referred to as "nature." The term 'nature' indicates *what kind* of a being is in question. If one has a human nature, then one is human and so is sensitive, creative, intelligent, responsible for one's own life, capable of intimacy and love, worthy of respect and reverence, and all the rest. These are the characteristics that determine human beings in contrast to other beings—rocks, trees, animals. In today's usage "person" means what the classical term "nature" meant. At the same time, the contemporary term "nature" is still used fairly often to mean what the classical term "nature" meant. When I say "That man has a vile nature," or "His behavior is an insult to human nature," I am indicating what kind of an individual someone is. In this case, I am suggesting someone's behavior is far below the quality it can have and ideally should have. The term 'nature' can still generally indicate *what*, or *what kind* of thing, something or someone is. Therefore, in today's usage both "person" and "nature" generally mean about the same thing as the classical term 'nature' meant. The result is that there is no term left over to indicate what the classical term 'person' indicated. So the notion is foreign to us. It is very difficult to construe. It even seems irrelevant.[7] It is not part of our common thinking. Still, the issue is critical. It is part of what was at stake at the Council of Ephesus.

According to Ephesus, to be a person and to be human are not the same thing. Ephesus insists on a distinction between *who* was born of Mary and *what kind* that one was as born of Mary. Jesus Christ as born of Mary was human; that is what kind of being he was. But *who* was born of Mary? A divine someone, the Eternal Word. So *who* one is and *what kind* one is are not the same thing. The term 'person' indicates the "who." The term 'nature' indicates that "what" or "what kind." *What* Jesus is because of his birth from Mary is human. He is what all of us are. He is now the same kind of being as we are. He shares the same nature as we do. But *who* Jesus is, even though born of Mary, is not determined by that birth from Mary. His ultimate identity is not a human thing. He was in God eternally before he was born of Mary. He has an eternal identity. This determines *who* he is. The same one who was born eternally of the Father was born in time of Mary. That one is a divine one, the Eternal Son of God. A divine someone took on a human way of being. A divine person took on a human nature. That one who was eternally in God took on a new way of being, a human way of being. His way of being was then human. But who he was was not human. That is to say, Jesus Christ is a divine person, even though through Mary he took on a human way of being. Ephesus insists that to understand Jesus Christ properly, we must make a distinction between the *who* and the *what* in Jesus.

The point of the last paragraph is, I hope, clear enough. It is nothing more than the point of Ephesus. To say, then, that Jesus is a divine person may also seem clear enough. At least the phrase is familiar; it is traditional teaching in traditional terminology. Yet what happens if we remain faithful to Ephesus and draw out the logical implication? If Jesus Christ is a divine person and there is only one person in Jesus Christ, then *Jesus Christ is not a human person.*[8] This conclusion is acceptable enough as long as the terms are understood in their classical meaning. But take that same statement out of the context developed here, take it out onto the street or into the pulpit, confuse the systematic with the kerygmatic, and what would be heard would be offensive. What that statement means according to common usage of the terms is, indeed, heretical. According to everyday usage, to say "Jesus is not a human person" is to say "He is not human, he is not really like us." Not only is this offensive to Christian piety, it is a position condemned by Constantinople I and III, as we have already seen. For Jesus is completely, wholly human. Obviously, the real issue here is terminology. The dilemma is clear. What is fully ortho-dox to the classical ear: "Jesus Christ is not a human person," is fully heretical to the contemporary ear: "Jesus Christ is not really human."

The above exposition of the Council of Ephesus avoided this terminological dilemma. That exposition did not employ the term 'person' but offered substitutes: "who," "the one and the same one who," "the subject," "someone," "one," "an individual," "an iden-tity," "ultimate identity." These substitutes are far from perfect. Bor-rowed from commonsense usage, they are used to *suggest* a technical meaning. The clearest of them is the first. It suggests a distinction between *who* someone is and *what* someone is: I am Daniel and I am human, I am a theologian, I am an American. Yet English grammar renders this substitute least manageable. In German one could speak of *das Wer* and *das Was*. In English it is awkward to make a noun of "who" and speak of a divine "who" who took on a human "what," or to say there is only one "who" in Jesus and that one "who" is divine. It is to be hoped that, despite the strange grammatical form, the meaning comes through. For that meaning is quite precisely what the classical terms 'person' and 'nature' intend.

Something similar must be said about the other suggested substitutes for the classical term 'person.' Take "identity," for example. In every case—except Jesus'—an identity is determined by one's biography. I indicate *who* I am by giving my name and by stating who my parents are, where I was born, and what I've done. My history determines my identity. According to common understanding, who I am is what I have done. Commonly, identity is determined by the "what's" in one's life. So "identity" is not a perfect substitute for "person." This is clear in the case of Jesus Christ. His identity is determined eternally in his relationship with the Father. One cannot truly say who he is by indicating his birth at Bethlehem and noting his life's achievements. Of course, by analogy one could suggest who he is—his identity—by stating who his Eternal Parent is and where he was born: eternally "in heaven." Yet the imagery here begins to boggle the critical mind. So in suggesting "an identity" as a substitute for the classical term "person," I am also suggesting a new meaning for the term 'identity'. And this is so for all the other suggested substitutes as well.

The substitute terminology offered here is kerygmatic in form. It attempts to meet popular need by creative use of ordinary terms. Whether anyone understands these terms correctly depends on whether he or she grasps the meaning of the terms in the descriptive, suggestive use made of them. Unfortunately, the subtleties of christological doctrine cannot be expressed accurately in easy, popular statements. In popular usage words mean different things to different people. Popular formulations simply cannot be adequate for precise theology. Somewhere, someone has to be able to explain the beliefs in precise, technical terms. Otherwise, beliefs, like metaphors gone berserk, come to mean whatever anyone wants to make them mean.

136

Hence the need for systematics. If these suggestive accounts of the teaching of Ephesus have sparked deeper understanding in some people, the intended purpose is well on its way to being achieved. Then perhaps these alternative terms may be useful for popular preaching and teaching. If for others the issue is still opaque, this is understandable. What exactly the terms 'person' and 'nature' mean can be expressed only systematically. The following section will present such a systematic definition.

The subtle distinction between who and what someone is arises only in Christianity. The distinction is critical to all Christian theology. Not only does this distinction allow us to speak of one divine person—Jesus Christ, the Eternal Word—in two natures, human and divine. It also allows talk of three divine persons—Father, Son, and Holy Spirit—in one divine nature. Hence, it is a key to the doctrine of the Trinity. And the same distinction allows talk of many human persons—I, you, and all others—coming to share in the one divine nature. So it is also a key to the doctrines of Church, grace, and divinization, ultimate "beatitude" is "heaven." The distinction is central for an account of the Christian understanding of Christ, Trinity, Church, and human salvation. The distinction locks together the understanding of the core doctrines of Christianity. The distinction is a master key to a comprehensive Christian systematic theology. Yet the distinction arises only because of Christian belief about Jesus Christ. With what other issue would one be pushed to make such a distinction? None. The source of this distinction is certainly not Hellenism or excessive rationality. The source is Christian belief about Jesus, as clarified at the Council of Nicea and presupposed in the New Testament writings and grounded in the historical Jesus. In Jesus Christ alone do we have an instance of a human being whose ultimate identity is not human. Every other human being we know is also a human "who." Who would suspect that the two are not necessarily the same thing? No one. So it is that common usage gets by easily enough without this distinction. Common usage can ignore the possible difference between "person" and "nature." It can identify who one is with what one is and what one does. But systematic christology cannot get by without this distinction. In Jesus Christ it is crucial to distinguish who he is: the Eternally Begotten of the Father, from what he is: divine and through Mary also human. Eliminate this distinction and not only does Christian doctrine about Jesus Christ dissolve, but so do the doctrines of the Trinity, Church, and grace. The essence of Christianity is at stake here.

Systematic Definition of Person and Nature

With a variety of approaches, I have been suggesting the meaning of Ephesus' teaching about Jesus Christ. Inherent in this teaching and central to it is the distinction between person and nature. As noted above, contemporary usage has no term to indicate what "person" meant in classical usage. The meaning is not part of our everyday awareness, so there is no term to point to it. Nor is it part of the awareness in most contemporary philosophical thought. Today's thought about human beings focuses on the psychological, sociological, historical, and relational—on the existential, on *the experiences of living*. Elaboration of this dimension of human reality is the contemporary contribution to our on-going understanding of the human. Classical thought, on the other hand, focuses more on the ontological, on the determination of what is or is not as *the conditions for the possibility of any human experience whatsoever*. Current psychological and existential awareness have redefined the classical terms that originally indicated ontological understandings. Today, concern for the ontological is generally lacking and, where it does emerge, it is often belittled and disallowed. The resulting terminological dilemma is not easy to resolve. In the last analysis, since the main issue is ontological, adequate terminology can only be developed within an ontological mentality, and the requisite terms must be systematic in form. Therefore, to bring this discussion of "person" and "nature" to its ultimate resolution, there follows also a systematic understanding of these terms, grounded in the epistemological presuppositions expressed in Chapter Two.[9]

Recall that knowledge is the result of a process. The process involves three levels of conscious operations: 1) awareness of data, 2) understanding of the data, and 3) verification of the understanding in the data. The result of level 2) is an idea, a hypothesis, a possible explanation of the data. The result of level 3) is fact, correct and accurate understanding, formulated expression of what really is. These three levels articulate human consciousness insofar as it moves from experience of reality to knowledge of reality. These levels articulate the cognitive structure of human consciousness.

138

The operations on the second level—wondering, understanding, conceiving, formulating—are responses to the question, What is it? What kind is it? The operations on the third level—reflecting, marshalling and weighing the evidence, judging—are responses to the question, Is it? Is it so? Accordingly, these two levels are parallels in the structure of human consciousness to two aspects of reality: what something is and that it is or, said otherwise, to be something and to be. This analysis grounds in consciousness the classical philosophical notions, essence and existence.

As is obvious, to be something and to be—essence and existence—are inseparable. We never know something unless it is, and nothing is unless it is something. We could never determine the essence of a thing unless it were there existing to be known, and everything that exists has an essence that can be determined. These two aspects are inseparable. Nevertheless, they are distinct. They are distinct both in consciousness and in reality.

They are distinct in consciousness. The operations that determine the second and third levels of consciousness are different from one another. Understanding what something is is different from judging that an understanding is correct. Understanding that something is a particular kind of thing is different from affirming that that something actually exists. Moreover, it is possible to conceive something that does not really exist. The unicorn is a popular example. In the mind essence and existence are not only distinct but also separable. So the second and third levels of conscious operations are certainly distinct in consciousness.

Essence and existence, that which these two levels of consciousness intend, are also distinct in reality. This can be realized by considering that existence is not a necessary part of anything we know in this world. Nothing has to exist. The fact that things do exist must be posited over and above any understanding of what is existing. No reality we know in this world has existence as a necessary aspect of its essence. Take humanity, for example. Human nature, in and of itself, does not include existence as an essential factor. Granted, we know no human who does not exist. Yet we are well aware that the existence which any one of us has is contingent. It could not be. In fact, we exist. But that existence is simply a matter of fact, not a matter of necessity. It is contingent. It is completely possible that we—some of us or all of us—could not exist. There is a real distinction between any essence and its existence. The one aspect is not the other. According to classical theology, only in God is existence necessarily included in essence. God exists necessarily. To exist is an essential quality of what God is. One could say that God's essence is existence. The same cannot be said for any creature. The very meaning of the term "creature" implies as much. Everything created only happens to be. It does not exist necessarily. Its essence does not entail existence. It is not self-explanatory. It requires something outside itself, God, to explain its existence. In reality, as well as in consciousness, essence and existence are really distinct.

Persons in General and Human Persons

Within this background, the meaning of "nature" and "person" becomes clear. The real distinction between the second and third levels of consciousness grounds the distinction in reality between essence and existence. The real distinction between essence and existence in reality grounds the distinction between nature and person.[10] "Nature" is a parallel to the second level of consciousness. It refers to one's essence. It responds to the question, What? or What kind? And the answer is, Human, and one can then go on to specify what it means to be "human." On the other hand, "person" is a parallel to the third level of consciousness. It refers to one's existence. It responds to the question, Is it? And the answer is, Yes, this is a really existing human: a person. As a correlate of the third level of consciousness, the term "person" indicates the reality of one's being, it focuses on the existence that makes one really be. As a correlate of the second level of consciousness, "nature" indicates the "whatness" of one's being, the humanity. One's human nature distinguishes one from other possible kinds of persons—say, divine or angelic or, in a science fiction world, Martian or Plutonian persons.

Mark this well. "Person" is not a synonym for "existence." A human being is not a combination of person plus nature. Rather, the person is the whole individual. The person is that which is—or more accurately, the one who is. Still, the emphasis of the term 'person' is on the actual existence of the one existing. And the emphasis of the term 'nature' is on the qualities or characteristics—the kind—of the one existing.

Thomas Aquinas defines person as *subsistens distinctum in natura intellectuali:* a distinct subsistent (or existent) in an intellectual nature. The first part of the definition indicates what is determinative of person: a person is an existent, that is, one that really does exist; and a person is a distinct existent, that is, one who is this one and no other. The second part of the definition indicates what kind one is: one in an intellectual nature, that is, one that has mind and will, one that can understand, know, and love. According to the medieval mind, there are three kinds of intellectual natures: divine, angelic, and human. So there are three possible kinds of persons: divine, angelic, and human. Modern speculation on intelligent life on other planets introduces the possibility of still other kinds of persons. In any case, wherever there is an instance of one of these natures really existing, there also is a person. Because these existents are special compared to all other things that exist, a special term designates them. They are not called "things" but "persons."

Granted this understanding, one could go on to spell out more about what a person is like. One could fill out an understanding of the reality that the definition specifies. Observing the persons that we know best, humans, contemporary thought does just that. We conclude that persons are perceptive, intelligent, thoughtful, self-determining, creative, sensitive, loving, interrelating, communicative, developing, worthy of respect, and all the rest. So contemporary concerns and understandings about persons do fit into the classical understanding of person—but they fit as filling out the understanding of human *nature.* They say more and more about *what kind* a *human* is. They speak about *human* persons and really do not attempt to specify what persons in general are, as medieval thinkers did.

Indeed, the classical definition of person does highlight a valid and important consideration. In the classical understanding, the determinative factor about a person is the actual existence of the person. This actual existence, so often taken for granted, is crucial. It deserves to be highlighted. After all, in the case of all created reality, existence is contingent. It is not a necessary given. It cannot be taken for granted. The classical understanding of person highlights this crucial factor. In the classical definition, that which makes a person a person is the *actual existence* of an intellectual nature. In this sense, person correlates with existence and so with the third level of consciousness. In contrast, according to contemporary usage, the term "person" indicates all those qualities that make one human—it points to *what* or *what kind* one is. And contemporary usage has no easy way of highlighting the forgotten factor, created existence. But according to the classical definition, actual existence determines "person." 'Person' means a particular kind of actual existent—not something but someone, a "person."

On this understanding, my ultimate identity is determined not by *what* I am as human or even by *what* I am as having a biography different from every other human's biography. Rather, my ultimate identity is determined by the creative act of God that makes me be. My "who" is the direct historical expression of the existence, given by God, that makes me be.

On this basis, it is possible to understand how I am irreducibly unique and distinct from every other human being. The distinctness of my identity, determined ultimately by the existence that makes me and no other be, is inviolable. Consider the possibilities.

Abstractly conceived, I am human, just as is every other human being. Still, no one else is I. My humanity is uniquely mine because of the created existence that makes me—a really existing human—be. That I am makes me be myself and no other. Though in the abstract my humanity is the same as every human's, the existence that makes me me also makes me distinct from every other human. The same holds true also in the concrete. My biography may overlap that of others. We may have much in common. From the point of view of what we have made of ourselves in our actual lives, concretely, we may be the same. Think, for example, of people of the same nationality group or family members or spouses or longstanding friends. In many ways *what* they are in the concrete is the same. We become like the people with whom we associate. Project this to an ideal level where everything I have become in the concrete is the same as what others have become. My thoughts and values, all that I stand for and am, all that makes me be what I am, all this I share in common with others. I am the same as they in everything. Here I am thinking of that ultimate state of perfection that Jesus prayed for: "that they may all be one; even as thou, Father, art in me, and I in thee, that they also may be in us. . . . that they may be one even as we are one, I in them and thou in me, that they may become perfectly one" (Jn. 17:21–23).[11] According to Christian belief, such ultimate unity with Christ, the

142

Father, and all others is possible in the Holy Spirit. Nonetheless, even if what I am concretely becomes the same as what others are concretely, even if there is no difference whatsoever in *what* I am as compared to *what* others are, I still maintain my unique identity as determined by the existence that makes me be. This is never held in common with others. It is the ultimate determinative of me as a unique, distinct individual. In classical terms, my 'person' is inviolable. Even when I might become perfectly one in Christ with God and all other humans, as 'person' I remain myself, distinct. I never lose my uniqueness as 'person'. The existence that makes me be is never the same as the existence that makes someone else be.

The Case of Jesus Christ

I have been developing a systematic understanding of the terms 'person' and 'nature'. 'Person' is a correlate of the third level of consciousness and focuses on the existence that makes one be and be what one is. On the other hand, 'nature' is a correlate of the second level of consciousness and indicates what one is. Conceived in this way, 'person' and 'nature' are really distinct. In reality the one is not the other. This real distinction opens the *possibility* that someone could have a human nature and not be a human person. Said otherwise, someone could be as a human but not be determined in ultimate identity by a created existence. Obviously, the present possibility is a suggested account of what happened in Jesus Christ. Christ's "who" is his eternal identity as Born-of-the-Father. As Born-of-the-Father, the Eternal Word shares the same divine way of being as the Father. The Word is consubstantial with the Father. The Word exists eternally in the divine nature. He is, indeed, identical with the divine nature, for the Word is God. The distinction between a divine person and the divine nature is not real but only conceptual, for God is one, and in God there are no real distinctions except those among the Father, Son, and Holy Spirit.[12] The divine person, the Eternal Word, exists eternally in the divine nature. But the Word became flesh and dwelt among us. This divine one took on also a human way of being. The one born eternally of the Father was born in time of Mary. The "who" remains the same, yet the kind of being is new. A divine "person" is now existing in a human "nature." *Who* the Word is remains the same,

143

but *what* the Word is has changed. The Word is now also human. The humanity of the Eternal Word is real; it really exists. Yet, unlike in the case of any other really existing humanity, in Jesus Christ there is not human "person." The human "whatness" of Christ is not sustained in being by a created existence, which would determine a human "person." For there is only one "who" in Christ, namely, the Eternal Word. Rather, Christ's humanity, concrete and real and really existing, is sustained in existence by the existence of the Word himself—which is sufficient as such to account for everything that is: it is the existence of God. When absolute divine existence is in question, appeal to nothing else is needed to account for what is. So in Christ there is no need for separate created existence to account for the reality of Christ's humanity. It is the humanity of the Etenal Word himself; its existence is that of God the Word himself.[13]

It is, indeed, strange and awkward to realize that the infinite existence of the Eternal Word could be the very existence also of a limited, created humanity. That such a thing could occur is precisely the mystery of the Incarnation. The present account does not explain the mystery; it merely points out where exactly the mystery lies.

Granted in faith that the Incarnation did occur, the present account also offers a reasonable account of it.[14] The real distinction in the human case between the "who" and the "what"—between "person" and "nature"—allows that there could be a human being who was not a human "who." And the divine existence of the one in question—the Eternal Word—is sufficient to account for the existence of this humanity apart from a distinct created existence. Here there is no attempt to prove that this is what happened in Jesus Christ. There is only the suggestion that this is a reasonable account of what Christians believe about Jesus Christ. I have accepted the distinction—between "who" one is and "what" one is—inherent in the Council of Ephesus. I have elaborated the distinction and grounded it on the rockbed of all human understanding, human consciousness itself. The whole provides a coherent, reasonable account. One can accept the Council of Ephesus without mythologizing it, on the one hand, and without being a fool, on the other.

From the prior councils, Jesus Christ was known clearly to be both human and divine. Thus, the main issue at Ephesus was to account for the unity in Jesus Christ. Ephesus taught that Jesus Christ is one because in him there is only *one "who"* was both human and divine. The technical Greek term finally accepted to express this point of unity was *hypostasis,* usually translated as "person." Cyril of Alexandria argued that the unity in Jesus Christ was *kath' hypostasin,* according to the *hypostasis* or on the basis of the *hypostasis.* This Greek usage is the source of the term, hypostatic union. The union of humanity and divinity in Jesus Christ is called the hypostatic union. The term indicates precisely what was determined at the Council of Ephesus: there is in Christ only *one "who"* is both human and divine. The unity of Christ rests in this, that Jesus Christ, the Eternal Word and Son of God, is only one identity. Humanity and divinity are united hypostatically—that is, because of the only one hypostasis—in Christ.

No Confusion of Natures in Christ: Chalcedon

The Council of Ephesus did not definitely resolve the discussion about how the humanity and divinity were united in Jesus Christ. In actual history, the issue was much more complex than I have presented it. The terms did not have the clear definitions that I gave to them. There was still much room for confusion, difference of opinion, and misunderstanding. Cyril of Alexandria himself, insistent on a union *kath'hypostasin,* also used other phrases to express what he meant. His phrases were not understood in the sense he meant them—and perhaps he himself was not always sure what he meant. Cyril did accept the two-nature formula. Nonetheless, he continued to use the phrase, "the one incarnate nature of the God-Word." Cyril was using the term *phusis*—Greek for "nature"—in a sense different from what I defined above. For another sense was still accepted—at least it was accepted in Alexandria, if not in Antioch. *Phusis* was used to mean one single reality, one something. In this sense it was practically a synonym for *hypostasis.* In any case, the scene was set for more discussion.

The archimandrite of a Constantinople monastery, Eutyches, became the focus of the next christological debate. Eutyches heartily objected to the duality that Nestorius' position introduced into Christ. Furthermore, he adhered zealously to Cyril's statements, themselves sometimes ambiguous and overstated. Intent on preserving the unity of divinity and humanity in Christ, Eutyches proposed yet another way to understand that unity. His understanding exalted Jesus Christ to a superhuman—indeed, a non-human—reality. Eutyches refused to acknowledge that Christ's human nature was "of one nature" with ours. Rather, he insisted, "our Lord is of two natures before the union, but after the union I confess one nature."[15] Eutyches' suggestion was that the two natures united in such a way that the result was just one nature. It was as if water and dye had mixed. The result was a blend of the two. Both were changed because of the mixture. This christological position is called monophysitism—from the Greek: *mono* means one, and *physis* means nature. According to Eutyches, Jesus Christ had only one nature, a divine-human one.

Eutyches' concern is obvious and it is legitimate enough—to preserve the unity in Christ. Moreover, an understanding of humanity being "absorbed" into divinity offers an appealing way to imagine how humanity is saved in Christ. Nonetheless, the objection to Eutcyches' position is also obvious. The Christ that results is neither truly human nor truly divine but rather a nondescript mixture of humanity and divinity. The supposed resulting "one nature" is a hybrid, a monster.

Eutyches' understanding of Christ is really not far from what many pious Christians believe today. Because of catechetical overemphasis on the divinity of Christ, many have an impoverished understanding of Jesus' humanity. The picture is that of a magician, a wonder-worker—a supposed man who, however, has divine power and knowledge and invokes these whenever he chooses. This Jesus is not really like us in all things, for his mind outstrips the experience in which he is involved, and at will his powers extricate him miraculously from any situation. He is more Superman than Son of Man. In fact, this is the picture of Jesus presented in the gospel of John—but only when this gospel is misunderstood, ripped from its literary and historical context, and read as a literal account of Jesus' earthly life. One purpose of John's gospel was to highlight the divine status of Jesus Christ. This purpose was accomplished by writing back into the life of Jesus an appreciation gained only after his resurrection. The form is kerygmatic. Unfortunately, only in the last century have we become clearly aware of the kerygmatic character of the gospels. Popular teaching about Jesus is still far from presenting an adequate understanding. Thus many well-intentioned Christians are crypto-monophysites.

The ecumenical Council of Chalcedon in 451 c.e. declared the monophysite position unacceptable. Recalling the christological teaching of the previous councils—Nicea, Constantinople I, and Ephesus—Chalcedon presented a summary formula of Christian belief about Jesus Christ: one person in two natures. The decree of Chalcedon reads in part as follows:

> In imitation of the holy Fathers we confess that our Lord Jesus Christ is one and the same Son . . . , the same perfect in his divinity, perfect in his humanity: truly God and the same truly man of a rational soul and body; of one nature with the Father according to the divinity, and the same of one nature with us according to humanity. . . . (We confess) one and the same Christ, Son, Lord, Only-Begotten, in two natures, without confusion, without change, without division, and without separation. The difference in natures is not removed through the union, but the property of each nature is preserved and they coalesce in one person *(prosopon)* and one independence *(hypostasis)*.[16]

As in the previous councils, Chalcedon's teaching is also a direct response to the objectionable position. So, besides conveniently summarizing conciliar teaching thus far, Chalcedon also adds one more clarification. Against Eutyches, Chalcedon insists that the two natures in Christ are not mixed, not changed. Christ's divinity and his humanity remain intact. He is divine even as the Father is divine; he is human even as each of us is human. Chalcedon's "without confusion, without change" and the subsequent elaboration make this point absolutely clear. The humanity and divinity of Jesus do not flow into one another.

This teaching is supremely important for our contemporary concern for the humanity of Jesus Christ. From this teaching it follows: when Jesus, Eternal-Son, is in the flesh, he exists and lives and acts through his human nature and through it alone. Any suggestion of divine knowledge and power "seeping into" and influencing the activity of Jesus' humanity is in violation of the teaching of Chalcedon. When the Eternal Word becomes human, it is as if he "gives up" his divine way of being; he puts this aside; he stops acting through his divinity and limits himself to acting only through his

147

humanity. In the words of Paul, formerly thought to refer to the incarnation, he "emptied himself, taking the form of a servant" (Phil. 2:7).[17] The Greek word Paul used here is *kenoun*, to empty. So this kind of understanding about Jesus is called "kenotic."[18] Obviously, the Word does not "give up" his divinity in the sense that he literally stops *being* God. Such a thing is impossible. Jesus Christ *is* God, the Eternal Son. But he does prescind from use of divine prerogatives. As human, he stops *acting* as God. He stops *acting* through the divine nature and acts through his human nature. So all his activities are limited to what is humanly possible, just as are our own. Whatever Jesus does needs to be explained on the basis of his humanity.[19] To invoke his divinity to explain Jesus' activities is to suppose that from time to time the divine power erupted into Jesus' human life. It is to suppose that his divinity mixed with—and disrupted!—his humanity. Such an explanation violates the Council of Chalcedon.

Of course, this is not to say that God was in no way acting in Jesus' life. Just as God acts in our lives, so God also acted in Jesus' life. Just as we are created human beings, dependent on God's creative and sustaining power for our continued human being, so was Jesus. Jesus did not have a claim on the divine power so that he could exercise it whenever he wanted. On earth, Eternal-Son gave up his divine power. He relied on faith, prayer, and trust, even as we all must. He was not like Superman, an other-worldly being, here among us in disguise, never really one of us.[20] He did not from time to time doff his human garb and flex his divine muscle. According to such an understanding, he would be neither really human nor really divine. Rather, he would be some capricious mixture of the two. Like a chameleon, he would switch back and forth from human to divine whenever he chose. He would not be like us, who are human and limited to the human condition. He would not be like God, all-powerful, all-knowing, eternal, and necessary. He would be some hybrid. Such an understanding is monophysite. Chalcedon necessitates that while on earth, though Eternal Son, he gave up his divine powers and lived within the limitations of humanity. If the divine power played an active part in Jesus' life, it did so just as it can and does in our own lives.

How is such a thing possible? How can God, while still being God, stop acting as God and limit himself to acting only as human?

Ah, here the mystery of the Incarnation comes clear again. Now we appreciate what the mystery is.

All that can be said is this. First and by way of faith—obviously such a thing *is* possible. It happened. Jesus Christ is the Eternal Son. Then—and by way of reasonable account—the unity with divinity in Christ does not result because his two natures are mixed together but because the one and the same one who is Eternally-begotten-of-the-Father became human through Mary. Jesus Christ is known to be Eternal-Son not because on earth he had and exercised the power of God; this is precisely what he gave up. He is known to be Eternal-Son because that is *who* this human being is. Not his divine nature but his divine identity is what lets us affirm that this man is God. For in the flesh he does not act through his divine nature, so his divine nature is not available for our observation. We say that this man Jesus is God because of who he is, not because of what he is. As far as the "what" goes, he appears obviously human and only that.[21] Yet his "who" is Eternal-Son, Begotten-of-the-Father. This allows us to say he is God. His identity is our link between his humanity and his divinity. The union in Christ is hypostatic. For this reason Chalcedon affirms that humanity and divinity in Christ, while "without confusion, without change," are also "without division, without separation" and "they coalesce in one person."

Review of Conciliar Teaching

This account of the Council of Chalcedon completes this presentation of conciliar teaching about Jesus Christ. The contributions of two councils subsequent to Chalcedon have already been noted: Constantinople II taught that the one "who" in Christ was one of the Blessed Trinity, and Constantinople III insisted that Jesus Christ has a human will as well as a divine will and so exercised human freedom during his earthly life. A summary of conciliar teaching about Jesus Christ can be brief. According to Nicea, Jesus Christ is truly God. He is *homoousios* with the Father. Subsequent understanding interprets Nicea to mean that Jesus Christ, the Eternal Son, shares the divine nature with the Father. According to Constantinople I and III, Jesus Christ has a complete human nature as well. Specifically, he has a human mind and human freedom; he has a complete human psychology, a complete human consciousness. According to Ephesus, there

149

is only one who in Christ has both a human and a divine nature. That one who as divine is born eternally of the Father was, as human, born in time of Mary. That one is, then, no other than the Eternal Word, as is confirmed by Constantinople II. Finally, according to Chalcedon the union of humanity and divinity in Jesus Christ does not result in some new, third reality, some monster. The unique characteristics of each respective nature are preserved. This means that, while on earth, the Eternal Word acted as human. He acted always and only through his humanity and did not invoke the powers of his divinity. *For all practical purposes*—that is, insofar as his activities are concerned—*while on earth Eternal-Word was only human.* He acted only through his human mind, human psyche, human freedom, human body. The one principle of all his activities on earth was his human nature. In all his activities he was limited to his human state just as all of us are limited. On earth, his was a human way of being. Yet the one so limited was none other than Eternal-Son-of-God. This, in summary, is the christology that emerges from the councils of the Christian Church.

This summary makes obvious how narrow the conciliar concern about Jesus Christ really was. Much that *we* would want to understand about Jesus was never treated. From beginning to end, the focus was on the incarnation: the union of humanity and divinity in Jesus Christ. Granted, soteriological concerns lay behind the conciliar debates, but the goal was to clarify the mystery of the incarnation. The perspective of this traditional christology, as we inherited it, was purely that of a christology from above. Traditional preaching and catechesis so emphasized the incarnational aspect—God became human—that even conciliar teaching about Jesus' full and unmixed humanity was generally underplayed. With special care the above account of the councils highlights this other aspect of the tradition, for in the overall picture it is easily lost to view. It should now be clear that the doctrinal concern of the first seven centuries is the source of the one-sided christology we generally know.[22] History explains why things are today as they are. Obviously, there is room for further development in Christian understanding about Jesus. This is not to say that the conciliar teaching was inaccurate. Rather, it is to say that the conciliar teaching is incomplete. Contemporary emphasis on the earthly life, death, and resurrection of Jesus begins to fill in the picture. Sketching out a fuller picture of Jesus will be the task of the following chapter.

Summary Thus Far

This study began by insisting that christology is reflection on Jesus Christ. The point was to distinguish clearly between the reality to be understood: Jesus, and reflection on the reality: christology. Inherent in this starting point is a set of critical-realist epistemological presuppositions, which gradually unfolded. Two main approaches to christology were noted: "from above" and "from below." These two are useful for naming the general line of thought and resulting general focus a christology takes. Thus, the above paragraph was able to describe the christology of the ecumenical councils as a christology from above. Nonetheless, under critical analysis, these two approaches are seen to be kerygmatic in form. They make their point by means of a story; they employ image and metaphor to convey their message. That is to say, they are not systematic formulations. Their storyline as such is not to be taken literally. Kerygmatic and systematic statement are the expression proper to functional and ontological mentality respectively. The distinction of these two mentalities and, in particular, the legitimation of the ontological mentality allowed both a sketch of the development of New Testament christology within a functional mentality and a retrieval of the development of conciliar christology within an ontological mentality. Granted these presuppositions, the whole tradition is valid and valuable, the whole is coherent and reasonable. An account of it portrays the gradual, centuries-long increase of Christian understanding about Jesus Christ. An account of it summarizes the history of the development of christology. This development brings us to the present day. Contemporary concern for the life, death, resurrection, and saving work of Jesus Christ still needs to be addressed. What the tradition provides—retrieved, legitimated, and unified—is the solid ground on which further development can stand. The remainder of this book will begin that still-needed construction project. The result will be a picture of Jesus Christ that is true to traditional teaching about Jesus and enriched by contemporary scholarship on Jesus.

PART III

A Contemporary Christology

CHAPTER EIGHT

Jesus, the Human True to Himself

This study has finally come to its promised conclusion. We have discussed the major problems that contemporary thought poses regarding an understanding of Jesus. We have summarized the conclusions that contemporary biblical scholarship offers about Jesus himself and about the New Testament understandings of Jesus. We have reviewed the teaching of the christological councils and offered an interpretation of them in light of subsequent speculation and contemporary concerns. Now Part III of this book presents a synthesis of all this material. It develops a coherent presentation of Jesus Christ as is allowed by contemporary scholarship and demanded by traditional belief. The present chapter presents an overview of this contemporary christology. Chapter Eight is a summary statement. The following two chapters treat in detail certain important issues and implications of this understanding about Jesus. Here begins my answer to the question, How can one understand Christian belief about Jesus Christ today? What do you make of Christ?

A New "Model" of Jesus

In 1981, John F. O'Grady published *Models of Jesus*. Emulating Avery Dulles's very useful and widely acclaimed *Models of the Church*,[1] *Models of Jesus* presents six different contemporary pictures of Jesus.

The idea is that Jesus Christ can be understood in different ways. He is different things to different people. Jesus is "The Incarnation of the Second Person of the Blessed Trinity," God become flesh, passing through our world. Jesus is "The Mythological Christ," an inspiring and saving message which, however, would hardly be true to the historical Jesus. Jesus is "The Ethical Liberator," the hero and inspiration of Liberation Theology, calling for social justice, for economic, social, and political liberation, in anticipation of the Kingdom of God on this earth. Jesus is "The Human Face of God," a remarkable human being who changed our notion of both humanity and divinity. Jesus is "The Man for Others," the servant of others in this world. Finally, Jesus is "Personal Savior," the transformer of people's lives, known especially within the charismatic renewal movement.

Models of Jesus provides a useful, popular overview of contemporary christology. Each chapter summarizes a major approach to Jesus. The resulting array of models evidences the plurality of opinions prevalent today. The very shift from one authoritative statement to a variety of models in christology is a noteworthy phenomenon. It suggests that no comprehensive christological account is available. In the end the reader is left to decide for himself or herself which is most adequate, most congenial. The uncertainty that currently rules the field is obvious. *Models of Jesus* is an excellent exhibit on contemporary christology.

By the same token, that book also exhibits the major shortcomings in the contemporary scene. It is astonishing in itself that "Jesus as the Incarnation of the Second Person of the Blessed Trinity" would appear as one model among six, all claiming to account for Jesus Christ. Granted, there are many ways of understanding Jesus; Jesus means different things to different people. But what Jesus means for me or for you is one thing; what he is in himself may be quite another. The many faces of Jesus in Christian piety is one thing; a comprehensive and adequate theological account of Jesus Christ is another. Yet in an array of models, Jesus-for-me and Jesus-in-himself are mixed together. The difference between the two may be lost. The traditional Christian understanding of Jesus Christ in himself may appear as just another instance of what some people consider Jesus to be for them. The shift from ontological to functional thinking—indeed, the implicit devaluation or obliteration of ontological thinking—goes unnoticed.

A methodology that is useful for study of the church is not

156

necessarily also adequate for the study of Jesus Christ. Ecclesiology is a very new theological specialization. It is still far from achieving any widely accepted systematic formulation. In this field, kerygmatic statement still leads the way.[2] The same can be said about the question of revelation and so justify Dulles's later book, *Models of Revelation*.[3] However, the same is not true for christology.

Already by 325 C.E. Christianity achieved a fundamental clarification about Jesus Christ, formulated in a nascent systematic form. Subsequent thought and official teaching went far beyond Nicea's first step. The usual process of human explanation seems to move from poetic inspiration and suggestion, to standardly accepted metaphors and images, to consolidation of images into overriding models, and finally to theoretical breakthrough and systematic formulation.[4] In christology, to revert again to models is to step backwards.

O'Grady does not suggest, of course, that all six models are of equal value. He evaluates each, noting its advantages and liabilities. Moreover, he insists that a complete christology would have to take into account the contributions of all six models. Yet, here is the telling issue: no single model appears capable of effecting the synthesis. Only the first, Jesus as the Incarnation, and the fourth, Jesus as The Human Face of God, qualify as *possible* paradigms—master-models that could become the basis for a comprehensive, adequate christology. As is obvious, these two models are expressions of the two basic modes of contemporary christology, from above and from below.

What is needed is a seventh "model" of Jesus. It would combine the valid insights of the more traditional christology from above with those of the more contemporary christology from below. This new "model" would give full emphasis both to Jesus' eternal divinity and to his historical humanity. It would use the ontologically conceived distinctions between creature and creator, person and nature, and humanity and divinity from traditional christology to construct a basic understanding of Jesus Christ. Onto this it would engraft an understanding of Jesus' humanity and its potential, its development, and its social significance, as developed in contemporary thought. That is, this seventh model would integrate an ontological understanding with psychological and existential understanding.

Such a synthesis is possible today because the modern "turn to the subject" has finally resulted in a systematic account of human

157

subjectivity and its development. Moreover, an analysis of this dynamic subjectivity can ground metaphysics. This achievement provides a systematically constructed bridge over the gap between classical metaphysical and modern psychological concerns.[5] Applied to christology, the result would be more than a "model." It would be a systematic account of Jesus Christ. It would provide the basis and the criteria of validity for any piety's model of Jesus. It would be a paradigm.

The complete name of this "model" would necessarily be cumbersome: "Jesus as the Eternal Son of God Become Human and in His Humanity Divinized so that All Humans Might Likewise Be Divinized." More concisely, it could be called "Jesus, the Human True to Himself." Here "the Human" indicates Jesus' complete and unmixed humanity. The term is a substitute for the more familiar but sexist term "The Man." No doubt Jesus was a man, but the significant issue is not that he was male but that he was one of us, human.[6] "Himself" indicates his divine identity as Eternally-Begotten-of-the-Father and so presupposes the incarnation. "True to" serves to indicate the human, historical achievement of his perfect fidelity—fidelity, first of all, to himself and so automatically also to his heavenly Father. This fidelity resulted in his death and glorification—which, transforming this one human being, by implication also transformed the ultimate meaning of all human life. This "model" would combine incarnational, resurrectional, and soteriological emphases into one, comprehensive, coherent understanding of Jesus Christ. This "model," a paradigm, would be capable of absorbing and integrating all the other models of Jesus. The following presentation sketches such a paradigm, a systematic christology.

Two Movements in Christology

A complete understanding of Jesus Christ comprises two movements. The first is the movement of God to us. The supreme moment of this movement was the incarnation of the Eternal Word as the son of Mary, Jesus Christ. This first movement introduced into human history an absolutely unique human being. Of course, in one way every human being is unique. Each is himself or herself and no other. None will be repeated. But the uniqueness of Jesus Christ goes beyond this common uniqueness. Jesus' identity was not human but divine. The one born of Mary was none other than Eternally-Begotten-of-the-Father. The uniqueness of Jesus Christ is that he was God born into human history. This movement of God into history is the first christological movement. It is the movement from above.

The second is the movement from below, the movement of the human being to God. It is the movement of historical, human growth common to all human beings. Yet in the case of Jesus Christ, this movement takes on unique significance. Because of who he is and simply by being in history who he is, Jesus Christ had the possibility of a human fulfillment that was unique to him. The second christological movement is Jesus Christ's human growth toward perfect historical expression of himself and, as a result, to ultimate human fulfillment in God. Through his human life and not until his resurrection, the human Jesus Christ achieved as perfect as humanly possible a participation in divine qualities. Such human participation in divinity could and should have been his from the beginning. After all, he was Eternal-Son. But it was not. In divine wisdom his Father conferred it on him only in the end because in his human life he was perfectly faithfully Son of the Father.

The first christological movement, the incarnation, is the condition for the possibility of the second movement, the divinization of the human Jesus. Because of who he is, Jesus' human life is open to a human consummation unlike any before him. Even as human, if he but be himself, he will share in qualities proper to God alone. Furthermore, the completion of the second movement in Jesus' case has implications for every other human being ever to live. Through the confluence of these two movements and because of his connection with all through the human history he entered, Jesus Christ changed the ultimate possibility for human fulfillment. Attaining that fulfillment in himself, he opened a new possibility to all. With the help of the Holy Spirit, all people could now likewise attain that fulfillment. He saved humankind.

I will elaborate in turn each of these two christological movements and then their implication for human salvation.

The Movement from Above: the Incarnation of the Eternal Word

The presentation of the development of conciliar christology in Chapters Six and Seven already significantly details the movement from above. Here a brief summary will suffice.

159

A Comprehensive Christology/Soteriology

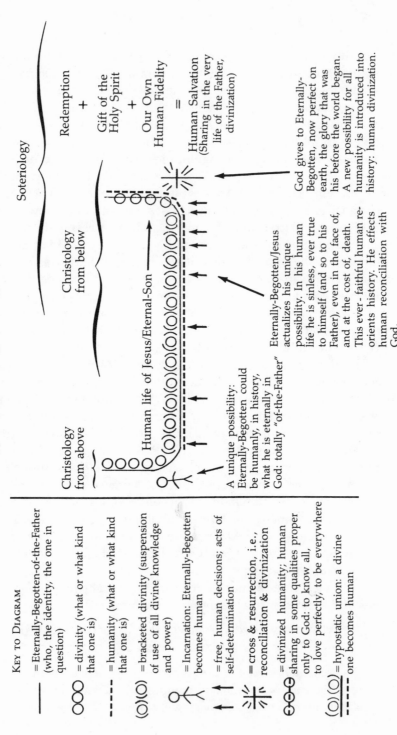

KEY TO DIAGRAM

—— = Eternally-Begotten-of-the-Father (who, the identity, the one in question)

OOO = divinity (what or what kind that one is)

----- = humanity (what or what kind that one is)

(O)(O) = bracketed divinity (suspension of use of all divine knowledge and power)

⊥ = Incarnation: Eternally-Begotten becomes human

→ = free, human decisions; acts of self-determination

※ = cross & resurrection, i.e., reconciliation & divinization

⊖⊖⊖ = divinized humanity; human sharing in some qualities proper only to God: to know all, to love perfectly, to be everywhere

(O)(O) = hypostatic union: a divine
----- one becomes human

Christology from above

Christology from below

Human life of Jesus/Eternal-Son →

Soteriology

Redemption
+
Gift of the Holy Spirit
+
Our Own Human Fidelity
=
Human Salvation (Sharing in the very life of the Father, divinization)

A unique possibility: Eternally-Begotten could be humanly, in history, what he is eternally in God: totally "of-the-Father"

Eternally-Begotten/Jesus actualizes his unique possibility. In his human life he is sinless, ever true to himself (and so to his Father), even in the face of, and at the cost of, death. This ever-faithful human reorients history. He effects human reconciliation with God.

God gives to Eternally-Begotten, now perfect on earth, the glory that was his before the world began. A new possibility for all humanity is introduced into history: human divinization.

To say that the Word became flesh, that the Eternal Son became human, is to affirm that a particular preexisting individual became human. The one in question is the Eternal Son. This one is not the Father; nor is he the Holy Spirit. Only the Son became human, the Son as distinct from the Father and the Holy Spirit. They are two *others who* are God but who did not incarnate. The exact identity of the one who became human is Begotten-of-the-Father. The Son's "begottenness" distinguishes him from the Father, for the Father is not begotten. Rather, he is Without-Source. That "begottenness" likewise distinguishes the Son from the Holy Spirit, for the Holy Spirit is also not begotten. Rather, he is Proceeding-from-the-Father-and-the-Son. The exact distinguishing quality of the Son, that which gives him identity in contrast to every other, human and divine, is his eternal "begottenness" from the Father. His identity is to be begotten of the Father. Who he is is Begotten-of-the-Father.[7]

As Begotten-of-the-Father, the Eternal Son is distinct from the Father and the Holy Spirit. Yet what or what kind the Son is as God is the same as what the Father and the Holy Spirit are—namely, divine, God. Since the Eternal Son is God, it is accurate to say that in Jesus Christ God became human, despite Nestorius' objection. Still, considering that the Father and the Holy Spirit are also God, the statement "God became human" is not altogether without ambiguity. This statement in itself could be taken to refer to the Father or to the Holy Spirit or even to a unitarian God where distinct subjects in God are disallowed. The absolutely precise and unambiguous statement is "The Eternally-Begotten became human."

The point of insistence is this: some*one* became human, not some*what*. What the Eternal Word brought into the world with him was himself, his identity, and not his divinity. His divinity he "gave up" when he became human. That is to say, as human, Begotten-of-the-Father no longer acts through his divine nature. His way of acting is now solely human. In the incarnation, the Eternal Word "stripped himself of glory,"[8] he "emptied himself" (Phil. 2:7).[9] He limited himself to a human way of being. His divine prerogatives—infinite knowledge and power—he left behind. In all his activity on earth, he prescinded from those divine qualities. He surrendered his former principle of activity, divinity, and limited himself to a new principle of activity, humanity. This does not mean that he stopped being God.

His divinity is indistinguishable and inseparable from himself as Eternally-Begotten-of-the-Father. Nonetheless, he prescinded from acting as divine when he became human. Chalcedon's teaching that Christ's humanity and divinity were "without confusion, without change" insists on this. There is no inflow of omniscient knowledge and omnipotent power into the human Jesus. The Eternal Word did not bring divine power and knowledge with him when he came into this world. That is precisely what he left behind. He did bring himself. Then Eternally-Begotten-of-the-Father began living as one of us, fully and completely human, and only so.[10]

Jesus' Miracles What, then, about Jesus' miracles? Do they not show his divine power? Certainly popular presentation sees Jesus' miracles as signs of his divine power. Yet, it must be remembered, every miracle Jesus performed has some precedent in the Old Testament. Only Jesus' resurrection has no precedent in the Old Testament. Besides, Christians and non-Christians today are rediscovering the gift of healing and again doing miracles. If such miracles are an indication of divinity, then we must conclude the Old Testament prophets and many other people are also divine, just as Jesus is. The conclusion is unacceptable. According to Christian belief, Jesus is unique in his divinity. It follows, his miracles are not correctly understood as expressions of his unique divinity. They are better understood as expressions of extraordinary humanity.

As human beings, all of us have powers far beyond what we imagine. Some people are especially gifted in these extraordinary powers. Especially holy people tend to have such special gifts.[11] Jesus, an extraordinary human being and a uniquely holy human being, knew how to use powers that God has given to many—or even all—human beings. This is to say, Jesus' miracles are not necessarily signs of divinity; they are rather signs of developed humanity.

The same can be said about Jesus' extraordinary knowledge on many occasions. It is not at all uncommon to meet people who in one way or another can "read" other people. They pick up "vibes." They can sense what someone is feeling or thinking or likely to do. They have this ability not because they are God but because they are human beings deeply in touch with themselves and with others. Jesus' extraordinary awareness could also be understood in this way.

We are learning more and more about the powers of the human

162

mind. In the process, we have less reason to suppose that the verified extraordinary activities of the historical Jesus were expressions of his divinity. Rather, they indicate his extraordinary humanity. Such an interpretation is in full accord with the teaching of Chalcedon, which forbids mixing human and divine powers in Jesus.

At the same time, any extraordinary occurrences—miracles—can be occasions to consider God's action among us. In some way God is behind everything that happens, so he is also behind Jesus'—and anybody else's—miracles. In this sense, miracles are signs of God's work among us. They point us to God. They become indicators of something more than themselves, unusual occurrences. Understood in this sense, Jesus' miracles are indications that he is from God and that God is in him. Indeed, it is in this sense that the gospel of John speaks of Jesus' deeds not as miracles but as signs.[12]

The Word Became a Real Human Being   While on earth, the Eternal Word limited himself to acting humanly. He was restricted by the confines of space and time, just as all humans are. He could only be in one place at one time, and his life moved on minute by minute, hour by hour, day by day. Where it was going remained to be seen. Whatever he knew, he knew with a human mind. Whatever he did, he did with human freedom and human potential. His experiences, his feelings, the joys and longings of his heart—all were those of a human being. He had no memories of his eternal life in God. His memories were those of a human mind, and that human mind had its beginning at his birth.[13] His personality and his ways of behaving were developed among his family and associates. He grew up in a small town in early first-century Palestine. This experience formed his language and thought patterns and general outlook on things. Like all of us, he was a product of his environment. As noted in Chapter Five, we know very little detail about Jesus' concrete biography. Still, what must be said in general about any human being must also be said about Jesus. Once come to earth, *for all practical purposes* the Eternal Word was human and solely so.[14]

O'Grady's model of Jesus as The Incarnation of the Second Person of The Blessed Trinity summarizes faithfully the standard presentation of the christology from above. According to it, the incarnation is the central event of Christianity. In the incarnation humanity and divinity come together. Nothing more is to be expected. Jesus' earthly life is the automatic consequence of that central event. His teachings announce that marvel, and his deeds confirm his words. His death is a lesson about the wickedness of sin, and his resurrection, the ultimate confirmation of the truth of the incarnation. Jesus' life, death, and resurrection add nothing that was not already there in the incarnation. The story is over as soon as it begins.

The present account unfolds differently. By giving equal and balanced emphasis to the teaching of all the councils—Nicea's insistence on the absolute divinity of Jesus Christ, Constantinople I and III's insistence on his complete humanity, Ephesus' implicit distinction between the who and the what in Jesus Christ, and Chalcedon's exclusion of mixture between his humanity and divinity—this account presents the christology from above not as the sum of the story but only as its beginning. To recognize that Jesus Christ has a full humanity, unmixed with his divinity, is to acknowledge the introduction into human history of a human being whose future is yet to be determined. Eternal Word though he is, Jesus must live his own human life starting from birth, just as every other human being. What he will do with his life remains to be seen. How he will exercise his human freedom and use his exquisite talents is his own to decide. The movement from above set a beginning, but it did not resolve the whole issue. Uninformed speculation on the case might suggest that things could or should or did occur differently. Yet history alone reveals God's good wisdom. As it in fact was, this beginning only opened the possibility for the consummate union of God and a human, but the full actuation of that possibility remained to be achieved. Not only the incarnation but also the human freedom of Jesus throughout some thirty years of living would determine the outcome. The first movement of christology leads to a second. Without it the first was not to be completed. What was possible in the first movement still needed to be made actual in the second.

The Movement from Below: The Divinization of Jesus

The second movement is that from below. It is the growth of the human Jesus. Its goal is his glorification, his divinization. Divinization does not mean that somehow the human being became God. Jesus Christ already was God; he did not have to become God. Besides, no one, nothing, can become God. Jesus Christ was not a human being

who became God. Still, something did happen to him between the
incarnation and his return to the Father. His life did make a difference.
The change was in his humanity. He was divinized. Divinization
means that Jesus' humanity came to participate to some extent in
certain qualities proper only to divinity. According to this account,
christology from below does not deal with a supposed move from
humanity to divinity; a human being does not become God. Rather,
christology from below deals with the perfection of a human being to
the point even of sharing to some extent in divine prerogatives. The
human who is divinized remains human. Yet certain ideal human
potentials, which one would not ordinarily expect to be actualized,
are actualized. The result is still human, yet the humanity is transformed. It reaches a perfection that surpasses ordinary expectation.
The human remains human. By the same token the human remains
also created. A creature does not somehow suddenly become uncreated. Yet the creature shares in qualities proper only to divinity. In
question is a created participation in divinity. Precisely such a created
participation in divinity was the final result of Jesus' human life. More
explanation is necessary.

Jesus' Unique Possibility   When he entered human history, the
Word-made-flesh, Jesus Christ, had a unique possibility. No one
before had ever been a divine one made human. Of course, born as
human, Jesus shared a common possibility with all other humans: he
could be true to himself. But as Eternally-Begotten-of-the-Father become human, this possibility was unique in his case. By being true to
himself, he would live out in human history the identity he has
eternally in God. He would express historically who he is eternally.
Now, his whole identity, that which is his alone, is to be begotten of
the Father. This is what distinguishes him from the Father and from
the Holy Spirit. His whole self is to be "of-the-Father." That which
makes him uniquely himself is absolute, total dependence on the
Father. Accordingly, to be himself in history is to be totally dependent
on the Father, to live in complete surrender to the Father, to spell out
in word and deed a constant awareness of utter "self/gift-edness"
from the Father. The Eternal Word's historical expression of himself
would be absolute fidelity to the Father.[15] And he would be absolutely faithful to the Father simply by being faithful to himself. By
being himself he would be in history perfectly Son-of-the-Father. To

165

be himself, and so to be in history perfectly Son-of-the-Father, was Jesus Christ's unique possibility.

Obviously, this "being true to himself" implies no such thing as following his own whim.[16] Its meaning is not that of the current slogan, "Do your own thing." The sense here is more that of Shakespeare's

> This above all: to thine own self be true,
> And it must follow, as the night the day,
> Thou canst not then be false to any man.[17]

The sense is that of John Donne: "No man is an island, entire of itself; every man is a piece of the continent, a part of the main."[18] The sense is that of Paul:

> Now there are varieties of gifts, but the same Spirit; and there are varieties of service, but the same Lord; and there are varieties of working, but it is the same God who inspires them all in every one. . . . For the body does not consist of one member but of many. . . . If one member suffers, all suffer together; if one member is honored, all rejoice together. (1 Cor. 12:4–6, 14, 26)[19]

Were Jesus Christ to be absolutely true to himself in his human life, *ipso facto* he would be in history perfectly Son-of-the-Father, and *ipso facto* he would be perfectly faithful also to the Father. To be true to himself would automatically be to be true to the will of God. To be true to the will of God would likewise automatically be to be true to all that is right, good, noble, and worthwhile for all others.

By being true to himself, he would "historicize" his eternal "begottenness." That is to say, he would express in history what he is in eternity. He would effect an historical expression of his own self. Historically as well as eternally, humanly as well as divinely, he would be Son-of-the-Father. In contrast, by being himself, he would *not* be "historicizing" his divinity. Divinity is his divine way of being. That is precisely what he left behind. That is what he has in common with the Father and the Holy Spirit. Divinity is not what would be expressed historically if in history the Eternal Word were completely himself. Rather, total and absolute dependence on the Father, "bornness" of the Father, "self/gift-edness" from the Father, is what would be expressed. Who he is—not what he is—is the link between his eternal being and his historical being. The union is hypostatic. Jesus' human life does not express the divine nature. It expresses a divine identity.

166

Jesus' human life is the historical expression of Begotten-of-the-Father.

Jesus, Ever Faithful   In fact, Eternal-Son-of-the-Father was true to himself in his human life. At great cost, at the price of death, he was ever true to himself.

The New Testament insists on this, though it gives precious little detail about Jesus' moments of anguish. The temptation accounts[20] and the passion narratives[21] suggest that Jesus did face the uncertainty of life, as we all do. Each time he chose the path of faith. He entrusted himself to the love of his Father. What he had was a flame burning in his soul. There was a love he felt, which he chose never to abandon. Where it would take him was yet to be seen. What it would cost him was becoming ever more clear. But that he would be faithful to it was never in doubt. The path of worldly possessions, the path of power and fame, the path of selfish use of talent—all these were options for him, and he refused them all. They were discordant with who he was. He would not be untrue to himself. In Jesus we have one who is able "to sympathize with our weaknesses . . . one who in every respect has been tempted as we are, yet without sinning. . . . In the days of his flesh, Jesus offered up prayers and supplications, with loud cries and tears, . . . and he was heard for his godly fear. Although he was Son, he learned obedience through suffering" (Heb. 4:15; 5:7–8).

Like every human being Jesus lived with the awesomeness of life's uncertainty. He had no script to follow. No plan was written out. No mission was spelled out for him. The "plan of salvation," the Son's "mission on earth,"—the things *we now* speak of—were known after the fact. They were written down and spelled out after they happened. Their marvelous coherence is seen only in hindsight. It was Jesus who worked them out. It was he who determined their course. It was he who took on, as every human must, the overwhelming responsibility for each moment's decisions. It was he who decided, from the depths of his loving heart, what he would do. He acted—not because some script called for it, but because the moment called for it. Ever true to himself, ever faithful to his Father, he did what was called for by every unpredictable, contingent moment of human life.[22]

The flame burning in his heart was his only guide. Invisible to the eye, elusive to concepts, inexpressible in words, impossible to define,

167

it was nonetheless real. In touch with the depths of his very self, he was in touch with that flame. He had a sense of himself. It would be too much to say he knew who he was. Knowledge is clear and precise and articulate. He had no such easy thing to go on. What he had to follow was more elusive than that—a hunch, an intuition, some vague but insistent sense.[23] It was obscure, hidden, secret. But it was real, and he followed it. Despite what it cost, despite where it led, he would be true to himself.

Jesus, Challenged As We Are: A Homily   Poor Jesus! Poor, poor Jesus! Sometimes we think we have it hard. We wonder what we should do with our lives. Consider his case. What he was had never happened before. There was no precedent for him to follow, no model to imitate. There were no words even to suggest it, no concepts to fix it in mind. he could not "become a carpenter," or make a career as a "teacher," or become a "doctor" or a "lawyer" or a "businessman." It would not do to "get married" or "get into sales" or become a "writer" or "typist" or "house contractor." He would not be himself were he simply to "raise a family" or "take up a hobby" or "hang loose for a while." Whatever he would make of himself would fit no pre-formed mold. He would inevitably fall through the cracks of society's structures and categories. Who in history was so alone as Jesus? Who else so clearly had to determine his or her own fate? Who ever had to live with such trust in God? His only guide was his sense of himself, his sense of utter dependence on his Father. Neither he nor others could comprehend it.

Sometimes I like to imagine what might have been happening at Caesarea Philippi.[24] Of course, the Gospels do not give us enough information to make accurate conclusions about Jesus' emotional and psychological experiences. Unlike us, the early Christians did not seem to be much interested in such things. Nonetheless, I like to speculate. And since Jesus is as human as we are, there is some basis for speculation. Jesus was becoming more and more aware of where his chosen path was taking him. He was disturbed by this. He did not want to provoke hostile reactions. He did not want people to be confused. And he did not want to get himself killed. Yet he would not be untrue to himself, unfaithful to his heavenly Father. In his anguish he turned to his friends. He hesitatingly began to share with them his life's scenario as he saw it inevitably unfolding. He wondered how

168

they saw him. What were people saying about him? He hoped his friends would support him. He wanted some encouragement to adhere to the path he knew he had to follow. It is easier to be virtuous when others give their support. So he dared to expose himself, to reveal his anguish. And the reaction: "Oh, come on, Jesus! Don't talk that way. You're going to be great. Forget this talk about suffering." And it was Peter who led the group—as always. Jesus could not share the questions of his innermost heart. Not even his closest friends understood.

Of course, this account is purely speculative. It is completely homiletic. It is at least one remove from Mark's account, which is itself is at least one remove from the actual historical occurrence. It is a kerygmatic statement.[25] Who knows if Jesus and his followers talked so personally? Who knows what they were really feeling on any particular occasion? The gospels simply do not give us that kind of information. Such speculation is purely homiletic. But it does serve a purpose, just as all good preaching does. It helps to translate Jesus' life among us into terms that we can understand. It helps us to appreciate that he was just like us.

I also like to speculate about what might have occurred at Jesus' trial. Again, actual Gospel evidence is meager even regarding the procedure of the trial(s). Nonetheless, could this have happened? They call in the witnesses. Jesus blatantly broke the Sabbath law. He disrupted the regular functioning in the temple. He uses blasphemous ways of speaking about and praying to God. He counters the Law of Moses and claims to have authority over it. He is disrupting the stability of Judaism and the peace of the province. It was clear where all this was leading. Legal or not, they were going to get rid of him. And Jesus? How easy it would have been to back off. "Wait a minute.. Don't take these things so seriously. You misunderstand me. Let's talk this over. Just let me explain." A few words is all it would have taken. Jesus could so easily have hedged a bit, toned down his words, covered himself. A little bit of compromise goes a long way in tight situations. He would have been safe. Dishonest—yes. Discredited—well, a little bit. But safe, safe to live out his now petty life in the fear of again offending the authorities, in the self-contempt of compromised integrity. No, for Jesus it was not to be that way. He was who he was, and he would be true to himself. He said what he said, and he was honest in that. He would not take it back. Better to die hanging on a cross than to extinguish the flame of love in his soul. Death would easier to bear—and more promising—than dishonesty. His yoke was light and his burden, sweet.

Jesus' Human Freedom   Things might have been different, but they were not. In fact, Jesus was true to himself throughout his life. He was faithful to his heavenly Father. Despite the cost, despite even death, he was ever true to himself.

His fidelity was the effect of his human freedom. Whatever he did, he did freely. He chose his own life each step of the way. He himself made himself to be what he was as daily decisions slowly expressed and forged the historical expression of his unique identity. The freedom he exercised was human freedom. As a human being, the Eternal Word freely lived his human life in absolute fidelity.

Death, the Definitive Human Act   In human freedom Jesus Christ chose to be himself. Even in the face of death, he did not deny himself. He was who he was, and he expressed that faithfully. Death itself gave the final and best opportunity for Jesus to express in perfect fidelity his absolute "self/gift-edness" of the Father.

With every decision of life, we determine our fate, we create the historical expression of our selves. Life is a process. To be humanly is to become.[26] Where I will live, what work I will do, what people I will befriend—all these decisions make me concretely to be who I am. There is a cost attached to each: to live here I cannot also live there; to do this work I give up that; to have these friends I invest the time I might have spent with those. These costs are little deaths. They draw the line between what for me is and, on the other hand, what could have been but now is lost forever. But all such decisions are incomplete, and none is irreversible. As long as we are alive, we may not be able to retrieve the past, but we can change our minds. We can change our lives. We can change ourselves. In this respect, our actual physical death is different. Death is final, complete, and irreversible. The choice that death expresses is complete. The surrender of self in death leaves nothing more to give. The choice that death expresses is irreversible. At death the time for choices ends. Thus, death becomes the perfect expression of oneself. In death one's whole self is at stake, and irreversibly. How one dies becomes the consummate expression of one's life and self.[27]

The Consummation of Jesus' Human Becoming   Even in death Jesus was true to himself. He went to his death because of his fidelity. So his death expressed perfectly, completely, and irreversibly the self that he was all along: totally dependent on the Father, totally Begotten-of-the-Father. Jesus' moment of death was the culmination of his life: "Father, into thy hands I commit my spirit" (Lk. 23:46). Through his fidelity even unto death, in a definitive way he made himself to be historically who he is eternally. He spelled out in history his eternal identity. He who is completely "of-the-Father" became by human self-determination wholly the Father's. He who is eternally Son-of-the-Father became also historically perfectly Son-of-the-Father. Because of his fidelity, even to the end, Jesus' human life became the historical expression, most perfectly possible for a human being, of his ultimate identity. Through his human life and consummately in his act of death, Jesus Christ became in historical concreteness what he is eternally in God. He ever chose to be who he was. Daily he confirmed that reality in his life. Finally, through his death, completely and irreversibly, he became in history who he is in eternity—totally of the Father.

Jesus' Fidelity, Not his Death, as Valuable   Obviously, the important issue was Jesus' absolute fidelity—fidelity even at the cost of death. Not the physical suffering, not the emotional anguish, not the actual experience of death itself, but the fidelity expressed through all these, the fidelity constant despite all these, made Jesus' death valuable. Of course, Jesus' absolute fidelity did not come to expression apart from his death. Nonetheless, when the distinction is drawn, not his death but his fidelity was what mattered. God neither willed nor wanted nor enjoyed the murder of his Son. However, with his Son's perfect integrity and constant fidelity the Eternal Father was, indeed, well pleased.

Jesus, Faithful Son, Raised from the Dead   Jesus' human life did make a difference. At the end of it he was different from what he was at the beginning. Through his human living, by every free decision of every day, he developed. Like all of us, he made himself be what he would be. With every new decision, he expressed his very self more and more fully in history. Humanly he expressed his eternal identity, that which constitutes him as distinct from the Father and the Holy Spirit in eternity, his being born of the Father. Throughout his human

171

life, he was being himself. In his fidelity unto death, completely and definitely, as perfectly as is humanly possible, he was Son-of-the-Father on earth. Poured out in death, as human he became empty and nothing of himself, totally dependent on the Father for his very being, even as he is eternally Begotten-of-the-Father. So the Father raised him up. It was not proper that Eternal-Word, wholly the Father's on earth as he is eternally in heaven, should lie in the defeat of death. For, in fact, death was no defeat but rather the point of victory for Christ. Christ used death as a tool. Through it Eternal-Word became himself completely in his humanity. Not even by appearance, then, not even to the shallow eyes of history, should death appear to have the last word. Eternal-Son, who became wholly Son on earth through his human life, should be glorified in a way fitting for Only-begotten-of-the-Father. So God raised up his Son. He restored to him the glory that was his before the world began.[28] God gave divine glory to Jesus Christ—not only in his divinity; for in his divinity the Son is glorified eternally. God gave divine glory to Jesus Christ in his humanity. Eternal-Son-become-human was raised up not merely to the height of human perfection. Through his death Jesus had already achieved this. Rather, he was raised up to perfection beyond what is proper to a human. Insofar as it is possible for a human to share in the divine way of being, Eternal-Son as human would so share. For him such sharing would be appropriate. Because of who he is, he ought to share that fullness. For him it would be expected. Indeed, from the point of view of human wisdom, such fullness should have been his from the beginning. Once made human, he should already have enjoyed the fullest perfection proper to a human—and more. In fact, following just this line of thought, a former and commonly accepted christology did attribute to Jesus divine prerogatives even during his earthly life: he knew all things from the first moment of his human existence, he was able to do all things. Misunderstanding of the Gospels' intent made such a christology possible. Yet, as we now understand in still another context, God's ways are not our ways. According to divine wisdom, Jesus Christ—Eternal-Son though he is—was to live our human life as every other human does. Through the process of ordinary human life, he was to determine what he would be in the concrete reality of history. He must be faithful to himself, faithful to his eternal identity in God. He would complete that human task by

172

the passage through death. Only then would the fullness of glory be given to him.

So Jesus rose from the dead. The kind of human life he could and should have had from the beginning was given to him. In his humanity he was divinized.

Divinization   I use the term "divinization" to indicate what happened to Jesus in his resurrection. Divinization means that a human being shares, insofar as possible, in God's own qualities. What exactly this entails cannot be fully explained in itself. It is something we affirm in faith and only gropingly approximate in understanding. We do not understand what the resurrection is. We know what it is not: a mere resuscitation to our ordinary human way of being. Beyond that, we can only hint. Even to say it is "a human sharing in God's own qualities" does not explain it. All our conceptions of God—total understanding, perfect knowledge, complete power, infinite love, all perfection eternally—are but human suggestions that attempt to make some sense of "God."[29] We do not know what God is.[30] Then we can hardly understand what it might mean to share in God's way of being. Still, some suggestion can be made to help understanding. Indeed, to make that suggestion is the task of theology.

Consider that our minds are insatiable in their curiosity. We want to know more and more. We want to understand everything. As things are, perhaps only some people sometimes actually allow such unbridled curiosity. Perhaps for most people, life is routine and dull, and questions are rare. They say that children are full of questions. With bright and excited eyes, they are constantly asking "What is it?" and "Why?" They also say that most children lose most or all of that initial curiosity. By the sixth grade they have learned well. They have learned not to ask questions. Instead, they have learned to pass exams! In reality, there is little place left in the contemporary world for the "pure" and "unrestricted desire to know."[31] Few pursue pure scholarship or science, asking questions and seeking answers, simply for the joy of knowing. Nonetheless, if unleashed, our minds do have an insatiable curiosity. We want to know and understand everything about everything.

More than this, from one point of view, our minds are geared to know everything about everything. Knowledge is the correct affirmation of what really is. What is correctly affirmed as so, is what is.[32] On

173

this understanding, reality and knowledge are correlates. The structure of our minds parallels the structure of reality. Reality is all there is
to be known. Conversely, whatever there is to be known is real. Our
minds are open to whatever there is to be known. Our minds are
open to whatever is real. They are open to all reality. In fact, the ideal
goal of our minds is to know everything about everything.

Nonetheless, there is a discrepancy here. The ideal goal of our
minds may be to know everything about everything. Moreover, we
may indeed want to know everything about everything. In fact,
however, we do not know everything about everything; and bound
by the limitations of ordinary human life, we cannot know everything
about everything. Though our minds in themselves might be ideally
open to such a thing, in fact, they do not attain it. For other factors
enter in. Our learning is a process of accumulation. We know bit by
bit. Our knowing is limited. So we cannot know everything about
everything, for such knowledge would represent the ideal goal of the
process of human knowing. To know everything about everything
would take us beyond the pale of human knowledge. Moreover, we
are embodied beings. We are not simply pure mind turned loose on
all there is to be known. Our potential to know is limited: we know in
the body, and we only know what is also somehow in the body.
Whatever is not somehow embodied—like God—we could not know.
Within the ordinary limitations of human knowledge, we cannot
know God. In fact, then, we cannot know everything about everything.

There is a tension built into the actual human situation. Our
minds themselves are open to and want to know everything about
everything. Yet the limitations of our earthly life preclude such an
achievement.[33] But suppose that somehow these limitations were
lifted. Suppose the ideal potential of the human mind were freed.
Suppose that the space-time limitations of the physical world were
transcended and that God were present to a human being through the
immediate presence of a human to himself or herself. If in being
present to himself or herself that human were *ipso facto* present to God
and if the space-time, bit-by-bit boundedness of human knowledge
were surpassed, then that human would know God and in knowing
God would know everything about everything. That human would
know even as God knows. He or she would share in God's way of

knowing. In such a case, he or she would share humanly what is proper to God alone. A human would share in a quality of divinity. To this extent, it could be said that a human was divinized.

A similar analysis can be made about the human desire and capacity to love. We would like to love everything that is lovable and to love it to the extent that it can be loved. We would like to love perfectly. Moreover, in the ideal there seems to be no real reason why we could not love that way. People who love deeply claim some apprehension of such perfect love. It appears to be the elusive but nonetheless ideal goal of human loving. In fact, however, our loves are quite imperfect. And the scope of even our most perfect love is restricted by the sheer limits of space and time. The same tension, inherent in the human situation, appears again. But suppose that these limitations were lifted. Suppose a human being were enabled to release the powers of love and love everything insofar as it is lovable. Suppose a human could love perfectly, absolutely, without bounds. In such a case, a human would love even as God loves. A human would share in what is proper to God alone—to love, in fact, all that is lovable insofar as it is lovable. A human would share in a quality of divinity. To this extent, it could be said that a human was divinized.

These considerations explain what divinization means: to share, insofar as it is possible for a human being, in qualities proper to God alone. So conceived, divinization is a created participation in divinity. It is a participation *in divinity* because it allows a human to enjoy certain qualities proper to God alone, like universal knowledge and perfect love. It is a *participation* because a human shares not what is proper to humanity but what is proper only to divinity; a human shares in what is other than his or her own. Moreover, it is but a participation in divinity because a human shares only certain qualities of divinity, like infinite knowledge and love, but does not share other qualities, like God's eternity or God's necessity. A human does not become God. No creature can become Creator. Finally, the participation is *created* because that which is shared is not the eternal, uncreated existence of God. Rather, God grants a human the disproportionate perfection of his or her created humanity and sustains in being this human and her or his disproportionate perfection. The participation in divinity exists and perdures through God's creative power. Divinization is a created participation in divinity.

The disproportionate nature of this created participation in divinity must be emphasized. To know and love with infinite and perfect knowledge and love is not proper to human beings. These acts exceed humanity's expected achievement, as explained above. Infinite knowledge and love are proper to God, not to humans. Said more generally, divinization is possible, but it is disproportionate to humanity. Though not in opposition to humanity's intrinsic potential, it is a fulfillment that is beyond human. It is unexpected, gratuitous, gift—precisely in this sense: it is not proper to humanity.[34]

Now, in the resurrection Jesus Christ was divinized. This is my understanding of the resurrection. He is that human being who attained a created participation in divinity. Because of his fidelity even unto death, Jesus Christ, Eternal-Word, expressed as perfectly as humanly possible in history precisely who he is eternally in God. Ever true to himself, through his every human decision and consummately in death, Eternal-Son-of-the-Father made himself to be also in the concreteness of his contingent, historical existence perfectly Son-of-the-Father. What he was—indeed, what he became by his own doing—on earth expressed as perfectly as humanly possible who he is eternally. So the Father raised him up and gave him a glory that surpassed that which is proper to any human being, but a glory proper to Son-of-the-Father even as human. Jesus was divinized. The limitations of his human life were suspended. His human mind and heart shared in ideal measure the knowledge and love of God. This human being now knows and loves even as God does. In his resurrection, Jesus Christ himself moved to a perfection beyond what is proper to human beings. In Jesus Christ a human being was divinized.

The Objective Reality of the Resurrection   It is obvious that I presuppose an objective and a concrete understanding of the resurrection. The resurrection was something that happened to Jesus Christ. It entails a transformation in that man, Jesus. It indicates the entry of an objective new reality on the human scene, though the point of entry is on the crossover between history and eternity. Granted, Jesus' resurrection also has implications for his disciples. In one sense, it was their experience and not Jesus'. The resurrection does mean the disciples' post-crucifixion experience of Jesus. Granted, too, the New Testament seems more concerned to explicate the resurrection's faith-transforming implications in the disciples than to detail its transforming effect in Jesus himself.[35] Nonetheless, to suggest that the resurrection is *merely* a way of indicating the transformed faith of the disciples is to evacuate the resurrection of any ontological significance. To confess that Jesus Christ rose from the dead is to say something about Jesus as well as something about the faith of the confessors.[36] This presentation takes concretely the faith affirmation about something that happened to Jesus and attempts to provide some reasonable account of what that something might be. New Testament scholars generally agree that the empty tomb accounts are later additions to the original Easter kerygma. But this does not imply that those accounts are false. They intend to say something about Jesus' body and about his tomb—the body rose, the tomb was empty. They are not merely another way of insisting that the disciples found themselves somehow revitalized in faith after Jesus' death.[37] Jesus himself was transformed in the resurrection. He, in his human, physical body, was raised from the grave. This is the meaning of Christian Easter faith.

The above presentation on divinization gives some account of the spiritual dimension of Jesus' transformation in the resurrection. His human capacity for knowledge and love was advanced to its furthest possible perfection. This presupposes that in some way his physical dimension was also transformed. His physical body was freed from its space-time-bound limitations. What might this physical transformation be? With a limited knowledge of physics, I confess that I am working here from pure imagination—imagination formed, no doubt, by artists' conceptions and childhood musings about Jesus' resurrection, but confirmed by the contemporary realization that the ultimate nature of physical matter remains a mystery. Extensive treatment of the doctrine of the resurrection of the body remains to be done. Twentieth-century developments in the field of physics make this a challenging and exciting area of research.[38] Be this as it may. It is part of Christian belief that Jesus' resurrection affected Jesus himself, the whole human race of which he is a part, and the physical cosmos in which he also shares. Unable to explain it, Christianity nonetheless affirms a very concrete understanding of the resurrection.

It must be so. If one would make the life, death, and resurrection of Jesus on integral part of christology—if one would unite the movement from above with that from below—the resurrection must be as real as the incarnation. Relying on Nicea and the constant belief of the Christian Church, Christians affirm the reality of God-become-human in Jesus Christ. Relying on Easter faith and constant Christian hope for salvation through Christ, Christians affirm the reality of the resurrection in Jesus Christ—a transformation of him that entails a transformation of us. The incarnation reaches its completion in the resurrection, and the resurrection is the link between the Eternal Word's human life and a concrete transformation, the salvation, of the world. Just as something new really happened when the Word became flesh, so something new really happened when Christ rose from the dead. The Christ of the incarnation is not the same as the Christ of the resurrection. Something happened in between. A human life intervened—and if it was real, it made a difference. At the incarnation Jesus had a unique possibility. At the resurrection that possibility was fully actualized. The human being, Jesus Christ, was divinized. And that made all the difference in the world—the real world, the human world, the world of spirit *and* body.

Complementarity of the Two Movements

This account speaks of the divine in Jesus Christ in two senses. First, Jesus Christ is God the Only-begotten-of-the-Father. His ultimate identity is eternal and divine. He is the one born eternally of the Father. Second, through the resurrection the man Jesus Christ came to share in certain qualities of divinity even in his humanity. He was divinized. The first indicates Jesus' eternal and natural divinity. Because of it we can rightly say Jesus Christ is God. The second indicates Jesus' created human participation in divinity. Because of it we can say Jesus Christ was divinized. Through the resurrection, also as human he came to share in some of the prerogatives of divinity. The first is Christ's necessary and eternal divinity. As Eternal-Son-of-the-Father, he is eternally God. He does not ever and cannot stop being God. In this sense, even during his pre-resurrectional earthly life when he prescinds from acting through his divinity, he is God. This is the issue clarified in the discussion at Ephesus. The second is Christ's contingent and human participation in divinity. It had a beginning, namely, at the point of Jesus' glorification in the resurrection. The first is the adequate meaning of the decree of Nicea: Jesus Christ is God from God, Light from Light, true God from true God, begotten not made, one in being with the Father. The second is a legitimate understanding of Jesus Christ's resurrection from the dead. The first is key to the first christological movement, the movement from above. The second is key to the second christological movement, the movement from below.

The two senses of the divine in Christ—just as the two movements in christology—are complementary. In God's plan of salvation *as it actually is,* each without the other is incomplete. The incarnation without the resurrection would have been an interesting experiment, a fascinating historical curiosity. But in the last analysis, it would have been without significant effect on human history. It would have been a Jewish version of the Greek myths about the gods. It would have left us—had we ever come to know about it—with the memory of an extraordinary human being, a great hero and model, a remarkable teacher, to be recalled with nostalgia and romantic aspiration. Another prophet, another great philosopher, would have passed through human history. But it would have changed nothing. Such, at least, is one possible scenario, produced by imagination turned to that utterly useless speculation about what *might have been.* On the other hand, the resurrection without the incarnation would be without an adequate base. As things *in fact* unfolded, the one who was raised to divinized glory is no other than Eternal-Son, human and faithful to the end. That such a one be divinized is completely understandable and appropriate. This one deserved divinization. Divinization is his birthright. Human wisdom would have granted it to him from the first moment of his human existence. That divinization should come to him at the end is, finally, as it should be. The resurrection is the rightful completion of the incarnation. The two are complementary.

The Effect of Jesus' Divinization: Salvation to Humankind

The confluence of the two christological movements results in a new reality in creation: a divinized human being. This occurrence has implications for every human being. It introduces into history a new possibility for human becoming. It changes the ultimate meaning of human life.

The Parameters of Human Possibility   Human reality, historical reality, is contingent reality. It is what it is, not because it must be so, but merely because it happens to be so. Only God is necessary; all else is contingent. So human life is limited by possibilities, though the outer limits of those possibilities have still to be clarified. Thus, history is an open system.[39] Not all that is possible already is. There is room for speculation about what humanity might still become. On the other hand, all that already is is certainly possible. Real possibility is known through what is actual. What is, certainly can be. What is mere speculation perhaps could be; then, again, perhaps it really could not be. In a contingent world, we know what is really possible by noting what has already actually occurred. That a human and a horse could mate to produce an intelligent horse or a swift footed child is impossible. It has never happened. That a child could be born with six fingers on each hand is, unfortunately, possible. It has happened. What has happened indicates what is really possible.

The Divine-Human Possibility   When Jesus Christ, a human being, was divinized, a new possibility was introduced into human history. What happened to one human could happen to others. It is really possible. What was for the incarnate Word a unique possibility became, given the proper conditions, a possibility for everyone. In the resurrection the very meaning of humanity changed. The ultimate possible fulfillment proper to humans was surpassed.[40] A human being shares in divine qualities. The goal of human development is no longer merely human. Now it is also divine. To be human means more than it used to mean. So everyone who is human is by that very fact involved in something beyond the human. Each one is opened to participation in the divine. Humanity now shares a divine-human possibility.

The Solidarity of the Human Race   The achievement of Jesus Christ opens a new possibility for all humans because of the solidarity that binds the human race as one.[41] By our very nature, we humans are solidary beings. It is folly to suppose that the human individual is ever an isolated being. One may be an individual, but the very humanity that makes one human binds one with every other human.

The family offers the clearest and most immediate example of this. Members of the same family resemble one another. This is so not only physically. Shared genes, shared eating habits, shared personal health and hygiene practices, and living together explain physical resemblance in shape and behavior among family members. But the resemblance also includes values and interests, patterns of thinking, outlooks on life. Not only physically but also in much of their thinking and acting, family members are like one another. They become what they are through their relationships with one another. The humanity which they share in common with all humans is specified in its concrete development through shared experiences. What they in fact become depends on one another. Human becoming is conditioned by human sociality.

The example can be expanded, for the same issue applies also to larger social groups—communities, regions, nations. Though it is foolish to assume that the people of any nation are all alike, it is also foolish to deny any common nationality traits. In broad and general ways, people who live together become like one another. They influence one another's becoming what they are.

The human is a social phenomenon. Individual and social are but different perspectives on the same phenomenon. Our most prized human qualities are social in nature. The language we use to speak and to think is a social product, a social inheritance. Only through social interaction does a child learn to speak. And, granted that thinking is internalized conversation,[42] only through social interaction does a child learn to think. The very development of mental capacity and the eliciting of responsible choice occur in social interaction. Even a hermit who goes off alone to a cave takes along a whole set of social encounters that, internalized, evince their presence in the hermit's very feeling and thinking and acting.

Human consciousness itself is no private possession. If it were, communication through symbols—language—could never be explained.[43] How does one know what the symbols mean? Does one deduce the meaning of present symbols on the basis of past ones? Then how explain the functioning of the past ones? Explanation by infinite regress will not do. The same question, pushed back a few steps, still remains. How does the process start? Somewhere along the line—everywhere, in fact—something more than external signs, visible and auditory, passes between people. We are in touch with one another on levels of mind that generally escape our notice. In some way our very minds interpenetrate one another. Otherwise how do we know what we and one another are thinking? One and the same thought is in more than one mind. Consciousness itself, the basis of thought, must be a shared reality. At heart the human is social.

The whole human race is bound up as one. Our hopes for advancement lie with one another. What one has achieved through a lifetime of labor, once achieved, can soon become the common property of all. The solidarity of the race even bridges generation gaps. We stand on the shoulders of giants, and they see farther through our eyes. The successes of ancestors provide the base for life today, and the dreams of today are the achievements of tomorrow. Those who have gone before us live on in us, as we will live on in our children. In some way each of us embodies the history of the race. Success for those who went before us depends on those who come after us. The destiny of all is bound up together. We stand or we fall as a whole. The life and the world that anyone has is never that one's alone. Our life is shared, and our world is shared. A solidarity binds all humans as one.

Human Solidarity, the Basis of Our Union in Christ   In Christ the solidarity of the human race becomes the vehicle for divine life. Because he is a member of the human race, his achievement affects all humankind.[44] The divinization of this one human introduces the real possibility for divinization in all. For all share the same life and world; all share the same destiny. The fulfillment of the human race is one, common to all. By entering the human race, Eternal-Son introduced a new ingredient into the pot of human history. By living true to himself, he fulfilled the unique human possibility of his calling. By rising from the dead, he achieved a new highpoint in human advancement. Henceforth, under the proper circumstances, some participation in divinity is possible for all humans. The link is the humanity that he and all share.

Divinization is a disproportionate fulfillment for humankind. Obviously, then, something more than common humanity is needed if divinization for all is to be explained. That more is the Holy Spirit, and I will treat it presently. Here, another critical point must be stressed. The solidarity of the human race is essential to the spread of Jesus' achievement to other human beings. Too easily we attempt to explain our unity with and in Christ by appeal to "mysterious" factors. The result is almost magic or fantasy. We suppose some "mystical" bonds, some "rays of supernatural force." We appeal to metaphors—radio waves, invisible to sight yet acting through the air. Yet our link with Jesus is the same one that binds us to one another and to every human being ever to live. The solidarity of our race—nothing more mysterious than that, though marvelous it is—the solidarity of our race is the vehicle by which the divinization of Jesus becomes a real possibility for us.

Salvation is transmitted through the concrete realities of our worldly living. The elements of history become the conveyers of grace. The bodies in which we live, the consciousness we share, the meanings and values that make us concretely what we are—that which binds us as one people also conveys divine fulfillment to us. For Jesus Christ has transposed the significance of all these things. They are now caught up in the glory of that human's divinization. For this reason Christianity understands faith and grace to come to us through earthly word and sacrament. Concrete historical elements are our source of divine life. We have saving contact with Christ through the Church's living tradition—a "handing down" that passes through the signs and objects of the Christian religion and especially through the hands and very being of Christians who precede and surround us. And we ourselves, the contemporaries of our race, stand on the moving front of salvation in Christ as it passes on through history. In Christ the solidarity of the race becomes the communion of saints. Our very sharing in humanity is our link with the human who was divinized, Jesus Christ.

The Need for the Holy Spirit   Jesus Christ introduced into history a new possibility for human becoming. The model was set. The possibility was actualized. Through the solidarity of the race, divinization is now a real, universal human possibility. However, another factor is needed before the achievement of Christ can be reproduced in us. Something more is required before the possibility becomes actual in us. Jesus' divinization in the resurrection was contingent on his becoming perfectly Son-of-the-Father also in his human life. And that, in turn, was contingent on his actually being Son-of-the-Father. His divine identity set the unique possibility that, when actualized in his humanity, resulted in his divinization. Divinization is a fulfillment disproportionate to humanity. It is explained in Jesus Christ because of who he is. This divine factor in Jesus makes his divinization understandable. By being true to himself, he was on the way to

183

divinization. Disproportionate to humans, divinization for him was nonetheless appropriate; indeed, it seems required. He is Only-begotten-of-the-Father.

That the fulfillment appropriate to Jesus might also be appropriate to us, God sent the Holy Spirit to dwell in our hearts. The Holy Spirit is the final factor needed to account for our divinization. The Spirit given to us is God, Breathed-forth by the Father and the Son. God now dwells in us. Given to us as our very own, the Spirit becomes a divine principle in us. In this we become like Jesus Christ, the divine one who, in taking on our humanity, became like us. In Jesus and in us there are now both a divine and a human principle. The divine principle in us, the Holy Spirit, is God's own life in us. Through the Holy Spirit, a new life is ours. We are reborn. Like Jesus, each of us is now a child of God. By pouring the Holy Spirit into our hearts and so renewing us, God has made us adopted sons and daughters.

The Work of the Holy Spirit   Poured into our hearts, the Spirit dwells in us as a constant companion. The Spirit is our Paraclete. Inspiring and motivating and guiding our ways, the Spirit transforms the movements of our hearts. The Spirit is present in the very depths of our being, closer to us than we sometimes are to ourselves. Being present to ourselves, in the same act we are present also to God, the Holy Spirit within us.[45] Like a flame burning in our souls, the Spirit leads us forth. Invisible to the eye, impossible to define, elusive to concepts, inexpressible in words, that burning presence is nonetheless real. It leads us to where we do not know. We follow only in faith. Like Jesus now in all things, we lead our lives trusting in our heavenly Father, who leads us through the Spirit within. Being true to ourselves, we are true to the Spirit within, and true to the Spirit, we are faithful to the Father. Faithful to the Father, we become more and more in our concrete selves sons and daughters of the Father. We reproduce in our own lives what Jesus achieved in his. We conform ourselves more and more to the image of God's Son. We become more totally like Jesus, our brother. Heeding the Spirit within and freely choosing day by day to become what we will be, we follow the path that Jesus first trod. We go the way he opened for us. We move toward the divine glory that that human first achieved. When in death we confirm our fidelity, as Jesus Christ did his own, the Father will bring to completion the divine life poured into our hearts. Divinization will be ours, as well. In our case, now, just as in Jesus' own, such fulfillment would be appropriate. For we are sons and daughters of the Father.

God, All in All   Our divinization in Christ is not widely preached. Nonetheless, human divinization is a central theme in the Christian tradition. 2 Peter teaches that we are called to God's own "glory and excellence" and we are to "become partakers of the divine nature" (1:4). 1 John 3:2 says that, indeed, "we are God's children now" and "we shall be like him." The early fathers of the Church preached at length about this mystery.[46] A prayer still used in the Roman Catholic Mass during the mixing of the water and wine sums up this patristic teaching: "By the mystery of this water and wine, may we come to share in the divinity of Christ, who humbled himself to share in our humanity."

Our ultimate salvation is the reproduction in us of the divinization that was first Jesus Christ's. He saved us by opening the way through human history to divinization. The Holy Spirit assists us by becoming the divine guiding principle in the depths of our own souls. Our own free self-determination in the Spirit leads us to disproportionate divine fulfillment. Our own daily life in Christ becomes the substance of divine life growing in us. The Father completes our salvation by granting final divinization. We come to share in the Father's divine way of being, shared eternally with the Son and the Holy Spirit, attained insofar as possible in his humanity by the incarnate Son, and, through the work of the Son and the Holy Spirit, given finally, in some measure, also to us. So God becomes all in all. The plan of salvation reaches its end.

Jesus and We as "Divine"   Human salvation is the reproduction in us of the divinization first achieved in Jesus Christ. Yet there are important differences between our case and Jesus'. Jesus is the natural Son of the Father. His "bornness" of the Father is eternal. It is what determines his eternal identity. He is God. On the other hand, we are "adopted children" of the Father. Our natural status is creature. We are not God; we cannot become God. For love of us, the Father chooses to share with us certain aspects of his own divine way of being. Over and above the life God gave us in creating us human, the Father also offers us a share in certain divine qualities. Pouring the

Holy Spirit into our hearts, the Father gives us a share in divine life and so adopts us as children. We are, then, adopted children in the divine life and natural children in our created, human life. But the Eternal Son is the natural child of God in the divine life and through Mary also makes his very own a second natural childhood in created, human life.

There is a second contrast. After the resurrection, Jesus can be said to be divine in two senses. First, he is eternally divine—he is God—as Eternally-Begotten-of-the-Father. Second, he is also divine insofar as his humanity shares in certain qualities proper to divinity; he is divinized. On the other hand, we are divine in only one sense, the second. We can be said to be divine insofar as we are divinized. More accurately, we *will be* divine when we share fully in the new possibility Jesus Christ opened to us. We are divine only in an analogous sense of the term. We are not God. We merely share in certain qualities proper to God.

It might be suggested that we are divine also in another sense, insofar as the Holy Spirit is poured into our hearts. But that would be inaccurate. It is the Holy Spirit in us who is divine, not we ourselves. Though the Spirit touches the depths of our being and transforms us, that intimacy does not cancel the distinction between the Holy Spirit and us. All retain their distinct identities. We are not swallowed up into and lost in the Divinity. The divinity that is within us is the Spirit's, not our own. The transformation that the Spirit effects in us is our sanctification, our growing salvation. It is none other than our incipient divinization. Even though the uncreated, divine Holy Spirit is given to us, only in the second sense can we ourselves ever be said to be divine.

A third contrast summarizes the others. Our divinization is derivative. It depends on that of Jesus Christ. His is originative. It is the source of our own. Because of him and in him we share in divine life. That is why we profess that Jesus Christ is our savior. Our salvation—our divinization—comes through him. It depends on his own.

Implications for Spirituality   These contrasts between Jesus Christ and us take on critical importance in view of increasing contemporary interest in spirituality. For these contrasts determine the uniqueness of Christianity in comparison with other accounts of supposed human divinization. Some Eastern accounts also propose that

186

we are to share in divine life. Yet their understanding is significantly different.

The Christian understanding holds that we are not God; we are creatures. Our creation in God's "image and likeness" (Gen. 1:26) does not suggest that we are God. Rather, we are *like* God—like God in that we are made responsible for creation and we are to "create" our own life and world. We are given a human spirit, alert, intelligent, reasonable, responsible. We are given capacities that set us over all creation. In this we are like God. We share with God in the work of making and caring for our world. If Christianity allows that there is, indeed, a divine principle in us, that principle is the uncreated Holy Spirit given to us. The Christian understanding is rooted deeply in the Jewish awareness of God's inviolable transcendence. The Christian understanding never confuses the created human spirit with the uncreated Holy Spirit, God in us.

On the other hand, some Eastern accounts assume that we will share divine life because we, in fact, are divine from the beginning. Our deepest nature is supposedly a "spark of the divine." Our most hidden self is supposedly God. Such accounts suggest that all humans are more or less what Christianity affirms only about Jesus Christ. This is to say, they blur the distinction between what is human and what is divine.

The further result is that these accounts do not affirm the validity of the physical world in which we live. Obscuring our own created status, they undervalue our experience in this world. Then, not worldly experience but some supposed reality beyond this world is considered really real. The doctrine of reincarnation follows—I cannot be sure if you are really you or someone else reincarnated in you. Such a view devalues the world as we know it. Its goal for spiritual growth is to free oneself from this world and to attain ever more subtle degrees of internal "spiritual" experiences. This view is basically dualism: a devaluation of the physical and an exaltation of the spiritual. That both physical and the spiritual in us are created is overlooked. The spiritual, because it is more subtle, is identified with the divine; and the physical is thought to be an opposing—or even an evil—principle.

Such an understanding is in clear conflict with Christianity's basic incarnationalism, the affirmation of the worthiness of God's creation, capable even of conveying divine life. The practical implications of these different views for lived spirituality are far-reaching. What Christians believe about Jesus tends to determine how we understand and live our own lives. It is important to keep clear the contrasts between the divine in Jesus Christ and in us. No less than the preservation of Christianity is at stake here.[47]

A New Paradigm

This present christology is intended to be a comprehensive understanding about Jesus that reconciles contemporary concerns with traditional Christian belief. It locks together in one systematic presentation an understanding of the incarnation, Jesus' human life, death, and resurrection, and the salvation of humankind. Might this christology serve as a new paradigm? Can it stand as the master-model that integrates the available data, addresses the relevant questions, and incorporates all other models? Judgment on the first score will rest on what is already said or will be said elsewhere in this book. Here there is need for a brief statement about this christology's ability to include other contemporary models of Jesus. The focus of this book has required extensive treatment of doctrinal and philosophical issues. It may appear that the resultant christology is overly abstract, tediously technical, and above all, narrowly traditional. A comparison with John O'Grady's six models of Jesus will show that this is not the case.

Obviously, the present christology is a combination of the two most important contemporary models: The Incarnation of the Second Person of the Blessed Trinity (the christology from above) and The Human Face of God (the christology from below). The present christology retains what is valid and useful in both while avoiding the shortcomings in each.

Like the first, the present christology is faithful to official church teaching, clearly preserves the divinity of Jesus, and allows for much theoretical expansion, integrating Jesus' mission, miracles, knowledge and lack thereof, resurrection, and relationship to the Christian community, the Church. In addition, the present christology does find a basis in Scripture, does not eclipse the meaning of the humanity of Jesus, does not stifle theological thinking—or responsible Chris-

188

tian living—by adhering to defined doctrine, and furthers Christian piety by insisting that the believer identify with the human Jesus.

Like the second model, The Human Face of God, the present christology affirms Jesus' human life in every detail not only as the expression of revelation of God, but indeed, as the very life of God, the Eternal Son himself. Furthermore, this christology relates Jesus to real human life like our own. It avoids any false dichotomy between the human and the divine by affirming a union of the two—hypostatic in Christ and through the Holy Spirit in us. It restores a balance by emphasizing the material as well as the spiritual. By highlighting the role of the Holy Spirit, it emphasizes the importance of the present and does not either canonize the past or live in the future. It is in full accord with contemporary biblical scholarship about Jesus. And it is open to effective pastoral application. Unlike the second model, this christology is not likely to lose awareness of the divinity and degenerate into a mere humanism, nor to forget the afterlife, not to become anti-intellectual, nor to lose the distinction between God and humans and so fall into a form of pantheism.

The present christology also integrates the insights and meets the concerns of the other four models of Jesus. Like the model, The Mythological Christ, the present christology retains a message that inspires and challenges, and it is pastorally relevant and frees dogma from imprisoning rigidity. Yet unlike this model, it affirms the objective truth of Christian belief; it grounds its inspiration in objective reality.

Although the present christology understands ultimate salvation in terms of divinization, it does not discredit partial expressions of the ultimate in finite history. This christology can incorporate the model, Jesus, The Ethical Liberator. The present christology sees the Holy Spirit within us as the root of all true liberation—freedom from sin and ultimate death and so freedom for justice and love, peace and virtue, and advancement of all that is right and good among humankind. In his own time and place and as was appropriate then and there, Jesus made the coming of God's Reign the central theme of his preaching and even knew God's Reign to be present in himself. Become somehow like Jesus through the indwelling of the Holy Spirit, yet in our own time and place and in ways appropriate here and now, we, too, must proclaim a Reign of Justice and Peace and exercise our part in the transformation of our world. In all this, the Holy Spirit takes the lead, enabling us to do in our historical situation what the man Jesus did in his own. Here there is no slavish imitation of Christ. Rather, there is the faithful response to the Holy Spirit, who brings to completion in us in our concrete case what Jesus brought to completion in his particular case. The Holy Spirit inspires us to achieve in our lives what Jesus achieved in his, perfect fidelity to the Father. But the Holy Spirit does not lead us to do always exactly what Jesus did; indeed, activities appropriate in Jesus' culture may not be appropriate or even right in our own. Moreover, the lead of the transcendent Holy Spirit keeps us from identifying definitively with any particular social order. No order is perfect; each needs to be corrected. The Reign of God is not identical with the structures of this world.

As is obvious, the present christology does not advocate a pie-in-the-sky notion of salvation. It is not oblivious to this-wordly concerns. Our ultimate salvation, divinization, is intrinsically linked to and is the fulfillment of faithful living in this world. According to this christology, avoidance of this life for the sake of one to come entails the loss of both. Thus, the present christology can integrate the model, Jesus, The Ethical Liberator.

However, in principle the present christology is perhaps even more revolutionary than this other model. The Ethical Liberator model seeks a basis for human liberation in Jesus, the liberator,[48] but is hard pressed extensively to develop that image of Jesus on the basis of contemporary information about the historical Jesus. The present christology has no need to find in Jesus a model of liberation that corresponds to contemporary political needs. Rather, in this case and in every other that concerns our own daily living, the present christology gives way to a pneumatology. It highlights the Holy Spirit's role in guiding us through our lives. By Spirit-guided fidelity to the heavenly Father, through our human pursuit of justice, we will achieve that ultimate salvation that includes all others and that the incarnate Son made available to us—participation in the very life of God.

By the same token, the present christology can incorporate the model of Jesus as The Man for Others. This christology presents Jesus as a real human being. There is no docetism here. Jesus is deeply engaged in this world, responding to life's challenge moment to moment and so determining his own fate. His fidelity to himself, Eternal Son, does not separate him from concern for others. On the contrary, true to himself in his human state, he is aware of his connection with all humanity, and he lives out his life in loving service. His very fidelity to himself in every concrete situation *is* his service to others.[49] Through it he makes the contribution that he alone among all human beings could make. In this he gives us, each unique in his or her own way, an example. Now it comes clear that the dichotomy between "self-serving" and "altruistic" is misconceived and misleading. The telling difference is rather between "authentic" and "inauthentic."[50] The path to Jesus' own divinization and the path to the redemption of others is one and the same. It is a path of fidelity to oneself and so the path of life-giving and lasting service to others— in and through this world and even beyond this world. For us, then, the one supremely true to himself is the supreme example of the servant of others.

Here again, there is no room for pie-in-the-sky religion. The Holy Spirit in us leads us to do in our lives as Jesus did in his. Moreover that Spirit links us most powerfully with all others—all humankind— who possess the same, one Spirit. We are all one body.[51] To be true to ourselves is to serve one another, and vice versa. In the Spirit and so in Christ, we grow in divine life precisely through our living in this world, not by fleeing this world. The very human life we all share has, in Christ, become the vehicle of divine life. The present christology gives solid theological basis for this-worldly Christian concern and service. It easily incorporates the model of Jesus as The Man for Others without neglecting other aspects of traditional christological belief.

Finally, the present christology can also incorporate the model, Jesus, Personal Savior. This christology includes soteriology as an integral part of its conception. More narrowly, then, this christology and its soteriology include concern for personal salvation. Moreover, emphasis on the role of the Holy Spirt in human salvation makes the present christology attractive to the charismatic renewal movement, where the model, Jesus, Personal Savior, is most prominent. And acknowledgement of Jesus' miracles as acts of a particularly gifted human being doing God's work gives a nuanced and theologically sound basis for enthusiastic acceptance of charismatic gifts like tongues and healings.[52] On the other hand, the solid doctrinal basis of the present christology, its correlative emphasis on both Jesus and the Holy Spirit, its firm insistence on the social nature of the human, its dependence on historical-critical interpretation of the Scripture, and its emphasis on human freedom and responsibility in all human activities counter the excesses to which the model, Jesus, Personal Savior, is prone. It appears, then, that the present christology can easily incorporate this model and all the other models of Jesus. It recommends itself as a master-model. It can become the new paradigm that contemporary christology is seeking and contemporary Christianity needs.

Summary

Here is a new "model" of Jesus, indeed, perhaps a new paradigm. It is a comprehensive systematic christology[53] that integrates the christology from above, the christology from below, and an account of Jesus' saving work, the redemption of the human race. It is a master-framework into which other models of Jesus can be integrated. The focal features of this comprehensive christology are the identity of Jesus Christ as Only-begotten-of-the-Father and his perfect human fidelity to himself and so to his heavenly Father. Only-begotten-of-the-Father surrendered his divine prerogatives and became human. He would live fully within the limitations of humanity. Then his divine identity would present him a possibility unique in human history. By being faithful to himself he would at the same time be faithful also to his Eternal Father. Moreover, he would express in historical concreteness that which makes him be who he is eternally: total dependence on his Father. By each moment's free human decision, in historical reality he would be a perfect Child of God. At the price of misunderstanding, persecution, and death, he was faithful. The Father raised him from the dead, transforming his humanity so that it could share in divine qualities—insofar as such a thing is possible to any human being. The human Jesus was divinized. The personal integrity of a lifetime culminated in the definitive transformation of this human being. He was now perfectly humanly—as he is eternally divinely—Son of God. However, because of his entry into human history, this change in Jesus' humanity had effects beyond Jesus himself. The ultimate possible perfection of a human being was now divinization. So the divinization of Jesus Christ introduced a new possibility for all humankind. Jesus Christ had opened humanity to new life in God. Jesus had redeemed the human race. Through the Holy Spirit all humans could now follow the path of Jesus to participation in God's own divine qualities. This "model" shows Jesus as "The Eternal Son of God Become Human and in His Humanity Divinized so that All Humans Might Likewise Become Divinized." More briefly, this is the "model" of "Jesus as the Human True to Himself." Jesus' human fidelity to his divine identity is the source of divinization for himself and all humankind. Chapters Nine and Ten will treat certain aspects of this christology that call for further elaboration.

CHAPTER NINE

Jesus' Human Mind and Heart

The previous chapter presented a picture of Jesus such as contemporary christology allows. This picture is sketchy. It gives no details about "human interest" aspects of Jesus' life, for we simply have no such historical information about Jesus. Instead, the above picture outlines the doctrinal issues that constitute Christian belief about Jesus. The picture relates these issues to one another and to our own salvation. The whole is a coherent and reasonable account of Christian belief, in accord with official Church teaching and with the historical data we do have about Jesus. Yet more can be said. Certain questions still remain, and contemporary theology has some answers for them. The final two chapters will address these questions. The present chapter will treat Jesus' consciousness and knowledge and Jesus' freedom and sinlessness. The final chapter will treat the mystery of our salvation in Christ.

Jesus' Consciousness and Knowledge

The popular rock opera of the late 1960's, *Jesus Christ Superstar*, highlighted a question already prominent in most people's minds:

Jesus Christ Superstar
Do you think you're what they say you are?

The question is about Jesus' knowledge. Did Jesus Christ know he was God? I have already suggested an answer to this question. I argued that Jesus could still be God even if he did not know he was God. For reality, and thought about reality are two different things. And even if the thought is Jesus' own—granted that it is human thought—it might not be wholly adequate to the reality. Indeed, no human being knows himself or herself perfectly. Since Jesus is as human as we are, there is no reason to expect him to know himself fully. He could still be God even if he did not know, in his human mind, that he is God.

Obviously, the suggestion is that he did not think he was who we now say he is. He did not *know* he was God. But the issue is more complex than this direct answer allows. For its meaning is ambiguous. Unless the answer is correctly understood, it is incorrect. The only completely correct response to the question is another question: What do you mean by "know"? Depending on what "know" means, the correct answer would be "Yes" or it would be "No." Adequate treatment of the question, Did Jesus know he was God? requires some detail.

Former Opinions about Jesus' Knowledge   Until about 1950, the standard teaching about Jesus insisted that Jesus had three kinds of knowledge. Because he was a human being with a human mind, he had experiential knowledge as all of us do. He learned by his experiences. Because he had a specific mission to fulfill, he had infused knowledge. God placed in his human mind information and understanding that allowed him to fulfill his mission. His predictions of his passion[1] or his knowledge about Judas' betrayal[2] would be examples of such extraordinary knowledge. Finally, because he is God, he enjoyed the beatific vision. The beatific vision is that direct presence to God which the saints have in heaven. As immediate presence to God, beatific vision entails perfect blissful fulfillment and understanding of everything about everything.

According to this standard teaching, Jesus certainly did know that he was God. From the first moment of his human existence, he had full understanding of himself, his life, his mission, and its saving effect on others. He lived his life in accordance with this understanding. His fidelity consisted in following perfectly the manifest will of the Father, even as it led him to death. He followed

196

it perfectly because he knew that his expiatory sacrifice was necessary to save the world.[3] The obvious difficulty with this understanding is that Jesus hardly seems human; and the Father, demanding that Jesus pass the test of nerves by leading himself to crucifixion, appears to be a sadistic ogre.

From where did that standard teaching come? Mostly from theological speculation about the Incarnation. Theologians pondered what would *have to be* the case if a divine individual became human. To human reason it seems proper and, indeed, necessary that the Incarnate Word enjoy the beatific vision and have extraordinary knowledge about his life and its purpose. Moreover, read uncritically, the New Testament fostered such an interpretation about Jesus. The source of this teaching, then, is speculation about what ought to be the case and misunderstanding of the intent of New Testament writings.

Nonetheless, this position was so prevalent that relatively recent teaching of the ordinary magisterium of the Roman Catholic Church supports it. In 1918 the Holy Office decreed that it is dangerous to question the certainty of these statements: while on earth, Christ had the beatific vision, as do the saints in heaven;[4] and Christ's soul had no ignorance, but in the Word, by knowledge of (beatific) vision, knew everything, past, present, and future, that is, all that God knows.[5] The specific judgment of the Holy Office at that time was that it is not safe to teach anything contrary to these statements. In 1943, Pope Pius XII's encyclical letter, *Mystici Corporis*, reaffirmed this general teaching and insisted: Christ had a most loving knowledge which surpassed any possible human power; through the beatific vision, even while in the womb, he had present to him all members of the Mystical Body and embraced them in his saving love.[6]

Obviously, the picture of Jesus presupposed here is the Jesus of traditional piety. It is the picture presupposed in the introductory paragraphs of this book. But the picture of Jesus is changing. Why? Because there have been significant advances on two fronts—the study of the Scriptures (Chapter One) and the understanding of human consciousness and knowledge (Chapter Two). These advances allow a different picture of Jesus. And these advances, now secure and commonly accepted, make it safe today to propose this different picture.

Current Opinion about Jesus' Knowledge   A former understanding of Jesus was highly speculative. It reasoned what must be so in Jesus' case. The contemporary understanding of Jesus is empirical. It studies the evidence to determine what in fact was so in Jesus' case. Critical-historical interpretation of the New Testament reveals that Jesus had no extraordinary information about himself and his mission. All talk of the "plan of God"[7] resulted from reflection after the fact. Jesus had no script to follow. Rather, his life wrote the drama and revealed the plan about which we now speak. Human wisdom might grant the incarnate Son special knowledge. But according to the evidence of the New Testament, divine wisdom withheld any such thing. The Son was to be like us in all things but sin.

In fact, on the one hand, the Gospels recount numerous examples of ignorance on Jesus' part.[8] He did not know who touched him in the crowd.[9] He confused Old Testament figures: Ahimelech, not Aviathar, was high priest when David entered the sanctuary;[10] Zechariah, who was killed between the sanctuary and the altar, was son of Jehoiada, not son of Barachiah.[11] Jesus refers to Jonah as a historical figure,[12] yet Jonah is only a literary figure. Jesus insists that he does not know when the end is coming; only the Father knows.[13] And, as already noted, there is no certainty whether Jesus saw himself as the eschatological Son of Man. Nor was Jesus clear about his role as Messiah/Christ or Son of God or Suffering Servant. On the other hand, what extraordinary knowledge is attributed to Jesus is not unlike that attributed to the prophets of old: he knew from where would come the bread to feed the crowd, that Judas would betray him, that the Pharisees were thinking he was a blasphemer, that Nathanael had been under the fig tree. In summary, according to a critical reading of the Scriptures, Jesus did make mistakes, and he had no infused knowledge about his mission. A change in our interpretation of the New Testament makes that former understanding of Jesus untenable. It simply does not square with the evidence.

Consciousness and Knowledge A change in our understanding of human consciousness and knowledge also affects that former understanding about Jesus. The central issue is, What is knowledge? In Chapter Two I defined knowledge as interpretation that is verified in data. Knowledge is accurate understanding. Thus, it is clear that knowledge is a complex reality. It is the result of a process, and the process contains a number of activities. To know, one must not only be aware of something; one must, in addition, not only have understood that something; one must also have determined the validity of one's understanding. Only then does one know. This analysis of knowledge suggests that there is a difference between being aware of something and knowing something. It should be obvious that the term "to be aware" has taken on a technical meaning here. In everyday usage "to be aware" means the same as "to know." Here a distinction between awareness and knowledge is introduced, a distinction between consciousness and knowledge. Now, to understand what consciousness is becomes the main issue.

Simply stated, consciousness is awareness. Nonetheless, this statement remains ambiguous, for there are different kinds of awareness. There is the subject's awareness of some object, and there is the subject's awareness of himself or herself as the aware subject. Even as I am aware of anything else, I am simultaneously but *in another mode* also aware of myself as the aware subject. Call the subject's awareness of some object "reflexive consciousness." Through reflexive consciousness the subject stands over and against some object. The subject reflects on the object. This understanding was presupposed in my initial definition of christology as reflection on Jesus. Call the subject's awareness of self as subject "non-reflexive consciousness." Through non-reflexive consciousness the subject is present to himself or herself not as an object reflected upon but rather as the subject who is reflecting. Whenever I reflect about anything, I am not only aware of the object of reflection, but simultaneously and in another way I am also aware of myself as the "reflector." I, the conscious subject, am simultaneously reflexively aware of the object of my concern and non-reflexively aware of myself as the concerned subject.[14]

In non-reflexive consciousness one is present to oneself as subject. This presence of the subject to self as subject is awareness in another mode. It allows that one can know not only another object but also oneself as object. It allows that one can become an object to oneself. One can know oneself. In itself it is an awareness that is not reflected, not thought, not articulated. On the contrary, it is that upon which one reflects when one begins to reflect on oneself. It is that about which one thinks when one begins to think about oneself. It is that which one speaks when one begins to articulate oneself. It is that

199

which allows one, the subject, to become also an object to oneself. It is a condition for the possibility of one's knowing oneself. Only because I am present to myself non-reflexively can I later reflect on myself and express the self that I was. And even as in the present moment I am expressing the self who was, I am simultaneously but non-reflexively also aware of myself again as the subject, now reflecting on himself. I could continue in this way, "trying to catch my tail," but I would never fully possess myself in reflexive consciousness. Each time I achieved a new level of reflexive awareness of myself, there would still be the reflecting subject, present to myself non-reflexively, adding to the still possible, further, reflexive awareness of myself. This reflexive self-awareness is the unfolding of an always prior non-reflexive self-awareness. Thus, I can grow in knowledge of myself. Yet, my non-reflexive consciousness of myself always exceeds my explicit reflexive awareness and possible knowledge of myself.

In summary, there are two kinds of human awareness: non-reflexive consciousness whereby the subject is present to himself or herself as the aware subject, and reflexive consciousness whereby the self-aware subject is also simultaneously present to something—or even to himself or herself—as object. What is non-reflexively present to the subject can become reflexively present and so become data for the process of knowing. The product of this process, knowledge, is understanding that is verifiable in the data.

Consciousness and Knowledge Revisited   Another consideration, less accurate but more suggestive,[15] may help to clarify the point. Since the advent of Freud's depth psychology, we are all familiar with talk of "levels" of awareness. We commonly accept that there are experiences buried deep within us. We are not "aware" of them, and we cannot articulate them. Nonetheless, they are there, and they are operative within us. They influence our behavior. Though we cannot now name them, we grant the reality of these deeper levels within us because on occasion we have become reflexively aware of something which, though there, we had not previously realized. It seems, then, that there are deep levels of self-awareness that generally elude our inspection. The very purpose of psychotherapy and all self-help programs is to raise these experiences to a reflexive level where they can be acknowledged and dealt with.

Our dreams offer an easy, concrete example. Researchers tell us that all healthy people dream nightly. In our dreams we work out various issues that affect our daily, waking life. Yet many of us are seldom aware of dreaming. We do not remember our dreams. Still, they are there. At some level of awareness, we are in touch with them. They do express themselves in what we do during our waking hours. Sometimes during the day we suddenly become reflexively aware of a dream we had not remembered. Its meaning may become starkly apparent to us. We realize it had been with us, and actively so, all along. It may be "coming true" on the spot.

Evidently, we are "aware" of more than we "know." Expressed otherwise, we "know" more than we are "aware" of. The words may be confusing; they shift meaning in popular expressions. Yet the point is the same. There are different ways in which we are present to ourselves. Consciousness is both reflexive and non-reflexive.

By means of human consciousness, every human subject is present to himself or herself. Precisely such self-presence and the subsequent capacity to reflect on self are what distinguish humans from brute beasts. Because human consciousness is what it is, we not only experience, we also reflect on our experience. We think about ourselves and our world. We assess them. We determine what they will become. This is to be human. At its root is consciousness, inextricably and simultaneously dual in nature: reflexive and non-reflexive.

In contrast with "consciousness," the meaning of "knowledge" also becomes more clear. Knowledge in the popular sense of the word may be understood as movement within consciousness, movement from non-reflexive to reflexive awareness. To know something is to be aware of it reflexively, to think about it, to verbalize it. More precisely, however, knowledge entails more than movement from non-reflexive to reflexive awareness. What has become reflexively present must also be questioned and understood, and the understanding must also be checked against the evidence. Reflexive awareness merely provides data. Only the addition of insightful interpretation of the data and reasonable verification of the interpretation promotes the reflexive awareness to knowledge in the strict sense of the term.

Jesus' Two Consciousnesses   Apply this analysis to Jesus.[16] As both human and divine, Jesus has two consciousnesses. This one individual, Jesus, has both a human consciousness and a divine consciousness. The two differ.

Divine consciousness can be understood to be one perfect act of understanding that understands everything about everything. Since the act of understanding in God is perfect and infinite, in God there are no real distinctions between being aware and understanding and knowing.[17] For God, to be aware is to understand is to know. Merely by being present to himself—self-aware in divine consciousness— God knows himself. Besides, since God is the source of all else, present to himself, God is also present to everything else, understands all else, and knows all else.

On the other hand, human consciousness is a potential moving toward actualization. It is not a perfect act of understanding. It is not infinite actuality. Rather, through finite acts of understanding, it comes gradually to know more and more. In the human, active consciousness is a process. Consciousness entails a movement from non-reflexive awareness to reflexive awareness, from reflexive awareness to understanding, and finally from understanding to sure knowledge. In the human, there are real distinctions between each of the steps in the process. To be non-reflexively aware is not the same thing as to be reflexively aware. Nor is it the same as to understand, nor is it to know, nor is any of these separate acts the same as any other. So it is possible that consciousness may be actualized in a human being on any of the lower levels without being active also on the higher. That is, one may be aware of something without being reflexively aware that one is aware. Then, of course, one could have no understanding or knowledge of that something. Or one may be reflexively aware of something but as yet have no understanding of it and so, certainly, no sure knowledge of it. Or one may have an understanding of something but, if the understanding is wrong, have no real knowledge of it. Human consciousness is a potential that moves toward full actualization. The same is not true for divine consciousness.

Jesus has both human and divine consciousness. Furthermore, the two are unmixed. In Jesus, the divine mind and the human mind remain unconfused, undistorted by each other. This means that Jesus Christ is one individual with two modes of presence to himself and two modes of knowledge. He is present to himself by divine consciousness and human consciousness. He has both divine consciousness and human consciousness. He has both divine and human knowledge. The implications are complex.

Jesus' Divine Consciousness   First, consider Jesus' divine consciousness. As God, Jesus had divine consciousness. It follows that by
divine consciousness he was perfectly present to himself and in himself knew all things. That is to say, he was God. On this basis, the 1918
teaching of the Holy Office is accounted for: "in the Word" he had no
ignorance. As God he certainly knew all things. However, these
considerations are irrelevant when the pre-Easter Jesus, the man who
walked the earth, is in question. Granted, as God, Jesus knew all
things. Yet it is precisely the power and knowledge of God that he
gave up when he became human. These divine qualities are no longer
active in Jesus—not because he ceased being God but because he
stopped acting through the divine nature and began acting only
through human nature. That means that the divine consciousness is
completely irrelevant when one asks about Jesus' knowledge while
on earth. To insist that *as the Eternal Word Jesus knew* all things is no
more than to insist that God knows all things. But becoming human,
he surrendered the prerogatives of God. Or again, *to know as the
Eternal Word* is nothing other than to know as God. The focus in this
statement is on divine knowledge. Divine knowledge is a function of
divine consciousness, a facet of the divine nature. As such, it is held
in common by Father, Son, and Holy Spirit. That is, it pertains to
divinity and not specifically to the individuality of the Three who
share divinity. The focus here is not, then, on the individuality of the
Divine Word as Born-of-the-Father. Yet, the Bornness-of-the-Father,
his distinct identity, is what the Eternal Son brought with him into the
world; and the divine nature and its prerogatives is precisely that from
which he prescinded when he became human. Therefore, the question about what Jesus knew while on earth has to be answered solely
by consideration of Jesus' human consciousness. The fact that as God
he knew all things is irrelevant when asking about Jesus during his
earthly life.

How could Jesus really be God and still not have divine knowledge? The answer, already presented in Chapter Seven, is simply
this. In the first place, we believe that the Eternal Son became incarnate as Jesus Christ. Only by faith do we know this. That such a thing
is possible is the presupposition of Christian faith that conditions this
essay. Secondly, the Incarnation is and remains a mystery. We will
never fully understand it. But thirdly, a reasonable account of this
Christian belief can be given. The union of humanity and divinity in

203

Jesus Christ is not accounted for by the mixture of the divine and human natures. In such a case, divine consciousness and knowledge would be relevant to understanding the human Jesus while on earth. But such a position was condemned by Chalcedon as monophysitism. Rather, the union is to be accounted for by the unicity of identity in the one who, born eternally of the Father, was born of Mary in time. So Born-of-the-Father took on a human way of knowing, and all questions about what that human being knew while on earth are conditioned by the reality of his human consciousness.

The unlimitedness of divine knowledge does become relevant to an understanding of the human Jesus—but only at the point of his glorification. For then, according to the present hypothesis, his human consciousness was transformed to share in the knowledge that is proper to God. His divinization entailed the full disproportionate actualization of his human consciousness. Then, certainly, the human Jesus knew he was God, and he knew each of us directly and distinctly. In this sense the traditional pious belief is true: when he died on the cross—at that moment of pass-over from this life to glory—Jesus was aware of, and knew, each of us, sinners, yet human brothers and sisters whom he loved and willingly saved. But this is true only at the moment of his glorification.[18] While he was alive and hanging on the cross, he did not have knowledge of each single human being ever to live. Until he was glorified, his operative consciousness was human and limited, and his knowledge was limited accordingly.

Jesus' Human Consciousness   Next, let us consider Jesus' human consciousness. Now the full answer to the question, Did Jesus know he was God? can be given. For the assumption is that the question is asked about the man Jesus while he was on earth.

Distinguish between consciousness and knowledge. As human, Jesus had a human consciousness. Assuming that by human consciousness we are present to ourselves—even before we might reflect on ourselves—it follows that the incarnate Word was present to himself by human consciousness. By human consciousness the Eternal Son was present to himself non-reflexively, as every human is. This is to say, by human consciousness a divine one, Born-of-the-Father, was present to himself. He was conscious of himself. And since he was God, the Eternal Son, he was conscious of himself precisely as God, the Eternal Son. Jesus, God the Eternal Son incarnate, was conscious that he was God.

At the very least, as a human being with a human consciousness, Jesus was non-reflexively conscious of himself as God, the Eternal Son. It is also likely that this non-reflexive consciousness advanced to some degree of reflexive awareness in Jesus. The total integrity of the human being in question would suggest as much. Then this self-awareness in Jesus would be experiential data calling for some kind of interpretation. It would be only this—data. It would not be conceptual or articulate. It would be experience in need of conceptualization and articulation. It would show itself in feelings and urges and spontaneous images arising in the psyche from the depths of his being. That is, it would show itself in the primordial currency of the internal communication system proper to the human organism.[19] It would be the wellspring of Jesus' activities and teachings that scholars call "implicit christology" and that make people ask, "Who did he think he was?" But, of course, it is unlikely that he himself had clear thoughts on this point. The evidence does not suggest that he understood what he was experiencing in himself. Yet some degree of self-experience must have been there. After all, he was human. He had human consciousness. By means of that consciousness, he was present to himself—non-reflexively and so in some inarticulate way also reflexively.

We have seen that Jesus certainly thought of himself as a prophet. There is debate whether or not he also called himself Son of Man. If one grants that he did, this second self-designation could be seen as Jesus' halting and hesitant attempt to make further sense of his experience of himself. He was trying to understand and put into words what he experienced in himself. It seems that he never did understand it, though he was willing to die for it.

Here is one possible answer to the question, Did he know he was God? If "know" means conscious, then the answer is certainly "Yes." At some level of his being, by means of his human consciousness, the divine Word was non-reflexively present to his divine self, and this non-reflexive self-awareness very likely resulted in some perceptible experience. Yes, Jesus was conscious that he was God, the Only-Begotten.

I referred to this self-consciousness elsewhere in more descriptive and popular terms: he had some sense of himself; he was in touch with himself at a deep level; there burned in his heart some vague yet real awareness of himself. By those metaphorical statements I meant precisely the consciousness now under discussion. That self-consciousness in Jesus was real and active. It expressed itself in the way Jesus acted and in the things he taught. These deeds and teachings, expressions of Jesus' inarticulate self-awareness, allowed his followers, bolstered by the Easter experience, gradually to come to an explicit acknowledgment of who he was. Then, if Jesus was but *conscious* that he was God, Christians came to *know* that he was God.

However, Jesus himself did not know he was God. Here "know" is taken to mean conceptual and accurate understanding of reflexively conscious data. So the answer to the question is "No, Jesus did not know he was God." This is to say, Jesus did not complete the process of human self-knowledge. So he did not think about or speak of himself as God or Son of God or any such thing. Though as human he was certainly aware of himself—and precisely as the divine Son who he was—according to all available evidence he had not advanced this awareness to correct understanding and accurate articulation. That human process of knowing was completed definitively only by his followers at the Council of Nicea.

In summary, Jesus was conscious of himself as God, the Eternal Son, but he did not know he was God.

Jesus and Beatific Vision   One last question remains. The 1918 and 1943 statements of the ordinary Roman Catholic magisterium—that is, teaching authority—insist that Jesus knew all things because he had the beatific vision while on earth. Having already denied that Jesus knew all things, including his own divinity, this book must also address this related concern about Jesus' beatific vision. For to deny knowledge of all things in the earthly Jesus is also to deny the beatific vision in Jesus.

The beatific vision is that state of blessedness proper to the saints in heaven. That state of blessedness, described in terms of vision, is suggested in the New Testament: "Blessed are the pure in heart, for *they shall see God*" (Mt. 5:8). "For now *we see* in a mirror dimly, but then face to face. Now I know in part; then I shall understand fully, even as I have been fully understood" (1 Cor. 13:12). "Beloved, we are God's

children now; it does not yet appear what we shall be, but we know
that when he appears we shall be like him, for *we shall see him* as he is"
(1 Jn. 3:2). This state of blessed vision is generally thought to entail the
soul's immediate presence to God. The result is perfect happiness and
fulfillment, a sharing in God's own perfection. In the terms I have
developed, it is none other than human divinization. It is the full
actuation of human consciousness to the point of understanding
everything about everything and loving all that is lovable. It is a share
in what is proper to God alone. As such, it entails absolute bliss,
perfect human fulfillment, and the greatest possible intimacy with
God.

It is suggested that because he was God Jesus enjoyed this beatific
vision of God from the first moment of his human existence. There
follows the insistence on his knowledge of all the members of his
Mystical Body and knowledge of all things, past, present, and future.
The suggestion is that Jesus, because of who he was, always enjoyed
that ultimate fulfillment that among humans would be proper to him
alone. This book has argued repeatedly against such an understanding. The Scriptures give evidence of no such thing. Although human
wisdom might accord such blessedness to Jesus, divine wisdom did
not. Jesus attained human divinization only through his resurrection.
Until then his human mind enjoyed no all-enveloping rapture in the
divine being.

However, this is not to suggest that there was nothing peculiar
about Jesus' human consciousness. Some valid intent in the former
insistence on Jesus' beatific vision can be indicated. As the Eternal
Son incarnate, Jesus was immediately present to himself as God
throughout his life. That is to say, he was humanly non-reflexively
conscious of himself as Eternal Son. In this, Jesus was unique in
comparison to every other human ever to live. This uniqueness in his
conscious experience is rooted precisely in his divine identity. Because
he was God the Eternal Son, throughout his life he was immediately
present to God simply by being humanly present to himself. Jesus'
non-reflexive self-consciousness is in one way similar to beatific vision: it is immediate presence to God. It differs, however, in that it
does not entail the perfection of the capacities of human consciousness, and so does not confer full beatitude on Jesus before his

207

resurrection. Despite this difference, this interpretation respects the concerns of the Roman Catholic magisterium. A uniqueness in Jesus' conscious experience is linked immediately with his divine identity. So there is no danger of denying Jesus' divinity simply because one denies in Jesus knowledge of all things and heavenly beatific vision. The distinction between consciousness and knowledge and the further distinction between Jesus' non-reflexive self-consciousness and divinizing beatific vision now allow one safely to teach that Jesus did not know all things and did not possess the beatific vision from the first moment of his conception.

Summary　　With these clarifications christology again makes a step forward. Understanding about Jesus advances. Moreover, both the insistence on traditional doctrine and the insights of further scholarship are saved. Again the new position cuts down the middle between two seemingly sole alternatives. In accordance with traditional belief, contemporary christology can insist that Jesus Christ is, indeed, the Eternal Son of the Father and so always immediately present to God and still, in accordance with newly determined scriptural evidence, deny that Christ knew all things or had the beatific vision throughout his lifetime. Applied to the case of the human Jesus, contemporary understanding about human consciousness and knowledge allows this development. A clear answer to the question, Did Jesus know he was God? emerges. No, he did not know; but Yes, he was conscious of his divinity. No, he did not have the beatific vision; but Yes, through his non-reflexive human consciousness he was immediately present to himself and so to God throughout his lifetime.

Jesus' Freedom and Sinlessness

According to Christian belief, Jesus Christ did not sin. The New Testament is clear on this point: he "knew no sin" (1 Cor. 5:21). He is our high priest "who in every respect has been tempted as we are, yet without sinning" (Heb. 4:15). "He committed no sin; no guile was found on his lips" (1 Pet. 2:22). In John's gospel Jesus asks, "Which of you convicts me of sin?" (8:46). The Council of Florence in 1442 taught that our Lord Jesus Christ was conceived, was born, and went to his death without sin.[20] And, as we have seen, the Third Council of Constantinople taught that there was no opposition between his human and divine will. This belief calls for explanation, for it raises questions: Subject to his own divine will, was he really humanly free? Totally without sin, was he really human?

Jesus' Human Freedom   Constantinople III insisted that Jesus has both a human and a divine will. There were in Jesus two principles of activity, two wills. This must be so if Jesus is truly human as well as truly divine. It would be too easy to explain his holiness by insisting he had no human will and for this reason he always followed the divine will. Without a human will, he would not be human. Since he was human, he certainly had a human will. So the Council argued. Yet, if his human will was always subject to the divine will, was he really free? He may have had a human will, but did he have human freedom? Was the exercise of that will free?

According to New Testament insistence, Jesus certainly exercised human freedom. In the garden he prayed, "My soul is very sorrowful. . . . Father, if it be possible, let this cup pass from me; nevertheless, not as I will, but as thou wilt . . . if this cannot pass unless I drink it, thy will be done" (Mt. 26:38, 44). Jesus' prayer presupposes human freedom. In John's gospel Jesus states explicitly, "For this reason the Father loves me, because I lay down my life, that I may take it again. No one takes it from me, but I lay it down, and I have power to take it again" (10:17–18). 1 Peter 2:18–25 argues that there is credit in bearing suffering, though one is innocent. Such was the example of Christ. This argument presumes that Jesus was free, for there is no credit where there is no freedom. Furthermore, there can be no question that Jesus exercised human freedom. If he did not, he was not human. This was the intent of the teaching at Constantinople III.

The question that remains is this: How was Jesus Christ, the Eternal Son, who was the subject of a divine will as well as of a human will, really humanly free? This question is easy to answer. In fact, Jesus' case is no different from our own in this instance. According to Chalcedon, his divine nature did not impinge on his human nature. After the union, the two remained unchanged and unmixed in Christ. Just as divine knowledge did not flow into and distort the natural functioning of Jesus' human mind, so the divine will in Jesus did not interfere with the natural functioning of Jesus' human will and freedom. When the question is about the human Christ, all considerations of divine qualities are irrelevant: he gave those up. Therefore, though the divine will was his very own as God, as human Jesus was no more subject to or free from the influence of the divine will than we are. He was human as we are!

Human Freedom and Divine Omnipotence   Now the question about Jesus' freedom appears in its true light. It is not a particularly christological question but rather a general theological one. It is the question about divine omnipotence and human freedom. How can we—any of us humans—be free when God is omnipotent? The simple answer is that God omnipotently makes us free. God created us as free beings, and his very creative omnipotent power sustains us in that free status.

This answer is not a cop-out. It does not avoid the issue. It is completely adequate when one understands the unique nature of God's action on us. Too easily we conceive God's action to be like that of other influences. God's influence is imagined to be one more among all the others that impinge on us. And since God's influence is omnipotent, we imagine—and rightly so, according to this misguided scenario—God's influence is wholly irresistible; it completely cancels any possibility of human freedom. But God's influence is not like any other. It is not one more among the others impinging on us. Rather than being in competition with our freedom and the other influences on us, God's action is precisely that which constitutes us as free and sustains also the other influences on us. God's influence is what makes us and all things be and be what we are.[21]

The supposed opposition between God's power and freedom rests on a misconception. At the core of the misconception is the denial of human freedom and responsibility. The relevant question is not, How can God's omnipotence and human freedom be reconciled? The relevant question is, Do I know myself to be free in my decisions and responsible for them? If so, then I am free; and God's power—by definition—is sustaining me in my free being. There is no opposition. Rather, there is concurrence between God's action and my own. On the other hand, if I do not know myself to be free, then the question about God and human freedom—and all questioning, all thought, all discussion—becomes pointless, for none of it leads anywhere and everything is pre-determined. Even in this second case the question is resolved—or more accurately, dissolved! In either case and in sum-

mary, the question about Jesus' freedom is merely a specific application of the question about human freedom in general. The
christological consideration of Jesus' two wills adds no complication to
the issue.

Jesus' Sinlessness   The more fruitful question asks about Jesus'
sinlessness. It is a question that strikes closer to home. Was Jesus
really human if he never sinned? We tend to believe that sin is a part
of being human. When people are involved in wrongdoing, we excuse them with the observation, "To err is human, to forgive divine."
Or we say, "It's only human." The presupposition is that to be human
is to sin. And we wonder how we can identify with Jesus if he never
sinned.

What Sin Is Not   What is most needed is an appreciation of sin;
for confusion about sin leads to confusion about Jesus' sinlessness.
Too often the first thing that comes to mind when we think of "sin"
and "morality" is sex. There is an all too pervasive belief—happily in
recent years a better balance is being struck—that anything dealing
with sex is wrong. Then, to say Jesus was sinless suggests that he was
sexless. He had no sexual feelings or bodily reactions. Since we are
hardly like that, we wonder how he could have really been human.
However, not sex itself but what we do with sexual feelings and
impulses is the stuff of sin. Sexual feelings and bodily reactions are a
normal part of being human. Undoubtedly Jesus experienced them
just as we do. There is nothing of sin here. Of course, the New
Testament gives no information whatsoever about this. It was not the
concern of the gospel writers. Only pathological preoccupation and
prurient interest focus always on sex. Still, it is clear that Jesus had
deep, feeling-filled relationships with his family, friends, disciples,
and enemies, both men and women. To be sinless merely means that
in the midst of deep, human relationships one always responds as is
proper and good. Jesus' sinlessness does not mean he was asexual.[22]

Nor does Jesus' sinlessness mean that he never got angry or
impatient. Again, popular overzealous piety considers all anger to be
sin. However, not anger but what one does with one's anger is the
stuff of sin. In fact, Jesus was angry with the Pharisees when he cured
the man with the withered hand.[23] He acted violently when he drove
the money changers out of the temple.[24] He was impatient with the
dullness of his disciples.[25] He cursed the fig tree that offered him no

211

fruit when he was hungry.[26] And he sharply rebuked the disciple who cut off the ear of the high priest's servant in the garden.[27] In all this there was no sin.

Once a group of seventh graders posed this question to me: How can you say Jesus was sinless when he stayed in the temple for three days, not even bothering to tell his parents? He should at least have called home to say he would be late! With that group I ignored the fact that this story is more the expression of Luke's theology than an account of Jesus' biography.[28] I noted—and luckily the kids were satisfied with the explanation—that Jesus was still quite young and perhaps did not yet know any better. But be sure he did not do that a second time!

That answer was appropriate for seventh graders, but the incident holds a lesson for everyone. Obviously, the evangelist did not hesitate to portray Jesus as launching out on his own as he grew older. That his parents were grieved by his action does not necessarily mean what he did was sinful. Time and again Jesus broke taboos and even religious laws; he did not always act as others expected him to. That does not mean he sinned. Conformism is not the equivalent of virtue. To raise the objection of others, even of authorities, does not necessarily mean one sinned.

I developed a further speculation with that seventh grade class. Considered from a psychological point of view, the temple scene portrays Jesus as a typical adolescent. He was just becoming aware of his individuality. He was fired with the enthusiasm of youth. He overlooked the practicalities of life. It never occurred to him that his parents might be worried. After all, he was out to fulfill his life's mission!

Of course, I am reading into Luke. Concern for developmental psychology is proper to the twentieth century, not the first. The gospels simply offer no empirical basis for proposing a psychological portrait of Jesus. I am giving another homily here. My statement is kerygmatic. My point—and not my actual words—is what is intended here.

Then note that Luke does end that passage with a statement about Jesus' growth: "And Jesus increased in wisdom and in stature, and in favor with God and humans" (2:52). Elsewhere the New Testament again notes Jesus' growth in virtue: "Although he was a Son, he learned obedience through what he suffered; and being made perfect he became the source of eternal salvation to all who obey him" (Heb. 5:8–9). Obviously, to be sinless is not to be perfect.[29] Jesus grew in virtue and only in the end became perfect. His ignorance and errors noted above and his unexpected actions noted here show him limited and imperfect, as is every finite human being. He lived within human history. He was confined by space and time. To say he was sinless means only that, given his concrete situation, he did what was best— every time. Still, he grew in his ability to determine what was best, and he increased in freely chosen responsibility for what he did.

What Sin Is   Sin is not equated with sexuality nor with being angry or impatient nor with being imperfect. The essence of sin is the deliberate choice of what is known to be wrong. Sin is a matter of the heart. It expresses one's stance before God, who is Right and Good. To choose what one knows to be wrong is *ipso facto* to choose against God. This is so even if one may be mistaken in what one considers wrong. To choose what I believe to be wrong, even if my act is not wrong at all, is to set my heart against what is right and good. Similarly, to choose what I believe to be good, even though what I choose may really be wrong, is nonetheless to set my heart for what is right and good. So to do wrong is not necessarily the same thing as to sin. Sin is willful wrong. This is not to say that whether something is right or wrong makes no difference, as long as I think I am doing right. Our actions have effects, despite what our intentions might be. Besides, each of us is responsible to seek to know what is really right and good. Indeed, those whose hearts are set only on the good would have minds increasingly sensitive to good, would easily revise their thinking in accordance with what is good; and so would come to know what is really good in itself. Nonetheless, it is the determination of the heart, and not any external action, that indicates sin or virtue. The essence of sin is the deliberate choice of what is known to be wrong. Such choice is self-deviation from God.

Humanizing and Dehumanizing Behavior   From the beginning this book has presupposed that there is in us a natural inclination toward truth. We continue to ask questions. We want to understand things. When we do understand, we still wonder whether our understanding is correct or not. We do not rest until this desire to know is satisfied. And we do know when our question has been answered, for the same source that raises the question—our own minds—also sets the criterion for satisfaction with the answer. Thus, our inclination toward the truth is the condition for the possibility of knowing the truth about everything.

Similarly, there is in us a natural inclination toward the good. Spontaneously we wonder whether something is really good in itself or only seemingly good. We deliberate with ourselves and others whether something is merely satisfying or is actually of real value. We do not want to waste our lives on what is a sham. We do not want to invest in what is not really worthwhile. We ponder, we deliberate, we weigh our decisions. We have a natural inclination toward the good.

Whoever would dispute this claim would object to this whole discussion. "Stop wasting time discussing what is nonsense. Your supposed 'natural inclination toward good' is merely the effect of an overly intense religious upbringing. It's neurotic and not worth pursuing." Yet this very objection exhibits commitment to a particular view. The objection belies any feigned lack of concern for what is worthwhile. Indeed, the objection appeals to worth. Words and actions contradict one another. What the words deny, the act of objection affirms. No one can object without, by that very act, making an issue of what is worthwhile or not. So it appears that we do have a natural inclination toward the good. We spontaneously seek what is worthwhile.

It follows that to deliberately choose what one knows to be wrong is to act against the very structures of one's own being. To sin is to do violence to oneself. Alternatively, to choose always what one knows to be right is to act in harmony with one's deepest intrinsic drives. It is to do what is natural in oneself.

It appears, then, that we humans are in a peculiar situation. Our human freedom allows us to make or break ourselves.[30] We can act in accordance with the inherent structures of our makeup, or we can act in ways that oppose our very selves. Our choices form ourselves. On the one hand, to act in accordance with our natural inclination toward the good is freely to choose the good. Freely to choose the good entails not only choosing some good external to ourselves but also choosing to be what we ourselves are. When we choose good, we increase our sensitivity toward the good and increase our subsequent ability to choose the good. We involve ourselves in a snowballing effect. Choosing, through every choice of the good, to be what we are, we become increasingly what we are; we enhance our drive toward the good and so lead ourselves ever more deliberately toward the good toward which we naturally tend. We perfect ourselves. On the other hand, when we choose what we know to be wrong, we set up a process that diminishes our inherent tendency toward the good and our ability to choose the good. We debilitate ourselves.

Therefore, to sin is not human. Rather, it is dehumanizing. Only the one who always chooses what is right, only the sinless, is perfectly human. A proper understanding of sin turns the tables on us. Rather than judge Jesus against ourselves and conclude that he was not human because he did not sin, we must judge ourselves against Jesus and conclude that we are dehumanized because we are sinners.

The Meaning of Sinlessness   To be sinless is to be in endless and unerring pursuit of the true and the good. It is to be on the path of open-ended self-fulfillment that points to the fullness of Truth and Goodness Itself, God. To be sinless is to respond in every situation as one ought to respond. Then each human decision, necessarily limited yet unswervingly set on what is really good, becomes the stepping stone to a new situation, open itself to yet another step forward in goodness. To be sinless is to continue to create oneself and one's world along a line of development that leads to no dead ends.[31] It is to participate in an on-going renewal that transforms the world into what would be intended by God.

This is not to say that one has access to an eternal blueprint or that one is merely going along with some foredetermined cosmic plan. To be sinless is to act freely and to respond in the concrete world which is itself determined by the free choice of others. But to be sinless is to respond always in accord with what is good in every concrete situation and so to advance that situation toward a state of further possible development toward the good. The whole movement is free, for it is movement within a human world. If God knows the outcome, God does not know it in order to insure that such an outcome will be achieved; rather, God knows it because in eternity— where there is no past, present, or future—God is already present to the outcome freely determined by the human agents leading the world to its future. So to be sinless is not to act as God has foredetermined that one should act; it is always to choose the good in every situation and so to act as God, who is Goodness, would have one act under the circumstances.

Jesus' Human Sinlessness   The above account has been describing Jesus as the sinless one. To be sinless is to be truly human and ever more self-humanizing. Jesus was not unhuman because he was without sin; he was supremely human. We dehumanize ourselves when we sin. By sin we undo ourselves. We diminish our God-given human dignity. We deviate from the true and the good and make ourselves deviates. On this understanding, Jesus' sinlessness is not in itself the expression of his divinity. Rather, it is the expression of his perfect humanity. Undoubtedly, his being Eternal Son of God did influence his sinlessness. The presence of God burning in his heart— his non-reflexive presence to himself as Eternal Son—urged him to choose always only the good. But the actual choice, the sinlessness itself, was human.

The Tibetan Buddhist goal of enlightenment corroborates this conception of sinlessness as a human ideal. The enlightened one is fully open to all that is occurring in any situation. He or she acts always spontaneously, that is, from the depths of a pure mind. As a result, the enlightened one responds only as every situation demands. One does what is called for. One is not determined by external laws or social expectations. Rather, one is determined by what is really going on and by one's trust in the spontaneous intelligence of one's mind. So one acts always as is appropriate. Others may deem one mad. They may take offense. But the enlightened one trusts in his or her "crazy wisdom" and continues confidently to act as one knows one ought.[32]

Jesus acted with "crazy wisdom." Confronted with the woman caught in adultery,[33] he responded in none of the expected ways. Rather, responding to what was really going on, he devastatingly cut through the facade presented to him. He dissolved the issue and moved the situation to a whole new level of possibility. The same can be said for his response about giving tribute to Caesar,[34] about curing even on the Sabbath,[35] about eating with sinners and Publicans, [36] about cleansing the temple,[37] about the source of his authority,[38] about his guilt or innocence,[39] and much more. In all this, Jesus was being perfectly human. Even in a tradition that does not speak of God but is concerned only for enlightened humanity, Jesus would still be recognized as a model. Though Tibetan Buddhism does not speak of sin, its ideal of enlightened behavior appears to be an equivalent to sinlessness. It is a human ideal.

Unfailing Human Integrity   Now sinlessness appears to be an expression of human integrity, not the result of slavish adherence to external laws. Jesus was sinless because he was ever true to himself, not because he followed a pre-set program without deviation. He was ever faithful. And, because of who he was, being true to himself, he was automatically true to the right and the good. Of course, the New Testament does speak in terms of Jesus' "obedience."[40] The term "fidelity" is preferable. In a Christianity deformed by legalistic preoccupation, the biblical term "obedience" is too easily misunderstood. Then it obscures the reality of Jesus' experience. "Fidelity" better translates the meaning of the biblical term.[41] Jesus was virtuous because he was true to himself, not because he was true to some law imposed from without. He himself discerned what was good, and in so doing he determined what the law was in any instance. He determined the law; the law did not determine him. Strikingly, the reality of the situation is the inverse of what we too often imagine.

Something similar can be said about us. Like Jesus, we ourselves are sinless to the extent that we are true to ourselves, transformed by the gift of God's Holy Spirit in us. The sinfulness or sinlessness of our behavior is not determined by external law. Nor is it determined by slavish imitation of the deeds of Jesus—for, indeed, he lived his life in an age and culture significantly different from our own. To do simply what he did would hardly be to meet the needs of our day. Rather, our virtue or vice is determined by fidelity to God's Spirit, who speaks in our hearts; it is determined by our being true to our graced selves. Following the Spirit is true imitation of Christ.[42] As Paul argues at length in his major epistles, we are freed from the law and indebted to the Spirit. The law kills, but the Spirit gives life. Nor does this situation result in social chaos, for one and the same Spirit is the source of all God-inspired behavior. Those who are free in the Spirit are free, indeed. Always following the Spirit, they do only what is good. Doing only what is good, they are sinless. Now sinlessness is seen for what it is: the expression of unfailing human integrity.

Sinlessness as the Fullness of Freedom   Jesus' sinlessness—like our own—consisted in doing what was natural to him. He was being himself. On this understanding, it was easier for Jesus to be sinless than to do otherwise. To sin he would have had to do violence to himself. Obviously, to that magnificent human being, the external violence of physical death was to be preferred to the internal violence of spiritual self-destruction. So Jesus was faithful even unto death.

I have a friend who helps me appreciate this extraordinary quality in Jesus. My friend is alcoholic and a dedicated member of AA. He remembers well his former drugged life. He would wake up in a strange bed in a strange city, not knowing where he was or how he got there—though he was reassured that he had had a good time! He went through his savings and his family's, and he still lives with the consequences of the injustice he wrought. His body deteriorated; his mental and spiritual strength waned. Only by the grace of God, he insists, did he find the slow and arduous path to recovery. He remembers well. Now he is so grateful for the simple joys of every sober day. Now I find him unbelievably self-disciplined. Not only did he give up drinking; he also stopped smoking. He is content, for the time being, with a simple job, whose stress he can handle. He cancels social engagements when he needs to attend an AA meeting. He makes time for his rest, for his health, and for his prayer. He is available to help his fellow alcoholics. And he recently began a part-time graduate program in business administration. He does nothing that would lead him back to the hellish life he escaped, but slowly and patiently he rebuilds himself and his life, grateful that he is still alive.

To me, my friend's behavior is virtue; to him, mere necessity. When I compliment his self-discipline and wish I had more of it myself, he simply answers, "I have no choice. It's this or drink myself to death." Now more in touch with the core of himself, he finds it easier to live as he does than to slip toward drunken death. To drink again becomes increasingly impossible for him. His growing capacity for self-determination does not allow it. To drink he would need to do violence to himself.

Throughout this discussion of Jesus' freedom and sinlessness, a particular understanding of "freedom" has been emerging. Is my friend free if he, by his own determination and admission, *cannot* drink again? Is he free when he rebuilds his health and his life? The answers depend on how one understands freedom.

According to one understanding, freedom is the ability to choose what one will. Freedom is free choice. To be free means I can do what I please. The epitome of such "freedom" shows itself in the adolescent mentality that needs to do whatever is challenged and so prove it is free. One cuts off one's nose to spite one's face. The missing nose, the inability to breathe properly, is proof that one is free.

According to another understanding, freedom is self-determination. It is the ability to act without constraint. What one does, one does because one wants to do it. According to this understanding, whether or not one could do otherwise is not the issue. What one does do, one does freely.

They say there are only two things one has to do: die and pay taxes. Here there is no free choice. Yet one can die freely, or one can die kicking and screaming. One can freely pay taxes, or one can have them wrenched from oneself. Though there is no possibility of choice, there is still the possibility of free decision and self-determination.

Moreover, when what one must do is what is good, freely to choose it is not only to effect some good but also to reaffirm one's own freedom as inclined toward the good. Freely choosing what is right, I grow in my ability freely to choose what is right. I affirm my own nature and move increasingly toward the fullness of good, the goal of my own being. Conversely, to do what is wrong and so prove that I have free choice is not only to effect evil but also to ensnare myself in restrictive patterns of behavior. It is to enslave myself to wrong. It is to make it ever more difficult for me to choose good. Choosing evil increasingly limits my freedom. It confirms in me what is contrary to my natural inclination. It moves me ever further toward a dead end.

In his debates with Pelagius on the nature of grace, St. Augustine distinguished two notions of freedom like the two just explained. Augustine called the first *libertas:* freedom. It is the ability to choose what is good. It opens one to unending development. Augustine called the other *liberum arbitrium:* free choice. It is the ability to choose between this or that, and when that which is chosen is wrong, it is enslavement rather than freedom. So only *libertas* is really freedom; it is the essence of freedom. Free choice only appears to be freedom; it is not the heart of the matter.

These considerations help us appreciate how very human Jesus was. That he was without sin does not mean he was not human. On the contrary, it means he was a more fully developed human than others who sin. He was a person of such high integrity—so faithful to himself and therefore faithful to his heavenly Father and to all that is right and good—that his every decision confirmed him ever more in such fidelity. He made himself to be a perfectly faithful child of his heavenly Father. He developed an all-encompassing habit of fidelity. His every decision was radically in harmony with the noblest thrusts of his being. His whole being moved relentlessly toward all that is true and good. He expressed in his every act the best of what it means to be human. He was the epitome of humanity. If like my alcoholic friend who "cannot" drink, Jesus just "could not" sin, this does not mean that he was not free. It means, rather, that he had actuated his human freedom to its utmost possibility. Of course, Jesus did have free choice; he could have sinned, just as my friend really still could take a drink. But from another point of view, Jesus could not sin, and my friend cannot drink. Such a thing is so contrary to what they have chosen to be that they simply could not—would not—do it. Better life, simple and unexciting though it be, than death on a binge. And better death on a cross, painful though it be, than betrayal of self and God and goodness. In the face of such options, for certain people, there really is no choice. Nonetheless, there is no diminution of humanity here. Rather, there is a flowering of humanity. These considerations help us make sense of Jesus' sinlessness as an expression of—and not a contradiction to—his real humanity. They help us understand how, precisely as human, Jesus was sinless.

Jesus' Supposed Impeccability　　Some theologians hold that Jesus not only did not sin. In fact, he was not able to sin. This "not able" is not meant as in the case of my alcoholic friend and Jesus noted above. There a moral or virtual impossibility was in question. This "not able" is meant absolutely. According to this opinion, not only was Jesus sinless, he was also impeccable, utterly incapable of sinning.[43]

The argument runs as follows. Jesus is the Eternal Son, God. If Jesus sins, God the Eternal Son sins. This is clear from the discussion at Ephesus. If the Eternal Son was born of Mary, then God was born of Mary and Mary is rightly called Mother of God. Likewise, if Jesus sins, God sins. Said otherwise: the sole subject who acts in Jesus Christ is Eternal-Son, a divine one. If a divine one sins, God sins. But that God sins is self-contradictory. What is self-contradictory cannot

220

be. Therefore, it cannot be that Jesus, Eternal-Son, God, sin. Not only did Jesus not sin; he also could not sin.[44]

This position is unsatisfactory. If Jesus had no possibility of sinning, what meaning could temptation have for him? If Jesus absolutely had no possibility of doing wrong, was his freedom like ours? Granted, freedom is more than just free choice. Still, free choice is part of freedom as we experience it.[45] Without free choice, would Jesus really share our human lot? I think not. But Jesus *was* really human. He *was* like us in all things but sin. He *was* tempted as we are. So he must have had at least the possibility of sinning.[46]

A further argument can be developed. Indeed, "God sins" is self-contradictory and so metaphysically impossible. "Metaphysically impossible" means forbidden by the intrinsic reality of the issue in question. For example, a square circle is a metaphysical impossibility. The meanings of the terms cancel each other and nothing is left. A square circle is nothing, so not even God can make a square circle. It is nothing to be made. It is a metaphysical impossibility. The same is to be said about the supposed rock so big that God cannot lift it. This is a metaphysical impossibility. It is nothing to be made. A contrast is moral impossibility—something very unlikely, highly improbable, yet in theory still really possible.

That God sin is metaphysically impossible. The sense is this. What God does is good. This is so by definition. But to sin is evil. Evil and good are contradictions. So that God sins is self-contradictory. It cannot be.

This can be said otherwise. What God does determines what is. All being depends on God's divine creative activity. All that is is good; it is the result of God's doing, which is always good. But to sin is to effect evil. By definition God cannot effect evil, so God cannot sin.

Again, this can be said otherwise. That God sin is self-contradictory. "God sins" is a metaphysical impossibility. It is nothing. The terms cancel one another. Nothing remains. There is nothing to be considered. "God sins" is nothing to be, it cannot be that God sin.

Of course, the presupposition all along is that we are speaking of God as God. We are speaking of God acting through the divine nature. We are speaking of God as the ultimate, necessary, creative cause of all being. On this understanding it cannot be that God sin.

221

However, it does not seem that the same applies in the case of Jesus, the Eternal Son incarnate. For here the presupposition shifts. Now we are speaking of God acting through a human nature, not through the divine nature. In this case, the acts of God are not determinative of being but are merely finite human acts. The same argument about self-contradiction does not apply. The same ontological contradictories—being and nothing, good and evil—are not at stake here. The human acts of Jesus are not the creative acts of God, determinative of being itself. Jesus' human acts—God though he is— are secondary causes, like the acts of every other human being. They are not acts of primary causality, strictly divine acts, explanatory of all created acts and of all that is. So Jesus' human acts need not be perfect, infinite, free of all limitation. They could even be mistaken or sinful, as are the finite acts of other humans. Such acts on the part of the human Jesus imply no self-contradiction in God, the eternal, infinite, and necessary source of all being. It could be that Jesus' human acts be sinful. Such a turn of events would not be appropriate. Jesus' acts should not be sinful. After all, he is God's Only-Begotten-One. Still, theoretically it would be possible.

Other considerations confirm this conclusion. In Jesus' case, to phrase the issue in terms of "God sins" is to obscure the issue. Certainly Jesus is God since he is Eternal-Son. So, rightly understood, what Jesus does, God does. But to say "What Jesus does, God does" also obscures the fact that the subject of Jesus' activity is Eternal-Son, a distinct someone. The subject is not the Divinity, not God in any unqualified sense. When he became human, Eternal-Son surrendered all prerogatives of divinity. Then what is said about his activities is said of him not as divine but as human, though the one spoken about is Eternal-Son. So things can be said about Jesus and so about God—and correctly so—that otherwise simply cannot be said about God. In the case of Jesus, it is true that Eternal-Word was born at a particular time, and died. So it is also true in his case to say that God was born and God died. But the understanding is clearly that he was born *in his humanity* and he died *in his humanity*. To take the statement otherwise results in nonsense. Taken absolutely, "God dies" is nonsense, just as "God was born" is nonsense. Divinity is eternal, so these notions, taken absolutely, are metaphysical impossibilities. Therefore, if it is self-contradictory that God sin, it is likewise self-contradictory that God have a beginning in time and that God die. But since we know that in Jesus Christ God *was* born and God *did* die—not as God, however, but precisely as human!—then in the case of Jesus we can correctly say about God what otherwise would be self-contradictory. And since there is no greater self-contradiction in "God sins" than in "God dies" or "God is born," "God sins" could also be a legitimate statement in Jesus' case. Just because Jesus was who he was does not mean it was metaphysically impossible for him to sin. If it was not metaphysically impossible for him, a divine one, God, to die, it was not metaphysically impossible for him, a divine one, God, to sin.[47] Jesus was sinless but not impeccable. His temptations were real.

Summary

Insistence on Jesus' sinlessness does not deny Jesus' humanity. Rather, it calls us to a more accurate and loftier understanding of what it means to be human. While humanity failed in Adam and Eve, it reached its God-intended goal in Jesus Christ. Jesus lived in a world conditioned by the sin of our first parents and of all humans after them. Nonetheless, Jesus freely and unfailingly did only what was good. He never sinned. So rooted was he in God and so radically in tune with his deepest self, he simply would not sin. This does not mean that he fully understood himself, his mission, and all the implications of his activities. He did not have before him a copy of "the divine plan," a script that dictated his life-course and that he had to follow. Like all of us, he lived in faith. Unlike us, he was ever faithful. He never sinned. He is what humans are to be. He is the measure of our humanity. And because of him, we too can now become what we were intended to be. He restored the possibility that human sinfulness destroyed from the very beginning. The implications for us of Jesus' fidelity even unto death are the concern of the next chapter.

CHAPTER TEN

Jesus and Human Salvation

Traditional christology followed the pattern "from above." The moment of the incarnation was the focal point. The primary concern was to explain how humanity and divinity came together in Christ. All else paled in significance. As a result, the correlative mystery of human salvation in Christ got sidetracked. Christology, the study of Christ, and soteriology, the study of human salvation, were separated. The redemption, Christ's work that effected our salvation, was never fully integrated into the study of Christ. One of the concerns of contemporary christology "from below" is precisely to integrate Jesus' life, death, and resurrection into christology and so provide a single, coherent account of the mystery of Christ and the mystery of human salvation. The christology presented in Chapter Eight sketches such an account. The present chapter will fill in some detail in that sketch by treating four issues: Jesus' role in salvation, the contingencies within the plan of salvation, what Jesus revealed to us, and the salvation of non-Christians.

Jesus' Role in Salvation

A central affirmation of the New Testament is that Jesus saved us: he freed us from our sin and reconciled us to God. "God was in Christ reconciling the world to himself, not counting their transgressions against them" (2 Cor. 5:19). "Christ died for our sins" (1 Cor. 15:3). "Through him we have redemption, the forgiveness of our sins" (Col. 1:14). This affirmation is so central to Christian faith that *it* determined the outcome of the Council of Nicea. The argument was, "If he is not divine, we have not been saved." And since we know we were saved through Christ, he must be God. Nonetheless, despite the centrality of this belief, how exactly Jesus saved us had yet to be determined. Beyond question the belief was there; but a satisfactory understanding of it was lacking.

The Theory of Satisfaction   Only at the end of the eleventh century did the now generally accepted explanation of redemption emerge.[1] Its author was Anselm of Canterbury. It is usually called the "theory of satisfaction" or the "theory of atonement."[2] Anselm presumes Augustine's understanding of the sin of Adam and Eve. This sin—and all sin—is an offense against God. The merciful God is fully willing to forgive sin, yet the order of justice demands that some reparation be made. With his medieval contemporaries, Anselm shared a concern for the right order of things: the hierarchy of kings, lords, nobles, and knights; the duties and rights owed one to another; the requirements regarding insults, offenses, and reparation. Medieval life was hard and oftentimes cruel. Blood, gore, and death were familiar scenes. In the depth of its psyche, the harsh values of barbarians still colored the age. Chivalry and unflinching bravery presented a noble and socially necessary ideal. With his contemporaries Anselm also shared a misunderstanding of the New Testament metaphors that speak about Christ's saving work: ransom, expiation, shedding of blood, canceling a debt. All these were understood too literally and too legalistically. A product of his own time, Anselm put heavy emphasis on the requirements of justice, and he interpreted the redemption in these terms.

Anselm reasoned that only a human being could make up for human sin. But an offense against God is infinite in weight. So, on the other hand, only God could make reparation to God. Thus, it was necessary that God become human, for only a divine-human one could satisfy for our sins. His reparation would be of infinite value and could undo an infinite offense. Moreover, this divine-human one, Jesus Christ, was himself free from sin. Born of a virgin, he did not contract the sin transmitted through the ordinary process of human conception, sexual intercourse. (On this latter point, Augustine's warped understanding of original sin still held regrettable influence.) So Jesus suffered the punishment of sin—suffering and death—but was himself wholly innocent. The infinite merit of his guiltless and voluntary death was then applicable to other humans. By his suffering and death Jesus made satisfaction for our sins, redressed the order of justice, and so reconciled us with the Father. The resurrection figured only incidentally in this account. The common understanding in Anselm's day was that the resurrection served the purpose of making known that the crucifixion had achieved salvation.

Anselm himself did not speak of vicarious suffering—that Christ suffered in our place. But this notion was prevalent in his age. And Anselm's own formulations readily lent themselves to such an understanding. So this theory came down even to our own time: Jesus saved us by taking on himself the punishment for our sins. Suffering and death was that punishment. Jesus freely bore it out of obedience to the Father. "Indeed, it was for this purpose that he came—to die for sinners."[3] That was his mission. He knew this. He wished he could avoid it. Yet out of obedience to God and love for us, he gave himself over to death on the cross. By his death, we were saved.

The theory generally attributed to Anselm appears repeatedly in church documents, liturgical texts, and Christian piety across denominational lines. Even when the notion of vicarious suffering is not intended, the traditional terms suggest it. The idea of dying in our place or of paying the price of sin is the obvious meaning of words like sacrifice, dying for our sin, making reparation, reconciling us with God, and the like. Yet the question is still open to considerable theological discussion. The Roman Catholic Church, for example, has never made an official definition about the redemption. The Council of Trent specifically uses the terms "merit" and "satisfaction" to speak of the redemption: "Our Lord, Jesus Christ . . . merited justification for us by his most holy passion on the wood of the cross and made satisfaction to the Father for us."[4] Still, that Council did not intend to give official approval to Anselm's or any other theory of redemption. As is clear from the context, these conciliar statements merely use terms, used in various senses since the third century, to paraphrase the Scriptures and indicate Christ's saving work. This means that theologians are still free within broad limits to propose an explanation of the redemption.

An Alternate Theory of Redemption   A new understanding of the redemption is certainly needed. The current theory, removed from its medieval context and deformed by questionable piety, is no longer acceptable. God appears to be an ogre, delighting in blood and death, demanding the crucifixion of his own Son. Suffering appears to be valuable in itself: supposedly, it was Jesus' suffering and death themselves that saved us. So any increase in the excruciating pain of Jesus' execution is thought to have added to the redeeming value of his death. And Christians themselves are supposed to welcome suffering. Indeed, they should seek ways of increasing their discomfort, doing penance for their own and others' sins. In this way they are thought to be reproducing in themselves the sufferings of the Lord. Such an understanding completely overlooks the love and mercy of God and misrepresents the human virtue of Jesus Christ. It is offensive to the Christian sense of God, and it distorts the best of the Christian tradition on this subject, especially the New Testament. Moreover, it is repugnant to the contemporary world, which values human dignity and emphasizes the positive. It makes Christianity unintelligible and unacceptable to a world craving spiritual nourishment. For it misidentifies the scandal of the cross, and unwittingly sets up guilt, punishment, and death in place of the God of mercy, love, and life.

The christology presented above in Chapter Eight suggests a two-part alternate account of the redemption. In the first place, it is *Jesus' fidelity* that redeemed us, not his death. His suffering and death are but the occasions for perfect expression of his love and fidelity. His fidelity even in the face of death is what redeemed us. Moreover, his fidelity was not some iron-willed, masochistic obedience to an external decree. Rather, he was first of all faithful to himself; and because of who he was, he was then automatically faithful also to his heavenly Father. His being himself cost him his life and was saving for us. He redeemed us by being himself. In the second place, *Jesus' divinization* resulted as the concrete effect of his loving fidelity and of God's loving plan. Thus, Jesus introduced a new possibility for human becoming into human history. In Jesus, for the first time, a human being

228

attained the goal intended by God from the beginning for Adam and Eve and their descendants. In effect, Jesus changed the meaning of human existence. That is, he redeemed us by rising from the dead.

However, the saving work of Jesus, the redemption, does not alone account for human salvation. In addition to Jesus' saving work—his fidelity unto death and his resurrection—the work of the Holy Spirit must also be noted. For the new possibility opened to us through Jesus' resurrection cannot be actualized in us apart from the Holy Spirit, who becomes our very own. The gift of the Holy Spirit makes us adopted sons and daughters of God. Then, as children of God, by being faithful to ourselves we are automatically faithful to God, the Holy Spirit. Then we reproduce in our lives what Jesus did in his. Our lives become the concrete lived expression of children of God. Thus we share on earth the human life of Only-Begotten-of-the-Father, and so we can expect to share in his glorification. Glorified with him, through the Holy Spirit we live eternally with him in the life of Father. The work of Jesus Christ, of the Holy Spirit, and of ourselves together brings us God's life. Salvation is accomplished. God becomes all in all.

This overall account of human salvation requires further comment. In particular, the emphasis of Jesus' fidelity, a contrast to the Anselmian theory of atonement, needs legitimation. A brief study of New Testament teaching will provide this.

The New Testament Metaphors   I have repeatedly noted how contemporary biblical studies have changed our understanding about Jesus. Here the same phenomenon appears again. A historical-critical understanding of the New Testament metaphors about our redemption in Christ disqualifies the legalistic interpretations usually given to them.

The metaphor of *ransom* occurs only in a few places in the New Testament sources: "The Son of Man . . . came . . . to give his life as a ransom for many" (Mk.10:45); "there is one mediator . . . Christ Jesus, who gave himself as a ransom for all" (1 Tim. 2:5–6). More frequent is the closely related metaphor of *redemption*—a "buying back": "they are justified by his grace as a gift, through the redemption which is in Christ Jesus" (Rom. 3:24); "He [God] is the source of your life in Christ Jesus, whom God made our wisdom, our righteousness and sanctification and redemption" (1 Cor. 1:30).[5] Basically, ransom and redemption refer to business transactions—buying back a slave, paying the price to buy back a pledge, redeeming a pawned object.

Applied to God's saving action, both in the Old and New Testament, the notions are metaphorical. Unfortunately, the early fathers of the Church took them literally. Debate ensued asking to whom the ransom was paid: to God or to the devil? That a ransom for souls was paid to the devil was soon deemed unthinkable. But a problem also remained about paying the ransom to God. After all, God was the one redeeming us. Should he pay a price to himself? Anselm's ingenious contribution was to propose that payment was due neither to the devil nor to God but to justice itself. Brilliant as this resolution was, the initial problematic was mistaken. The Bible never intended that payment was literally made to anyone or anything.

In the Old Testament the metaphors of ransom and redemption were used to express *the experience* of God's mercy. God was the one who saved, redeemed, delivered, ransomed. One felt *as if* one had been pulled back from death, freed from slavery, released from the guilt of sin: "They remembered that God was their rock, the Most High God their redeemer" (Ps. 78:35). The same meaning applies to the New Testament usage of these metaphors. Through Jesus Christ God has freed us from sin and given us life again. The experience is like being bought back from slavery, saved from death, ransomed from the power of sin.

Colossians 2:14 introduces still another metaphor, *the bond of indebtedness*. But the point is the same: "And you . . . God made alive together with him, having forgiven us all our trespasses, having canceled the bond which stood against us with its legal demands; this he set aside, nailing it to the cross." That is to say, God's love cancels out any supposed debt of sin we might have. God sweeps away any legal considerations. God's mercy forgives us and restores our life. Nothing is held against us. Through Jesus and consummately through his handing himself over to death on a cross, it was as if debt (Col. 2:14) and law (Eph. 2:15; Gal. 4:4–5) and sin (2 Cor. 5:21) and curse (Gal. 3:13) were themselves crucified. These were destroyed and taken completely out of the picture. The idea is not that Jesus' death was payment of the debt or fulfillment of the legal requirement. The idea is that through Jesus the case was dismissed, legal considerations

230

were set aside, the debt was forgiven. There is no idea that Jesus paid off a debt. Rather, through Jesus God turned humanity around to openness to his friendship. Through a human being, God removed all the barriers that humans themselves had set up. This is the marvel of God's love and wisdom that Christians experience. They feel as if they were dead and brought back to life, enslaved and set free, indebted and absolved of their debt. So they praise God through Jesus Christ! Is this not the lesson of the parable of the Prodigal Son?

The notion of Jesus' making *"expiation* for the sins of the people" (Heb. 2:17) also needs to be correctly understood. In classical and Hellenistic Greek usage, the term means to placate or propitiate an angry god or hero. It means to sacrifice in order to pay off or buy off an angry god. This is *not* how the Old Testament uses the term. There it is God who expiates, and expiation refers to being made ritually clean before God or to having one's sin wiped out or covered over. When this notion is applied to Jesus, it simply means that through Jesus our sins are forgiven. That's all. How this happens is not explained by the term "expiation." Romans 3:25 also uses the term: "Christ Jesus, whom God *put forward as an expiation* by his blood. . . ."[6] This verse means that through Jesus God wiped out our sins and displayed Jesus on the cross as the means of our forgiveness and of our access to the Father. Jesus' blood here is seen as a sign— like rebel paint splattered on a wall—pointing out Jesus as our reconciliation with God. The blood here is not a sign of suffering, not an indication of payment in human sacrifice. The heavy overlay of images in a Hebrew mentality and of repeated misinterpretation according to our own mentality makes it almost impossible to salvage these biblical images for contemporary use. I know of nothing in our own culture that even comes close to the Hebrew understandings. The meaning of those images can hardly be expressed accurately in contemporary images. But this much is clear and can be said outright. For the Hebrew mind, in no way does expiation refer to appeasing God's anger. Rather, expiation is a biblical way of referring to God's forgiving us our sins. When the Greek term "expiation" (*hilasterion*) was used to translate the Hebrew Old Testament notion, the term took on a very different and peculiar meaning.

Similarly, references to being saved by the *shedding of Christ's blood* need to be understood against the background of Old Testament

ritual practices. The New Testament authors borrowed on those practices to speak about God's saving work in Jesus. In the Hebrew mind,
"the blood is the life" (Dt. 12:23). Yahweh is the source of all life, so
blood is sacred to Yahweh. To be sprinkled with blood means to be
purified and reconsecrated to God. The key to understanding Old
Testament sacrifice in this case is not in the death of the animal but in
the use of its blood. The death of the victim is almost incidental; it is a
prerequisite to the sprinkling with blood. And to be sprinkled with
blood means to be in contact with life, which is Yahweh's. The New
Testament authors use this understanding, so foreign to our way of
thinking, to help interpret Jesus' bloody death on the cross as the
means of our reconciliation with God. In this sense Christ "entered
once for all into the Holy Place, taking not the blood of goats and
calves but his own blood, thus securing an eternal redemption. For if
the sprinkling of defiled persons with the blood of goats and bulls and
with the ashes of a heifer sanctifies for the purification of the flesh,
how much more shall the blood of Christ . . . purify your conscience
from dead works to serve the living God" (Heb. 9:12–14). By means of
his own blood, Jesus was totally consecrated to God on the cross. And
by means of his blood, especially in Eucharistic communion with it,
we are also purified and rededicated to God. So Christ's is the blood of
a new covenant.[7] In his blood we are reconciled to the Father. The
shedding of blood effects a consecration to God. Shedding of blood
has no reference to appeasing God or to paying any kind of price to
anyone.

In an attempt to make some sense of the crucifixion of Jesus, the
New Testament Christians latched onto the image of blood and its
shedding. They proposed interpretations of Jesus' death by using
notions available in their own culture—just as they attempted to
interpret Jesus himself under the titles of Son of Man, Christ, Lord,
and Logos, notions proper to their culture though foreign to our
own.[8] To understand the image of the blood of Christ correctly one
must understand the—to us bizarre—notions of sacrifice in the Old
Law. The New Testament was not concerned with blood, gore, suffering, and death in any sense that includes paying a price, paying off a
debt, appeasing a god, or offering human sacrifice. Though these are
the notions that come most readily to our minds when we read those
first-century metaphors, these repulsive notions are not what the

New Testament authors intended. One even sometimes wonders if we do not distort the Christian message rather than promulgate it when we insist too forcefully on metaphors so foreign to our way of thinking and therefore almost inevitably doomed to misunderstanding.[9]

This is not to say that there are no references to God's *wrath* in the New Testament. There are: "Jesus . . . delivers us from the wrath to come" (1 Thes. 1:10); "Since, therefore, we are now justified by his blood, much more shall we be saved by him from the wrath of God" (Rom. 5:9). But these references do not suggest that Jesus' death appeased the anger of God. As is obvious in these quotes, "wrath" refers to God's action at the end of time. As such, it is a frequent image throughout the Bible. It refers to the Day of Yahweh, when those who resisted God's saving will will be destroyed. It presumes the salvation already effected through Christ. It is an image for the catastrophe the wicked will experience when the only world they know comes to an end.

Interpreted in their own contexts, these New Testament metaphors point again and again to a God of mercy, forgiveness, and love. They do not portray a God who demands retribution for sin. They do not suggest that Jesus' death was required as the price of forgiveness. If, in fact, we were redeemed through Jesus' death on the cross, it was not because God required that death as the punishment due to sin. Some other explanation is needed. God's prime motive in our redemption was love for us. "God so loved the world that he gave his only Son" (Jn. 3:16). God "did not spare his own Son but gave him up for us all" (Rom. 8:31). "God our Father . . . loved us" (2 Thes. 2:16). The same must also be said for Jesus: "Christ loved us and gave himself up for us, a fragrant offering and sacrifice to God" (Eph. 5:2). "Christ loved the church and gave himself up for her" (Eph. 5:25)[10] Awareness of the love and mercy expressed in God's saving act for us in Christ discredits past legalistic emphasis on atonement. The medieval world and we ourselves may be concerned to preserve the demands of justice. The New Testament had no such preoccupations. Correctly understood, the metaphors of ransom and redemption and expiation by blood are ways of extolling the salvation effected for us in Christ. They are echoes of the main theme of the gospel: "God was in Christ reconciling the world to himself" (2 Cor. 5:19). That reconciliation was an act of mercy and love, made manifest by Jesus' death on the cross.

A Theory of Reconciliation   Jesus' death was not a payment for our sins. Another explanation is needed. Jesus' death was the occasion for expression of his ultimate act of human surrender to God.[11] Perfect even in the face of death, Jesus' fidelity saved us. Death in itself is worthless. Agonizing death was never intended by God. It is the result of sin. But through Jesus, God in his infinite wisdom used death to undo death. Death, the effect of sin, became the very occasion for the ultimate expression of love that would undo sin.[12]

When God created the world and gave it into the hands of humankind, humans betrayed the trust God put in them. The life given to us in creation was intended eventually to lead us to life in God. But because of sin, that goal was never achieved. Instead we brought upon ourselves misery, suffering, agonizing death, and separation from God. The fallen world was our own doing. Nonetheless, God's love is greater than we are and greater than our wickedness. God would respect the freedom he gave us in the beginning. God would even respect the death-dealing structures we had introduced into our world. God had given the world to us, and he would not now take it back. Rather, he would take the very world as we had made it and turn it into the vehicle of divine life intended for us from the beginning.

God sent his own Son to live among us, become like us in all things except sin. The world he lived in was a fallen world, the product of our sin. The very sinfulness of humankind resulted in his murder. Jesus' death was an injustice. It itself was sinful. Obviously, at least in this sense, "Christ died for our sins" (1 Cor. 15:3); that is, he died because of sin. But he himself was sinless. His fidelity perdured despite the threat of death. In Jesus, death became the ultimate expression of surrender to God: "Father, into thy hands I commit my spirit!" (Lk. 23:46) Death was undone; it became the passageway to life in God. Sin was stripped of its power; its ultimate victory, death, was no longer a threat. Through Jesus God used the very elements of the sinful world that we had made as vehicles for the life that he intended for us.

A similar reversal of meanings is seen when Christ is compared with Adam and Eve. The Genesis account of Adam and Eve is a

234

symbol of the sin that has been among us since the beginning of the human race. The infidelity of Adam and Eve derailed God's plan of divine life for the human race. Once sin entered the world, birth into the human world was no longer birth into a pathway to divine life. Rather, it was birth into sinfulness. Just by being born human, one was involved in a situation contrary to God's intentions.[13] One was in a state opposed to God's good wishes. Jesus reversed this state of affairs. In Jesus, for the first time, there was a human being who was completely faithful. Even in a world of sin and in the face of death, Jesus remained faithful. Passing through death and rising divinized, Jesus attained the goal of human life that God had originally intended for us. In Jesus this earthly life had become again a pathway to divinization.

Jesus' fidelity reversed the course of sinful human history. Jesus turned the path of human life around. Because of Jesus, one of our race, being born human no longer necessarily meant being inextricably embroiled in a state of opposition to God. Jesus' human life led to divine fulfillment. His life introduced a new possibility into human history. So his human life brought to human history a new opening to God. If in Adam and Eve human life was disobedience and led to separation from God, in Christ human life was on-going fidelity and led to divinization. Because of Jesus, human life is no longer what it used to be. Reversing the meaning of human life, Jesus restored humanity to friendship with God. Jesus reconciled humankind with the Father. Jesus redeemed the human race.

Here is another sense in which it is true that "Christ died for our sins" (1 Cor. 15:3). His fidelity unto death freed us from sin's control of human history. Through his death, he pulled us out from under the oppressive power of sin. "He died for our sins" in the sense that his death was the undoing of sin in the world.[14]

Here is also an alternative to Anselm's theory of atonement or satisfaction. It is a theory of reconciliation. Through his fidelity unto death, Jesus effected the reconciliation of the human race with God. Jesus did this not by changing God's attitude toward us humans, for God always loved us, even when we were sinners.[15] No, Jesus reconciled us with God when in himself he reoriented humanity to God. The change came on the human side, not on the divine side.

Here, then, is also an alternative answer to the title question of

235

Anselm's treatise on the redemption: *Cur Deus Homo? Why Did God Become Human?* God did not become human because only a divine-human one could make infinite reparation for a human offense. The presupposition of this answer is mistaken. God was not looking for repayment for sin. Jesus did not pay off any debt. The Scriptures say nothing of the kind. God did become human because, as it happened, it took the Son-of-God-become-human to remain ever faithful in our sinful world. Only the very Son of God, at tremendous cost to himself, succeeded in resisting the sinful structures of our fallen human world and so reversing the flow of sinful human history. No one else was ever able to achieve such a thing. So, in his unbounded love and wisdom, God effected the reversal himself—not by imposing his will from without and so destroying human freedom, but by sending his own Son to enter the human situation and from within and as a human being to effect the needed reversal.

The term "satisfaction" does have some status as a traditional and canonized way of speaking about Christ's work of redemption. But it also has the distinct disadvantage of misrepresenting the meaning of the redemption. Of course, as a technical theological term, it can mean whatever it is defined to mean. In physics, for example, technical terms like "energy," "mass," "distance," and "time" have precise meanings inscrutable to the lay person. Still, the technical meanings do have some discernable relationship with the popular meanings of those same terms. But the term 'satisfaction'—in its etymological derivation, its historical usage, and its popular meaning—is so far removed from the acceptable understanding of the redemption that the term appears to be downright misleading. I prefer to drop the term 'satisfaction'—and 'atonement', as well—and to speak of the *reconciliation* that Jesus effected by his fidelity unto death.

In summary, Jesus' human virtue, his fidelity unto death, is the cause of our redemption. His suffering and death themselves are not what saved us. He did not come to suffer and die. He came to live out in time what he was in eternity, perfect Son of the Father, and so from within to transform human history. His fidelity to himself and so to his heavenly Father was costly, especially in a sinful world. His fidelity eventually cost him his life. He did not shun that cost. He embraced it—not because it was valuable in itself and not because being innocent himself he could suffer in someone else's place and not

236

because the Father was requiring human self-sacrifice of him. No. He embraced suffering and death because he could not avoid them without being unfaithful. His death was the cost and expression of his fidelity. His fidelity is what was saving. By it Jesus turned the human situation Godward again. He, one of us, reconciled us with God.

The Meaning of Christian Asceticism. Jesus gives us a lesson about our own calling.[16] We are not Christ-like when we seek out suffering, take on penances, look for punishment. We are Christ-like when we are true to ourselves and the situation in which we find ourselves. We are Christ-like when we are being ourselves, making the unique contribution that we alone can make: when we develop our talents, when we contribute to our utmost, when we express our opinions, when we share our insights, when we insist on the truth, when we respond to the needs we recognize about us, when we persist in doing good, when we are the sons and daughters of God that the Holy Spirit makes us to be. If we follow such a course, we would not be lacking for suffering. Each choice for virtue would require discipline and self-denial in regard to other options. There would be sufficient room for "penance," not self-imposed but spontaneously demanded by the positive choice for good that we follow. Moreover, our virtue would inevitably provoke persecution by the unjust, and we would suffer abuse and possibly death. We would become like Jesus even in death—not because we sought suffering and death but because we followed a path of virtue even at the cost of death.

In fact, this is the New Testament teaching on asceticism. The only voluntary disciplines the gospels generally enjoin are fasting and almsgiving.[17] Sexual abstinence may also be advised, but it is not presented as something valuable in itself. It is accepted "for the sake of the kingdom of heaven" (Mt. 19:12) and "that you may devote yourselves to prayer" (1 Cor. 7:5).

Paul does say, "Well, I do not run aimlessly, I do not box as one beating the air; but I *pommel my body and subdue it,* lest after preaching to others I myself should be disqualified" (1 Cor. 9:26–27). But this must be understood correctly. The metaphor is that of a sports contest.[18] The Greek word translated "pommel" could also be rendered in popular English "to give an uppercut." Here it means "to strike a telling blow." "Body" had widely different meanings in Paul. It gener-

237

ally refers not to human physicalness but to human this-world-liness, to the weakness that works against God. The word "subdue" conjures up the image of the victor dragging the defeated opponent around the arena. The overall point is metaphorical. Paul's point is drawing a parallel. Just as a boxer takes his sport seriously, so Paul takes his devotion to Christ seriously. The point is not that Paul imposes harsh disciplines on his body. That is what a boxer does. The point is that Paul is serious about his commitment. He gives himself fully to his apostolate.

Even if this text were—mistakenly!—taken to refer to self-imposed penances, Paul gives no indication here about what practices he might use to "subdue" his "body." His writings elsewhere mention only fasts and vigils, nothing else. When Paul does speak of greater "disciplines," he refers to the persecution, hardships, and sufferings that come to him because of his apostolate.[19] These same disciplines must also explain what is meant by Colossians 1:24: "Now I rejoice in my sufferings for your sake, and in my flesh I complete what is lacking in Christ's afflictions for the sake of his body, that is, the church." This is no reference to self-imposed penances. On the contrary, the same epistle specifically warns of the futility of such practices: "These have indeed an appearance of wisdom in promoting rigor of devotion and self-abasement and severity of the body, but they are of no value in checking the indulgence of the flesh" (Col. 2:23). The last line could also be translated, "They are of no value, serving only to indulge the flesh." In any case, the point is clear: "If you have been raised with Christ, seek the things that are above" (Col. 3:1). We are to find salvation in Christ's victorious presence, not in any self-made asceticism.[20]

Likewise, the gospel injunction to take up one's cross and follow Jesus[21] refers to the cost of discipleship, not to the practice of voluntary penances. The Christian is to set the Reign of God above all things.[22] This is the supreme value. It is the single-minded, the pure of heart, who will see God.[23] In a sinful world, seeking the Reign of God single-mindedly, being true to oneself in the Holy Spirit—and therefore being a faithful follower of Christ—will inevitably entail bearing a cross. This is the asceticism required of the Christian. But bearing this cross brings joy, peace, and abundance in this world and the next. That is why Jesus' yoke is sweet and his burden light.[24]

Too often misunderstanding about the redemption deforms our understanding about Christian asceticism. The example of Jesus teaches us to place suffering in its proper perspective. Suffering is of no value in itself. It is not to be chosen for itself. Rather, virtue is to be chosen—despite its cost.

Other Dimensions of the Reconciliation The mystery of redemption in Christ also provides *the Christian response to the problem of evil.* God did not eliminate evil from the world in order to save us. God used the evil in the world to achieve good. And in Christ, the power of evil was broken. The resurrection is the ultimate victory over all evil and death. So Christians need not avoid the misery, suffering, and death of this world. They do not seek it out, but when it is unavoidable, they allow it. They suffer freely—not because suffering is of value in itself but because suffering provides another occasion to express their trust in the heavenly Father. Even in the face of death, like Jesus before them, they continue to be faithful sons and daughters. No evil or suffering is so great that God's love cannot use it for good. If God could use the atrocity of Jesus' murder to redeem the world and bring Jesus to glory, we need fear no hardship. This is the Christian response to evil in the world.

The New Testament teaches that *Jesus loved us* and willingly died for us. As noted in Chapter Nine, while on earth and limited by a human mind, Jesus did not have any explicit knowledge of each of us. That he loved us must be understood in a more general sense. That sense, I suggest, is that he loved the people he knew during his life and in his world, and in them he loved humanity. The popular way of making this point is to say that he "loved people." This love of people was an extension of his attitude toward his own self and his human situation. He embraced his situation. He was completely realistic in accepting the human situation which was his. He did not reject or withdraw from what he was: a human being bound to other humans in a human world. His lot was thrown in with that of his human brothers and sisters. He accepted it all, he loved us all.

Love shows itself in sincere concern. One of the most valuable things we can give one another is to be honest—honest about what we think, how we feel, how we experience others, what is important to us. In fact, that is the only thing we have that is really our own to give. That is the only thing that is unique to each of us. Our most precious

239

gift is our own self, shared honestly with others. To love is to give of oneself. And we need that gift. Too much of our lives is passed in a daze, lost in the fog of insincere but well-intentioned words, politically astute but false statements, socially required but dishonest behavior. The world prescribes what should be said and done if we would get along in the world, but the world is not often concerned honestly to admit the way things really are and to act accordingly. An honest word, a sincerely expressed sentiment breaks through the facade of social expectations and opens us to a new reality, to real reality. We need that opening. We shrivel up and die without that breakthrough. The gift of true self, shared honestly with others, is liberating; and this liberation, understood as part of God's working in our world, is saving.

Now, Jesus was fully himself in this world. Deeply in touch with himself and so with God and ever faithful, his words and deeds cut through the pretenses of life. He transformed situations for the better by moving them to a new level of reality. Undoubtedly, Jesus knew the saving power of human authenticity. Moreover, he undoubtedly shared the conviction prevalent in his own day, that the death of an innocent person benefited the people. The story of the ninety-year-old teacher of the Law, Eleazar, bears witness to this conviction. At the cost of his life, Eleazar refused even to pretend to eat pork for fear that his example would lead the young people away from their religious practice.[25] And Jesus was also undoubtedly aware that his behavior would eventually lead to his death. There is no reason to suppose that by his saving self-offering Jesus explicitly and in concrete detail willed the salvation of every single human being ever to live. Nonetheless, Jesus knew his integrity would cost him his life, he willingly accepted his inevitable fate, and he believed his innocent death would benefit others. Put all these pieces together and there is sound basis in the historical Jesus himself for the Christian belief, "Christ died for our sins," and "through him we have redemption."[26] Jesus' love for us and his fidelity to himself and so to his Father is the source of salvation for the world. By this Jesus redeemed us.

A rich appreciation of the saving human virtue of Jesus and of the cost he paid for it opens still another insight into the mystery of our redemption in Christ. We know Jesus as a brother. From our own experience we know how difficult it is to be always authentic. We can appreciate the cost of his fidelity. So *we identify with Jesus*, and we are moved to pity when we realize his sufferings. His love for us and the price of love that he paid move us. Our hearts go out to him. We begin to love him. And such love is saving. The love and fidelity of Jesus, expressed amidst the dehumanizing, vindictive, death-dealing structures of our sinful world, elicits love in us. God uses our very human affection and sympathies, our own self-pity called forth by the sorrow of others, to move us to love for Jesus. Our own isolation, loneliness, and secret hurts—all the result of sin—become the occasion of saving love in us as we sympathize with Jesus in the same situation. Because we love, we are forgiven. What is more, our love for Jesus is love for God. In multiple ways, by loving Jesus we are reconciled with God.

Summary on the Reconciliation   How profound is God's love for us! How wise his plan! The very effects of sin become the occasions of saving virtue. The divine life lost to us because of human sin is restored to us because of human virtue. The alienation between God and humankind, caused by humans, is overcome by the love and fidelity of a human being. The same human life that in Adam and Eve led us to death now in Christ is the pathway to divine life. The required surrender to God that caused humans to stumble is transformed in Christ into the need merely to be true to oneself. The very bearing with now unavoidable evil, the result of sin, becomes the expression of loving and saving trust in God. The suffering and death of our Lord, caused by our sin, move us to love that takes sin away.

Here is a new understanding of the redeeming work of Jesus' cross. The medieval world focused on this one aspect of the redemption and interpreted it primarily in terms of debt and payment and the demands of justice. This same aspect can and should be interpreted differently, in terms of fidelity and virtue, mercy and love, and the unsurpassed wisdom of God. Such an interpretation does justice to New Testament statements, to traditional concerns, and to official Christian teaching. It replaces the theory of atonement with a theory of saving fidelity, and the theory of satisfaction with a theory of reconciliation.

Jesus' Divinization as Redeeming   However, these considerations alone do not account for the redemption. They deal only with the

241

subjective aspects of the issue, with the change in relationship between humans and God. But Jesus did more than reorient our race to
God. He also effected an objective change in his humanity, and that
change in him entails a change in the concrete reality of all humanity.
His resurrection introduced a new reality into human history. Never
before was there a divinized human being. Now there is. Because of
Jesus' resurrection, the concrete possibility for human fulfillment is
different. Because of Jesus, human divinization is now possible. This
change affects every human being ever to live. It is a change not just
in attitude or understanding or relationship; it is a change in the
reality of things. It represents a quantum leap in human achievement.
This change in the goal of human becoming, effected by Jesus, is also
part of his contribution to our salvation.

So there are two aspects to Jesus' saving work: reconciliation and
divinization. On the one hand, through his fidelity at the cost of
suffering and death, Jesus reversed the themes of the human story.
The effects of sin became the occasion for virtue. Death became the
entrance into divine life. The creature that was sinful now proved fully
faithful. Jesus reconciled us with the Father. On the other hand,
through his resurrection, Jesus achieved the divine fulfillment God
intended for humankind. He became the first human to be divinized,
and as a result divinization became a concrete possibility for humankind. These two, reconciliation and divinization, are essentially complementary aspects of one mystery. The cross and the resurrection
comprise the one redemptive work of Jesus Christ. Either without the
other is inexplicable: reconciliation, as actualized in the case of Only-
Begotten-of-the-Father become human, is incomplete without divinization; and divinization without reconciliation is groundless. And
each is real: Jesus' reconciliation-effecting fidelity unto death is real
human virtue that resulted in his divinization; and his divinization is a
real change in him, not just the announcement that reconciliation has
occurred. The medieval theory gave short shrift to half of the mystery.
In the atonement theory the resurrection is almost incidental. But
Jesus' saving work, the redemption, is a complex mystery. It includes
both the cross and the resurrection, and neither without the other.

The Saving Work of the Holy Spirit   However, there is also more
to human salvation than the redemption. In addition to the saving

work of Jesus Christ, the redemption, there is also the saving work of the Holy Spirit. Firm insistence on Jesus' resurrection as an essential aspect of the redemption disallows a mere christo-centric account of human salvation, characteristic of the theory of atonement. Jesus' reconciliation of humanity with God does not exhaust the mystery. More than a juridical change occurred in the redemption. The change that occurred was also ontological. It was a change in human reality itself. The change occurred first in Jesus. He is the paradigm of human salvation. But the same change in others is not explained apart from the work of the Holy Spirit. So focus on the full mystery of the redemption, including the resurrection, demands focus also on the work of the Holy Spirit.

Jesus opened the way to human divinization. Because of Jesus, divinization is really possible for humankind. But unlike Jesus, other humans are not eternal children of God. We lack that internal divine principle that led Jesus to divine glory. In our case, the gift of the Holy Spirit supplies that divine principle. God gives us the uncreated, divine Holy Spirit. The Spirit is then our very own. From deep within us the Spirit transforms our created human spirits. A complete account of the effect of the Spirit within us is the task of the theology of grace. That task remains to be done. Here some general and suggestive indications must suffice.

The Spirit opens us to the things of God. The Spirit reforms our hearts so that we easily and spontaneously love God above all things. The Spirit influences the very core of our being, and we increasingly become one with the Holy Spirit. Then, just by being sensitive to the stirrings of our own hearts, we are sensitive to the things of God. By being faithful to our selves, we are faithful to the Holy Spirit within us. Adopted children of the heavenly Father, our human life can parallel that of Jesus, the natural Son of God. Then, through a life of fidelity we, in our concrete historical being, become more and more children of God. The culmination will be life in God, divinization as Jesus himself experienced in his resurrection.

The Holy Spirit leads us along this path to divine glory, our salvation. We are not saved without the gift of the Spirit. Yet the path we follow in the Spirit is the one opened up by Jesus. Our faithful living in the Holy Spirit will lead us to divinization only because of

Jesus, who went before us. He made that path a reality in human life as he reoriented humankind toward the Father. Without Jesus' redemption, the work of the Holy Spirit in us has nowhere to lead. Without the Holy Spirit, the work of Jesus comes to no fruition in us. The Spirit and the Son work together to bring us the life of the Father. In this way our salvation is accomplished.

The work of the Holy Spirit and the work of Jesus Christ are both necessary for our salvation. It is true, then, that Jesus is our Savior. But it is also true, then, that the Holy Spirit is our Savior. And, in fact, the Father has his role in human salvation as well. The Father is the one who sent the Son and with the Son sent the Holy Spirit. So we obscure part of the truth when we say simply that Jesus is our Savior. For, in another way, so is the Holy Spirit. Understandably, our hearts readily go out to Jesus, our human brother; and rightly so, for it is precisely in his humanity that he redeemed us. However, we also love the elusive yet powerful Spirit, who wells up in our hearts. It is the Holy Spirit who is our companion, our paraclete, our friend. The Spirit is our immediate contact with God. Only through the Holy Spirit do we have contact with Christ. Only because of the Spirit do we look to Jesus as a model for human living. Only because of the Spirit do we recognize Jesus as Only-Begotten-of-the-Father incarnate. Only because of the Spirit do we make our own the life of Jesus among us. Only because of the Spirit are we united to Christ and in Christ to one another. From this complementary point of view, the Holy Spirit is closer to us and more central to our Christianity than is Jesus. The Holy Spirit, as much as Jesus Christ, is our Savior.

As contemporary christology puts more emphasis on the saving humanity of Jesus, the resultant contemporary soteriology must put more emphasis on the Holy Spirit. The often one-sided christo-centric emphasis of the past gives way to a trinitarian emphasis in the present. Further insight into the mystery of Christ provokes further insight into the other mysteries of our faith. A better balance is struck.[27] The Christian message of salvation is further nuanced. Another step in the development of doctrine emerges.

In summary, human salvation is a complex mystery. It entails the work of the Father, the Eternal Son, and the Holy Spirit. The Father sent the Son, who surrendered the prerogatives of divinity and became human. He lived his earthly life faithfully unto death. As a result, he rose to divine glory. His humanity was transformed and, even as human, he came to share in qualities proper only to God. By his fidelity unto death and his resurrection from the dead, Jesus reoriented humanity to God and changed the ultimate goal of all human life. In brief, he redeemed us. The Holy Spirit, sent by the Father and the Son to dwell in our hearts, allows us to achieve the goal of human life that Jesus established for us. Through the Holy Spirit, we, like Jesus and because of him, can be divinized. We share in the life of the heavenly Father. This is our ultimate salvation. That ultimate is ours only in heaven. But this is not to say that the mystery of our salvation has no effect while we still live on earth. Through Jesus Christ and in the Holy Spirit our every human thought and deed plays a part in the on-going divinization of ourselves and our world. All that was said at the end of Chapter Eight—about Jesus as The Ethical Liberator and as The Man for Others—needs to be recalled here. A wealth of contemporary thought about salvation in this world needs to be fitted into the outline presented here. Only then does a full picture of human salvation emerge.

Contingencies Within the Plan of Salvation

A revised understanding of the redemption highlights another aspect of the mystery of Christ and human salvation: its contingency. Anselm's theory of atonement presumed that only a divine-human one could make reparation for human sin, so God *must* become human; that human sin offended the order of justice, so justice *must* be redressed; that death was the punishment for sin, so Jesus *must* suffer and die. Anselm's argument suggested that the redemption occurred as it did by necessity. In contrast, the theory presented here insists on the *de facto* status of human salvation: it is as it is because, in fact, that is how things *happen* to be. Throughout, human salvation depends on *free* decisions. Human redemption in Christ did not have to happen, and it did not have to happen as it did. We cannot say what *must* have been. All we know is what in fact did happen. The whole was contingent, not necessary. This issue deserves comment.

To be sure, the very creation of the world and of human life was a free act of God. God did not have to create. Creation itself is contingent. But salvation involves a level of reality that goes beyond creation. We are not only created to live a human life. Through Christ

245

and the Holy Spirit, we are also invited to share in God's own life. We are to be divinized. Divinization entails a fulfillment that is disproportionate to what is human. It introduces us into what is proper only to God. Therefore, it entails a contingency beyond that of creation. The disproportionate order of salvation is an additional free gift of God over and above the gift of human life. It is "grace" in the proper and technical sense of the term.[28]

Within the order of salvation, the realm of grace, a number of contingent moments can be specified. Some represent divine freedom, and some, human freedom. First, the Father did not have to send the Son into the world for our salvation. The incarnation was a contingent event, dependent on divine love. Second, once in the world, the Eternal Son, Jesus Christ, did not have to be faithful to himself and so to the Father. Jesus' virtue was the result of free human choices.[29] Third, after his death, the Father did not have to raise Jesus from the dead. The resurrection, Jesus' divinization, may be presupposed in God's prior free act in the incarnation; but according to God's wisdom the resurrection was contingent on Jesus' human fidelity. Therefore, the resurrection did not have to happen. As the paradigm and epitome of all grace, it represents the effect of human and divine freedom acting in harmony. Fourth, God did not have to send the Holy Spirit to dwell in us so that we, like Jesus, could also attain to divinization. The mission of the Holy Spirit, though related in the divine plan to the mission of the Son, is not necessitated by the Son's mission. The Holy Spirit is God's free and loving gift to us. Finally, our salvation will not be achieved without our own free cooperation with the Holy Spirit. Grace leaves us free to respond or to refuse. The whole order of salvation in Christ depends on contingencies.

Contemporary speculation about christology from below tends to overlook the contingent character of the actual plan of salvation. Once effected and completed, the overall plan appears completely coherent, amazingly integral. In hindsight, so perfect is the unity of this plan that it seems that the plan not only in fact worked out this way; it also seems it obviously *had to* work out this way. There is no other possibility. What happened *necessarily* happened. It is in the nature of things.[30]

Then other unwarranted conclusions follow. A christology from below, standing alone and taken literally, pretends to be an adequate account of Christian faith about Jesus Christ.[31] Because now it is in fact common human destiny, divinization is thought to be natural for humans. So the resurrection is disconnected from the incarnation and thought to stand on its own. Divinization, the result of Jesus' resurrection, is confused with the divine status accorded Jesus in the christological councils, where the incarnation was the prime focus. And our own salvation is likewise seen as the natural perfection of humanity, following, of course—but now almost incidentally—the path that Jesus first trod.

This latter scenario is not absurd in itself. Indeed, the notion of human divinization, once worked out, lends credence to it. Divinization appears to be a universal human possibility. However, there is a glaring methodological flaw in this scenario. It takes the fruit of one account, pulls the fruit from its branch, and presumes to have the fruit apart from the tree. Where in Western civilization did the notion of a human-divine one arise if not in the constant belief of the Christian Church? Why is contemporary christology so concerned somehow to account for the divine status of Jesus Christ if not because of the decree of the Council of Nicea? Within the Judeo-Christian tradition the question of a divine-human one arises in all its literalness only when Jesus Christ is affirmed true God from true God. Otherwise, any proposed union of divinity and humanity is considered blasphemy. Only Christian revelation through Jesus Christ introduces such a novel understanding.

But the Christian understanding is not that divinization is a universal human possibility with Jesus as a prime example. Rather, the primary Christian understanding is that Jesus is Son-of-God become human. The subsequent understanding is that divinization is uniquely proper to the faithful Jesus because of who he is in the first place. The final understanding is that, because of Jesus' human divinization and the gift of his Spirit within us, all can be divinized. Only because of the Christian understanding of Jesus Christ as God incarnate did awareness of the reality of human divinization emerge in Christianity. Therefore, to propose Jesus' divinization or anyone else's apart from the reality of the incarnation of Eternal-Son in Jesus Christ is to deny one's actual presupposition. It is to present an account that is inconsistent with itself. It presents a conclusion, divinization, without its actual basis, the incarnation.

This is not to suggest that God could not have chosen to bring humans to divinization apart from the redemption in Jesus. Indeed, humans do have a capacity for sharing certain qualities that are proper to God alone. This capacity is one factor in the explanation of the divinization of the human Jesus in the resurrection and of all humans through the Holy Spirit in Christ. Since there is nothing self-contradictory in the notion, it is evidently possible that in some way apart from Christ God could have actualized that human capacity and so brought humans to divinization. Still, in the face of this speculative possibility, two things must be affirmed. First, the fact of the matter is that God did not choose to save humankind apart from the redemption in Jesus Christ. Second, the fact of the matter is that we are discussing the possibility of human divinization only because of what occurred in Jesus Christ. Apart from the facts of the matter, all speculation is idle. In a contingent world, musing about what could or might or would have been is fruitless. Such musing is a mere exercise in fantasy. It is not theology. It is not methodical explanation of a given. It is not science. Hope for eventual correct understanding of any contingent phenomenon requires that one stay close to the data, close to the given, close to the facts of the matter. Mere speculation is useless in understanding historical reality.

Of course, other religions and philosophies—like Hinduism, Gnosticism, Platonism—also speak of something like human divinization, and they posit no incarnation in the strict sense that Christianity affirms. Is the notion of divinization, then, not peculiar to Christianity? Consider this. There is a methodological flaw in those presentations, too. For them divinization enters easily. The human is considered from the beginning to be divine. Some "divine spark" is the essence of the human. The human spirit is an "emanation" of the divine. In such an understanding, that the human "regains" divine status is not startling at all. The human is divine all along. And the obvious flaw is this: the distinction between divinity and humanity is ignored. In his or her secret core, every human being is God. Such a notion, akin to a misconceived christology from below, is far from Christian. In fact, such a notion is far from Jewish. It obscures the heart of Old Testament faith: Yahweh alone is God. The presuppositions of those other positions on "divinization" are significantly different from the Christian presuppositions. If other religions do speak

248

of divinization, their explanations of the issue are incoherent. They contain a fundamental flaw. If one insists on those explanations none-theless, one changes the issue so completely that one is no longer addressing the question, How can humans, created beings, become divine? This question and its answer are peculiarly Christian con-cerns.

The position developed here seeks to provide a coherent account of human divinization. Central to this account is an appreciation of the contingency within the plan of salvation. Being human does not automatically or necessarily imply divinization. A string of historical contingencies must intervene before divinization becomes a concrete human possibility: the incarnation, the fidelity of Jesus unto death, the resurrection of Jesus, the sending of the Holy Spirit, and the Christian's own fidelity to the Holy Spirit. All the pieces of the puzzle interlock marvelously to produce a picture of God's good plan for us. In hindsight, this is clear. But the fact that the pieces fit so well does not suggest that they all have to be there or that they have to be there as they are. For all we know, God could have saved us in some other way. Indeed, God could have worked out myriad other plans by which to save us or decided not to save us at all.

Undoubtedly, much could be said about the marvel of God's wisdom in general, and Christians will go on to speculate in detail about each of the particular contingencies in the plan of salvation. However, my present concern is limited to two issues.

The Nature of Christian Theology   First, these considerations highlight once again the nature of christology and, indeed, all the-ology. Theology is traditionally understood as faith seeking under-standing. Theology is the believer's attempt to make some sense of what is believed. Likewise, christology is the believer's attempt to give a reasonable account of Christian belief about Jesus Christ. The ac-count that results is precisely that: an account of the matter. Christology is a hypothesis, a theory that relates the known facts in an intelligible way. There is little of necessary deduction or proof in it. Rather, christology and all theology is an account of the way in which God, in fact, but not necessarily, chose to deal with us.

Over the centuries our puny intelligence may increasingly dis-cern an amazing intelligibility in God's chosen plan. We realize better and better how the pieces fit together. Strikingly, God has chosen to introduce us to divine life while still preserving the humanity formed in creation, while still respecting human freedom—indeed, while even using human freedom to effect salvation—and while utilizing the very effect of sin as occasions for redeeming virtue. We can be overwhelmed by the depth and beauty of God's plan of salvation. Nevertheless, we should not flatter ourselves, thinking we have unlocked the ultimate mystery of the universe. We have in some way understood God's plan for saving us through contingent human history. But we have not understood what must be. We have not understood anything predictable. We have not understood The Necessary: we have not understood God. We have merely taken the facts of faith as they come to us in our tradition and have discerned something of the meaning latent in those facts.

Christology and all theology is a process of faith seeking understanding. The presupposition of the whole is the faith that accepts as true the mysteries revealed in Jesus Christ. These mysteries are, indeed, true; and they are real. But they are also contingent. They are merely what, in fact, happens to be the case. Theology courts arbitrariness—if not outright absurdity—when it forgets the contingency of the facts from which its further conclusions derive. Specifically, when the incarnation is overlooked, theological speculation about human divinization is a castle hanging in mid-air. Its foundation is missing.

The fact is that all humanity is invited to share in God's own life. Divinization is the actual goal of all human life. But the further fact is that things need not be this way. Divinization is not natural for humans. It is a fulfillment that is completely disproportionate to humanity. Divinization is in no way intrinsic to human nature. Only because of God's unsurpassed love, divinization happens, in fact, to be our life's goal. Human divinization is a contingent reality. Real as it is, it depends on a string of contingencies.

In practice, we must remain humble before the plan of God, revealed to us in its actual unfolding. And we must be wary. We must not be so taken by one facet of the plan—like divinization—that we overlook the actual presuppositions of that facet. Otherwise, we end up with a theology that is not only not Christian but also not even coherent. Giving attention to the contingencies within the plan of

250

salvation highlights the nature of theology and averts one-sided approaches and untenable conclusions.

Jesus' Human Contribution as Redeemer   Second, these considerations help us to appreciate what Jesus Christ did for us and why Christians love him. Among the contingencies within the plan of salvation, the human fidelity of Jesus is central. When the Word became flesh, he did not have to be faithful to himself and so to his heavenly Father. Jesus' fidelity even unto death was not a necessary occurrence. It was the result of human freedom. The redemption of the human race depended on the free human virtue of Jesus Christ. By a human being we were redeemed.

From this point of view, we were redeemed not by divine power or love. We were redeemed by Jesus' human fidelity. For this reason Christians love Jesus.

From this point of view, we love him not because he is God but because he was an ever-faithful human being. He is the paragon of human virtue. He is admirable and most noble in his human life. And his virtue and his nobility are the source of new life for all humankind. For this reason Christians praise him.

He has been what each of us is called to be. He is what each of us, in some secret alcove in the depth of our being, longs to be. So our hearts go out to him. Our love and loyalty are fixed on him—on Jesus, that human being whose life changed the meaning of history.

For too long we have looked on him only as God. We loved him because he was God. And since we could pretend to love God, whom we cannot see, while ignoring our brothers and sisters in the flesh, we could also pretend really to love Jesus. All that has changed. Such self-deceit is no longer easy. Contemporary christology retrieves appreciation for Jesus as human. It allows us to love him—nay, it demands that we love him—precisely as human. It allows us to realize more clearly that it was precisely as human that he redeemed us. The free, contingent, unconstrained, human virtue of Jesus is what redeemed us. So we love and prize and exalt and reverence him, the human being, Jesus Christ. And in loving him we are saved. And in loving him we realize that in God's wisdom there is no other way for humans to be saved but by loving one another.

Awareness of the crucial role of Jesus' human freedom in our salvation draws attention also to the role of other men and women in salvation history. We are not saved apart from Mary's "Let it be to me according to your word" (Lk. 1:38). The gospel did not come to us apart from the honesty and dedication of the early disciples and apostles. Ours is an apostolic faith. We do not have contact with Christ apart from the generations of Christians that faithfully link us with him. Our own salvation and that of the whole world will not be achieved apart from our free cooperation with the Spirit working within us.

In God's wisdom human salvation depends not only on God but also on human beings. Chief among these is Jesus Christ. Loving him, we do love God. Loving God, we love one another and together come to the divine fulfillment that Jesus, our first love, opened to us. The whole plan of salvation is woven through with contingencies. Beyond the divine, there are also the contingencies of human freedom. Jesus' ever faithful love for his Father and for us, our Spirit-inspired love for him, for one another, and for God—all work together to achieve God's goal for history, life in God.

What Jesus Revealed to Us

Common Christian belief insists that Jesus revealed God to us. One basis for this insistence is certainly Christian belief that Jesus is God. Jesus is God come among us, and so in Jesus we see what God is like. Another basis is scriptural quotes like John 1:18: "No one has ever seen God; the only Son. . . has made him known."

How Jesus "revealed God"   The present christology requires that this insistence be nuanced. Jesus was God, the Eternal Son. Yet, when he became human, he suspended his divine way of being and limited himself to a human way of being. This is precisely what the incarnation means. But if Eternal-Son suspended his divine way of being during his earthly life, Jesus could not very well model God for us. In fact, the Jesus which contemporary scholarship uncovers would present a pretty poor picture of God: ignorant, tired, angry, weak, sad, among other things. What we see in Jesus is not God but a human being.

On the other hand, Jesus was not just any human being. If he surrendered his divine knowledge and power when he became human, he did bring into the world his divine identity.[32] Who he is

252

remained the same on earth as in eternity. His specific identity, that which distinguishes him from the Father, the Holy Spirit, and every other individual in existence, is Eternal-Son-of-the-Father. So the human life of Jesus on earth is the human life of Eternal-Son-of-the-Father. And what Jesus shows us is himself, Son-of-God. Faithful to his eternal identity in every act of his earthly life, Jesus spelled out in human terms what it is to be Begotten-of-the-Father. But again, the valid conclusion is not that Jesus, Eternal-Son, therefore showed us what God is like. Rather than in a general way revealing God to us, Jesus' earthly life shows us himself, perfect Child-of-God. By implication he shows us how to be children of God,

Then is there truth in the statement that Jesus revealed God to us? Yes, but that truth must be accurately stated. Through the events of Jesus' human existence, we have come to understand what God is like. This is not to say that Jesus himself presented a human picture of God for us. But the saving events that occurred in Jesus of Nazareth are the culmination of God's action in our regard. So Jesus' human life summarizes and makes known the whole of God's dealing with us. By realizing that in a preeminent way God was at work in Jesus' human life and by noting how God acted there, we learn something about God. By recognizing the overall plan of salvation, as it unfolds consummately in Jesus, we come to know God. Thus, the letter to the Ephesians reads, "Blessed be the God and Father of our Lord Jesus Christ. . . . For he has made known to us in all wisdom and insight the mystery of his will, according to his purpose which he set forth in Christ as a plan for the fullness of time" (1:3, 9–10). Through Jesus Christ the Father finally made known his gracious purpose for the world. So, as we understand Jesus better—who he was, what was happening through him, how he affected all of us—we understand more about the God behind all this. In this sense Jesus revealed God to us.

There is also a second sense in which Jesus revealed God to us. Jesus' actual teaching about God makes God known. The core of Jesus' preaching was the coming of God's Reign on earth. The main theme of Jesus' public career was God's saving action among us. Jesus taught us about God. Jesus' parable about the weeds growing up among the wheat shows God to be patient with us. Jesus' story of the Prodigal Son and the Loving Father show God to be remarkably forgiving. Jesus' words about the lilies of the field and the birds of the air show God to be intimately concerned for every aspect of everyone's life. These and other teachings of Jesus teach us about God. Of course, Jesus also lived what he preached. As a perfect child of God, he mirrored in his own life the God whom he knew and loved and about whom he taught. So Jesus himself was concerned and compassionate, forgiving, patient. The very actions and teachings of Jesus are lessons about God. In this sense too, Jesus revealed God to us.

In summary, Jesus revealed God to us in two ways. First, the events that made up and surrounded Jesus' earthly life are expressions of God's dealing with us. Second, Jesus' own living and preaching taught us directly about God.

The Mysteries Revealed in Christ   What is it that we have come to know about God? A number of things. Above all, we realize the depth of wisdom and love with which God deals with us. God so loved us that he sent his only Son. Here the lessons of Nicea come back again. God did not send some created intermediary. God did not remain safely distant from us. The Father's Eternal Son himself came to dwell among us. God loves us that much.

Further, while among us the Eternal Son did not remain aloof, never really becoming part of our life, merely disguising himself in the form of a human being. On the contrary, he surrendered all prerogatives of divinity and became as human as we, limiting himself to the created world of space and time as we are limited. His action gives an ultimate validation to us and our world; we are worthy of God. Again God's love shines forth.

Further, in Jesus we see that God respects our freedom, even to the point of allowing the evil we produce. But in his love he transforms that evil and uses it to accomplish good. Suffering becomes the occasion of virtue, death becomes the doorway to life in God. Jesus' resurrection makes this clear.

Further, God's own Spirit has been given to us. God's own life is ours. The Holy Spirit abides with us and guides us in the footsteps of Jesus. This, too, has been made known through Jesus.

Moreover, we have come to know that God is a community, three dwelling in perfect unity—Father, Son, and Holy Spirit—sharing all in common, yet all retaining their individual identities.[33] This insight into the very being of God is certainly accurate. For if the Eternal Son is God even as the Father is God, and if the Holy Spirit is also God, then God is a tri-unity. Now we know this. God has allowed us to share in the intimate secrets of the inner divine life.

Moreover, the relevance of this knowledge about God's inner life is also clear. The tri-unity of God explains our divinization. Like the human Jesus before us, Eternal-Son made flesh, through the Holy Spirit we are also to share in the divine life of the Father. Our divinization is the expression of the Trinity in history. Divinized, and so sharing in God's own knowledge and love, we will know God even as God does and we will love with the love of God. This is the ultimate destiny God has in store for us.

Finally, we realize that not everyone believes, appreciates, or rejoices in this understanding of God's plan for us. Only some do, those who are Christians. This means that to some God has given a special role in the working out of this plan for salvation. Greater understanding implies greater capacity. Christians are empowered to further God's work explicitly by living out the love of God in this world and so making it known to all. This is the mystery of the Church.

All this has been revealed to us through God's action in Jesus. These paragraphs summarize the central beliefs of Christianity: Creation, Sin, Incarnation and Redemption, Trinity, Grace and Salvation, and Church. The whole of Christian belief can be traced back to the first-century Jesus-experience.

Of course, there is no suggestion here that this complete understanding was given in one fell swoop or that the New Testament itself explicitly expresses this whole understanding. A main purpose of this book has been to show that Christian understanding about the mystery of Christ has developed. We grow in our understanding of the faith. Not only as individuals but also as a community of believers, we understand more today than we did previously. But what we are understanding is the selfsame mystery that came into our world in its fullness through Jesus Christ. If our understanding continues to grow, what we understand does not.[34] What we understand only after centuries of prayerful reflection is nothing other than what was revealed in Jesus Christ. And what was revealed in Christ awaits even further understanding as the ages go by.

The Fullness of Revelation   God has already made his definitive intervention into human history. If Jesus is really who we say he is and if the Holy Spirit has really been poured into our hearts, there is nothing more to be expected from God. God the Eternal Son himself has come into our world. The Holy Spirit is ours. All has been given. There is nothing more. We look in vain for something else, blind to what is already ours. God has entered our world in a way that cannot—simply cannot—be surpassed: nothing more than God can be given to us. God has given us his all. And with God we are given everything else besides. It is simply for us to acknowledge what is already here, to understand it better, and to begin living the new life that is ours through the Holy Spirit in Christ.

God made his definitive revelation in the saving events culminating in Jesus Christ. This is not to say that nothing of God and God's way is known apart from Jesus. Indeed, the whole of creation makes God known.[35] "The heavens are telling the glory of God; and the firmament proclaims his handiwork" (Ps. 19:1). And God makes himself known through other religions besides Christianity. God's Spirit is at work everywhere. Yet through Jesus Christ God's self-communication to the world has reached an unsurpassable apex. If Jesus is God the Eternal Son become human and raised to divine glory, as Christians know him to be, he represents the fullness of divine revelation. His human life exhibits the paradigmatic realization of God's definitive plan for us; in him we have the most perfect instance of God's self-expression in history. Then, all else points to Jesus Christ, and all else is a participation in Christ's fullness.

Summary   The point in broaching the question of revelation is to clarify how Jesus makes God known to us. Even with a not so traditional emphasis on the development of doctrine, a rather traditional understanding of revelation still follows from my contemporary christology. However, this christology necessitates a nuanced treatment of Christ as revealer. When the humanity, as well as the divinity, of Jesus is given its due, revelation of God through Jesus must be attributed not to the human Jesus as somehow embodying God— Eternal Son though he is—but to the overall action of God as exemplified above all in the human life, death, and resurrection of Jesus. And appreciation of God's action in the life of Jesus will depend on the work of the Holy Spirit among us. The Holy Spirit emerges clearly as our immediate contact with God. Through the Holy Spirit we know Jesus Christ as God and Redeemer and so acknowledge God's revelation in Christ. And through the Holy Spirit our understanding of that revelation develops throughout the centuries.

In fact, a close reading of the New Testament confirms this understanding. This is the real intent of John's statements, recognized not as Jesus' own words but as the theology of the Johannine community.

> No one has ever seen God; the only Son, who is in the bosom of the Father, he has made him known. (1:18)

> Not that anyone has seen the Father except him who is from God; he has seen the Father. (6:46)

> Whoever has seen me has seen the Father. (14:9)

> I have manifested thy name [the Father's] to the men whom thou gavest me out of the world. (17:6)

> But when the Spirit of Truth comes he will lead you to the complete truth, since he will not be speaking as from himself but will say only what he has learnt. . . . He will glorify me, since all he tells you will be taken from what is mine. (16:13–14)

The point is that the experience of Jesus reveals a reality beyond Jesus, the Father, whose loving plan is at work in Jesus. "God so loved the world that he gave his only Son" (3:16). This is what is made known through Jesus. This is what the Spirit brings to light.

Paul's account of the matter is similar. What is revealed through Jesus is "the mystery which was kept secret for long ages but is now disclosed" (Rom. 16:25), "the mystery of his will [the Father's], according to his purpose which he set forth in Christ" (Eph. 1:9).

In summary, Jesus did not reveal God by being God in a human form. Such a notion is self-contradictory. It also violates the Council of Chalcedon. Rather, Jesus showed us in himself how to be perfectly human and what a true child of God is like. Because he was perfectly faithful to himself, Eternally-begotten-of-the-Father, in history, he became for us in his humanity the prototype of child of God. Nonetheless, it is true that in Jesus God is revealed to us. This is true insofar as Jesus is the supreme locus of God's loving action in our world, the anticipatory culmination of God's saving plan, and so the definitive manifestation of that plan within history. We know God because of God's action in Jesus. It is also true that Jesus revealed God to us insofar as Jesus himself, by his deeds and preaching, explicitly taught us about God.

Jesus and Non-Christian Religions

The christology presented here integrates contemporary concern and shows Jesus to be as human as any of us. Nonetheless, it insists firmly on Jesus' ultimate identity, Eternal-Son-of-the-Father. Jesus is God, the Eternal Son. So this christology is a "high" christology. It affirms Jesus' absolute divinity without question.

The Essence of Christianity   As a result, Christ is seen as the central mystery of Christianity. Belief about Jesus determines all the rest—Redemption, Trinity, Grace and Human Salvation, Church. Thus, the essence of Christianity, in contrast to other religions, is clear acknowledgment of the possible union of humanity and divinity. Jesus Christ is the paradigmatic instance of this divine-human union—God made flesh and in the flesh, divinized.

Indeed, no other world religion reverences its "founder" as God. Moses and Mohammed are reverenced as instruments of God, prophets of God, intimates of God. But they are certainly not thought to be God. The case of Buddha is harder to express. Eastern thought has its own starting point and mindset. It hardly makes the same firm distinctions between humanity and divinity that are found in Western thought. Still, it must be said that Buddhism and its derivative religions do not reverence Budha as God in any meaningful sense. If we must speak about God at all and if Buddha could be said to be God, he is God no more than you and I are. He has achieved ultimate enlightenment, perfect harmony with his true self—with God, if you will. We have yet to achieve that goal, though it is already real at some point within us. So Buddha is the model for the rest of us. That alone makes him different from us. He is not "divine" in any unique sense. Moreover, Buddha is thought to reincarnate periodically in different individuals throughout history. This makes one wonder how seriously one is to take the historical reality of any incarnation. Clearly, this conception differs sharply from the Christian, which insists on the absolute distinction between humanity and divinity, the absolute reality of both, the absolute divine identity of Jesus Christ, and the absolute incarnation of the Eternal Word once and for all in a single personage limited to earthly space, time, and ordinary human experience. No other world religion reverences its "founder" as God. Only Christianity does. This difference specifies the essence of Christianity.

The Scandal of Christianity   The divinity of Jesus Christ is the Christian scandal of the contemporary world. In the earliest days of Christianity, the scandal to the Jews was that the Christian-acclaimed Messiah suffered and died on a cross. A bit later the scandal to the Greeks and Romans was that the Christian-acclaimed Savior from heaven had really become flesh. Once Christianity became the established religion, it offered little scandal to anyone, except Christians who were seeking fidelity to the gospel message and Jews and other outsiders who were persecuted. With the dissolution of Christendom and, indeed, the secularization of Western civilization, the scandal was Christian concern for something beyond the palpable, the rational, the empirical.

Today, in many sectors, our world is experiencing an upsurge of spiritual renewal. Its prime concern is the development of our amazing human potential. A multitude of religious and secular movements offer competing conceptions of the spiritual ideal and methods for attaining it. Talk of the spiritual is no longer so scandalous. The scandal has changed again. In the contemporary situation the scandal of Christianity is its insistence that Jesus of Nazareth was God-incarnate on earth. Today's scandal is to suggest that Jesus was divine in a way that no other human being was or can be. Today's scandal is to believe that all spiritual growth is dependent on Jesus, derivative from him, and a participation in his achievement of divinization.

At the very least, the Christian claim is challenging, and to the unsympathetic ear, it is simply preposterous. It seems too otherworldly, still too involved with a passé "mythology," a supposed layered view of the universe. Besides, Christian exaltation of Jesus seems to belittle the obviously rich traditions of non-Christian religions. It seems to set Christianity in opposition to them at a time when the unification of the human race through the unification of religions is an ever more urgent need. The temptation to excise the scandal is great, especially when the historical and philosophical problems it raises even within Christianity appear insurmountable. The temptation is to ignore the ontological claims of traditional Christianity or, at least, to reinterpret them, to suggest they were merely a

259

peculiar way of expressing existential conerns.[36] The temptation is to consider Christianity only as a practical affair, one religion among many others, each particular in its emphasis but all equally valuable, all equally valid.[37]

This book is a response to the need of the day. It rejects the temptation to gloss over the doctrinal core of Christianity and offers at least to Christian believers a reasonable account of Christian faith, traditional and contemporary. The scandal remains. The unique divinity of Jesus Christ is clearly affirmed. Moreover, if my account is correct, this particular scandal must remain. Today's Christian scandal finally rests on the essence of Christianity. It is what is specific to Christianity in contrast to all other religions. Without it, what still may go by the name "Christian" is simply not Christian at all.

This stance is harsh, but it is also realistic. It calls for no apology. It is merely the acknowledgement of the truth. As the present review of the Christian tradition shows, Christianity remains in irreducible contrast with Judaism and Islam, Buddhism and Hinduism, and all other religions. The essential difference cannot be erased. All ecumenical concern must start from this fact. If Jesus Christ is really God-incarnate, Christianity, like Jesus before it, is utterly unique on the face of the earth.

Religion, a Complex Phenomenon   However, the uniqueness of Christianity does not prevent dialogue and sharing of concerns with other religions. Indeed, isolating that which is specific to Christianity casts in relief the other aspects of Christianity that are truly held in common with others. A differential analysis allows the legitimate interrelationship of world religions without prejudice to the specific and distinctive. Such differential analysis is needed, for any religion is a complex reality.

Within one system a religion embraces diverse aspects of lived experience and diverse levels of theological concern. Primitive religions offer the most obvious example.[38] They actually include every aspect of life within their purview: art, music, property rights, family relationships, business contacts, calendar determinations, and much more.[39] Relationship to gods, worship, and ritual are only one aspect of primitive religion. The book of Leviticus documents this state of affairs in Judaism.

The same state of affairs existed in Christianity. As Western civilization developed, more and more facets of life separated from religion and achieved autonomy and secular legitimation. Theatre, for example, emerged from religious ritual. The medieval mystery plays are the well-known link here. Art provides another example. Only in the early nineteenth century did artists insist that their creations needed no moral, religious, or spiritual justification.[40] Even today one still occasionnally hears quaint-sounding protests against "art for art's sake." Or again, marriage today can be celebrated religiously or civilly. Not everyone agrees on where the acceptable locus of authority over marriage lies.

Every religion has embraced and still does embrace many aspects of life that may not be essential to the particular faith of the religion. So highlighting what is specific to Christianity and determinative of it clarifies the line beyond which intercourse with secular culture or other religions may freely and profitably proceed.[41]

Christianity and Non-theist Religions   Even non-theist religions share much in common with Christianity. Concern for honest living and for what is right and good in life constitutes the prime emphasis in every major religion. Tibetan Buddhism offers an example. The highest virtues in that non-theist religion are called the *paramitas*. They include the following: honest openness to what really is, right action in every situation, generosity to all without prejudice, joyous energy in every activity, and compassion toward every living being.[42] This list reads like the Christian list of the gifts of the Holy Spirit: "love, joy, peace, patience, kindness, goodness, faithfulness, gentleness, self-control" (Gal. 5:22). Though the doctrinal basis for each list is significantly different, the practical consequences in each case are the same.

What is right and good for humans—if it is really right and good—must be the same for all, regardless of religion. What is authentically human for some must be authentically human for all; otherwise it is not really authentically human. Said otherwise, ethics is not a specifically Christian nor even specifically theist concern. Ethics is a human concern. In ethics, what is at stake is human authenticity, not theism. So Christians may and must discuss and resolve moral questions with all people of good will everywhere—whether those others believe in God and Christ or not.

Christian belief in Jesus as the paradigm of authentic humanity

261

does not introduce a stumbling block into this dialogue with non-believers. For here focus is not on the specifically Christian, the affirmation of Jesus' unique, divine identity. Rather, focus is on the humanity of Jesus, shared in common with all humankind. Chapter Nine has already noted how the Buddhist ideal of enlightenment is quite compatible with the Christian understanding of Jesus's sinlessness.

Christianity and Theist Religions   With theist religions Christianity shares belief in a God who is the source, sustenance, and ideal goal of all authentic humanity. Belief in God does not change the content of authentic humanity; it merely grounds it in a broader theoretical base. So the theist factor in Christianity not only does not isolate Christians from non-theists; it also links Christians closely with other theists.

With all who believe in the one God of the Universe, Christians may and must adore and repent, thank and petition. Where the one and the same God is truly the object of cult, all who reverence God may worship together. Few today would disagree with these statements.

It is noteworthy that worship of God, when distinguished in differential analysis from other functions of religion, is not a controversial issue at all. In truth, the specifically theist question is very narrow. Though theologians do need to clarify the exact understanding of God in each respective religion, theological questions—intellectual, doctrinal issues—are not the determining factor in the practice of any religion; sincere worship is. If one were to sort out the differences in theological formulation within almost any congregation today, one would likely find as divergent an array of views within each religious body as across the lines of religions. It would appear, then, that the troubling differences among theist religions are not rooted in specifically theist concerns. More likely the differences lie in humanist concerns, in non-theist questions about how life ought to be lived and how it ought to be structured. If this is really the case, these differences should be resolved on the criteria of human authenticity and not by theology. When theology is invoked to settle such disputes, theology is used, like political rhetoric, to legitimate falsehood and to obscure the truth of the matter. For the real questions in this instance are not about God. The real questions are about people and their learned preferences, about their politics and power.

All who believe in the one God, Christian and non-Christian alike, worship the same God. Christian belief in God unites Christians with all others who also believe in God. The fact that Christians also acknowledge Jesus Christ as God does not prevent them from identifying with others who also believe in God. What Christians know and believe about God because of Jesus in no way invalidates what others may rightly know and believe about God apart from Jesus. On the contrary, Christian faith confirms and validates belief in the mercy and love, the wisdom and power, of the one God who created us all. Christians know no other God than the God of the Universe, and this God all theists adore.

The Specifically Christian   That which makes Christianity different from other religions is an addition to what is shared in common with the major non-Christian religions, theist or non-theist. Belief in a divine-human one, Jesus Christ, Eternal Son of God incarnate and divinized Redeemer, is the distinctive core of Christianity. This belief about Jesus entails an understanding of God as a Tri-unity, the divinization of the human race, and a special mission for Christians as Church. These four basic and interlocked beliefs—Incarnation and Redemption, Trinity, Grace and Salvation, and Church—set Christians apart from all others. Compared with others, Christians have a different understanding of the human situation.

This is not to say that the Christian understanding is in opposition to that of others. As just explained, in varying degrees Christian belief is in accord with that of all people of good will. It is to say that the Christian understanding goes beyond that of others. The Christian understanding affirms what others believe and more. It claims a deeper insight into the meaning and unfolding of life. Our life is not just human (non-theist conception). It is not even just human and lived before God (theist conception). Our life is a process that increasingly catches us up in the very life of God (Christian conception). In an important way, our life is a process of divinization. Only Christians hold this understanding about life, and they claim it is the accurate understanding of reality, human and divine.

Universal Salvation in Christ   Of course, this understanding presumes that through Jesus Christ and in the Holy Spirit divine life is offered to all humankind. This understanding presumes that Jesus' redemption affects every human being, whether each knows it or not. The present christology requires such a conclusion. Indeed, this re-

263

quirement is a major strength in that christology: all human salvation is inextricably linked with the mystery of Christ.

Jesus' resurrection was not simply an announcement that redemption had been achieved in the crucifixion, as the medieval mind would have had it. The resurrection entailed a real change in Jesus himself. This change was a change in reality, not just a change in understanding or knowledge. The resurrection entailed an ontological change. Jesus' humanity was transformed. He was divinized. More than just a new idea in history, the resurrection introduced a new human reality into history. So human reality has never been the same. The resurrection inaugurated a new age in human history.

Anyone who shares humanity is now involved in something new, and this is true for any human being who ever lived at any time whatsoever. The human race is one. Its history is one. Its goal is one. Any change in the meaning of humanity affects every human being ever to live.[43] Jesus' resurrection constituted divinization as the highest achievement of history, the goal of all human life. So through Jesus Christ, divinization became the ultimate goal for all human beings. Since the Holy Spirit is given universally, not Christian faith but simply sharing in human life constitutes our primordial contact with Christ. Then all who are human are affected by Christ. By mere birth into the human race, they are involved in a movement toward divine life.

There is some scriptural support for this universalistic understanding of salvation in Christ. 1 Timothy 2:5–6 reads: "For there is one God, and there is one mediator between God and humans, the human Christ Jesus, who gave himself as a ransom for all . . ."[44] Jesus is the one mediator between God and *all* humans, and his redemption was also for *all*.

A Fundamentalist reading of the New Testament would quote John 3:5, "Unless one is born of water and the Spirit, one cannot enter the kingdom of God," to insist that, unfortunately, the only access to the one mediator is Christian faith and Baptism. Such non-critical reading forgets that John was writing for Christians. Among Christians it is certainly true that eternal life comes through Baptism. But John did not consider the question of those who had never heard of Christ. We should not read into the Scriptures answers to questions that the Scriptures themselves never posed. First-century Christianity simply did not address the question of the possibility of salvation for non-Christians. Indeed, even the medieval world never imagined the magnitude of this issue. When pushed on the issue, Thomas Aquinas himself gave the credulous response that to save those few who had not heard of Christ, God would send an angel or a missionary![45] The history of this question is long, and it offers yet another example of the development of Christian doctrine.

In Roman Catholicism the Second Vatican Council conveniently summarized the most recent conclusion of that development. The following is the current official Roman Catholic teaching on this question:

> All this [the mystery of Christian salvation] holds true not for Christians only but also for all men of good will in whose hearts grace is active invisibly. For since Christ died for all, and since all men are in fact called to one and the same destiny, which is divine, we must hold that the Holy Spirit offers to all the possibility of being made partners, in a way known to God, in the paschal mystery.[46]

All somehow share in the Easter mystery of Christ. All are involved in one and the same salvation. That is to say, all are graced. All have received the Holy Spirit poured out in the world, the Holy Spirit is active wherever good is being achieved. Wherever the Spirit is active, human salvation is being furthered. In innumerable human beings, unbeknown to themselves, human virtue and the Holy Spirit are together advancing lives that lead, as Jesus' own did, to divinization.

If what Christians believe distinguishes them from non-Christians, what they live does not. For all are graced. According to the good plan of the Father, all are caught up in the salvation effected by Jesus Christ and the work of the Holy Spirit.

The Differences Between Christians and Non-Christians   This is not to gloss over the difference between Christians and non-Christians. In the first place, Christians know and increasingly understand the marvel of God's work among us. This is the primary difference. It suggests that there are varying degrees of awareness of the one and the same reality that all live. As argued in Chapter Two, reality and understanding of reality are not the same thing. Some understand only to the extent that they do pursue honest and right living. They are committed to human authenticity and to the fullest development of our created human potential. Over and above this, others also realize that all we are is, indeed, created, that it comes from a God who loves us, that our lives and their most noble expressions point to an Absolute Perfection. So, in addition to living rightly, they also praise and worship God. Finally, Christians realize that God has chosen to share divine perfection with us in a way completely disproportionate to our created human nature. This sharing is accomplished through Jesus Christ and the Holy Spirit. Christians know and understand what others do not, so another difference follows.

Knowing and understanding God's work among us, Christians can also live that saving reality more deeply than others. They can live it not only in fact but also with full knowledge and with deliberate choice. Though it is perfectly good to do a good thing, it is better to do it knowingly and deliberately. Similarly, it is one thing to be in love; it is another to acknowledge and avow that love. The reality itself, the love, remains the same reality. But once avowed, it takes on a new degree of perfection.[47] Likewise, it is one thing to be created by God; it is another to acknowledge and respond to the Creator. Finally, it is one thing to be redeemed by Christ and graced with the Holy Spirit; it is another to acknowledge and celebrate and deliberately embrace the divine life offered to us. Explicit knowledge and deliberate choice raise any human reality to a new level of perfection. They transform the reality and make it more fully human, more fully adequate to human beings, whose distinctive quality is the capacity to know, understand, and freely determine their own destiny. So Christians have the possibility to live the same reality that all live but to a degree of perfection not possible to others.

It does not follow that Christians are necessarily better people than others. Israel was clearly reminded that God's love and not their merit was the cause of his choice.[48] The same is true for Christians.[49] Moreover, Christians are not always faithful to the faith given to them. Many who bear the name "Christian" are not Christian at all. And many who do not believe in Christ nor even in God are noble, virtuous, outstandingly good people. Oftentimes the work of the Holy Spirit is more obvious among the supposedly godless than among those who profess to be Christian. The frequency of saintly secular humanists—who work for the poor, struggle for justice, crave spiritual fulfillment, die seeking peace—condemns a disgraced "Christianity" in the contemporary world. This latest disgrace merely lengthens the list of inquisitions and crusades and religious wars and persecution of Jews and suppression of thinkers and more. The history of Christianity is tainted with evil, with inhumanity, with sin.

And Christianity also has its saints.

In the face of all that, the fact remains, the faith that distinguishes Christians from others does provide a possibility for greater perfection in living God's life. What Christians actually make of that possibility is another question. What theology tells us about the mysteries of the faith is not always what is lived out in the lives of believers.

The Mission of the Church   The distinctiveness of Christianity does not confer on Christians the right to smugness and self-righteous conceit. Nor does it require that they glory in their difference and shun other people or else obnoxiously impose their distinctive beliefs on all. Rather, faith calls Christians to a fourfold task that constitutes them as Church, a distinctive community, and ordains them to the service of God's Reign coming into this world.

First, faith calls Christians to *kerygma*, proclamation. It calls them to proclaim God's work among us. Those who not only live by the Holy Spirit but also know the Spirit by whom they live can easily recognize the Spirit's work wherever it occurs, in whatever form. They highlight this wonder. They support the good others do. Christians encourage others to pursue virtue as best those others know it and to praise God however they can. The Christian's message is one of validation and affirmation and hope. It is Gospel, Good News. In its fullness it is the Good News about Jesus Christ, God's Only-Begotten, come among us for our salvation.

Second, faith calls Christians to *koinonia*, community. It calls them to love one another. They offer themselves as a test case of what they believe and proclaim. They present a sign of hope to our world, a sign of God's Reign on earth.

Third, faith calls Christians to *diakonia*, service. It calls them to serve the world with an intensity and for reasons that others would not comprehend. Christians engage themselves in the world. Our world was deemed worthy of God. Christians love other people. All

267

are brothers and sisters, members of the divine family. Christians work for justice and peace in the world as they await the comsumation of God's plan of salvation among us.[50]

Finally, faith calls Christians to *eucharistia*, praise and thanksgiving. It calls them to praise God and to celebrate the life we have in Christ. In their own name and in the name of all humanity, Christians raise a human voice to acclaim the Father of the Lord Jesus Christ, whose Holy Spirit gives us new life.

Summary   The distinctive core of Christianity is the affirmation that Jesus Christ is Eternal-Son-of-God, who transformed the meaning of human life by opening the way to divinization. This distinctiveness does not set Christians apart from other religions. Rather, in various ways it allows Christians to relate deeply with all people of good will. Besides, it provides Christians with something more to offer, something found only in Christianity.

Sacred communion with all human beings is possible for Christians because it is central to the mystery of Jesus Christ. Although Jesus Christ is God, he surrendered the prerogatives of God and became one of us, a human. Through his fidelity unto death and his resurrection, humanity became the vehicle of divine life for all human beings. Jesus Christ, in his humanity, is the source of divinization for all humankind. Although divinization is the ultimate human salvation and according to God's gracious plan there is no other, the humanity we all share is the entryway into that divinization. Our common humanity is the primordial basis of our communion with one another and with Jesus. So anyone who shares humanity is automatically involved with Jesus and Jesus with her or him. All are saved through Jesus. And all are saved only through Jesus. Jesus, by sheer dint of his humanity, plays a part, known or unknown, in every authentic religion. So Christians, *precisely because of their Christianity,* have a connection with all their human brothers and sisters. Christianity has a distinctive link with all the other religions of the world. Far from setting Christians apart from other religions, Christianity unites Christians with them. This is the necessary implication of a christology that gives full emphasis to the humanity of Jesus. And this implication is not disqualified by equally full emphasis on Jesus' divinity.

Overall Summary

At the outset it was noted that historical-critical study of the Bible forces us to rethink our understanding about Jesus. We began that rethinking by insisting that christology is reflection on Jesus. This starting point requires a clear awareness that Jesus Christ himself is one thing and Christian attempts to understand and articulate the mystery of Jesus Christ are another thing. This starting point also presupposes that we can, indeed, distinguish between a reality in itself and our own understanding about that reality, and that we can increasingly achieve accurate understanding about reality. The underlying issue is epistemological.

Thinking about thinking reveals that there are different kinds of thinking and so different ways of presenting an understanding about Jesus. Contemporary christologists speak about christology "from above" and christology "from below." Yet, further consideration shows that both these approaches are instances of kerygmatic statement. They are stories that convey a truth in a gripping, inspirational way. They are the product of, and they appeal to, functional mentality—thinking whose overall concern is what something means for me. But there is another way of thinking: ontological mentality, whose overall concern is to understand things in themselves correctly and precisely. Ontological mentality achieves precise understanding by relating things to one another. Systematic statement is the result. Emerging as differentiations of intellectual potential within one ongoing process of reflection on Jesus, both functional and ontological mentality can be distinguished, validated, and developmentally related. Such an understanding of understanding enables appreciation of both kerygmatic New Testament christologies and systematic-like Nicene and post-Nicene conciliar christological teaching.

On the basis of these presuppositions and following historical-critical interpretation of the Scriptures, contemporary scholarship can separate New Testament information about Jesus himself from early Christian faith testimony about Jesus, which is also weaved into the same New Testament accounts. The picture of Jesus that emerges is much more human than the picture Christian piety has generally proposed. Nonetheless, again allowing the above epistemological presuppositions, a reasonable account of christological development from Jesus himself through the New Testament and beyond can be presented. Christological development within the New Testament occurs within a functional mentality. The final indubitable evidence of the New Testament is that Christians look on Jesus as God. But is Jesus really God? The Council of Nicea answered this further and inevitable question in the affirmative, but not without shifting into an ontological way of thinking. This same ontological mentality continued to influence subsequent conciliar definitions, which clarified the relationship of divinity and humanity in Jesus Christ. Jesus is truly divine, God even as the Father is God. Jesus is fully and completely human, like us in all things but sin. There is only one who is in Jesus Christ, the Eternal Word, born eternally of the Father and the same born in time of Mary. The humanity and divinity of Jesus Christ, united in the single identity of Begotten-of-the-Father, remain in Christ intact, unchanged and unmixed.

General Christian belief about Jesus, resulting from the conciliar teachings, has tended to emphasize the divinity of Jesus to the detriment of his humanity. The christology from above has prevailed. Nonetheless, the same conciliar teaching offers a firm basis for emphasis also on Jesus' humanity, full and complete, undistorted by the influx of divine qualities. This official Christian teaching, retrieved through legitimation of the ontological mentality, provides a framework into which contemporary biblical scholarship and contemporary concerns—both emphasizing Jesus' humanity—easily fit. While on earth, the Eternal Word surrendered all prerogatives of divinity and lived only as human, lived a life completely like our own. His life's task, like all of ours, was to be true to himself. But because of who he is, his fidelity even unto death has unique implications. He would become also in his historical humanity perfectly Son-of-the-Father, who he is eternally in God. By so doing, he would reverse the course of human history. Finally a human being would be fully faithful. Humanity would be reconciled with God, and the Father would glorify Jesus, raising him from the dead.

Contemporary emphasis on christology from below—once purged of the absurd supposition that any human could literally become God—suggests an understanding of Jesus' resurrection as the divinization of the human Jesus. Insofar as is possible, the human being, Jesus Christ, came to share in qualities—like universal knowledge and perfect love—proper only to divinity.

This overall conception entails a confluence of two movements in christology—from above and from below: the movement of God to humanity and the movement of a human to God. In God's loving wisdom, the two movements complete one another. Neither alone makes sense. The ideal fulfillment of these movements occurred in Jesus' resurrection. Then, for the first time in human history, a human being had been divinized.

Since Jesus is part of the human race, this occurrence in him could not be without effect on the whole of humanity. Every human occurrence has some effect on the whole of humanity—all the more so, the perfect fidelity and glorification of Eternal-Word become human. Because of the solidarity that binds the human race as one, his fulfillment unto God irreversibly changes the ultimate meaning and goal of all human life. Jesus opens to humankind the possibility of divinization. His own glorification is inextricably entwined with the salvation of the human race. Through the Holy Spirit, poured into the hearts of humans everywhere, all can now follow the same path that Jesus trod. A disproportionate human fulfillment, the sharing in God's own way of being, is opened to all humankind. Any human concern for honesty, justice, peace, and love is an inchoate participation in the very life of God. Jesus Christ, Eternally-begotten-of-the-Father, Son of God become human, ever faithful Son, firstborn of the dead, prototype of human divinization, is redeemer of the world.

All the elements hold together in one coherent, reasonable account. This presentation does justice to contemporary concerns for a really human Jesus and a really just world, to contemporary New Testament scholarship about Jesus, to the contemporary effort to reunite christology and soteriology, and to official conciliar teaching about Jesus.

The picture is the contemporary picture of Jesus Christ, focus of all Christian devotion and faith, source of the uniqueness of the Christian religion. Some details are different from former pictures of Jesus. Yet the changes are accounted for; they square with the tradition. Nothing has been lost, if highlights have been added.

271

Christology continues to move forward. The picture is clearer than it used to be, and unaccustomed clarity may be disconcerting. The suit is new; it better fits our times. He looks a lot more like us. Still, we know who he is. We still recognize him, Jesus our Lord. At heart, it is still the same Jesus.

Endnotes

Introduction

1. E.g., Raymond E. Brown, *The Community of the Beloved Disciple* (New York: Paulist Press, 1979), *Jesus God and Man: Modern Biblical Reflections* (Milwaukee: The Bruce Publishing Co., 1967); Oscar Cullmann, *The Christology of the New Testament* (London: SCM Press, Ltd., 1959); C. H. Dodd, *The Founder of Christianity* (New York: Macmillan Publishing Co., 1970); James D. G. Dunn, *Christology in the Making: A New Testament Inquiry Into the Origins of the Doctrine of the Incarnation* (Philadelphia: The Westminster Press, 1980), *Unity and Diversity in the New Testament: An Inquiry Into the Character of Earliest Christianity* (Philadelphia: The Westminster Press, 1977); Joseph A. Fitzmyer, *A Christological Catechism: New Testament Answers* (New York: Paulist Press, 1981); Reginald H. Fuller, *The Formation of the Resurrection Narratives* (New York: The Macmillan Co., 1971), *The Foundations of New Testament Christology* (New York: Charles Scribner's Sons, 1965); Reginald H. Fuller and Pheme Perkins, *Who Is This Christ? Gospel Christology and Contemporary Faith* (Philadelphia: Fortress Press, 1983); Martin Hengel, *The Son of God: The Origin of Christology and the History of Jewish-Hellenistic Religion* (Philadelphia: Fortress Press, 1976); Willi Marxsen, *The Beginnings of Christology* (Philadelphia: Fortress Press, 1979), *The Resurrection of Jesus of Nazareth* (Philadelphia: Fortress Press, 1970); Albert Nolan, *Jesus Before Christianity* (Maryknoll, New York: Orbis Books, 1978); Gerard S. Sloyan, *Jesus in Focus: A Life in its Setting* (Mystic, Connecticut: Twenty-Third Publications, 1983); Bruce Vawter, *This Man Jesus: An Essay Toward a New Testament Christology* (Garden City, New York: Doubleday & Co., 1973); Geza Vermes, *Jesus the Jew: A Historian's Reading of the Gospels* (Philadelphia: Fortress Press, 1973).

2. E. g., Aloys Grillmeier, *Christ in Christian Tradition: From the Apostolic Age to Chalcedon (451)*, trans. John Bowden (Atlanta: John Knox Press, 1975); J. N. D. Kelly, *Early Christian Doctrines* (New York: Harper and Row, 1960); Bernard J. F. Lonergan, *The Way to Nicea: The Dialectical Development of Trinitarian Theology*, trans. Conn O'Donovan (Philadelphia: The Westminster Press, 1976); Jaroslav Pelikan, *The Christian Tradition: A History of the Development of Doctrine*, 3 vols. (Chicago: The University of Chicago Press, 1971, 1974, 1978); James M. Robinson and Helmut Koester, *Trajectories through Early Christianity* (Philadelphia: Fortress Press, 1971); P. Smulders, *The Fathers on Christology: The Development of Christological Dogma From the Bible to the Great Councils*, trans. Lucien Roy (De Pere, Wisconsin: St. Norbert Abbey Press, 1968).

3. E.g., Oscar Cullman, *Christ and Time: The Primitive Christian Conception of Time and History*, trans. Floyd V. Filson (London: SCM Press, Ltd., 1951); Monika K. Hellwig, *Jesus, The Compassion of God* (Wilmington, Delaware: Michael Glazier, Inc., 1983); John Knox, *The Humanity and Divinity of Christ: A Study of Pattern in Christology* (Cambridge: Cambridge University Press, 1967); Bernard J. F. Lonergan, *De Constitutione Christi Ontologica et Psychologica* (Rome: Gregorian University Press, 1958); John McIntyre, *The Shape of Christology* (Philadelphia: The Westminster Press, 1966); Sebastian Moore, *The Crucified Jesus is No Stranger* (New York: The Seabury Press, 1977); W. G. Most, *The Consciousness of Christ* (Front Royal, Virginia: Christendom College Press, 1980); William M. Thompson, *Christ and Consciousness: Exploring Christ's Contribution to Human Consciousness* (New York: Paulist Press, 1977).

4. E.g., Leonardo Boff, *Jesus Christ Liberator: A Critical Christology for Our Time*, trans Patrick Hughes (Maryknoll, New York: Orbis Books, 1978); Jean Galot, *Who is Christ? A Theology of the Incarnation* (Chicago: Franciscan Herald Press, 1981); Walter Kasper, *Jesus the Christ* (New York: Paulist Press, 1977); Hans Küng, *On Being a Christian*, trans. Edward Quinn (New York: Pocket Books, 1978); Bernard J. F. Lonergan, *De Verbo Incarnato* (Rome: Gregorian University Press, 1964); James P. Mackey, *Jesus the Man and the Myth: Contemporary Christology* (New York: Paulist Press, 1979); John F. O'Grady, *Models of Jesus* (Garden City, New York: Doubleday and Co., Inc., 1981); Wolfhart Pannenberg, *Jesus—God and Man*, trans. Lewis L. Wilkins and Duane A. Priebe (Philadelphia: The Westminster Press, 1968); Norman Pittenger, *Christology Reconsidered* (London: SCM Press, Ltd., 1970); Karl Rahner, *Foundations of Christian Faith: An Introduction to the Idea of Christianity*, trans. William V. Dych (New York: The Seabury Press, 1978); Karl Rahner and Wilhelm Thusing, *A New Christology* (New York: The Seabury Press, 1980); Lucien J. Richard, *A Kenotic Christology: In the Humanity of Jesus the Christ, The Compassion of God* (Washington, D.C.: University Press of America, 1982); Edward Schillebeeckx, *Christ: The Experience of Jesus as Lord*, trans. John Bowden (New York: The Seabury Press, 1980), *Jesus: An Experiment in Christology*, trans. Hubert Hoskins (New York: The Seabury Press, 1979); Piet Schoonenberg, *The*

Christ: A Study of the God-Man Relationship in the Whole of Creation and in Jesus Christ (New York: Herder and Herder, 1971); Jon Sobrino, *Christology at the Crossroads: A Latin American Approach*, trans. John Drury (Maryknoll, New York: Orbis Books, 1978); William M. Thompson, *Jesus, Lord and Savior: A Theopathic Christology and Soteriology* (New York: Paulist Press, 1980); Frans Jozef Van Beeck, *Christ Proclaimed: Christology as Rhetoric* (New York: Paulist Press, 1979).

5. Gerald O'Collins, *Interpreting Jesus* (New York: Paulist Press, 1983), written as a textbook, falls into this same category.

6. Bernard J. F. Lonergan, "Christology Today: Methodological Reflections," in *Le Christ Hier, Aujourd'hui et Demain*, eds. Raymond Laflamme and Michel Gervais (Québec: Les Presses de l'Universitié de Laval, 1976), 45–65.

7. Cf. especially Bernard J. F. Lonergan, *Insight: A Study of Human Understanding* (New York: Philosophical Library, 1957) and *Method in Theology* (New York: Herder and Herder, 1972).

8. Cf. Bernard J. F. Lonergan, *Grace and Freedom: Operative Grace in the Thought of St. Thomas Aquinas*, ed. J. Patout Burns (New York: Herder and Herder, 1971) and "The Natural Desire to See God," in *Collection*, ed. Frederick E. Crowe (Montreal: Palm Publishers, 1967), 84–95.

9. Daniel A. Helminiak, "How to Talk About God," *Religion Teacher's Journal* 15:5 (September, 1981): 24–26.

10. Daniel A. Helminiak, "God Shares Secrets," *Religion Teacher's Journal* 16:5 (October, 1982): 32–34, "Yes, There is a Perfect Love," *Religion Teacher's Journal*, 16:7 (January, 1983): 4–6.

Chapter One: *A New Way of Reading the New Testament*

1. Cf. Fitzmyer, *Christological Catechism*, 11–17.

2. Cf. Herbert Butterfield, "Historiography," *Dictionary of the History of Ideas: Studies of Selected Pivotal Ideas*, ed. Phillip P. Wiener, 4 vols. (New York: Charles Scribner's Sons, 1973), 2:464–98; George Peabody Gooch, *History and Historians in the Nineteenth Century* (New York: Longmans, Green and Co., 1913); and Lonergan, "History" and "History and Historians," *Method*, 175–234.

3. Cf. Butterfield, "Historiography," 485.

4. Cf. Hans Küng, *The Church* (New York: Sheed and Ward, 1967), 410–11.

5. Cf. Bernard J. F. Lonergan, "The Transition from a Classicist Worldview to Historical-Mindedness," *Second Collection*, eds. William F. J. Ryan and Bernard J. Tyrrell (Philadelphia: The Westminster Press, 1974), 1–9

6. Cf. Lonergan, *Method*, xi, 29, 301–2.

7. Cf. the classic study of Ruth Benedict, *Patterns of Culture* (Boston: Houghton Mifflin Co., 1934).

8. Cf. Leslie Dewart, *The Future of Belief: Theism in a World Come of Age* (New York: Herder and Herder, 1966); Gregory Baum, ed., *The Future of Belief Debate* (New York: Herder and Herder, 1967); and Van A. Harvey, *The Historian and the Believer: The Morality of Historical Knowledge and Christian Belief* (New York: The Macmillan Co., 1966).

9. On the historical connection between historical-critical method and philosophical relativism, cf. Georg G. Iggers, *The German Conception of History* (Middletown, Connecticut: Wesleyan University Press, 1968), and "Historicism," *Dictionary of the History of Ideas: Studies of Selected Pivotal Ideas*, ed. Phillip P. Wiener, 4 vols. (New York: Charles Scribner's Sons, 1973), 2:456–64. Friedrich Nietzsche, *The Use and Abuse of History*, trans. Adrian Collins (New York: The Bobb-Merrill Company, Inc., 1957) and Ernst R. Troeltsch, *Der Historismus und Seine Probleme* (Tübingen: C. B. Mohr, 1922) exemplify the connection.

10. For more detail, cf. standard works like Raymond E. Brown, *The Critical Meaning of the Bible* (New York: Paulist Press, 1981); John H. Hayes and Carl R. Holladay, *Biblical Exegesis: A Beginner's Handbook* (Atlanta: John Knox Press, 1982); Edgar Krentz, *The Historical-Critical Method* (Philadelphia: Fortress Press, 1975).

11. Cf. John L. McKenzie, "Qumran," *Dictionary of the Bible* (Milwaukee: Bruce Publishing Co., 1965).

12. Cf. O'Grady, *Models of Jesus*, 158–66; Pheme Perkins, *Reading the New Testament: An Introduction* (New York: Paulist Press, 1978), 191–255.

13. Cf. Joachim Jeremias, *The Problem of the Historical Jesus*, trans. Norman Perrin (Philadelphia: Fortress Press, 1964); James M. Robinson, *A New Quest of the Historical Jesus* (Naperville: Allenson, 1959).

14. Cf. James W. Sire, *Scripture Twisting: 20 Ways the Cults Misread the Bible* (Downers Grove, Illinois: Inter Varsity Press, 1980).

15. For the range of opinion, cf. Raymond E. Brown, " 'Who do men say that I am?' Modern Scholarship on Gospel Christology," *Perspectives in Religious Studies* 2(1975): 107–24.

16. Austin Flannery, ed., *Vatican Council II: The Conciliar and Post Conciliar Documents* (Northport, New York: Costello Publishing Co., 1975), 761.

17. For examples, see John Hick, ed., *The Myth of God Incarnate* (Philadelphia: The Westminster Press, 1977), and Knox, *Humanity and Divinity*.

Chapter Two: *Christology: Thinking about Jesus*

1. Richard Bach, *Illusions: The Adventures of a Reluctant Messiah* (New York: Dell Publishing Co., 1977; Laurel, 1981), 104–13, uses this same metaphor, but he means it literally. Life is a movie and nothing more, and each one writes his or her own story. Bach takes the legitimate insight about the constitutive function of meaning (cf. Lonergan, *Method*, 76–81 and *passim*) to the extreme

and devalues the reality of the historical, space-time world. This popular writer, author of *Jonathan Livingston Seagull*, articulates a worldview that is increasingly prevalent in Western society and at odds with the one presented here.

2. On the world mediated by meaning and motivated by value, see Lonergan, *Method, passim*, and "Dimensions of Meaning," *Collection*, 252–67.

3. Cf. Peter L. Berger and Thomas Luckmann, *The Social Construction of Reality: A Treatise in the Sociology of Knowledge* (New York: Doubleday and Co., 1967).

4. See Lonergan, *Insight* and "Cognitional Structure," *Collection*, 221–39.

5. Precisely the articulation of the structures of consciousness—the objectification of subjectivity—is the heart of Lonergan's achievement. Cf. Lonergan, *Method*, 6–24.

6. On the self-correcting process of learning, see Lonergan, *Insight, passim*.

7. *Ibid.*, 348–74.

8. Cf. Lonergan, *Way to Nicea*.

9. *Ibid.*, and Chapters Five, Six, and Seven below.

10. Cf. Bernard J. F. Lonergan, *Verbum: Word and Idea in Aquinas* (University of Notre Dame Press, 1967), 47–95.

11. On belief, see Lonergan, *Insight*, 703–18.

12. Here my Roman Catholic commitment—and what I believe to be a most valuable aspect of the Roman Catholic tradition—comes to the fore. For the classic statement of Roman Catholic insistence on the compatibility of faith and reason, see Vatican I's decree on faith and reason in *Enchiridion Symbolorum: Definitionum et Declarationum de Rebus Fidei et Morum*, eds. Henricus Denzinger and Adolfus Schönmetzer (Freiburg im Breisgau: Herder, 1965), par. 3015–3025 (henceforth cited as DS).

13. Here begins explicit treatment of the impact of the fourth level of consciousness—the responsible level, the level of decision—on the theological enterprise. Integration of existential consciousness into a comprehensive cognitional theory is one major achievement of Lonergan's *Method in Theology* over and above that of *Insight*. See Robert M. Doran, *Psychic Conversion and Theological Foundations: Toward a Reorientation of the Human Sciences* (Chico, California: Scholars Press, 1981), 19–21, 39–87.

14. Thomas S. Kuhn, *The Structure of Scientific Revolutions*, 2nd ed. (Chicago: The University of Chicago Press, 1970).

15. Lonergan, *Method*, 338.

16. On conversion and the shift of horizons, see *Ibid.*, 220–24, 235–66, and *passim*.

17. Cf. Rahner, *Foundations*, 213.

18. Cf. Lonergan, *Method*, 335–53, on systematics.

19. Lonergan, *Method*, 292; see also 265, 338.

20. On unauthentic tradition, see *Ibid.*, 80, 162.

Chapter Three: *Christologies "From Above" and "From Below"*

1. For useful summary discussions about these two christological approaches, cf. Gerald O'Collins, *What Are They Saying About Jesus?* (New York: Paulist Press, 1977), 1–34; *Ibid.*, revised edition (1983), 5–26; O'Grady, *Models of Jesus*, 36–57, 94–118.

2. Pannenberg, *Jesus—God and Man*, 189, testifies to the strength of contemporary insistence on Jesus' humanity: "Where the statement that Jesus is God would contradict his real humanity, one would probably rather surrender the confession of his divinity than to doubt that he was really a man."

3. Edna Heidbreder, *Seven Psychologies* (Englewood Cliffs, New Jersey: Prentice-Hall Inc., 1933).

4. Gail Sheehy, *Passages: Predictable Crises of Adult Life* (New York: E. P. Dutton & Co., 1976).

5. Cf. O'Grady, *Models of Jesus*, 98–102.

6. John A. T. Robinson, *The Human Face of God* (Philadelphia: Westminster, 1973).

7. It may seem unfair to the christology from below to propose the criterion, whether or not it shows that "Jesus is actually God." This criterion is ontologically conceived, whereas the christology from below generally relies on a more biblical—"functional"—mentality. See Chapter Five below. So christologies from below tend to speak of Jesus' divinity in more descriptive and circumspect terms: the human face of God (Robinson), the sacrament of God, God's saving presence (Schillebeeckx), the absolute savior, the climax of the total history of the human race (Rahner), God's advocate (Küng), the one in whom we meet the one true God (Mackey). Nonetheless, my overall argument presumes the definitions of the christological councils *and* their ontological mentality. See Chapter Six below. So only reference to this ontologically conceived criterion highlights my fundamental objection to the strict christology from below. At the same time, this insistence on ontology functions as a challenge to more precision in christological language.

8. Any claim to a pure christology from below that intends to present authentic Christian teaching (See No. 7 above) involves an internal contradiction—a contradiction between praxis and theory. In theory one moves from the historical Jesus to his divine status; that is, one presents a christology from below. But in practice one has already accepted as a presupposition the very conclusion of the christology from below. One actually invokes in practice what one claims to prescind from in theory. O'Grady, *Models of Jesus*, 115,

asks, "If the human expresses the divine, and if we therefore concentrate on the manifestation as very much part of ordinary human experience, then why continue to talk about the divine at all?" Why, indeed?

9. This, I believe, is the intent of The International Theological Commission, *Select Questions on Christology* (Washington: United States Catholic Conference, 1980), 4: "Apart from the assistance provided by the mediation of ecclesial faith, the knowledge of Jesus Christ is no more possible today than in New Testament times."

10. The "one" christology from below includes significantly different methodological approaches and often confuses epistemology and ontology. The categories "from above" and "from below" are not patient of strictly systematic application. See Chapter Four below. Brian McDermott, "Roman Catholic Christology: Two Recurring Themes," *Theological Studies* 41 (1980): 339–67, shows how widely the usage can extend when he understands "christology from above" as a term "affirming both God's initiative in Jesus' life and his response to that initiative" (366).

11. Richard McBrien, *Catholicism* (Minneapolis: Winston Press, 1980), 489, calls Ansfried Hulsbosch's christology "a christology 'from below' of a most radical kind." Other christologies that would fall under this category are Pittenger's and Schoonenberg's. John Macquarrie, "The Humanity of Christ," *Theology*, 74(1971):243–50, outlines a general approach that also qualifies as radical. He explains, "Manhood and Godhood are not taken to be fixed natures infinitely far apart. Rather, manhood is an open, emerging nature, which transcends toward Godhood, in virtue of that image of God in which humanity was created. Christhood may be understood as that critical point at which manhood and Godhood come together and in which Godhood is manifested not, indeed, in its pure majesty but mediated in finite being, in Godmanhood. There is indeed a *metabasis eis allo genos*, but such a transformation is not impossible because the human *genos* is open toward God." Macquarrie's later insistence (249, 250) that this *metabasis eis allo genos* can be maintained only in light of a prior incarnational christology does not redeem the position, the logic of which is unsalvageable. It projects a union in terms of natures and their fusion—Godhood, "Manhood," and Christhood or "Godmanhood." That is, its conception is monophysite and not hypostatic.

In his argument, Macquarrie relies on Karl Rahner's "transcendental anthropology," thus associating it, too, with this radical form of the christology from below. Indeed, Rahner's conception of the incarnation as the goal of human history within an evolutionary view of the world invites such an interpretation. This emphasis, though focused on the incarnation and not on the resurrection, allows one to view Rahner's christology also as one from below. On Rahner's christology, see Chapter Eight, n. 40 and Chapter Ten, n. 30 below. Schoonenberg's christology appears to be a logical unfolding of Rahner's position—minus the safeguards of a periodic assertion of conciliar decrees. This is especially clear in Schoonenberg's insistence on an evolutionary worldview and in the related blurring of the distinction between the natural and the supernatural, from which Schoonenberg's christology follows. See *The Christ;* "God's Presence in Jesus: An Exchange of Viewpoints," *Theology Digest,* 19(1971):29–38; "Process or History in God?" *Ibid.,* 23(1975):38–44; "Is Jesus 'man plus God'?" *Ibid.,* 59–70; "A letter from Piet Schoonenberg, S.J.," *Ibid.,* 224–25; "Chalcedon and Divine Immutability," *Ibid.,* 29(1981):103–07; Roch Kereszty, "The Pre-existence and Oneness of Christ," *American Ecclesiastical Review,* 167(1973):630–42; Lonergan, "Christology Today." Finally, Pannenberg, *Jesus—God and Man,* 344–45, n. 42, explicity appeals to Rahner's position for support of his own.

An exaggerated evolutionary/developmental mentality is one root of the radical form of the christology from below. This mentality pervades contemporary culture. By the same token, the radical christology from below is also more pervasive in contemporary christology than would seem likely in view of the blatant ontological flaw in that conception: the suggestion that a human being became God. But to recognize this as a flaw, one must appreciate the ontological mentality and rightly assess its strengths and limitations. But contemporary theology is more at home with the functional mentality. See Chapters Four, Five, and Six below.

12. I use the terms "imagination" and "Intelligent and reasonable thought" with specific meanings in mind. With Lonergan I distinguish between phantasm, imagination, or psyche, on the one hand, and aware, intelligent, reasonable, and responsible human spirit, on the other. When I speak of imagination here, I mean phantasm or psyche. But human psyche is "en-spirited"; human imagination participates in intelligence. Cf. Robert M. Doran, *Subject and Psyche: Ricoeur, Jung, and the Search for Foundations* (Washington, D.C.: University Press of America, 1977). Aware of this fact, but blurring the distinction between psyche and spirit while laudably attempting to overthrow modernity's limited rationalist model of mind as a mere logic machine, contemporary thinkers extol imagination as the source of creativity and "intuition." E.g., Donald L. Gelpi, *Experiencing God: A Theology of Human Experience* (New York: Paulist Press, 1978). I understand "intuition" to be but another name for insight, as explicated by Lonergan; insight to be proper not to imagination or psyche but to dynamic human spirit; and creativity to be the correlate of insight. Certainly, intelligence works most fruitfully—and so insightfully and creatively—in conjunction with psyche or imagination. However, the inherent norms of dynamic human consciousness (see Chapter Two above) and not imagination provide the needed critical control of insight, "intuition," and creativity. This conception of the issue—unlike the other—loses none of the essential factors but distinguishes and relates them coherently. Thus, I do not oppose the position that extols "imagination" in contrast to a rationalist view of mind. However, not holding a rationalist view of mind, I resist a terminology that shortsightedly seems to locate creativity in the psychic rather than in the spiritual. In this sense I reject as inadequate an appeal to imagination as the source of creativity. Perhaps the term "fantasy"

conveys my intention better than the term "imagination," whose contemporary meaning has probably become unsalvageably confused.

13. Association of the human spiritual capacity with divinity—though present in Augustinian thought precisely under the image of light—depends on the Platonic and Gnostic traditions rather than on the Judeo-Christian. Cf. Andrew Louth, *The Origins of the Christian Mystical Tradition: From Plato to Denys* (Oxford: Oxford University Press, 1981); Rowan Williams, *Christian Spirituality: A Theological History from the New Testament to Luther and John of the Cross* (Atlanta: John Knox Press, 1980).

14. The by then commonly accepted doctrine of *creatio ex nihilo* lay behind the debate at the Council of Nicea. The definition of the consubstantiality of the Son was simultaneously a rejection of certain aspects of Christian Platonism. Cf. Louth, *Christian Mystical Tradition*, 75–76. The absolute foundations of Christianity are at stake in contemporary christological discussion. Chapter Six argues that the Nicean definition did not result from the capitulation of Christian faith to Greek philosophy. The same needs to be said regarding the doctrine of *creatio ex nihilo*. So, Robert M. Grant, "Creation," *Miracle and Natural Law in Graeco-Roman and Early Christian Thought* (Amsterdam: North-Holland Publishing Co., 1952), 135–52: "the doctrine of creation in Christianity was not worked out in philosophical or even theological reflection. It is the expression of religious insight which finds in God the source of all existence" (135).

Chapter Four: *Kerygmatic and Systematic Statements*

1. See also 1 Cor. 1:21, 2:4; 2 Tit. 4:17.

2. In this book the term 'kerygmatic' has a technical meaning. Obviously, other terms might have been chosen: rhetorical, mythic, commonsense. Like kerygmatic, each would need to be defined since none means popularly exactly what is intended. The important issue is not the term but its meaning. Chapter Five relates kerygmatic statement to functional mentality and to Lonergan's notion of common sense. That relationship fixes the meaning of the terms. The terms are defined in relation to one another. They are systematic.

3. Cf. Van Beeck, *Christ Proclaimed*.

4. E.g., John Dominic Crossan, *The Dark interval: Towards a Theology of Story* (Niles, Illinois: Argus Communications, 1975); William James O'Brien, *Stories to the Dark: Explorations in Religious Imagination* (New York: Paulist Press, 1977); John Navone and Thomas Cooper, *Tellers of the Word* (New York: Le Jacq Publishing Co., 1981); John Shea, *Stories of Faith* (Chicago: Thomas More Press, 1980).

5. Cf. Mackey, *Jesus*, 33–34, 75–82, 215–16.

6. Avery Dulles, *Models of the Church* (Garden City, New York: Doubleday & Co., 1974), 20.

7. For an extended example of a critical analysis and a systematic formulation of the meaning inherent in biblical images—body of Christ, vine and branches, temple of the Holy Spirit—see Daniel A. Helminiak, "One in Christ: An Exercise in Systematic Theology" (Ph.D. Diss., Boston College and Andover Newton Theological School, 1979).

8. At issue is the move from *mythos* to *logos*. Cf. Lonergan, *Method*, 81–99, 257–62, 302–18; Bruno Snell, *The Discovery of Mind: The Greek Origins of European Thought* (Cambridge: Harvard University Press, 1953).

9. As the term 'kerygmatic', in this book the term 'systematic' also has a technical meaning. 'Systematic' refers to terms whose meaning is set by their relation to one another within a comprehensive system. Chapter Five presents systematic statement as a correlate of ontological mentality and of Lonergan's notion of theory. These terms—systematic statement, ontological mentality, and theory—are also defined by contrast to kerygmatic statement, functional mentality, and common sense. Thus, the terms' meanings are fixed. The terms are defined systematically.

Other terms could have been used in place of 'systematic', always with the same meaning. Since ontological mentality and systematic statement are correlates of what Lonergan calls the realm of theory (*Method*, 81–83), the term 'theoretical' would be appropriate. In *Insight (passim)* Lonergan speaks of "explanatory" statement and also borrows David Hilbert's conception and term "implicit definition" (10–13). Contemporary science speaks of "rigorous" definition and terminology or of "formal" argument and means what I intend by 'systematic'. Mathematics speaks of a certain set of interlocking terms and relations as an "algebra." All these terms—theoretical, explanatory, implicitly defined, rigorous, formal, algebraic—mean in their own realms what I mean by 'systematic.'

10. Cf. Lonergan, *Insight*, 291, 345; Garrett Barden, "II. The Symbolic Mentality," *Philosophical Studies* (Maynooth), 15(1966):28–57.

11. Lonergan, *Method*, 153–54.

12. *Ibid.*, 274, 346.

13. *Ibid.*, 95–96.

14. *Ibid.*, 97–99.

15. Such an understanding is the epochal achievement of Lonergan that allows the critically grounded reconciliation of New Testament statements with conciliar decrees. The task, as will be clear in Chapters Five and Six below, is to reconcile common sense with theory—or, in my terminology, to reconcile kerygmatic with systematic formulation, functional with ontological mentality. Lonergan's systematic articulation of the realm of interiority opens the way for that reconciliation as his articulation facilitates each one's own discovery and understanding of the realm of interiority. Then, self-appropriation allows each one to achieve "a basis, a foundation, that is distinct from

common sense and theory, that acknowledges their disparateness, that accounts for both and critically grounds them both" (*Method*, 85; cf. also 107).

16. It is clear that the term "systematic theology" is generally used in a sense different from the one proposed in this book. Cf. Lonergan's notion in his chapter on "Systematics" (*Method*). Thus, the very term "systematic" has both loose and strict senses. Even in the same field, theology, it means different things to different people. Here is an example of the terminological confusion referred to in the immediately preceding paragraphs above.

17. Küng, *On Being a Christian*, 133; Macquarrie, "The Humanity of Christ," 249–50.

18. Of course, the New Testament contents of the titles "Lord" and "Christ" are not the same as one another nor the same as that of the title "God." The only suggestion here is that the attribution of the titles follows a similar process. Moreover, "Lord" does have divine connotations in the New Testament. This is obvious in Phil. 2:6–11 where Old Testament attributes of the Lord Yahweh, Is. 45:23, are attributed to Jesus. See Chapter Five.

19. For a case in point, see Mackey, *Jesus*, and the analysis of his position in Chapter Six below. For a discussion of the issue, see Van Beeck, *Christ Proclaimed*.

Chapter Five: *Jesus in the New Testament*

1. For general sources on New Testament christology, see Introduction, n. 1.

2. Recall that I use the term 'kerygmatic' in a technical sense. My statement that the whole New Testament is kerygmatic in form does not deny the variety of literary genres found in the New Testament: liturgical, didactic, apologetic, creedal, etc.

3. Mk. 13:32; Mt. 11:25–27, 12:6; Lk. 10:72.

4. On this question (and others) about the historical Jesus, I find that O'Collins, *Interpreting Jesus*, 67, grants too much. Certainly his position does not emphasize the strict minimalist criteria enunciated above. In general, it seems, in order to justify later Christian doctrine, O'Collins finds a broad base for that doctrine in the self-awareness of the historical Jesus. I meet the same concern by accepting a thorough-going kenotic christology, by emphasizing the importance of Jesus' actions and teachings over his possible christological conceptualizations and statements, and by proposing a systematic account of the shift from functional to ontological mentality. On this basis there is no need for the human Jesus to have understood himself and his mission.

5. Cf. Fuller, *Foundations*, 109.

6. See also Mk. 8:38 and Lk. 12:8–9.

7. Cf. Lk. 11:49, Mk. 2:17, Mt. 11:4–6.

8. Mk. 14:36, Rom. 8:15–16, Gal. 4:6.

9. Ps. 68:6.

10. 1 Cron. 29:10.

11. Vermes, *Jesus the Jew,* 211.

12. E.g., Fuller, *Foundations.*

13. Cf. Robinson and Koester, *Trajectories;* Francis Schussler Fiorenza, "Christology after Vatican II," *The Ecumenist* 18, 6(1980):81–89.

14. The "Nicene" creed.

15. Dunn, *Unity and Diversity,* 269–270.

16. 1 Cor. 16:22, Rev. 22:20. See also Acts 10:42, 17:31.

17. See also Acts 17:3, 18:28.

18. Is. 42:1–4, 49:1–6, 50:4–9, 52:13–53:12.

19. Consider this statement by Macquarrie, "The Humanity of Christ," 249: ". . . those who, like van Buren, for instance, recognize the uniqueness of Christ and his unique claim, are confessing at least part of what has traditionally been expressed by saying that Christ is God. For in acknowledging the ultimacy of Christ, they are according to him a place and an allegiance which may not properly be ascribed to any finite entity."

20. This terminology derives from Lonergan, *Way to Nicea,* 127–28: ". . . the *ontological mentality* that finds expression in the affirmation that the Son is consubstantial with the Father" (emphasis added). The conception is also Lonergan's. Cf. *Ibid.,* 136: "Equally, it [the Nicene dogma] marks a transition from things as related to us to things as they are in themselves."

21. Cullmann, *Christology of New Testament,* 3–4, introduced a distinction between Christ's "nature" and his "function" and insisted the New Testament statements expressed the latter, not the former. So a "functional" understanding of Christ would be concerned about what he does. An "ontological" understanding would be concerned about what Christ is. Mackey, *Jesus Man and Myth,* 213, 243, 277; Eduard Schweitzer, *The Holy Spirit,* trans. Reginald H. and Ilse Fuller (Philadelphia: Fortress Press, 1980), 55; and Vawter, *This Man Jesus,* 122–23, 129, 130, use the term "functional" in this same sense. However, the issue becomes complicated because "what Christ does" is taken to mean "what he does *for me*"—or for us or for people in general; and Christ's activity (what he does) and the relationship (for me) are not clearly sorted out.

As a result, the term "functional" takes on other closely associated but different meanings. For Bonhoeffer functional christology is but another term for soteriology (Cf. O'Grady, *Models of Jesus,* 121–27). Galot, *Who Is Christ?* 5–8, showing little sense for the New Testament mentality, uses the term "functional" simultaneously in the same sense as Bonhoeffer and with the standard meaning derived from Cullmann and mixes the lot with an existential/psychological—but supposedly an ontological—understanding of "person."

How exactly Kasper, *The Christ*, 21, understands the term is hard to determine when he affirms the need for both an "ontologically determined Christology" and a " 'functional' Christology" but is primarily concerned to develop "a Christologically determined historical and personal ontology." The meaning of "functional" and "ontological" is not precisely defined anywhere.

I believe that my usage clarifies the valid intent of Cullmann's distinction. Since christology is *reflection* on Jesus, functional and ontological christology differ not because they focus on two different aspects of Christ—what he does or what he is—but because they represent two different ways of *conceiving* Christ. Functional mentality understands things insofar as they relate to myself; ontological mentality understands things by relating them to one another.

Note that on that understanding both functional and ontological mentality are concerned with both what Christ does and what he is. As Lord for me (functionally conceived), Christ does something, he saves; and he is something, God's supreme agent. As Eternal Son of the Father (ontologically conceived), he does something, he saves; and he is something, God, consubstantial with the Father. But these two mentalities conceive this doing and being differently. Note, secondly, that this distinction is not made in terms of the object known but in terms of the knowing subject. This conception sorts out the cognitive and the entitative—for that is the crux of today's problem—and highlights the fact that however Christ is conceived a human subject is doing the conceiving so a relationship between the known and the knower is always implicated. The notion that "ontological" thinking supposedly attains to some "objective" knowledge apart from a human subject is sheer folly. This notion, rightly rejected, is the counterpart of the now prevalent and equally muddled notion of "functional." Rather than rejecting this notion, too, I retrieve both and clarify them within a comprehensive theory of knowledge. Note, finally, that this conception allows that both mentalities result in statements that do say something about the object known. Both have entitative import, ontic significance. See note 23 below and Chapter Six, pp. 150–54. So the shift from functional to ontological thinking does not result in saying something different about Christ but implies a different way of saying something.

22. Lonergan, *Insight*, 173–244 and *passim*.

23. See Chapter Four, nn. 8–15.

24. Fuller, *Foundations*, 247–50, speaks of New Testament "ontic statements" about the Redeemer. (See also Vawter, *This Man Jesus*, 146: "the ontic formulae of the New Testament.") The term "ontic" is used to insist that the New Testament does say something about what Jesus Christ is. But Fuller contrasts functional and ontic statements, and presents the latter as an advance over the former. Functional statements express what Christ does; ontic statements suggest something of what Christ is; ontological considerations address the questions that ontic statements raise. Then ontic appears to be a

midway category between functional and ontological. Such usage is misconceived and misleading.

The term "ontic" is easily abused. Alan Richardson, *A Dictionary of Christian Theology* (London: SCM Press, 1969), p. 241, notes, "The precise significance of the word can usually be determined only from the context in which a particular theologian or philosopher uses it." In general, the term "refers to what really exists."

Accepting that general meaning, I hold that all the New Testament statements have ontic significance (See note 21 above) and all are functional. Likewise, the later ontologically conceived conciliar statements also have ontic significance. All must have or else be deemed the product of psychotics, completely out of touch with reality and articulating a world of pure fantasy, meaningful for them though it may be. Fuller's insistence on the ontic significance of the latest New Testament christological statements poses no challenge to my argument. Moreover, his insistence on the ontic significance *only* of those statements raises a question about the adequacy of the theory of knowledge behind his position.

Consider O'Collins, *What About Jesus?* (2nd ed.), 28: "In principle it appears impossible to speak of some person's value, significance, and role without making at least some implicit claims about the nature of that person. A merely functional Christology which sets aside ontological issues is simply not feasible."

25. Brown, *Community of Beloved Disciple*.

26. See also Jn. 3:16.

27. Also Jn. 1:18; 2 Cor. 4:4; Col. 1:15, 18; Heb. 1:6.

28. Also 1 Cor. 8:6; Col. 1:16; Heb. 1:2.

29. Brown, *Jesus God and Man*, 23–28, 34–38.

Chapter Six: *The Council of Nicea: A Double Development*

1. Pelikan, *Catholic Tradition*, I, 173.

2. E.g., Küng, *Being Christian*, 131–32; Sloyan, *Jesus in Focus*, 186–87.

3. Cf. Helmut Koester in Robinson and Koester, *Trajectories*, 270; Elaine Pagels, *The Gnostic Gospels* (New York: Random House, Inc., 1969), *passim.*

4. For detailed studies of the Council of Nicea and of the subsequent councils treated in Chapter Seven, cf. Introduction, n. 2. For the present chapter I am particularly indebted to Lonergan, *Way to Nicea*. The now classic study by John Courtney Murray, *The Problem of God: Yesterday and Today* (New Haven and London: Yale University Press), 33–60, is a corroborative presentation of this same material. Robert C. Gregg and Dennis E. Groh, *Early Arianism—A View of Salvation* (Philadelphia: Fortress Press, 1981), highlight other aspects of the Arian position, interpreting it first and foremost as a scheme of salvation, a scheme similar to the one presented here in the context

of a thorough-going kenotic christology. "At the center of the Arian soteriology was a redeemer, obedient to his Creator's will, whose life of virtue modeled perfect creaturehood and hence the path of salvation for all Christians" (x).

5. Arius' letter to Alexander, as cited in Lonergan, *Way to Nicea*, 70.

6. Arius' letter to Eusebius of Nicomedia, as cited in *Ibid.*, 72.

7. Arius' letter to Alexander, as cited in *Ibid.*, 71.

8. *Ibid.*, 70.

9. On authenticity, cf. Chapter Two, pp. 62–63; Lonergan, *Method, passim;* Daniel A. Helminiak, "Neurology, Psychology, and Extraordinary Religious Experiences," *Journal of Religion and Health* 23(1984):33–46.

10. On "dogmatic realism," cf Lonergan, *Way to Nicea*, 88, 90, 128–33, 135, 137; "The Origins of Christian Realism," *Second Collection*, 239–61.

11. See the example of Mackey, *Jesus Man and Myth*, criticized below.

12. An experience of "second naiveté." Cf. Paul Ricoeur, *The Symbolism of Evil* (Boston: Beacon Press, 1969), 347–57.

13. On meaning, cf. Bernard J. F. Lonergan, "Dimensions of Meaning," *Collection*, 252–67; *Method*, Chapter 3.

14. Athanasius' *De synodis* and *Ad afros.*, as cited in Lonergan, *Way to Nicea*, 99.

15. Cf. *Ibid.*, 2–3, 6, 9, 109; Lonergan, *Method, passim.*

16. Clement of Alexandria, *Stromata*, as cited in Lonergan, *Way to Nicea*, 117.

17. Cf. *Ibid.*, 128–33.

18. Athanasius, *Oratio 3 c. Arianos*, as cited in *Ibid.*, 100, and *Method*, 127.

19. Cf. Lonergan, *Way to Nicea*, 129–31, "The Dehellenization of Dogma," *Second Collection*, 11–32.

20. Fergus Kerr, *New Blackfriars* 60(1979): 283–84.

21. Dermot A. Lane, *Irish Theological Quarterly* 46(1979):202–09.

22. A survey of opinions indicates that Mackey's position is hardly idiosyncratic. In addition to the two reviews cited above, Paul F. Knitter, *Horizons* 7(1980):349–50, with the sole reservation that the book seems to make faith too dependent on history, recommends this book as an undergraduate text. And in his survey article, "Roman Catholic Christology: Two Recurring Themes," *Theological Studies* 41(1980):362–67, whose one focus is "the meaning of the Chalcedonian formulas for late-twentieth-century Roman Catholic theology" (339), Brian McDermott takes Mackey's book in stride, presenting in scholarly fashion a succinct and objective summary and at the end of the article placid and wholly uncritical "Reflections."

Despite his best efforts and intentions, Fuller, *Who is This Christ?* settles for a functional understanding of conciliar teaching on Jesus: "In his full humanity he is the definitive presence of God in-the-act-of-self-communication, *Deus pro nobis*, of the same God who was for us in creation, preservation, general revelation, and Israel's special revelation" (131). Again, Fuller summarizes the argument of Hans Grass, *Christliche Glaubenslehre* (Stuttgart: Kohlhammer, 1975), another merely functional understanding: "Can we not be content simply with confessing that we have found in the Christ event the definitive eschatological presence of God, a revelation and a salvation that can never be transcended, and leave it at that?" (126). Or again, in her introduction to *Jesus, The Compassion of God*, Hellwig expresses discomfort with, if not outright rejection of, theoretical christology; the freeing move must be back to symbols and analogies. Then, Hans Küng, *Being Christian*, questions the validity of the supposedly hellenistic conciliar teaching about Jesus and suggests not only that it is not identical with the New Testament message—which it is not—but also that it distorts or corrupts that original message (131–32). In the end Küng opts for an understanding of Jesus as God's advocate, a functional understanding. And Sloyan, *Jesus in Focus*, expresses the same lack of appreciation for ontological mentality and systematic formulation: "The Greek Christians and their Latin counterparts had to know how things were with God. Not surprisingly, they came to know" (186). "The Christian church . . . must expound the mystery of Jesus Christ and the Holy Spirit in a way comprehensible to the Jew and the Muslim, neither of whom thinks like a Greek or a Roman" (187).

Of the ten reviews of Mackey's book that I consulted, only three pinpoint serious historical and/or philosophical errors in Mackey's work. M. D. Goulder, *The Journal of Theological Studies* 31(1980):595–98, questions Mackey's interpretation of *homoousios* and *hypostasis* and calls on him to admit his apparent disbelief in certain traditional doctrines, including the divinity of Christ. Geoffrey Wainwright, *Scottish Journal of Theology* 34(1981):75–78, criticizes Mackey's interpretation of *ousia* and *hypostasis* and his representation of both the Alexandrian and the Antiochene concerns. And Frances M. Young, *The Expository Times* 90(1979):343–44, *cautiously* points to the methodological issue: "it will not do to say that all religious language is mythological. . . . it seems to me that there is something important being said, however crudely, by making this distinction between literal and mythical language."

Three other reviewers express some reservation, but they do not indicate the problem or its possible solution. Ralph P. Martin, *Interpretation* 34(1980):430–32, wonders if Mackey has done justice to the traditional insistence on Jesus' being *vere deus* while he praises the book as "a clearly conceived and well-executed presentation of a single thesis," namely, the contemporary approach from below. John P. Meier, *Journal of Ecumenical Studies* 17(1980):496–97, severely criticizing Mackey's use of New Testament material, has the further "impression that the popular Catholic excess of a fully divine and somewhat human Jesus is merely being replaced by the opposite excess (popular among academia) of a fully human and somewhat divine Jesus." Michael Slusser, *Theological Studies* 41(1980):403–04, states simply that the adequacy of Mackey's christology vis-à-vis the Christian myth is "open to question."

Evidently, the presuppositions that underlie Mackey's presentation are pervasive and powerful in comtemporary theology. They begin to control the field. Opposition tends to be hesitant and uncertain.

For another blatant example, cf. John Hick, "Whatever Path Men Choose is Mine," *Christianity and Other Religions: Selected Readings,* ed. John Hick and Brian Hebblethwaite (Philadelphia: Fortress Press, 1980; orig. in *The Modern Churchman,* 1974): Christian insistence that Jesus Christ is God is "a poetic, symbolic, or mythological statement" (185). "It is a way of saying that Jesus is our living contact with the transcendent God. In his presence we find that we are brought into the presence of God" (186). ". . . see the Incarnation as a mythological idea applied to Jesus to express the experienced fact that he is our sufficient, effective and saving point of contact with God. . . . We can revere Christ as the one through whom we have found salvation . . ." (186).

23. Mackey, *Jesus Man and Myth,* 234–35: ". . . Christian orthodoxy insists that in Jesus we meet true God and true man, since the fully human man of faith, Jesus of Nazareth, by inspiring others to live that same life of faith, enables us to encounter the one, true God. . . ."

24. *Ibid.*, 238: "It [the formula of Nicea] is a terse expression for a complex conviction, a conviction which contains at least the following constitutive elements: the conviction that the faith of Jesus . . . when it becomes ours, alone provides our encounter with the one, true God, whom we cannot directly 'see' or 'hear'; a conviction that the historic person of Jesus, himself a man of such faith, is for us the source of this faith, the one person in our history who inspires and empowers us to such faith; the one, therefore, in whom we encounter the one, true God."

212: ". . . the statement 'Jesus is God,' together with kindred references to the divinity of Jesus, is a kind of popular shorthand by which a very subtle relationship indeed between Jesus and the God he called Father is commonly indicated."

231: "To say that they encounter the one, true God in the faith of Jesus is to say what that faith is, to say simultaneously that it was the very life of the man Jesus, and that it is theirs because it was his; and all of this can be abbreviated in the formula that they meet in Jesus the one, true God."

25. In one place Mackey suggests what could be a third alternative in answer to the question, Is Jesus Christ, the Son of God, a creature? Arius' answer was that he was not God but a creature. Nicea's answer was that he was not a creature, but is God, though he is not the Father. Mackey seems to suggest he was God and was the Father.

I do not want to appear petty in my criticism. Certainly, Mackey in no way wants to suggest that Jesus Christ was actually God, the Father. This is clear. But more accurately, it seems, Mackey would not want to distinguish persons in God at all, and so the name "Father" would be just another name for God. All this must be speculation on my part, precisely because Mackey's position is not clear. Yet note what he writes: ". . . Jesus as *hypostasis*, as substantial object, now very much an 'object' in the world's history besides other objects, is the *hypostasis* or objectification which makes the *hypostasis* of God as Father a reality in our lives. That is what is meant by explaining in terms of *hypostasis* the confession of Jesus as Son or Word of God as Father" (p. 240).

Mackey is not using the term *hypostasis* in the sense the tradition developed. No matter. Take the terms as Mackey himself uses them, and this point is sufficiently clear. For Mackey Jesus is the historical, concrete manifestation of God the Father. If one is to take this statement literally, it means Jesus is the Father incarnate. This is not likely what Mackey wants to say. But it is what he seems to say. Moreover, it is doubtful we could ever discover what Mackey really means, for he shuns systematic statement with its technically defined terms and relies solely on kerygmatic statement—under the name "myth." The conclusion is obvious: Mackey's presentation persists in presenting the Christian message in a pre-Nicene form. Ambiguous as it is, it is no longer an accurate statement of Christian belief.

26. *Ibid.*, 235: "It would not be fair, of course, to complain so about Arius and not to acknowledge that most of us have entertained the idea of a literal generation process in the heavens, giving to God a divine Son who then took flesh as Jesus of Nazareth and brought to the human race literal revelations of the nature of God and of God's detailed will and purpose for human kind. We have consequently thought of the Christian faith primarily as intellectual assent to a set of revealed truths. The fully human nature and life of Jesus was an article of that faith . . . but it scarcely belonged to its source and essence: and a lesser divine being could certainly have brought us the truth to which our intellectual assent was demanded. The philosophers and historians . . . who insisted that the essence of Christianity consisted not in the confession of supernatural mysteries, but in a moral life which engendered hope of a happy after-life with God, were closer to the truth, for all the limitations of their rationalist models, than were many of their opponents."

27. I add the last phrase, "as well as correct affirmation," to give Mackey the benefit of the doubt. His understanding of myth hardly seems to allow objective cognitive implication. This is obvious especially in his treatment of the resurrection, which has been most severely criticized: M. D. Goulder, *The Journal of Theological Studies*, 31(1980):595–98; O'Collins, *What About Jesus?* rev. ed., 44–50. The resurrection accounts express experiences of the early disciples. Whether they also say something objectively real about Jesus himself, the named object of those experiences, is unclear in Mackey's presentation.

28. Mackey, *Jesus Man and Myth*, 239.

29. *Ibid.*

30. I find that Mackey's position does go too far. For example, ". . . all talk which seems to proceed from God's side and to explain how the utterly transcendent God relates to our empirical world is really talk which proceeds from the human side and explains how the human spirit can travel toward the utterly transcendent God. So when one hears talk about sons of God, whether from Jew or Greek, one must never be tempted to think that the talkers possess any priviledged information of any generation-process which took place within the divinity. One must realize, rather, that the talkers are presenting some person, whether real or imaginary, because they think they have reason to believe that this person, more than any other, bears God's image in the world. . . . The movement, as far as the human spirit is concerned, is always from below upward, from human experience in and of this world to intimations of divinity. This is always the case, no matter how much the finished schemata of any theology might tempt us to think otherwise" (220–21).

". . . questions begin to be asked, and unfortunately answered, about the complement or make-up of these natures" (244).

"It [the trinitarian formula] has tempted Christians to think that they had some direct vision of the inner being of God, that they could see three 'somethings' in there, 'three little mannikins', in Calvin's acid phrase. It has tempted otherwise worthy christian theologians to build theologies of the church or moral theologies on the trinitarian formula; ambitious projects indeed, except that too often the Trinity comes out of it looking like a second holy family in heaven, a somewhat superfluous parallel to the holy family of Jesus, Mary and Joseph on earth, a very talented and cooperative, happy and harmonious group" (241).

31. *Ibid.*, 214–15, emphasis added.

32. *Ibid.*, 243, emphasis added.

33. *Ibid.*, 245: "What Grillmeier here suggests, and what is in fact assumed by much of the Christian tradition, is that the one *proposon,* the one *hypostasis,* the one 'subject' in question in Chalcedonian orthodoxy is that of the Word of God. . . .All that can be said here is that it is quite possible to conclude as much; though it is scarcely possible to prove beyond any doubt that the Chalcedonian formula itself requires that we should so conclude."

34. See Chapter Two, pp. 58–60.

35. See n. 3 above.

36. Mackey, *Jesus Man and Myth*, 245.

37. DS 424: The Word become human "is only one hypostasis, namely, the Lord Jesus Christ, one of the Holy Trinity." DS 426: "the Holy Trinity did not suffer the addition of another Person or hypostasis by the incarnation of one of its number, namely, the Divine Word."

Chapter Seven: *Christological Development after Nicea*

1. For bibliography, cf. Introduction, n. 2.

2. The relevant teaching of Constantinople II was already treated in Chapter Six, p. 172.

3. Athanasius, *Tomus ad Antiochenos*, 7, as cited in Smulders, *Fathers on Christology*, 75.

4. For an entertaining and sobering account of these outlandish goings-on cf. Philip Hughes, *The Church in Crisis: A History of the Twenty Great Councils* (London: Burns and Oates, 1961).

5. Cf. Lonergan, "The Origins of Christian Realism," *Second Collection*, 239–61.

6. For further explanation of human divinization and its contrast with the divinity of Jesus Christ, see Chapter Eight, pp. 231–38.

7. Cf. Vawter, *This Man Jesus*, 146: ". . . the well-known philosophical objection to Chalcedon . . .: "What formerly was called nature is now accepted as person; what formerly was defined as person is now regarded as nonexistent.' "

8. I continue to support a doctrine of *anhypostasia*—Jesus Christ was not a human person (in the classical sense of the term). Others, e.g., Piet Schnoonenberg, *The Christ* and Hellwig, *Jesus, Compassion of God*, 13–14, 17, oppose this position. Current insistence that Christ was a human person generally does not appreciate the classical meaning of the term, person, and as a result does not really appreciate the change in that term's meaning. A compromise, *enhypostasia*, proposed by Leontius of Byzantium and John of Damascus, suggests that Christ does have human personhood but that this human personhood is included within the hypostasis of the Word. On my understanding of the issue, *enhypostasia* is unnecessary—and, indeed, erroneous. *Enhypostasia* represents an attempt to insure Christ's full humanity. But to suggest that without being a human person Christ would not be fully human is to misunderstand the distinction between nature and person. Nature is what makes one human or not. Christ has a complete human nature. Therefore, Christ is completely human. One indication of the misunderstanding is reference to person, hypostasis, as *something we have*: "Did Christ have a human hypostasis? We do. Then, if he did not, how can we claim he is fully human?" But hypostasis is not something someone has. The hypostasis is the someone who has whatever is had. If the divine hypostasis, the Word, has all the qualities that constitute someone as human—a human nature—then the Word, a divine hypostasis, is a human being, and fully so, period.

9. On the notion of person, cf. Lonergan, "Christ as Subject: A Reply," *Collection*, 164–97; "The Subject," *Second Collection*, 69–86; "The Origins of Christian Realism," *Ibid.*, 239–61; *De Constitutione Christi Ontologica et Psycho-*

logica (Rome: Gregorian University Press, 1958); *De Deo Trino: II. Pars Systematica* (Rome: Gregorian University Press, 1964).

10. The distinction between person and nature and their understanding as proposed here cannot be dismissed simply as left-over Aristotelian or medieval metaphysical gobbledygook. These terms are grounded in contemporary intentionality analysis and in a comprehensive cognitional theory, epistemology, and metaphysics. This same basis can ground contemporary science and provide a comprehensive context for interdisciplinary studies. Cf. Lonergan, *Insight; Method;* "The Example of Gibson Winter," *Second Collection,* 189–92; "An Interview with Fr. Bernard Lonergan, S.J.," *Ibid.,* 215–17; "The Ongoing Genesis of Methods," *Studies in Religion/Science Religieuse* 6(1976–77): 341–55; Frederick E. Crowe, *The Lonergan Enterprise* (Cowley Publications, 1980); and Robert M. Doran, *Psychic Conversion and Theological Foundations: Toward a Reorientation of the Human Sciences* (Chico, California: Scholars Press, 1981). Though the notions "person" and "nature" proposed here are in continuity with the classical tradition, they also represent an advance over that tradition.

11. Cf. Helminiak, "One in Christ."

12. Note that the definition of "person" needs a further qualification when applied to the Trinity. In God the divine existence is not what determines the persons, for all three in God share one and the same eternal and necessary existence. Rather, how each of the Three has divine existence determines the divine persons: the Father is without source; the Son is Born-of-the-Father; and the Holy Spirit proceeds from the Father and—or through—the Son. "Person," understood as a correlate of the third level of consciousness as "an existent in an intellectual nature," must be further qualified with the adjective "distinct" when applied to divine persons. The definition, when qualified and so rendered universal, still applies to human persons. So the notion of person, strictly defined, is not simply equivocal, *pace* Hellwig, *Jesus, Compassion of God,* 17 and Sloyan, *Jesus in Focus,* 186. Human persons are also distinct subsistents in an intellectual nature, but the basis of their distinctiveness is different from that of the divine persons. Humans are ultimately distinct because of the created existence that makes them respectively be. Divine persons are distinct because of their originative relations to one another. So neither is the notion of person, when applied to divine and human ones, strictly univocal. This further clarification is more pertinent to trinitarian theology than to christology. For when the question is about the Eternal Word in relation to his humanity and to other humans, his identity with the divine essence and its eternal and necessary existence is the key issue, and not the Word's distinctiveness vis-á-vis the Father and the Holy Spirit.

13. The reality of Christ's humanity is accounted for not on the analogy of other created realities but on the analogy of any contingent predication made of God. Cf. Lonergan, *De Deo Trino: II,* 217–19, 226–35; *De Verbo Incarnato*

(Rome: Gregorian University Press, 1964), 247–55. That a contingent statement made of God be true—e.g., God created this tree—it is necessary only that there really be the adequate contingent term of that predication, namely, this tree really existing. The predication of creation of God requires no change in God, for God is eternally sufficient to account for anything that is. If this created tree really exists, then it is true that God created this tree. If this tree does not really exist, then it is not true that God created this tree. Similarly, in order that the statement be true, The Word subsists in a created human nature, it is necessary only that that created human nature of the Word really exist. The divinity itself, the existence of the Word, is sufficient to account for the reality of that created human nature. Nothing more is needed. No additional created existence is needed. Now, according to Christian faith, that created humanity of the divine Word does exist, for the Word became flesh. Therefore, it is true to say that the Word subsists in a created human nature. Nothing more is needed, especially not appeal to some distinct created existence. Positing such a created existence would entail a human person alongside the divine Word, and it would not then be true that the Word subsists in a created human nature. What would be true is the adoptionist understanding: The Eternal Word indwells and so shares the humanity of a human person. Cf. Lonergan, "Christ as Subject: A Reply," *Collection*, 164–97.

14. Actually, this is a "reasonable account" only for those willing to enter into the patristic and medieval mindset out of which it arose and into the contemporary ontological mentality within which it is being developed. This mentality is generally foreign to us. As a result, these christological statements appear foreign. They do not speak to our culture. But neither do differential equations speak to the man and woman on the street. Yet no one, it is to be hoped, would conclude that differential equations are useless. On general bias, cf. Lonergan, *Insight*, 225-42. One basic contention here has been that there is a systematic formulation of the faith and there is a kerygmatic formulation. The present presentation is intentionally systematic. The immediate popular irrelevance of these statements does not make them invalid or inaccurate. They must be taken on their own terms. Those who want more easily accessible yet cogent explanation will have to look to another source, and I do not know what it is. Apart from other shortcomings, other contemporary approaches also eventually labor under the burden of intricately conceived metaphorical or philosophical terminology. Cf. O'Collins, *What About Jesus?* 2nd ed., 17–20; O'Grady, *Models of Jesus*, 114–16. Unfortunately, the contemporary questions about Jesus cannot be answered in easy, popular categories. It is no serious flaw if the present approach is not immediately relevant to popular needs. The more pressing need, it seems, is to determine precisely what Christian belief about Jesus actually is and how it can be understood intelligently. Once there is some consensus of these points—and today we are far from it—we may be able once again to proclaim authentic Christianity in a way easily accessible to all. Then, once again we

may also be capable of structuring a unified church and, perhaps, even a world civilization.

15. As cited in Smulders, *Fathers on Christology,* 128.

16. DS 301, 302, as translated in *Ibid.,* 3–4.

17. Cf. George Howard, "Phil. 2:6–11 and the Human Christ," *Catholic Biblical Quarterly* 40 (1978): 368–87.

18. Cf. Lucien Richard, *A Kenotic Christology: In the Humanity of Jesus Christ, the Compassion of Our God* (Washington, D.C.: University Press of America, 1982).

19. On miracles, see Chapter Eight, pp. 217–19.

20. Cf. John T. Galloway, *The Gospel According to Superman* (Philadelphia: A. J. Holman Co., 1973).

21. Then how do we ever arrive at belief in Jesus as God incarnate? See the discussion on christologies from below in Chapter Three, pp. 73–75.

22. Josef A. Jungmann, *Pastoral Liturgy* (New York: Herder & Herder, 1962) and "Christological Disputes and Their Influence on the Liturgy," *The Early Liturgy: To the Time of Gregory the Great,* trans. Francis A. Brunner (Notre Dame, Indiana: University of Notre Dame Press, 1959), 188–98, notes how excessive anti-Arian reaction exalted the divinity of Christ at the expense of awareness of his humanity. Monophysitism represented the extreme, fully eclipsing Christ's humanity. As a result, for centuries Christians have felt distant from Christ and refrained from receiving the Eucharist. Or again, out of concern to avoid any semblance of subordinationism, the formula of the doxology changed from *Gloria Patri per Filium in Spiritu Sancto* to *Gloria Patri et Filio et Spiritui Sancto.*

Chapter Eight: *Jesus, the Human True to Himself*

1. Avery Dulles, *Models of the Church* (Garden City, New York: Doubleday & Co., 1974).

2. Cf. Helminiak, "One in Christ," 74–177.

3. Avery Dulles, *Models of Revelation* (Garden City, New York: Doubleday & Co., 1983).

4. Cf. Lonergan, *Method,* 81–99; and Ian G. Barbour, *Myths, Models and Paradigms* (New York: Harper & Row, Publishers: 1974), which, however, does not integrate Lonergan's appreciation of theory.

5. See Chapter Four, n. 15; Lonergan, *Method,* 115: "For only through the realm of interiority can differentiated consciousness understand itself and so explain the nature and the complementary purposes of different patterns of cognitional activity"; *Insight,* 637: "logically unrelated sciences are related intelligently by a succession of higher viewpoints"; "The Subject," *Second Collection,* 69–86; Doran, *Subject and Psyche* and *Psychic Conversion;* Helminiak,

"Extraordinary Religious Experiences," "Where Do We Stand as Christians?" *Spiritual Life* 28 (1982):195–209.

6. *Inter Insigniores* (On the Question of Admission of Women to the Ministerial Priesthood), *Acta Apostolica Sedis* 69 (1977):98–116, insists on the fact that Jesus is male *(vir)*. This is the only official Church document known to this author that interprets Jesus' saving significance in terms of his being *vir*; all others relate him to us as a human being, using the generic terms— *homo* in the Latin and *anthropos* in the Greek.

7. In my text I avoid use of the now ambiguous term "person" (= *hypostasis*) and in its place substitute "identity" or other alternates, as explained in Chapter Seven. The intended meaning is the same.

8. Preface of Weekdays I, *The Roman Missal: The Sacramentary* (Collegeville: The Liturgical Press, 1974), 453.

9. But see Chapter Seven, n. 17.

10. This position is not a repetition of the late nineteenth-century liberal Protestant kenotic christologies. Cf. Richard, *Kenotic Christology*, 158–60. Those christologies, represented especially by Gottfried Thomasius, attempted to safeguard the full humanity of Christ by limiting the divine nature in the case of the incarnate Word. Thomasius posited a distinction in the divine nature between relational attributes: omnipotence, omniscience, and omnipresence, and essential or immanent attributes: power, love, truth, and suggested that by voluntary self-limitation the Word emptied his divine nature of the former but not of the latter. This theory implies a real change in the divine nature of the incarnate Word. Moreover, accommodation of this change requires redefining divine absoluteness: the absoluteness of God lies not in immutability but in the ability to change. Hence, a foreshadowing of a "process" God emerges. A further implication of this theory is that, while on earth with a debilitated divine nature, the Word is not equal to the other two Persons of the Trinity. Hence, the doctrine of the Trinity is threatened.

My position agrees that in the incarnation the Word limited himself by becoming human. This is standard Christian belief, and this is where agreement stops. First, the distinction between relational and immanent attributes of God is misconceived. All the listed attributes are essential—"immanent"— to God. Cf. Lonergan, *Insight*, 657–69. The distinction between "relational" and "immanent" attributes is reminiscent of the misconceived distinction between the "functional" and "ontological." Cf. Chapter Five, nn. 21, 24. Second, I do not understand the Word's self-limitation as a diminution of the divine nature. Rather, I affirm that in the incarnation the Word assumed a second nature, humanity, and while on earth limited himself to acting through that second nature. He prescinded from use of the divine nature, which necessarily remains intact. Remembering the argument at the Council of Chalcedon, I insist that the sole principle of activity of the incarnate Word was the human nature. I also suggest that the mystery in the incarnation lies precisely in the Word's prescinding from use of the divine nature while on earth. At the same time, this is not to suggest that during the time of Jesus' earthly life the eternal and transcendent Triune God was not able to continue the divine activities because one of the divine persons had in history limited his activities to what is humanly possible. Cf. International Theological Commission, *Questions on Christology,* IV, 8. This latter issue represents but another way of highlighting the mystery in the incarnation. For some explanation of this mystery, see pp. 199, 205, and what follows here. Third, an adequate understanding of the hypostatic union in Christ eliminates the problem inherent in the nineteenth-century kenotic christologies. They are actually monophysite in their approach. They try to reconcile divine and human qualities or attributes. That is, they attempt to combine, mix, mingle, divinity and humanity. Then, in an attempt to safeguard the humanity, they must debilitate the divinity. In contrast, union *kath' hypostasin* allows that both the humanity and divinity in Christ remain intact ("without confusion, without change") while being the principles of activity of one and the same one, namely, the Eternal Son, Jesus Christ, Our Lord ("without division, without separation"). Union *kath' hypostasin* also allows—indeed, if conciliar teaching and common Christian belief about the humanity of Christ are taken seriously, it requires—that the incarnate Word prescinds from activity through the divinity and limits himself to activity through his humanity. What this implies about the possibility of Jesus Christ's revealing God to us is treated extensively in Chapter Ten, pp. 329–35. Finally, I reject any suggestion of change in the divinity. The incarnation is predicated of the divine Word, not of the divinity. The Word became flesh; divinity did not become humanity. Cf. Lonergan, *De Deo Trino,* II, Chapter VI, "De Divinis Missionibus."

11. Cf. Charles T. Tart, ed., *Transpersonal Psychologies* (New York: Harper Colophon Books, 1975), 150–51; Helminiak, "Extraordinary Religious Experiences."

12. Cf. Jn. 2:11; 3:2; 6:29,30; 7:3,31; 9:16,33.

13. "Birth" is used figuratively, not literally. No claim is made regarding the moment when a human fetus becomes truly a human being, with a human mind.

14. The phrase, "for all practical purposes," suggests concern for doing things. Hence, it implies a "nature," a principle of *activity.* The intent here is that Jesus surrendered divine prerogatives and acted only through his human nature. This does not mean that he *was* no longer divine; it means he did not *act* through the divine nature.

15. Cf. O'Collins, *Interpreting Jesus,* 193: "The relation of the man Jesus to the Father is that of the preexistent Logos. Transposed into human conditions that relation becomes one of total, self-less obedience." But see Chapter Nine, n. 41.

16. On authenticity, cf. Chapter 6, n. 9, and nn. 49 and 50 below.

17. William Shakespeare, *The Tragedy of Hamlet, Prince of Denmark,* Act I, Scene ii, ll. 78–80.

18. John Donne, *Devotions Upon Emergent Occasions,* #17.

19. Cf. Helminiak, "One in Christ."

20. Mt. 4:1–11; Mk. 1:12–13; Lk. 4:1–13.

21. Mt. 26:36–46; Mk. 14:32–42; Lk. 22:39–46.

22. Brown, *Jesus God and Man,* 104–5: "A Jesus who walked through the world knowing exactly what the morrow would bring, knowing with certainty that three days after his death his Father would raise him up, is a Jesus who can arouse our admiration, but still a Jesus far from us. He is a Jesus far from a mankind that can only hope in the future and believe in God's goodness, far from a mankind that must face the supreme uncertainty of death with faith but without knowledge of what is beyond. On the other hand, a Jesus for whom the future was as much a mystery, a dread, and a hope as it is for us and yet, at the same time, a Jesus who would say, 'Not my will but yours'—this is a Jesus who could effectively teach us how to live, for this is a Jesus who would have gone through life's real trials."

For a superb statement about "The Faith of Jesus," cf. O'Collins, *Interpreting Jesus,* 190–93. My understanding differs from O'Collins' only on two details. 1) I agree that Jesus did not believe that he was God and Savior, but my reason is different. O'Collins suggests that Jesus *knew* he was God and Savior and so did not have to *believe* it. Here, again, it appears that O'Collins grants the historical Jesus what neither biblical evidence supports nor orthodoxy requires. See Chapter Five, n. 4. I understand Jesus' relationship to the fact of his being God and Savior to be one of non-reflexive and primordially reflexive consciousness, not one of knowledge. A detailed analysis of consciousness and knowledge, such as Lonergan presents, clarifies this issue. See Chapter Nine, pp. 262–72 and nn. 14, 15, 16, and 19. So, at the moment in salvation history when Jesus lived, the fact that he was God and Savior was not a necessary nor even possible appropriate content of *fides quae,* not even for Jesus. In this sense Jesus did not believe that he was God and Savior, nor did he know it. Rather, for Jesus this existential but not yet humanly known reality was an appropriate object of the third dimension of faith noted by O'Collins: confidence; even as O'Collins himself suggests: "Jesus trusted that he would be vindicated and that his death would bring salvation to the world. . . .At the end, even though he lacked full and clear knowledge about the future course of events, Jesus entrusted his cause to his Father" (192). Further theological analysis of this confidence also suggests that Jesus trusted his own internal experience—that which is formulated as implicit christology—and so taught and acted and died as he did. My second point of difference explicates this first. 2) Unlike O'Collins, I would not speak immediately of "Jesus' obedient commitment to his Father's will" (192). This is a theologization. Rather, explicating the experiential content of that phrase, I would speak immediately of Jesus' fidelity to himself and to his human situation and only mediately of his then *ipso facto* fidelity (obedience) to the

Father. Indeed, Jesus knew that he was being faithful to his Father's will, and he certainly intended that as an *a priori* heuristic of his every decision. But he, like all of us humans who live in significant obscurity in the face of life's most important questions—like Who am I? What is my life all about? Why do things have to be this way?—could determine the will of the Father only by responsibly assessing the situation in which he found himself. And he, like all of us humans, could gauge his fidelity to the Father only by honestly assessing the authenticity of his response to all he was experiencing, internally and externally. So I suggest that the immediate object of Jesus' commitment was his own self, for all that that meant and as best as he could determine it. *Ipso facto*, then, and mediately, Jesus was also committed to the will of the Father. This is simply to say, Jesus' was a human experience.

23. The reference is to non-reflexive consciousness. See Chapter Nine, pp. 262–66.

24. Mk. 8:27–33; Mt. 16:13–26.

25. See Chapter Four.

26. Cf. Lonergan, "Dimensions of Meaning," "The Subject," *Method*, 76–81.

27. Karl Rahner, *On the Thelogy of Death* (New York: The Seabury Press, 1973; orig. 1961).

28. John 17:5.

29. Bernard J. F. Lonergan, *Philosophy of God and Theology* (Philadelphia: The Westminister Press, 1973).

30. Thomas Aquinas, *Summa Theologica*, q. 3, a. 4, ad 2; q. 12, a. 12, ad 1; q. 12, a. 13, ad 1.

31. Lonergan, *Insight*, 350–52, 636–39.

32. *Ibid.*, 348: "Being, then, is the objective of the pure desire to know." Cf. 348–74.

33. Lonergan, "The Natural Desire to See God," *Collection*, 84–95; Aquinas, *Summa Theologica*, q. 12.

34. See Chapter Ten, n. 28.

35. Mackey, *Jesus Man and Myth*, 86–120

36. See Chapter Five, n. 24.

37. Cf. Raymond E. Brown, "The Resurrection and Biblical Criticism," *Commonweal*, Nov. 24, 1971, 235: " . . . it is disturbing to hear from Catholics the facile claim: 'My faith in the resurrection would not be disturbed if Christ's body were found in Palestine.' Much more to the point is the question whether the faith of the Eleven would have been shaken by such a discovery. This writer, for one, thinks that it would have been." On this very issue, see severe criticisms of James Mackey's and/or Eduard Schillebeeckx's treatment

of the resurrection in O'Collins' *What About Jesus?* (2nd ed.), 44–50, 59–62 and Fuller and Perkins, *Who This Christ?*, 28–38.

38. Cf. Paul Davies, *God and the New Physics* (New York: Simon and Schuster, 1983); Charles R. Meyer, *Religious Belief in a Scientific Age* (Chicago: Thomas More Press, 1983); Rahner, *Theology of Death.*

39. On emergent probability, see Lonergan, *Insight,* 115–28, 259–62, and *passim.*

40. Note an important contrast with Karl Rahner, "Christology Within an Evolutionary View of the World," *Theological Investigations,* vol. V, Karl-H. Kruger, trans. (Baltimore: Helicon Press, 1966), 157–92, where the Savior is "the climax of the history of the cosmos" and the incarnation is "the self-transcendence of the material in the spirit and towards God by His own dynamism inherent in the world (without thereby becoming constitutive of its being)" (178). This notion is essential to Rahner's christology and appears throughout. So also, "Current Problems in Christology," *Theological Investigations,* vol. I, Cornelius Ernst, trans. (Baltimore: Helicon Press, 1961), 149–200: "The Christ would appear as the summit of this history and Christology as its sharpest formulation" and "Christ has always been involved in the whole of history as its own proper entelechy" (167). Despite assertions to the contrary, this conception obscures the distinction between creation and redemption; it collapses the distinction between the natural and the supernatural. The position is deliberate: Cf. "Christology an Evolutionary View," 177–78: "For we are quite entitled to conceive what we call creation as a part-moment in that process of God's coming-into-the-world by which God actually, even though freely, gives expression to himself in his Word become part of the world and of matter; we are perfectly entitled to think of the creation and of the Incarnation, not as two disparate, adjacent acts of God *'ad extram'* which in the actual world are due to two quite separate original acts of God, but as two moments and phases in the real world of the unique, even though internally differentiated, process of God's self-renunciation and self-expression into what is other than himself."

On my understanding, Jesus' resurrection/divinization and not the incarnation is the high-point of the development of human history. This is one important point of difference from Rahner. The other difference is this: this high-point, though in principle open to humanity, is disproportionate to humanity. It is not merely the climax or summit of history's natural unfolding.

Another approach results in the same conclusion. On my understanding, in the actual order of salvation, Jesus' resurrection/divinization was contingent both on the incarnation and on his human fidelity. Significant contingencies mediate between the natural out-flow of historical process and its high-point, Jesus' divinization. Jesus' free, human decisions that led to his divinization are not simply of the natural order of history, for they are the acts of the Eternally-Begotten-of-the-Father. They are acts of one who is unique in history. They represent the confluence of what is both properly human: human freedom, and disproportionate to humanity: the incarnation of a divine individual. Is the presence of a divine one in history not history's natural fulfillment? No. Here the argument comes to the crunch as it turns to consideration of the incarnation. *Pace* Rahner, the incarnation itself is not merely the fulfillment of the "proper entelechy" of created reality; it is not the "self-transcendence of the material in the spirit and towards God." Rather, the incarnation represents an intervention by God in history over and above that of creation. According to Nicea, God was in Christ in a way that God is not present in the rest of creation. The difference is not merely quantitative. It does not represent the fulfillment of a historical, evolutionary process. On the one hand, God's "own dynamism inherent in the world" is creation, conservation, and concurrence. This is not God's presence in Christ through the incarnation. On the other hand, God's presence in Christ through the incarnation *is* "constitutive of (his) being." The attempt to affirm Christ's divinity by appeal to the evolutionary fulfillment of "God's own presence in the world" and at the same time to avoid thorough-going pantheism with the qualification "without thereby becoming constitutive of its being" effectively limits the presence of God in Christ to the same kind of presence that God has in creation. The divinity of Jesus as defined at Nicea is lost. So the evolutionary account is inadequate.

In summary, if the incarnation surpasses the created order, the divinization of the human Jesus, itself contingent on the incarnation, also surpasses what is proper to humanity—though not impossible for humanity. Then, neither is Jesus' divinization merely the summit of history nor is it the self-fulfillment—actual and still free, though it be—of the dynamism of human history. Human divinization *surpasses* what is proper to humans. It transcends the natural order of historical evolution. It is not merely its climax or summit. This is so not only because the intrinsic intelligibility of divinization—human participation in divine qualities—is disproportionate to humanity. It is so also because divinization is contingent on the incarnation, which is itself disproportionate to humanity. Neither the incarnation nor Jesus' divinization is the natural climax or summit of the evolutionary process of human history. Appreciation of the disproportionate nature of human divinization—a grasp of the two distinct, yet actually related and unified, intelligibilities in question—is the meaning of "supernatural." Cf. Bernard J. F. Lonergan, *Grace and Freedom: Operative Grace in the Thought of St. Thomas Aquinas*, ed. J. Patout Burns (New York: Herder and Herder, 1971), 13–19.

Other considerations confirm this conclusion. *Pace* Rahner, one is not free to conceive creation and incarnation as merely part-moments (a metaphor) of one process of God's coming-into-the-world. The intrinsic intelligibility of the two is different, so one is not the other (logical and reasonable conceptualization). If the two are nonethelss factors in one overall process, then that process presumes and embraces two radically different factors—a marvelous work of God! But the resultant unity of the process does not homogenize and so cancel the differences between the creation and incarnation.

Again, one wonders if "God's coming-into-the-world" adequately conceptualizes salvation, the goal of history as known in Christ. If it does, the goal is attained in the incarnation. Then what of the resurrection/divinization? What of Jesus' life? Do they add nothing? My distinction between the incarnation of the Word and the divinization of Jesus sorts out important issues that Rahner's christology confounds. Rahner's position here expresses his master notion, "spirit in the world." This notion generates problems when applied to christology because it fails to distinguish adequately betwen divinity and spirit. Then any developmental process of spirit gets interpreted as the entrance of God into the world. The intellectual capacity of the human spirit to know and love God, *potentia obedientialis*, is confused with the ontological capacity to be God. When this notion is applied to the incarnation, the distinction between spirit and divinity gets lost completely.

The argument of Chapter Three, n. 11 is relevant here. The attempt to account for the union of the divine and human in Jesus Christ on the basis of an evolutionary conception of God's self-expression in the world, present from the beginning and so free from the discontinuity of another distinct intervention on the part of God, results in monophysitism. It suggests that the humanity of creation is in and of itself, as the primordial yet pregnant effect of God's self-expression in what is other than himself, capable of becoming and in fact does become God—even if freely and only in one historical instance in Jesus Christ and only as predicated of God's Word. In this case humanity and divinity are united by the fusion of the two. And in this case insistence on the role of the Word, rather than preserving the real distinction between humanity and divinity, seems to call into question the real distinctions among the *hypostases* in God. On my understanding humanity and divinity in Jesus Christ are not united on the basis of any quality inherent in humanity—though something in humanity does make it appropriate for assumption by a divine *hypostasis*, namely, its being an intellectucal nature (and here Rahner's peculiar understanding of *potentia obedientialis* in regard to the incarnation has its legitimacy). Rather, humanity and divinity in Jesus Christ are united on the basis of a single hypostasis who, being divine, takes to himself a human nature. The union is hypostatic.

Again, it is correct to insist that in God creation and incarnation are not two separate, adjacent acts. God is simple; there are no real distinctions in God except those that determine three divine *hypostases*. But this does not mean that creation and incarnation are intrinsically the same reality, or are merely different degrees of expression of one and the same reality, namely, the dynamism of human history or of God's self-expression in history. Nor does it mean that the incarnation was not contingent. The incarnation did not need to happen. Just as any other contingent, historical occurrence does not necessitate a separate and really distinct act in God to assure its reality, neither does the incarnation. Yet every historical occurrence is real. And every historical occurrence is contingent, that is, not necessary, freely emergent, not necessitated by what went before. Unity of act in God does not imply the intrinsic identity of contingent, historical occurrences. The unity of creation and incarnation in God does not imply a totally homogenous process in the actual order of salvation. Appeal to acts in God is a red herring. The issue is not to distinguish or unite acts in God but to understand accurately the relationship between God's necessary, eternal being and created, contingent, historical being. For more on Rahner's obscuring the *de facto* status of the present order of salvation, see Chapter Ten, n. 30.

41. Cf. Helminiak, "One in Christ."

42. George Herbery Mead, *Mind, Self and Society,* ed. Charles W. Morris (Chicago: University of Chicago Press, 1934, 1974).

43. Max Scheler, *The Nature of Sympathy,* trans. Peter Heath (Hamden, Connecticut: Shoe String Press, Inc., 1970).

44. Cf. Rahner, "Current Problems in Christology," 165: "here we must remember that the world is something in which everything is related to everything else, and that consequently anyone who makes some portion of it into his own history, takes for himself the world as a whole for his personal environment." *Ibid.,* 167: "The Logos did not merely become (statically) man in Christ; he assumed a human history. But this is part of an entire history of the world and of humanity before and after it."

45. Cf. Chapter Nine, pp. 262–64, on non-reflexive consciousness.

46. Cf. Helminiak, "One in Christ," 53–74 and Henri Rondet, *The Grace of Christ: A Brief History of the Theology of Grace* (New York: Newman Press, 1967), 65–88, 365–77.

47. Cf. Chapter Three, nn. 13, 14.

48. Cf. Boff, *Jesus Christ Liberator:* Hellwig, *Jesus, Compassion of God;* Sobrino, *Christology at the Crossroads.*

49. Cf. Karl Rahner, "Reflections on the Unity of the Love of Neighbor and the Love of God," *Theological Investigations,* tr. Karl-H and Boniface Kruger, vol. VI (Baltimore: Helicon Press, 1969), 231–49.

50. Cf. Lonergan, *Method,* 57.

51. 1 Cor. 12:12–27; Eph. 4:1–16.

52. Cf. Helminiak, "Extraordinary Religious Experiences."

53. The present christology is systematic. (See Chapter Four, n. 16.) It expresses its understanding in terms and relations that define one another within one system. It begins with an understanding of one central issue and from it develops a complete explanation. That central issue is human consciousness. Lonergan's intentionality analysis provides an articulation of consciousness in terms of four "levels." These four are themselves interrelated and defined by their relationship to one another.

Distinction of the third, the reasonable level of judgment of fact (Is it? *An sit?*), in contrast to the second, the intellectual level of understanding (What is it? How is it? *Quid sit?*), isolates existence itself as a real and so a valid object of consideration.

Actual consideration leads to the distinction between contingent, finite, historical being and necessary, infinite, eternal being. This distinction between the *created* and the *uncreated* is also expressed in terms that relate to one another and define themselves precisely by that interrelationship.

At the same time, the same real distinction between the second and third levels grounds the real distinction between what one is and the fact that one is. The terms *'nature'* and *'person'* name the realities so distinguished. As a correlate of the third level of consciousness, the initial definition of person (see Chapter Seven, n. 12) as *subsistens—in natura intellectuali*—emerges. As a correlate of the second level of consciousness, the notion 'nature' signifies what or what kind something or someone is. Applied to God and to humans, the notion 'nature' gives rise to the notions of *"divinity"* and *"humanity."*

As for divinity: the notion of uncreated being already determines the meaning of divinity and in a definitive way distinguishes it from humanity. Cf. Lonergan, *Insight,* Chapter 19. Since in uncreated being the distinction between *Quid sit?* and *An sit?* is not real but only conceptual, the qualities of divinity are derived from a consideration of necessary being. That is, explication of the nature of divinity, a concern proper to the second level of consciousness, depends in this unique case on a proper understanding of existence, the explicit concern rather of the third level of consciousness. The analysis is metaphysical. These considerations do not pretend to explain God. Divinity can only be understood analogously. Here the analogue is dynamic human consciousness, the central issue of this systematic account. On this basis explication of divinity results only in a hypothesis, a proposed understanding of God. The often repeated wisdom of Aquinas, We know that God is but we do not know what God is, remains true. Nonetheless, if only a hypothesis results, the telling issue is that this understanding of God is intelligent and reasonable in itself and allows extensive and coherent treatment of all the important theological issues. It recommends itself.

As for humanity: explication of the meaning of human nature, a contingent reality, requires another approach, namely, empirical method. This method is specified most fundamentally by the same human consciousness that is the central issue of this systematic account. (See Lonergan, *Insight* on "generalized empirical method" and Lonergan, *Method,* Chapter 1.) Such empirical research about the human includes not only the concerns of contemporary human sciences and so, among other things, introduces a notion of radical *human sociality,* which serves systematically to link christological with soteriological considerations. Such research includes also the conclusions of modern philosophy and its *Wende zum Subjekt.* Accordingly, the present systematic account does not lose but systematically incorporates the legitimate conclusions of contemporary thought and science. In particular, analysis of human subjectivity—dynamic human consciousness, again—is obviously the source of understanding about human *consciousness* and *knowl- edge* and human *freedom, authenticity* and unauthenticity—and their compan- ion theological notions, *sinlessness* and sinfulness—and human self- determination or *self-constitution*, as they apply both to Jesus and to us. This same analysis also highlights consciousness as open to being, that is, open to knowing all there is to be known (and to loving all that is lovable). Here is the ground for the notion of human *divinization*.

It remains only to recall that the notions, *kerygmatic* and *systematic* state- ment, and their correlates, *functional* and *ontological* mentality, themselves defined in relation to one another (see Chapter Four, nn. 2 and 9), are likewise grounded in further analysis of dynamic human consciousness as it operates on the second level in various *differentiations of consciousness*.

This brief sketch of the systematic underpinnings of the present christology demonstrates its systematic nature. All the key notions in this systematic account are grounded in an analysis of human consciousness and defined in relation to one another within one overall system. The account is systematic.

As noted in Chapter Seven, n. 10, the present account is not a mere re- presentation of classical medieval philosophy or christology. Lonergan has taken a significant step beyond Aquinas by grounding theology in method. Lonergan's beginning point is not an inherited metaphysical system posited as a set of first principles. His beginning point is rather the realm of inte- riority. It and nothing else grounds his method and categories, which are applied here. Cf. *Method*, esp. 288–89. Note this revealing contrast. Whereas Aquinas begins his *Summa Theologica* with treatment of God, the present systematic account has its beginning in an analysis of human consciousness and from there develops the notions of created and uncreated, natures and persons, and all the others.

Chapter Nine: *Jesus' Human Mind and Heart*

1. Mk. 8:31–33; 9:30–32; 10:32–34.

2. Mk. 14:17–21.

3. For surprisingly recent reaffirmations of this position, see Galot, *Who is Christ?* 344–75, and W. G. Most, *The Consciousness of Christ* (Front Royal, Virginia: Christendom College Press, 1980).

4. DS 3645.

5. DS 3646.

6. DS 3812.

7. Eph. 1:9–11; Gal. 4:4–5; Rom. 16:25.

8. See Brown, *Jesus God and Man*, for a complete treatment of this ques- tion.

9. Mk. 5:30–33.

10. Mk. 2:26.

11. Mt. 23:35.

12. Mt. 12:39–41.

13. Mk. 13:32.

14. Cf. Daniel A. Helminiak, "Consciousness as a Subject Matter," *Journal for the Theory of Social Behavior* 14(1984):211–30; Lonergan, *Method*, Chapter 1 and *passim;* Karl Rahner, *Spirit in the World* (New York: Seabury Press, 1968), *Hearers of the Word* (New York: Seabury Press, 1968); Tarthang Tulku, "A View of Mind," *The Meeting of the Ways: Explorations in East/West Psychology,* ed. John Welwood (New York: Plenum Press, 1978), 40–44.

15. The apparent parallel between Freud's conscious and unconscious, on the one hand, and reflexive and non-reflexive consciousness, on the other hand, is deceptive and mistaken. First, the terminology differs. What for Freud is *unconscious* would have to be called conscious here. But second, and decisively, the difference in terminology presupposes a difference in understanding. Material in Freud's unconscious is present to the subject in objectified form: feelings, dream images, drives, whether the subject is alert to these or not. Though this objectification is primordial and far from conceptualization or verbalization, it is objectification nonetheless. But non-reflexive consciousness is precisely non-objectified. It is the subject's presence to himself or herself precisely as subject. It is that which finds its primordial objectification in feelings, dream images, drives. Therefore, appeal here to Freud's unconscious is a rhetorical move, a kerygmatic statement. The appeal here is to a metaphor, not to the actual reality in question. In the present context a popular presentation may bypass the technical precision presupposed in this note.

16. Cf. Frederick E. Crowe, "The Mind of Jesus," *Le Christ Hier Aujourd'hui et Demain,* ed. Raymond Leflamme and Michel Gervais (Quebec: Les Presses de l'Universite Laval, 1976), 143–56; Lonergan, *De Constitutione Christi;* Karl Rahner, "Dogmatic Reflections on the Knowledge and Self-Consciousness of Christ," *Theological Investigations,* vol. 5, 193–215.

17. Cf. Aquinas, *S.T.,* q. 3.

18. Here is invoked the theology of John 12:20–32, according to which the moments of Jesus' crucifixion and glorification coincide. On chronological questions within a systematic presentation, see Helminiak, "One in Christ," 439–70.

19. Cf. Robert M. Doran, "Aesthetics and the Opposites," *Thought* 52(1977): 117–33; "Aesthetic Subjectivity and Generalized Empirical Method," *The Thomist* 43(1979):257–78; "Psyche, evil, and grace," *Communio* 6(1979):192–211; "Psychic Conversion," *The Thomist* 41(1977):200–36.

20. DS 1347.

Endnotes

21. Cf. Lonergan, *Grace and Freedom*; Karl Rahner, "Grace and Freedom," *Sacramentum Mundi: An Encyclopedia of Theology*, vol. 2 (New York: Herder and Herder, 1968), 424–27.

22. Cf. Richard P. McBrien, "The Sexuality of Jesus," *Catholicism* (Oak Grove, Minneapolis: Winston Press, 1980), 532–38; Sylvia Chávez-García and Daniel A. Helminiak, "Sexuality and Spirituality: Friends not Foes," *Journal of Pastoral Care* 32(1985):151–63.

23. Mk. 3:5.

24. Mt. 21:12–13; Mk. 11:15–18; Lk. 10:19, 45–46; Jn. 2:13–17.

25. Mt. 15:17; 16:9, 11; Mk. 8:17, 21.

26. Mt. 21:18–19; Mk. 11:12–14, 20.

27. Mt. 26:51–52; Mk. 14:47; Lk. 22:51; Jn. 18:10–11.

28. Lk. 3:41–52.

29. Cp. Knox, *Humanity and Divinity*, 47–49.

30. On the constitutive function of meaning and self-constitution, see Lonergan, *Method*, 76–81.

31. Cf. Lonergan, *Insight*, 218–42.

32. Chögyam Trungpa, *Cutting Through Spiritual Materialism* (Berkeley: Shambhala, 1973), 210; cf. also 102, 109, 182, 243; *The Myth of Freedom: And the Way of Meditation* (Berkeley: Shambhala, 1976), 78.

33. Jn. 8:3–8.

34. Mk. 12:14–17.

35. Mk. 3:1–5.

36. Mk. 2:15–17; Lk. 15.

37. Mk. 11:15–17.

38. Mk. 11:27–33.

39. Mk. 15:5.

40. Rom. 5:19; Phil. 2:8; Heb. 5:8.

41. Cf. Johannes B. Bauer, ed., *Encyclopedia of Biblical Theology: The Complete Sacramentum Verbi* (New York: Crossroad, 1981): "The demand that the law shall be obeyed is freed from the formalism with which contemporary judaism has surrounded it. Jesus requires obedience as an attitude of mind and conscience" (617). "Obedience to revealed truth is not compulsory, but is an expression of the freedom of the children of God, devotion to God, the life of one who has been subject to God's dominion and permeated with divine life" (620). Xavier Leon-Dufour, ed., *Dictionary of Biblical Theology* (London: Geoffrey Chapman, 1967), 352: "The life of Jesus Christ was . . . obedience; that is to say, adherence to God through a series of intermediaries: persons, events, institutions, writings of His people, human authorities." Gerhard

Kittel, ed., *Theological Dictionary of the New Testament*, vol. 1 (Grand Rapids, Michigan/London: Wm. B. Eerdmans Pub. Co., 1964), 224, notes that the basic meaning of the Greek term retains the Hebrew sense of listening—receiving a divine Word and translating it into action.

The biblical notion of obedience as "listening to" parallels my metaphor of Jesus as "in touch with" himself and so with his whole situation. A systematic statement would speak in terms of non-reflexive and reflexive consciousness and authenticity. See Chapter Eight, n. 16. Jesus' ever appropriate response would be "obedience"—or "fidelity." Of course, a theology of "will of God" is presumed here. God's will is not understood voluntaristically as some external absolute imposing itself on a person but is understood as that to which one is called by responsible response in good conscience to every situation in which one finds oneself. My point here is that such an understanding is in accord with the biblical notion of obedience, critically interpreted. The present understanding is integral to a salvation-history and incarnational approach.

42. Cf. Frederick E. Crowe, "Son and Spirit: Tension in the Divine Missions," *Science et Esprit* 35(1983):153–69; Tad Dunne, "Trinity and History," *Theological Studies* 45(1984):139–52.

43. E.g., Galot, *Who is Christ?* 384–86; Lonergan, *De Verbo Incarnato*, 418–21; *Sacrae Theologiae Summa* ("The Spanish Summa"), 4th ed., vol. 3 (Matriti: La Editorial Catolica, 1962), 144–57

44. Other standard arguments for Jesus' impeccability—the possession of special preternatural gifts necessary for the fulfillment of his mission and the possession of the beatific vision—are disqualified by a critical reading of the New Testament and by contemporary understanding of the humanity of Jesus Christ.

45. DS 2003; Lonergan, *Grace and Freedom*, 94.

46. Cf. O'Grady, *Interpreting Jesus*, 194–95.

47. In contrast to the standard position (see n. 43), I affirm the parity of dying and sinning as predicated of God. Death is to God's being as sin is to God's willing. Dying is contradictory to God's being just as sinning is contradictory to God's willing. But since there are no real distinctions in God—except those that constitute the three divine *hypostases*—to be contradictory to God's being is to be contradictory to God's willing, and vice versa. The two are equally impossible to God as God. The one is the other. Then, if through incarnation a divine *hypostasis* can die, through incarnation a divine *hypostasis* can also sin. If the seemingly impossible is known to be possible in the one case—known to be possible because it actually happened—the seemingly impossible is *theoretically* also possible in the other case, though in this case no actual occurrence confirms that possibility.

It merely obscures the question to argue that sinning is intrinsically more opposed to God than is dying, that by definition sinning is opposition to God, whereas anguishing death is but the effect of sin. Both are inappropriate to a divine one become human and both are equally metaphysically impossible to God as such. On the one hand, *anguishing* death is opposed to human nature as it could and should be. Cf. Rahner, *Theology of Death*. Sinning is also opposed to human nature—as well as to God. Cf. the argument about the nature of sin in my text. Evidently, then, Eternal-Son in no way assumed an idealized—a supposed "perfect"—humanity when he became human. According to all human reckoning, the human condition that Eternal-Son in fact assumed was not appropriate for a divine one. Both dying and sinning are scandalous in the case of incarnate God. On the other hand, metaphysically both dying and sinning are equally contradictory to the divine nature and to God and so equally seemingly impossible predicates of a divine *hypostasis*. It is senseless to suppose any "more" or "less" in this either-or case.

Thus, the difficulty in this question appears to be one more of piety than of theology. Bad enough that God die on a cross; it is too scandalous that in Christ God might also have been able to sin. Quoting Suarez, "The Spanish Summa" admits as much: *"quamvis Verbum dicatur pati aut mori, dicere Deum peccare, 'pias omnium theologorum aures offendit'"* (151). The scandal of the incarnation is scandalous indeed. Furthermore, it appears that insistence on the impeccability of Jesus is part and parcel of a christology that over-emphasizes Jesus' divinity to the detriment of his humanity. Contemporary christology adjusts the balance.

Chapter Ten: *Jesus and Human Salvation*

1. With his usual mastery, O'Collins, *Interpreting Jesus,* presents a very useful summary of the classical theories of redemption: Aulen's emphasis on Christ as victor over sin and death, Anselm's theory of satisfaction, and Abelard's emphasis on the power of love to conquer all. In general, my position squares with O'Collins'. I especially affirm his insistence that the three theories complement one another but that the third "admits a certain priority" (160) over the others and, indeed, can subsume them.

I differ from O'Collins and others in that I disallow that suffering and death themselves are in any way saving. They may be the occasion and expression of saving acts, but they themselves are not what saves. So I reject the notion of vicarious sacrifice. Even O'Collins strongly opposes the penal substitutionary theory; but he considers this theory only in its strictest form, namely, as affirming that God treated Jesus himself "as a sinner" (150; cf. 153, 155), so burdened was he with the guilt of others. Otherwise, O'Collins allows some sense—not clearly explained—in which Christ and Christians can offer themselves in vicarious sacrifice (cf. 156, 157). Moreover, he seems to allow that suffering itself is somehow saving; "makes amends . . . through some purifying suffering" (149); "Christ came as a victim for sin and an offering for sinners" (155); "Christ's sacrifice . . . our sacrifices" (156); "suffering and death for others which Jesus *freely accepted*" (153). Certainly such statements are part of the Christian tradition, and they are deeply rooted in it. But were they intended to mean what we understand hearing them today? Does the New Testament really ever intend that Jesus' life was sacrificed for the sake of human salvation? Is God ever really presented as demanding Jesus' death? Is the point of the New Testament not rather that human salvation was achieved only at the cost of Jesus' life? The shift in emphasis is subtle but important.

O'Collins suggests that because Jesus is a representative—a voluntary victim from his side and a freely chosen Savior from our side—and not merely a substitute forced into service, the nature of the vicarious suffering in this case changes and so can be allowed as saving in itself (cf. 156). The International Theological Commission, *Questions on Christology,* IV, 2.5, 3.3, makes this same point. As I see it, the valid intent here is this. Jesus' murderous end was not the result of a dismal fate forced on him but was rather the result of his own free acceptance of the inevitable consequences in a sinful world of his loving fidelity—fidelity to himself, to the greatest good of all others, and so to his heavenly Father. The examples of Eleazar (1 Mac. 6:18–31) is telling here. So what was saving was not the suffering and death themselves but the loving fidelity that in a sinful world led to and expressed itself consummately in that suffering and death. The suffering and death may then be said to be saving, but only because of inextricable association with fidelity and love. The predication is analogous.

The idea of vicarious suffering inevitably carries with it either a notion of suffering in another's place (substitution theory, which almost all reject) or the notion of paying a price of suffering due for sins (which offends against divine goodness) or the notion that in some way suffering itself is useful, especially when freely chosen, and can be applied to another's benefit (which is pathological). In O'Collins' treatment of "expiation" I detect the entry-point of these unacceptable ideas about vicarious suffering when, with no account, the notion of "reparation" appears and begins to dominate (146–48). I would insist that it is Christ's love and fidelity, expressed through his suffering and death, that is saving and not the suffering and death themselves. Perhaps this is the intent of O'Collins' distinction between representation and substitution.

I differ with O'Collins in another important way. Over and above consideration of the saving effect of Christ's crucifixion—that is, of his fidelity unto death—for a complete account of the redemption I insist also on the implications of Christ's resurrection/divinization for the whole human race. This comprehensive and systematic account goes beyond the classical theories.

2. Cf. Pelikan, *Christian Tradition,* vol. 3, 108–18.

3. Tertullian, *De Pudicitia,* 22.4, as cited in Pelikan, *Christian Tradition,* vol. 1, 148.

4. DS 1529; cf. also DS, 1513, 1522, 1523, 1528, 3891. Tertullian introduced the term "satisfaction." Cf. Pelikan, *Christian Tradition,* vol. 1, 147–48.

5. See also Eph. 1:7; Col. 1:14; Heb. 9:15.

6. Note how *The Jerusalem Bible* (London: Darton, Longman, and Todd, 1966), mistranslates this verse, imposing a theory of atonement on it: "Christ Jesus who was appointed by God to sacrifice his life so as to win reconciliation through faith."

7. Cf. Mk. 14:24.

8. See Chapter Five.

9. For a more optimistic opinion, cf. O'Collins, *Interpreting Jesus*, 162–65.

10. See also Rom. 8:35, 37; Gal. 1:4, 2:20.

11. Cf. Rahner, *Foundations*, 248: "But he faced death resolutely and accepted it at least as the inevitable consequence of fidelity to his mission. . . ." Vawter, *This Man Jesus*, 131: "As in the hymn of Philippians 2, the Savior is represented [in 1 Pet. 3:18–21] as having suffered death in consequence of a life of service for others."

12. Cf. Rahner, *Theology of Death*, 61–62.

13. Cf. Karl Rahner, "Original Sin, d) Synthesis of the doctrine of original sin," *Sacramentum Mundi: An Encyclopedia of Theology*, vol. 4 (New York: Herder and Herder, 1969), 331.

14. These two senses accurately translate the Greek preposition *hyper*, for, our sins in 1 Cor. 15:3.

15. Cf. Rom. 5:8; 2 Tim. 1:9; Tit. 3:3–5.

16. Cf. 1 Pet. 2:20–21.

17. Cf. Mk. 9:29, 10:28; Mt. 9:15, 19:21; Lk. 9:57–62.

18. Cf. Richard Kugelman, "The First Letter to the Corinthians," *Jerome Biblical Commentary*, ed. Raymond E. Brown, Joseph A. Fitzmyer, Roland E. Murphy (Englewood Cliffs, New Jersey: Prentice Hall, Inc., 1968), 51:61.

19. Cf. 2 Cor. 6:4–10.

20. Cf. Joseph A. Grassi, "The Letter to the Colossians," *Jerome Biblical Commentary*, 55:24.

21. Cf. Mk. 8:34; Mt. 10:38; Jn. 12:25.

22. Cf. Mt. 13:44–46.

23. Mt. 5:8.

24. Cf. Mt. 11:30.

25. 2 Mac. 6:18–31.

26. See O'Collins, *What About Jesus?* (2nd ed.), 28–33, for a compatible and more extensive treatment of Jesus' "implicit soteriology." Also Rahner, *Foundations*, 254–55. But note my reservation about the extent of knowledge O'Collins attributes to Jesus. See Chapter Eight, n. 21. I also reject the notion of a "shift of consciousness" in Jesus. Cf. O'Collins, *Interpreting Jesus*, 187; Schillebeeckx, *Jesus*, 306. The present state of the Gospels gives little basis for

determining any chronology in the events in the ministry of Jesus. All the less is there evidence to propose a shift in Jesus' understanding, namely, that redemption would not be achieved by his preaching the Reign of God but would require his own death. Cf. Vawter, *This Man Jesus*, 130. Such a thesis appears to read a *post factum* understanding into the historical reality.

27. See Chapter Nine, n. 42.

28. The distinction between the natural and the supernatural results from the intelligent grasp of the difference between what is proportionate and what is disproportionate to human nature within the one, *de facto* human situation in Christ. Emergence of this distinction evidences the achievement of a higher viewpoint. Cf. Lonergan, *Grace and Freedom*, 13–19; *Insight*, 13–19. The distinction is not a separation; it does not suggest the possibility that some live only a natural life (pagans) and others (Christians) live a graced life. Likewise, the distinction does not suggest the image of a layered universe, grace being a second story built atop a separable ground floor. Finally, the essence of the distinction lies in the difference between what is proportionate and disproportionate to human nature as such. Appeal to gratuity alone is insufficient to secure the distinction, for nature as created gift and super-nature as gifted participation in the uncreated are both, in their own ways, gratuitous. The disproportionateness of the latter gratuity is precisely what distinguishes it from the former. The original meaning of the distinction is valid and important, yet it is widely misunderstood and, as misunderstood, rightly rejected: e.g., Langdon Gilkey, *Catholicism Confronts Modernity: A Protestant View* (New York: Seabury Press, 1975), 46–48; Juan Luis Segundo, *Grace and the Human Condition* (Maryknoll, N.Y.: Orbis Books, 1973), 62–69. For a brief historical sketch and some discussion about this supposed "burnt-out-model," cf. Gustavo Gutierrez, *A Theology of Liberation: History, Politics and Salvation*, trans. Caridad Inda and John Eagleson (Maryknoll, N.Y.: Orbis Press, 1973), 69–72, 76 n. 44.

29. On Jesus' freedom, see Chapter Nine.

30. Karl Rahner's position is a prime example here. Repeatedly and consistently Rahner speaks of necessity in the order of salvation when only contingency obtains. For example, "The Order of Creation and the Order of Redemption," *The Christian Commitment* as cited in *A Rahner Reader*, ed. Gerald A. McCool (New York: Seabury Press, 1975), 193: ". . . the incarnation of the Word of God *necessarily* took place because of sin and for our salvation" (emphasis added). Or again, *The Trinity*, trans. Joseph Donceel (New York: Herder and Herder, 1970), 28–29: ". . . is it true that *every* divine person might become man? We answer that it is not demonstrated and that it is false." Cf. also *Foundations*, 215, 223. Or again, "Nature and Grace," *Theological Investigations*, vol IV, trans. Kevin Smyth (Baltimore: Helicon Press, 1966), 176–77, argues at length against the understanding that "the connection between the Incarnation and grace is . . . merely *de facto*." Cf. also *Foundations*, 199, 200, 202, 207.

In that last case Rahner's oversight of contingency is easily demonstrated. One may obscure the issue of contingent divine acts by appeal to free acts in God and ask whether there is one or more of them. Cf. Chapter Eight, n. 40. But *human* contingency enters into the issue of the connection between the incarnation and grace. If "grace" is taken to mean the saving effect of redemption for us, then grace is certainly dependent on the free, human, acts of Jesus. Here not divine freedom but human freedom is in question. Then, grace depends on a series of contingent acts, Jesus' human acts. Then, to deny the merely *de facto* connection between the incarnation and grace is to deny this contingency and so to deny Jesus' human freedom and its part in the redemption.

A general oversight of contingency pervades Rahner's theology. The implications are serious and far-reaching, especially since Rahner situates his christology in an evolutionary worldview and a theological anthropology. There the incarnation is conceived as the fullest possible perfection of the human, and the mystery of the incarnation is confounded with the mystery of grace. But human openness to share in divine life is one thing; the incarnation of the Word as human is another. If the two were the same thing, in Jesus Christ we would necessarily only have a creature who somehow attained to participation in divine life. But a creature remains ever a creature, so it could not be argued in this case that Jesus Christ is truly God. In contrast, the christology in this book distinguishes two moments: the incarnation and the divinization/resurrection. For all practical purposes, Rahner's account of the incarnation as the high-point of historical evolution and the culmination of God's self-expression in the world is a parallel to an account of divinization. But divinization does not necessarily imply true divinity in the divinized one but rather only a sharing of certain divine qualities.

Another way of making this same point is to insist that the contingency of the incarnation is not the same as the contingency of human divinization based on the human *potentia obedientialis*. If divinization is understood as I present it, there is no reason why God could not have allowed it without the incarnation. In fact, this exact possibility is what traditional theology recognized in the unfallen state of humanity—a freely given gift of eventual participation in divine life. (Whether or not, further, such a thing would be possible without the gift of the Holy Spirit is another question, and it, like the present question, detours theology into more speculation.) Divinization is a *possibility* inherent in human nature as originally created by God. This is the proper implication of the human, created *potentia obedientialis*. But this *potentia* does not imply or in any way lead to incarnation. Granted, the same *potentia obedientialis* does say something about why a divine person could assume a human nature; intellectual nature—of different kinds, surely, but common to the Three in God and to humans—provides a link not given, for example, in the case of brute animals. See the discussion of "person" in Chapter Seven. But the incarnation entails a contingency not in any way implied by creation. The intelligibility intrinsic to the incarnation—that a divine one enter human history—is utterly disproportionate to anything created. Thus, the incarnation must be an utterly gratuitous occurrence. Its only reason is the love and wisdom of God. Though it is an act *de congruo*, it is in no way *de condigno*. Vis-à-vis creation, the incarnation is a *de facto* occurrence, not a *de jure* occurrence. It is a completely contingent event. It did not have to happen. By associating the incarnation with the *visio beatifica* and *potentia obedientialis* of the human, Rahner's dynamic anthropology obscures the contingency of the incarnation in contrast to the contingency of grace.

As a result, Rahner's christology implies that it is natural for humans to be divine, that there is in humans a natural openness to divinity such that when divinization occurs—as in Jesus Christ—a human being is literally God. This is tantamount to removing the distinction between humanity and divinity. The incarnation becomes a monophysite union, not a hypostatic one. Cf. Chapter Three, n. 11. Such a suggestion, resonating with echoes of German Idealism, is evident in Rahner's "Current Problems in Christology," 184: "Only someone who forgets that the essence of man . . . is to be unbounded . . . can suppose that it is impossible for there to be a man, who, *precisely by being man in the fullest sense* (which we never attain), is God's Existence into the world" (emphasis added). The fact that Rahner insists the incarnation is a unique occurrence—a perfection "which we never attain"—does not counterbalance the logical implications of his substantive argument. The repeated insistence on orthodox teaching is at variance with the systematic position. The systematic position is seriously flawed because it attempts to deal with a historical religion while obscuring the contingencies of history.

Likewise, O'Collins, *Interpreting Jesus*, 96–97, confuses the Jewish indication of divine providence (e.g. "The Son of Man *must* suffer many things" [Mk. 8:32]; "Was it not *necessary* that the Christ should suffer . . ." [Lk. 24:26]) with metaphysical necessity and so risks obscuring the contingencies in the redemption.

31. See Chapter Three.

32. See Chapter Eight, n. 7 and the related text, and for the presupposed distinction between who and what one is, see Chapter Seven.

33. Cf. Daniel A. Helminiak, "Yes, There is a Perfect Love," *Religion Teacher's Journal*, 16:7 (January, 1983): 4–6.

34. Cf. Lonergan, *Method*, 201–3, 347–50.

35. Cf. Wis. 13:1–9; Rom. 1:19–20.

36. E. g., see the discussion of Mackey's position in Chapter Six.

37. Cf. Lucien Richard, *What Are They Saying About Christ and World Religions?* (New York: Paulist Press, 1981).

38. The term "primitive religion" is not intended here in the technical sense developed by Robert Bellah, "Religious Evolution," *American Sociological Review* 39 (1964): 348–74.

39. Cf. Fustel De Coulanges, *The Ancient City: A Study on the Religion, Laws, and Institutions of Greece and Rome* (Garden City, New York: Doubleday and Co., Inc.); Mircea Eliade, *The Sacred and the Profane: The Nature of Religion* (New York: Harcourt, Brace & World, Inc., 1957).

40. I am grateful to Carol Solomon-Kiefer for this piece of information.

41. Cf. Helminiak, "Where Do We Stand as Christians?" "Four Viewpoints on the Human: A Conceptual Schema for Interdisciplinary Studies" *The Heythrop Journal* (in press).

42. Trungpa, *Cutting Through*, 167–84.

43. On human solidarity, see Helminiak, "One in Christ," and Chapter Eight pp. 241–45.

44. See also Rom. 5:15–19; 8:23; 2 Cor. 5:14–15, 19; 1 Tim. 4:10; Jn. 1:9; Acts 10:34–35.

45. *De Veritate*, q. 14, a. 11 ad 1, as noted in Rondet, *Grace of Christ*, 244.

46. *Gaudium et Spes*, art 22. *Vatican Council II: The Conciliar and Post Conciliar Documents*, ed. Austin Flannery (Northport, New York: Costello Publishing Co., 1975), 924. See also *Lumen Gentium*, art. 14, 15, 16 in *Ibid.*, 365–68.

47. Cf. Lonergan, *Method*, 112–13. On "degrees of being," cf. Lonergan, *De Constitutione Christi*, 98, 102–4, 127; Helminiak, "One in Christ," 345–46, 451–57.

48. Dt. 7:7.

49. 1 Cor. 1:26–31.

50. Richard P. McBrien, *Church: The Continuing Quest* (New York: Newman Press, 1970), 73.

Bibliography

Bach, Richard. *Illusions: The Adventures of a Reluctant Messiah.* New York: Dell Publishing Co., 1977; Laurel, 1981.

Barbour, Ian G. *Myths, Models and Paradigms.* New York: Harper & Row, Publishers, 1974.

Barden, Garrett. "II. The Symbolic Mentality." *Philosophical Studies* (Maynooth, 15 (1966), 28–57.

Bauer, Johannes B., ed. *Eycyclopedia of Biblical Theology: The Complete Sacramentum Verbi.* New York: Crossroad, 1981.

Baum, Gregory, ed. *The Future of Belief Debate.* New York: Herder and Herder, 1967.

Bellah, Robert. "Religious Evolution." *American Sociological Review,* 39 (1964), 348–74.

Benedict, Ruth. *Patterns in Culture.* Boston: Houghton Mifflin Co., 1934.

Berger, Peter L. and Luckmann, Thomas. *The Social Construction of Reality: A Treatise in the Sociology of Knowledge.* New York: Double-day & Co., 1967.

Boff, Leonardo. *Jesus Christ Liberator: A Critical Christology for Our Time.* Trans. by Patrick Hughes. Maryknoll, New York: Orbis Books, 1978.

317

Brown, Raymond E. *The Community of the Beloved Disciple*. New York: Paulist Press, 1979.

___. *The Critical Meaning of the Bible*. New York: Paulist Press, 1981.

___. *Jesus God and Man: Modern Biblical Reflections*. Milwaukee: The Bruce Publishing Co., 1967.

___. "The resurrection and Biblical Criticism." *Commonweal*, Nov. 24, 1971.

___. " 'Who do men say that I am?' Modern Scholarship on Gospel Christology." *Perspectives in Religious Studies*, 2 (1975), 107–24.

Butterfield, Herbert. "Historiography." *Dictionary of the History of Ideas; Studies of Selected Pivotal Ideas*, 4 Vols. Ed. by Phillip P. Wiener. New York: Charles Scribner's Sons, 1973, 2:464–98.

Chávez-García, Sylvia and Helminiak, Daniel A. "Sexuality and Spirituality: Friends Not Foes." *Journal of Pastoral Care*, 32 (1985), 151–63.

Crossan, John Dominic. *The Dark Interval: Towards a Theology of Story*. Niles, Illinois: Argus Communications, 1975.

Crowe, Frederick E. *The Lonergan Enterprise*. Cambridge, Massachusetts: Cowley Publications, 1980.

___. "The Mind of Christ." In *Le Christ Hier Aujourd'hui et Demain*. Ed. by Raymond Leflamme and Michel Gervais. Quebec: Les Presses de l'Universite Laval, 1976. Pp. 143–56.

___. "Son and Spirit: Tension in the Divine Missions." *Science et Esprit*, 35 (1983), 153–69.

Cullmann, Oscar. *Christ and Time: The Primitive Christian Conception of Time and History*. Trans. by Floyd V. Filson. London: SCM Press, Ltd., 1951.

___. *The Christology of the New Testament*. London: SCM Press, Ltd., 1959.

Davies, Paul. *God and the New Physics*. New York: Simon and Schuster, 1983.

De Coulanges, Fustel. *The Ancient City: A Study of the Religion, Laws, and Institutions of Greece and Rome*. Garden City, New York: Doubleday & Co., Inc.

Denzinger, Henricus and Schönmetzer, Adolfus, eds. *Enchiridion*

Symbolorum: Definitionum et Declarationum de Rebus Fidei et Morum. Freiburg im Breisgau: Herder, 1965.

Dewart, Leslie. *The Future of Belief: Theism in a World Come of Age.* New York: Herder and Herder, 1966.

Dodd, C.D. *The Founder of Christianity.* New York: Macmillan Publishing Co., 1970.

Doran, Robert M. "Aesthetic Subjectivity and Generalized Empirical Method." *The Thomist,* 43 (1979), 257–78.

———. "Aesthetics and the Opposites." *Thought,* 52 (1977), 117–33.

———. "Psyche, evil, and grace." *Communio,* 6 (1979), 192–211.

———. "Psychic Conversion." *The Thomist,* 41 (1977), 200–36.

———. *Psychic Conversion and Theological Foundations: Toward a Reorientation of the Human Sciences.* Chico, California: Scholars Press, 1981.

———. *Subject and Psyche: Ricoeur, Jung, and the Search for Foundations.* Washington, D.C.: University Press of America, 1977.

Dulles, Avery. *Models of the Church.* Garden City, New York: Doubleday & Co., 1974.

———. *Models of Revelation.* Garden City, New York: Doubleday & Co., 1983.

Dunn, James D.G. *Christology in the Making: A New Testament Inquiry Into the Origins of the Doctrine of the Incarnation.* Philadelphia: The Westminster Press, 1980.

———. *Unity and Diversity in the New Testament: An Inquiry Into the Character of Earliest Christianity.* Philadelphia: The Westminster Press, 1977.

Dunne, Tad. "Trinity and History." *Theological Studies,* 45 (1984), 139–52.

Eliade, Mircea. *The Sacred and the Profane: The Nature of Religion.* New York: Harcourt, Brace & World, Inc., 1957.

Fiorenza, Francis Schussler. "Christology After Vatican II." *The Ecumenist,* 18,6 (1980), 81-89.

Fitzmyer, Joseph A. *A Christological Catechism: New Testament Answers.* New York: Paulist Press, 1981.

Flannery, Austin, ed. *Vatican Council II: The Conciliar and Post Conciliar Documents.* Northport, New York: Costello Publishing Co., 1975.

Fuller, Reginald H. *The Formation of the Resurrection Narratives.* New York: The Macmillan Co., 1971.

——. *The Foundations of New Testament Christology.* New York: Charles Scribner's Sons, 1965.

Fuller, Reginald H. and Perkins, Pheme. *Who is This Christ? Gospel Christology and Contemporary Faith.* Philadelphia: Fortress Press, 1983.

Galloway, John T. *The Gospel According to Superman.* Philadelphia: A.J. Holman Co., 1973.

Galot, Jean. *Who is Christ? A Theology of the Incarnation.* Chicago: Franciscan Herald Press, 1981.

Gelpi, Donald L. *Experiencing God: A Theology of Human Experience.* New York: Paulist Press, 1978.

Gilkey, Langdon. *Catholicism Confronts Modernity: A Protestant View.* New York: The Seabury Press, 1975.

Gooch, George Peabody. *History and Historians in the Nineteenth Century.* New York: Longmans, Green and Co., 1913.

Goulder, M.D. Review of James Mackey's *Jesus the Man and the Myth. The Journal of Theological Studies,* 31 (1980), 595–98.

Grass, Hans. *Christliche Glaubenslehre.* Stuttgart: Kohlhammer, 1975.

Grassi, Joseph A. "The Letter to the Colossians." *Jerome Biblical Commentary.* Ed. by Raymond E. Brown, Joseph A. Fitzmyer, and Roland E. Murphy. Englewood Cliffs, New Jersey: Prentice Hall, Inc., 1968. Art. 55.

Grant, Robert M. "Creation." In *Miracle and Natural Law in Graeco-Roman and Early Christian Thought.* Amsterdam: North-Holland Publishing Co., 1952. Pp. 135–52.

Gregg, Robert C. and Groh, Dennis E. *Early Arianism—A View of Salvation.* Philadelphia: Fortress Press, 1981.

Grillmeier, Aloys. *Christ in Christian Tradition: From the Apostolic Age to Chalcedon (451).* Trans. by John Bowden. Atlanta: John Knox Press, 1975.

Gutierrez, Gustavo. *A Theology of Liberation: History, Politics and Salvation.* Trans. by Caridad Inda and John Eagleson. Maryknoll, New York: Orbis Press, 1973.

Bibliography

Harvey, Van A. *The Historian and the Believer: The Morality of Historical Knowledge and Christian Belief.* New York: Macmillan Co., 1966.

Hays, John H. and Holladay, Carl R. *Biblical Exegesis: A Beginner's Handbook.* Atlanta: John Knox Press, 1982.

Heidbreder, Edna. *Seven Psychologies.* Englewood Cliffs, New Jersey: Prentice-Hall, Inc., 1933.

Hellwig, Monika K. *Jesus, The Compassion of God.* Wilmington, Delaware: Michael Glazier, Inc., 1983.

Helminiak, Daniel A. "Consciousness as a Subject Matter." *Journal for the Theory of Social Behavior,* 14 (1984), 211–30.

____. "Four Viewpoints on the Human: A Conceptual Schema for Interdisciplinary Studies." *The Heythrop Journal,* in press.

____. "God Shares Secrets." *Religion Teacher's Journal,* 16:5 (October, 1982), 32–34.

____. "How to Talk About God." *Religion Teacher's Journal,* 15:5 (September, 1981), 24–26.

____. "Neurology, Psychology, and Extraordinary Religious Experiences." *Journal of Religion and Health,* 23 (1984), 33–46.

____. "One in Christ: An Exercise in Systematic Theology." Ph.D. Diss., Boston College and Andover Newton Theological School, 1979.

____. "Where Do We Stand as Christians? The Challenge of Western Science and Oriental Religions." *Spiritual Life,* 28 (1982), 195–209/

____. "Yes, There is a Perfect Love." *Religion Teacher's Journal,* 16:7 (January, 1983), 4–6.

Hengel, Martin. *The Son of God: The Origin of Christology and the History of Jewish-Hellenistic Religion.* Philadelphia: Fortress Press, 1976.

Hick, John, ed. *The Myth of God Incarnate.* Philadelphia: The Westminster Press, 1977.

____. "Whatever Path Men Choose is Mine." In *Christianity and Other Religions: Selected Readings.* Ed. by John Hick and Brian Hebblethwaite. Philadelphia: Fortress Press, 1980. Orig. in *The Modern Churchman,* (1974).

Howard, George. "Phil. 2:6–11 and the Human Christ." *Catholic Biblical Quarterly,* 40 (1978), 368–387.

Hughes, Philip. *The Church in Crisis: A History of the Twenty Great Councils*. London: Burns and Oates, 1961.

Iggers, Georg G. *The German Conception of History*. Middletown, Connecticut: Wesleyan University Press, 1968.

——. "Historicism." *Dictionary of the History of Ideas: Studies of Selected Pivotal Ideas*, 4 Vols. Ed. by Phillip P. Wiener. New York: Charles Scribner's Sons, 1973, 2:456–64.

The International Theological Commission. *Select Questions on Christology*. Washington: United States Catholic Conference, 1980.

Jeremias, Joachim. *The Problem of the Historical Jesus*. Trans. by Norman Perrin. Philadelphia: Fortress Press, 1964.

Jungmann, Josef A. "Christological Disputes and Their Influence on the Liturgy." In *The Early Liturgy: To the Time of Gregory the Great*. Trans. by Francis A. Brunner. Notre Dame, Indiana: University of Notre Dame Press, 1959. Pp. 188–198.

——. *Pastoral Liturgy*. New York: Herder and Herder, 1962.

Kasper, Walter. *Jesus the Christ*. New York: Paulist Press, 1977.

Kereszty, Roch. "The Pre-existence and Oneness of Christ." *American Ecclesiastical Review*, 167 (1973), 630–42.

Kelly, J.N.D. *Early Christian Doctrines*. New York: Harper and Row, 1960.

Kerr, Fergus. Review of James Mackey's *Jesus the Man and the Myth*. *New Blackfriars*, 60 (1979), 283–84.

Kittel, Gerhard, ed. *Theological Dictionary of the New Testament*. Grand Rapids, Michigan/London: Wm. B. Eerdmans Pub. Co., 1964.

Knitter, Paul F. Review of James Mackey's *Jesus the Man and the Myth*. *Horizons*, 7 (1980), 349–50.

Knox, John. *The Humanity and Divinity of Christ: A Study of Pattern in Christology*. Cambridge: Cambridge University Press, 1967.

Krentz, Edgar. *The Historical-Critical Method*. Philadelphia: Fortress Press, 1975.

Kugelman, Richard. "The First Letter to the Corinthians." *Jerome Biblical Commentary*. Ed. by Raymond E. Brown, Joseph A. Fitzmyer, and Roland E. Murphy. Englewood Cliffs, New Jersey: Prentice Hall, Inc., 1968. Art. 51.

Bibliography

Küng, Hans. *On Being a Christian*. Trans. by Edward Quinn. New York: Pocket Books, 1978.

——. *The Church*. New York: Sheed and Ward, 1967.

Kuhn, Thomas S. *The Structure of Scientific Revolutions*, 2nd ed. Chicago: The University of Chicago Press, 1970.

Lane, Dermot A. Review of James Mackey's *Jesus the Man and the Myth*. *Irish Theological Quarterly*, 46 (1979), 202–09.

Leon-Dufour, Xavier, ed. *Dictionary of Biblical Theology*. London: Geoffrey Chapman, 1967.

Lonergan, Bernard J.F. "Christ as Subject: A Reply." In *Collection*. Ed. by Frederick E. Crowe. Montreal: Palm Publishers, 1967. Pp. 164–97.

——. "Christology Today: Methodological Reflections." In *Le Christ Hier, Aujourd'hui et Demain*. Ed. by Raymond Laflamme and Michel Gervais. Quebec: Les Presses de l'Universite de Laval, 1976. Pp. 45–65.

——. "Cognitional Structure." In *Collection*. Ed. by Frederick E. Crowe. Montreal: Palm Publishers, 1967. Pp. 221–39.

——. *De Constitutione Christi Ontologica et Psychologica*. Rome: Gregorian University Press, 1958.

——. "The Dehellenization of Dogma." In *Second Collection*. Ed. by William F.J. Ryan and Bernard J. Tyrrell. Philadelphia: The Westminster Press, 1974. Pp. 11–32.

——. *De Deo Trino: II. Pars Systematica*. Rome: Gregorian University Press, 1964.

——. "Dimensions of Meaning." In *Collection*. Ed. by Frederick E. Crowe. Montreal: Palm Publishers, 1967. Pp. 252–267.

——. "The Example of Gibson Winter." In *Second Collection*. Ed. by William F.J. Ryan and Bernard J. Tyrrell. Philadelphia: The Westminster Press, 1974. Pp. 189–92.

——. *Grace and Freedom: Operative Grace in the Thought of St. Thomas Aquinas*. Ed. by J. Patout Burns. New York: Herder and Herder, 1971.

——. *Insight: A Study of Human Understanding*. New York: Philosophical Library, 1957.

____. "An Interview with Fr. Bernard Lonergan, S.J." In *Second Collection*. Ed. by William F.J. Ryan and Bernard J. Tyrrell. Philadelphia: The Westminster Press, 1974. Pp. 209–30.

____. *Method in Theology*. New York: Herder and Herder, 1972.

____. "The Natural Desire to See God." In *Collection*. Ed. by Frederick E. Crowe. Montreal: Palm Publishers, 1967. Pp. 84–95.

____. "The On-going Genesis of Methods." *Studies in Religion/Science Religieuse*, 6 (1976–77), 341–55.

____. "The Origins of Christian Realism." In *Second Collection*. Ed. by William F.J. Ryan and Bernard J. Tyrrell. Philadelphia: The Westminster Press, 1974. Pp. 239–61.

____. *Philosophy of God and Theology*. Philadelphia: The Westminster Press, 1973.

____. "The Transition from a Classicist Worldview to Historical-Mindedness." In *Second Collection*. Ed. by William F.J. Ryan and Bernard J. Tyrrell. Philadelphia: The Westminster Press, 1974. Pp. 1–9.

____. *De Verbo Incarnato*. Rome: Gregorian University Press, 1964.

____. *Verbum: Word and Idea in Aquinas*. Notre Dame: University of Notre Dame Press, 1967.

____. *The Way to Nicea: The Dialectical Development of Trinitarian Theology*. Trans. by Conn O'Donovan. Philadelphia: The Westminster Press, 1976.

Louth, Andrew. *The Origins of the Christian Mystical Tradition: From Plato to Denys*. Oxford: Oxford University Press, 1981.

Mackey, James P. *Jesus the Man and the Myth: Contemporary Christology*. New York: Paulist Press, 1979.

____Macquarrie, John. "The Humanity of Christ." *Theology*, 74 (1971), 243–50.

Martin, Ralph P. Review of James Mackey's *Jesus the Man and the Myth*. *Interpretation*, 34 (1980), 430–32.

Marxsen, Willi. *The Beginnings of Christology*. Philadelphia: Fortress Press, 1979.

____. *The Resurrection of Jesus of Nazareth*. Philadelphia: Fortress Press, 1970.

McBrien, Richard P. *Catholicism*. Minneapolis: Winston Press, 1980.

——. *Church: The Continuing Quest*. New York: Newman Press, 1970.

McCool, Gerald A., ed. *A Rahner Reader*. New York: The Seabury Press, 1975.

McDermott, Brian. "Roman Catholic Christology: Two Recurring Themes." *Theological Studies*, 41 (1980), 339–67.

McIntryre, John. *The Shape of Christology*. Philadelphia: The Westminster Press, 1966.

McKenzie, John L. "Qumran." *Dictionary of the Bible*. Milwaukee: Bruce Publishing Co., 1965.

Mead, George Herbert. *Mind, Self and Society*. Ed. by Charles W. Morris. Chicago: University of Chicago Press, 1934, 1974.

Meier, John P. Review of James Mackey's *Jesus the Man and the Myth*. *Journal of Ecumenical Studies*, 17 (1980), 496–97.

Meyer, Charles R. *Religious Belief in a Scientific Age*. Chicago: Thomas More, 1983.

Moore, Sebastian. *The Crucified Jesus is No Stranger*. New York: The Seabuary Press, 1977.

Most, W.G. *The Consciousness of Christ*. Front Royal, Virginia: Christendom College Press, 1980.

Murray, John Courtney. *The Problem of God: Yesterday and Today*. New Haven and London: Yale University Press, 1964.

Navone, John and Cooper, Thomas. *Tellers of the Word*. New York: Le Jacq Publishing Co., 1981.

Nietzsche, Friedrich. *The Use and Abuse of History*. Trans. by Adrian Collins. New York: The Bobbs-Merrill Company, Inc., 1957.

Nolan, Albert. *Jesus Before Christianity*. Maryknoll, New York: Orbis Books, 1978.

O'Brien, William James. *Stories to the Dark: Explorations in Religious Imagination*. New York: Paulist Press, 1983.

——. *What Are They Saying About Jesus?* New York: Paulist Press, 1977; revised ed., 1983.

O'Grady, John F. *Models of Jesus*. Garden City, New York: Doubleday & Co., Inc., 1981.

Pagels, Elaine. *The Gnostic Gospels*. New York: Random House, Inc., 1979.

Pannenberg, Wolfhart. *Jesus—God and Man*. Trans. by Lewis L. Wilkins and Duane A. Priebe. Philadelphia: The Westminster Press, 1968.

Paul VI. *Inter Insigniores* (On the Question of Admission of Women to the Ministerial Priesthood). *Acta Apostolica Sedis*, 69 (1977), 98–116.

Pelikan, Jaroslav. *The Christian Tradition: A History of the Development of Doctrine*, 3 Vols. Chicago: The University of Chicago Press, 1971, 1974, 1978.

Perkins, Pheme. *Reading the New Testament: An Introduction*. New York: Paulist Press, 1978.

Pittenger, Norman. *Christology Reconsidered*. London: SCM Press, Ltd., 1970.

Rahner, Karl. "Christology Within An Evolutionary View of the World." *Theological Investigations*, Vol. V. Trans. by Karl-H. Kruger. Baltimore: Helicon Press, 1966. Pp. 157–92.

____. "Current Problems in Christology." *Theological Investigations*, Vol. I. Trans. by Cornelius Ernst. Baltimore: Helicon Press, 1961. Pp. 149–200.

____. "Dogmatic Reflections on the Knowledge and Self-Consciousness of Christ." *Theological Investigations*, Vol. V. Trans. by Karl-H. Kruger. Baltimore: Helicon Press, 1966. Pp. 193–215.

____. *Foundations of Christian Faith: An Introduction to the Idea of Christianity*. Trans. by William V. Dych. New York: The Seabury Press, 1978.

____. "Grace and Freedom." *Sacramentum Mundi: An Encyclopedia of Theology*, 5 Vols. New York: Herder and Herder, 1968, 2:424–27.

____. "Nature and Grace." *Theological Investigations*, Vol. IV. Trans. by Kevin Smyth. Baltimore: Helicon Press, 1966. Pp. 165–88.

____. "Original Sin, d) Synthesis of the doctrine of original sin." *Sacramentum Mundi: An Encyclopedia of Theology*, 5 Vols. New York: Herder and Herder, 1968, 4:331.

____. "Reflections on the Unity of the Love of Neighbor and the Love of God." *Theological Investigations*, Vol. VI. Trans. by Karl-H. and Boniface Kruger. Baltimore: Helicon Press, 1969. Pp. 231–49.

——. *Spirit in the World.* New York: The Seabury Press, 1968.

——. *The Trinity.* Trans. by Joseph Donceel. New York: Herder and Herder, 1970.

——. *On the Theology of Death.* New York: The Seabury Press, 1973. Orig., 1961.

——Rahner, Karl and Thusing, Wilhelm. *A New Christology.* New York: The Seabury Press, 1980.

Richard, Lucien J. *A Kenotic Christology: In the Humanity of Jesus the Christ, The Compassion of God.* Washington, D.C.: University Press of America, 1982.

——. *What Are They Saying About Christ and World Religions?* New York: Paulist Press, 1981.

Richardson, Alan. *A Dictionary of Christian Theology.* London: SCM Press, 1969.

Ricoeur, Paul. *The Symbolism of Evil.* Boston: Beacon Press, 1969.

Robinson, James M. *A New Quest of the Historical Jesus.* Naperville: Allenson, 1959.

Robinson, James M. and Koester, Helmut. *Trajectories Through Early Christianity.* Philadelphia: Fortress Press, 1971.

Robinson, John A.T. *The Human Face of God.* Philadelphia: The Westminster Press, 1973.

The Roman Missal: The Sacramentary. Collegeville: The Liturgical Press, 1974.

Rondet, Henri. *The Grace of Christ: A Brief History of the Theology of Grace.* New York: Newman Press, 1967.

Sacrae Theologiae Summa ("The Spanish Summa"), 4th ed. Matriti: La Editorial Catolica, 1962.

Segundo, Juan Luis. *Grace and the Human Condition.* Maryknoll, New York: Orbis Books, 1973.

Scheler, Max. *The Nature of Sympathy.* Trans. by Peter Heath. Hamden, Connecticut: Shoe String Press, Inc., 1970.

Schillebeeckx, Edward. *Christ: The Experience of Jesus as Lord.* Trans. by John Bowden. New York: The Seabury Press, 1980.

——. *Jesus: An Experiment in Christology.* Trans. by Hubert Hoskins. New York: The Seabury Press, 1979.

Schoonenberg, Piet. *The Christ: A Study of the God-Man Relationship in the Whole of Creation and in Jesus Christ.* New York: Herder and Herder, 1971.

———. "God's Presence in Jesus: An Exchange of Viewpoints." *Theology Digest,* 19 (1971), 29–38.

———. "Is Jesus 'man plus God'?" *Theology Digest,* 23 (1975), 59–70.

———. "A Letter from Piet Schoonenberg, S.J." *Theology Digest,* 23 (1975), 224–25.

———. "Process or History in God?" *Theology Digest,* 23 (1975), 38–44.

Schweizer, Eduard. *The Holy Spirit.* Trans. by Reginald H. and Ilse Fuller. Philadelphia: Fortress Press, 1980.

Shea, John. *Stories of Faith.* Chicago: Thomas More Press, 1980.

Sire, James W. *Scripture Twisting: 20 Ways the Cults Misread the Bible.* Downers Grove, Illinois: Inter Varisity Press, 1980.

Sloyan, Gerard S. *Jesus in Focus: A Life in its Setting.* Mystic, Connecticut: Twenty-Third Publications, 1983.

Slusser, Michael. Review of James Mackey's *Jesus the Man and the Myth. Theological Studies,* 41 (1980), 403–04.

Smulders, Piet. *The Fathers on Christology: The Development of Christological Dogma From the Bible to the Great Councils.* Trans. by Lucien Roy. DePere, Wisconsin: St. Norbert Abbey Press, 1968.

Snell, Bruno. *The Discovery of Mind: The Greek Origins of European Thought.* Cambridge: Harvard University Press, 1953.

Sobrino, Jon. *Christology at the Crossroads: A Latin American Approach.* Trans. by John Drury. Maryknoll, New York: Orbis Books, 1978.

Tart, Charles T., ed. *Transpersonal Psychologies.* New York: Harper Colophon Books, 1975.

Tarthang Tulku. "A View of Mind." *The Meeting of the Ways: Explorations in East/West Psychology.* Ed. by John Welwood. New York: Plenum Press, 1978. Pp. 40–44.

Thomas Aquinas. *Summa Theologica.* In the public domain.

Thompson, William M. *Christ and Consciousness: Exploring Christ's Contribution to Human Consciousness.* New York: Paulist Press, 1977.

———. *Jesus, Lord and Savior: A Theopathic Christology and Soteriology.* New York: Paulist Press, 1980.

Bibliography

Troeltsch, Ernst R. *Der Historismus und Seine Probleme.* Tübingen: C.B. Mohr, 1922.

Trungpa, Chogyam. *Cutting Through Spiritual Materialism.* Berkeley: Shambhala, 1973.

_____. *The Myth of Freedom: And the Way of Meditation.* Berkeley: Shambhala, 1976.

Van Beeck, Frans Jozef. *Christ Proclaimed: Christology as Rhetoric.* New York: Paulist Press, 1979.

Vawter, Bruce. *This Man Jesus: An Essay Toward a New Testament Christology.* Garden City, New York: Doubleday & Co., 1973.

Vermes, Gaza. *Jesus the Jew: A Historian's Reading of the Gospels.* Philadelphia: Fortress Press, 1973.

Wainwright, Geoffrey. Review of James Mackey's *Jesus the Man and the Myth. Scottish Journal of Theology,* 34 (1981), 75–78.

Williams, Rowan. *Christian Spirituality: A Theological History from the New Testament to Luther and John of the Cross.* Atlanta: John Knox Press, 1980.

Young, Frances M. Review of James Mackey's *Jesus the Man and the Myth. The Expository Times,* 90 (1979), 343–44.

Index